MORMONISM AND EARLY CHRISTIANITY

The Collected Works of Hugh Nibley

The Collected Works of Hugh Nibley will
include volumes on the following subjects:

The Old Testament and Related Studies
Ancient History
The Pearl of Great Price
Early Christianity
The Book of Mormon
The Doctrine and Covenants and Mormonism
Education, Politics, and Society

Other volumes in this series:

Old Testament and Related Studies
Enoch the Prophet
The World and the Prophets

The Collected Works of Hugh Nibley: Volume 4
Mormonism and Early Christianity

MORMONISM AND EARLY CHRISTIANITY

Hugh Nibley

Edited by
Todd M. Compton
and
Stephen D. Ricks

Foreword by
Todd M. Compton

Deseret Book Company
Salt Lake City, Utah
and
Foundation for Ancient Research and Mormon Studies
Provo, Utah

Library of Congress Cataloging-in-Publication Data

Nibley, Hugh, 1910–
    Mormonism and early Christianity / by Hugh Nibley.
      p. cm.
    Bibliography: p
    Includes index.
    ISBN 0-87579-127-1 : $16.95 (est.)
    1. Church history—Primitive and early church, ca. 30–600. 2. Mormon Church. 3. Church of Jesus Christ of Latter-day Saints. 4. Bible. N.T.—Criticism, Interpretation, etc. I. Title.
    BR166.N53   1987
    270. 1—dc19   87-25291

Printed in the United States of America   84225-2726
R. R. Donnelley, Harrisonburg, VA

20 19 18 17 16 15

Contents

	Foreword	vii
1	Early Accounts of Jesus' Childhood	1
2	Evangelium Quadraginta Dierum: The Forty-day Mission of Christ—The Forgotten Heritage	10
3	The Early Christian Prayer Circle	45
4	Baptism for the Dead in Ancient Times	100
5	The Passing of the Primitive Church	168
6	The Way of the Church	209
7	Jerusalem in Early Christianity	323
8	What Is a Temple?	355
9	Christian Envy of the Temple	391
	Key to Abbreviations	435
	Scripture References	437
	Index	443

Foreword

In 1978, Hugh Nibley wrote, after referring to Brigham Young University's 1951 acquisition of the Greek and Latin *Patrologiae*, "here indeed was a treasure trove of hints. . . . At last we had something to work with in the *Patrologiae*."[1] Nibley has turned his scholarly attention in many directions throughout his career. He has dealt with Book of Mormon studies, LDS church history, Enoch, Abraham, Egyptology and the Book of Abraham, Jewish pseudepigrapha, the symbolism of statecraft and cosmology, Brigham Young, and the temple endowment. But from the outset of his career, he has been centrally concerned with primitive Christianity,[2] especially the shadowy era between the New Testament era proper and the emergence and triumph of the Catholic Church and Holy Roman Empire. In those early centuries of persecution, unrest, syncretism, uncertainty, and heresy, the Christian church eventually took strong steps to effect doctrinal and administrative unity. While Christian historians have traditionally described this as a victory,[3] Nibley, in the important series of articles contained in this book, has instead concentrated on what may have been lost in the transition from the New Testament church to the Christianity of Constantine's era and beyond. While this perspective may not be immediately popular in all circles, everyone should agree that it is a valid, even necessary, avenue of inquiry.

A number of themes that Nibley has focused on in these essays anticipated and received support from later scholarship. For instance, Nibley has frequently emphasized the importance of secrecy in early Christianity, showing that there were levels of esoteric and exoteric doctrine and ritual in the structure of the New Testament church.[4] A recent collection of essays entitled *Secrecy in Religions*[5] has shown that secrecy is an important component in all religions. Speaking of Christianity specifically, Kees Bolle, the editor of that volume, writes, "It does not take much of an effort to find examples for the notion of secrecy in Christianity, and the examples do not occur on the fringes of the doctrine of God's revelation; rather they point to the center."[6] Nibley's treatment of secrecy in early Christianity is valuable and persuasive.

Another issue that these essays are centrally concerned with, and that has been widely discussed in recent years, is orthodoxy and heresy in the Christianity that immediately followed apostolic Christianity.[7] Faced with the challenge of a Hellenized, ascetic Gnostic Christianity, how much did the more centralized and originally Judaic Christianity become like its enemy in order to compete? The very idea of a centralized Christianity has given way to a picture of early Christianity diverse and fragmented, where it is hard to define what is orthodox and what is heretical, what is Gnostic and what is "mainstream." For instance, William Phipps has recently argued that Augustine's influential doctrine of original sin derived from his Gnostic background and was, in reality, heretical, while Pelagius' opposition to the idea was orthodox. But it was Augustine's doctrine that won the day historically and has continued to influence Western theology and culture.[8]

One of the most remarkable things about these essays— "The Passing of the Primitive Church," "The Forty-day Mission of Christ," "Christian Envy of the Temple," and "Jerusalem in Early Christianity"—is that they were published in non-Mormon scholarly publications. Instead of being content to write only for a sympathetic if occasionally uncritical Mormon audience, Nibley subjected these essays to the scrutiny of non-Mormon editors and scholars in leading, influential journals (and one of the articles, "The Passing of the Primitive Church," spurred a brief, interesting debate in the pages of *Church History*).[9] In doing this, Nibley has set a valuable example for other Mormon scholars; such publication in non-Mormon journals enables a dialogue to be opened up between Mormon and non-Mormon scholars, and it will encourage Mormon scholarship to measure up to the highest possible standards of historical inquiry.

In other important essays in this book—"What is a Temple?" "Baptism for the Dead in Ancient Times," "The Early Christian Prayer Circle"—Nibley turns to another persistent concern in his writing—the temple and temple ritual. However we interpret the details of these articles (along with "Christian Envy of the Temple"), they show clearly that the earliest Christianity had strong ties to the temple, and that the earliest Christians had rituals that did not survive in subsequent Christianity, just as the Jerusalem temple did not survive. For instance, some important scholars have recently treated baptism for the dead as an authentic, if enigmatic, ritual of the earliest Christians. Wayne Meeks, in a widely respected book on the church in Paul's era, *The First Urban Christians*, describes baptism for the dead as "mystifying" but includes it in his section on ritual in the early Christian church.[10] Another commentator, Grosheide, is puzzled by the ritual but concludes that Paul could not have disapproved of the ritual if he used it as support for the resurrection of the dead.[11]

These essays and the others in this book are pioneering works, sharing both the virtues and the drawbacks of the pioneering vision. Nibley is the first to agree that they do not contain the final word on their subjects; they await further revision and refinement in the wake of new evidence and thought. We will be sifting for years through the sources that Professor Nibley has viewed from a Mormon perspective for the first time. As we evaluate and re-evaluate these important primary sources, we should remember that Dr. Nibley has continually described scholarship not as final and absolute proof, but as open-ended discussion.[12] Many of the conclusions and arguments in these articles will stand in future scholarship; others will be discarded. But Hugh Nibley's work has laid the foundation for all further discussion. These studies are an inspiring invitation to learning and thought and scholarly inquiry; they will deepen our interest in and our understanding of the apostolic church, and the church in the troubled centuries that immediately followed New Testament times.

I have edited "The Passing of the Primitive Church," "Evangelium Quadraginta Dierum: The Forty-day Mission of Christ—The Forgotten Heritage," "Christian Envy of the Temple," "The Way of the Church," and "The Early Christian Prayer Circle." The rest of the essays in this book have been edited under the direction of Stephen Ricks. I have, on the whole, merely checked footnotes, leaving the text untouched except where a direct quotation was involved, sometimes tightening up the citation or adding bibliographic data. On occasion, I have disagreed with the conclusions Nibley has drawn from his evidence, but this is only to be expected when two opinionated readers examine the same material. Readers interested in exploring Nibley's sources will find translations of many of them in two series, *The Ante-Nicene Fathers* and *Nicene and Post-Nicene Fathers*. A supplemental volume of *Ante-Nicene Fathers* (volume 9) contains a valuable bibliography that also serves as a table of contents for the series. Other works can be found translated in the series *The Fathers of the Church* (Washington, D.C.: Catholic University of America Press, starting 1947), and in *Ancient Christian Writers* (Westminster, Maryland: Newman Press, starting 1961). The original Greek and Latin texts of these writings can be found in the two extensive series of books, *Patrologiae Graecae* and *Patrologiae Latinae*, both edited under the direction of Jacques-Paul Migne. Many of these same writings, in vastly improved editions, can be found in the series *Corpus Christianorum* (CC) and *Corpus Scriptorum Ecclesiasticorum Latinorum* (CSEL). An indispensable guide to editions and translations of the early Fathers is Johannes Quasten's *Patrology* (Utrecht: Spectrum, 1950), in four volumes; see also Berthold Altaner, *Patrologie*, 5th ed., (Freiburg: Herder, 1958), and *Clavis Patrum Graecorum* (Turkhout: Brepols 1983; in CC), four volumes.

The Christian apocrypha can be found in Edgar Hennecke and Wilhelm Schneemelcher, *New Testament Apocrypha* (Philadelphia: Westminster, 1963), in two volumes; see also M. R. James, *The Apocryphal New Testament* (Oxford: Clarendon, 1924), and James Robinson, ed., *The Nag Hammadi Library* (New York: Harper & Row, 1977); Bentley Layton, *The Gnostic Scriptures* (New York: Doubleday, (1987). The Old Testament apocrypha, most of them used and adapted by the Christians, can be found in James Charlesworth, *The Old Testament Pseudepigrapha* (Garden City, N.Y.: Doubleday, 1983–85), in two volumes.

We wish to acknowledge our appreciation to the many individuals who helped us prepare this volume for publication, particularly John Gee, Gary Gillum, Gary Keeley, Jill Keeley, Brent McNeely, Mari Miles, Phyllis Nibley, Don Norton, Robert F. Smith, Morgan Tanner, and John W. Welch. We also wish to thank the Foundation for Ancient Research and Mormon Studies (F.A.R.M.S.) for their continued support in readying for publication *The Collected Works of Hugh Nibley*.

Todd M. Compton

NOTES

1. Hugh W. Nibley, *Nibley on the Timely and the Timeless* (Provo, Ut.: Religious Studies Center, Brigham Young University, 1978), xxv.

2. One of his first books was the patristic-oriented *The World and the Prophets* (Salt Lake City: Deseret, 1954), republished as volume 3 in these *Collected Works of Hugh Nibley*.

3. For example, William H. C. Frend describes "The Emergence of Orthodoxy" in the second century A.D. in *The Rise of Christianity* (Philadelphia: Fortress, 1984), 250.

4. See, for example, in this volume, "The Forty-Day Mission of Christ—the Forgotten Heritage," nn. 48–59 and 80; "The Passing of the Primitive Church," nn. 50, 105; "Baptism for the Dead in Ancient Times," nn. 1–16 and 46–50, with text.

5. Kees Bolle, ed., *Secrecy in Religion* (Leiden: Brill, 1987, projected date of publication). See also Joachim Jeremias, *The Eucharistic Words of Jesus* (New York: Scribner, 1966), 125–37.

6. Kees Bolle, "Secrecy in Religions," ch. 1 of *Secrecy in Religions*, preliminary typescript, p. 10. Some scholars have passed off ritual secrecy in the early church as influence from Hellenistic mystery religions, but Bolle shows that this oversimplification underrates the necessity for secrecy in any valid religious tradition; ibid., 16.

7. See "The Forty-day Mission of Christ," n. 60; "The Passing of the Primitive Church"; and "Christian Envy of the Temple."

8. William Phipps, "The Heresiarch: Pelagius or Augustine?" *Anglican Theological Review* 62 (1980): 130–31; cf. the treatment by E. Buonaiuti, "Manichaeism and Augustine's Ideas of 'Massa Perditionis'," *Harvard Theological Review* 20 (1927): 117–27. See also Walter Bauer, *Orthodoxy and Heresy in Earliest Christianity*, tr. and ed. by R. Kraft and G. Krodel (Philadelphia: Fortress, 1971); H. E. W. Turner, *The Pattern of Christian Truth: A Study in the Relations between Orthodoxy and Heresy in the Early Church* (London: Mowbray, 1954)—a response to Bauer; James D. Dunn, *Unity and Diversity in the New Testament* (Philadelphia: Westminster, 1977); J.M. Robinson and Helmut Koester, *Trajectories through Early Christianity* (Philadelphia: Fortress, 1971); Adolf von Harnack, *History of Dogma*, tr. Neil Buchanan, 7 vols. (New York: Dover, 1961), 1:128, n. 3 (Basilides influences Augustine); 263, n. 2 (Valentine influences Clement and Origen); 261, n. 1 (Gnostic Christology and the later church); Kurt Rudolph, *Gnosis, the Nature and History of Gnosticism*, tr. and ed. by Robert Wilson (San Francisco: Harper & Row, 1983), 368–73, 390 n. 187, 369, 372, which shows the influence of Gnosticism on the later Christian church.

9. Hans J. Hillerbrand, "The Passing of the Church: Two Comments on a Strange Theme," *Church History* 30 (December 1961): 481–82; Robert M. Grant, "The Passing of the Church: Comments on

Two Comments on a Strange Theme," *Church History* 30 (December 1961): 482–83.

10. Wayne Meeks, *The First Urban Christians* (New Haven: Yale, 1983), 162. Meeks notes that this is virtually the only reference to ritual relating to death found in the Pauline letters, which points up its importance.

11. F. W. Grosheide, *Commentary on the First Epistle to the Corinthians* (Grand Rapids: Eerdmans, 1953), 372–74. "If this type of baptism was actually practiced and if Paul had disapproved of it he probably would have written more about it than what this one reference contains. In any case the apostle could hardly derive an argument for the resurrection of the body from a practice of which he did not approve." Ibid., 372. This logical argument disposes convincingly of the view that Paul thought baptism for the dead was a heretical practice, a view that anti-Mormon polemic has understandably tried to put forth as fact. See also Herman Ridderbos, *Paul* (Grand Rapids: Eerdmans, 1975), 25, 540; Richard Lloyd Anderson, *Understanding Paul* (Salt Lake City: Deseret, 1983), 127, 403–16.

12. See, for example, Hugh W. Nibley, *Since Cumorah* (Salt Lake City: Deseret, 1967), v–vii.

1

Early Accounts of Jesus' Childhood

There are two widely separated traditions of the child-hood of Jesus. The older and more valuable one, whose chief representative is a writing known as the Protoevangelium of James, was condemned by St. Jerome, along with a great deal of ancient and authentic early Christian material, and so came under the ban of the Popes.[1] In its place there grew up another and later tradition, a mass of popular fables and miracle stories which captivated the minds of the Middle Ages and have come down to us as the official "Infancy Gospels."[2] These stories are unabashed daydreams in which Jesus is always the "super-boy" whose tricks are the dread and envy of all his fellows: Jesus slides down a sunbeam or hangs his water pitcher on a sunbeam, and when the other boys try it with disastrous results, Jesus instantly and magi-cally mends the damage; when Joseph the carpenter has a hard time fitting pieces of wood together, Jesus simply blesses them into place; when a local bully jostles Jesus in the street or breaks his sand castles with a stick, the offender is at a word from Jesus withered upon the spot; when the other kids will not play with Jesus, he turns them into goats, and so forth.[3] Of course, it is the school teacher who takes the worst beating, being struck blind or dead if he dares scold Jesus or tweak his ear—but only, of course, after Jesus has

"Early Accounts of Jesus' Childhood" first appeared in The Instructor, 100 (January 1965): 35–37.

brilliantly illustrated his own wisdom and the teacher's ignorance. [4]

Separated "by an enormous gap" from this popular literature which so vividly reflects the mentality of late antiquity
is the earlier tradition, sober, plausible, and of recent discovery. New Greek and Coptic manuscript finds now take
us back more than 700 years earlier than any childhood
accounts of Jesus heretofore known outside the Bible. [5] Yet it
turns out that both traditions deal with the same basic stories. If we strip the later legends of their fantastic accretions
(which are easily recognized because of the conflicts among
them), we may well ask whether the nonmiraculous elements
they all have in common might not go back to a foundation
of fact. What are these elements?

For one, all sources, early and late, Christian and anti-
Christian, agree that Jesus' family was often in trouble and
moved about a good deal. The early anti-Christian writers
made much of this: a family of improvident ne'er-do-wells,
tramping about the country looking for odd jobs; Mary a
woman of the lowest classes and the loosest morals, working
as a ladies' hairdresser, kicked out by her husband when she
had an affair with a Roman soldier (they furnished the name,
rank, and serial number), giving birth in disgrace to Jesus,
the ambitious boy who picked up a bag of magic tricks in
Egypt along with exalted ideas about his own divinity, and
who gathered about him a band of vagabonds and despera-
does with whom he ranged the countryside, picking up a living by questionable means. [6]

Implicit in all the early Christian accounts of Jesus,
Cullmann observes, is that they are obviously written *in
reply* to these scandalous stories that were spread about concerning the young Jesus and his family at a very early date. [7]
That is why they lay such stress on the spotless purity of
Mary, give full play to the journey to Egypt, and emphasize
the diligence of Joseph, who "never at any time ate the bread

of idleness," with the youthful Jesus always working hard at his side.[8]

Now we know who it was that gathered, embellished, and published the scandal-stories about the family—it was the doctors of the schools, the same "Scribes and Pharisees" who relentlessly pursued Jesus and John the Baptist during their ministries. Here again all our sources agree that the trouble was about Jesus and that it was the local scribes who stirred up the people against him and his family wherever they went.[9] And the people were easily stirred up since (again according to all reports) they were overawed by Jesus and rather afraid of him, like the widow who took the family in when they came to Egypt—"wrapped in strips of ragged stuff even as we are," says one early preacher—but turned them out of the house when Jesus (at the age of three) brought a dried fish to life.[10] The miraculous element is only to be expected, but would *pro-Christian* apologists all admit that the family was hated and persecuted because of Jesus if there was any reason for denying it? "These people [must] suffer and hate us and persecute us," Joseph complains to Jesus in a very early source.[11]

But what did Jesus do to make all that trouble? All the sources agree with Luke 2:52, that he was a good boy and everybody liked him. Even our collectors of miracle tales are careful to specify that there was nothing abnormal about his family life: "And He increased in stature like [any other] child, and He obeyed His parents, and performed all the other things which it was right for Him to do. . . . [He] called Joseph 'my father,' and Joseph instructed Him like a son, and the child obeyed him like a good son."[12]

It was not anything Jesus did (it will not be necessary to show what is wrong with the popular "super-boy" stories), but rather things he said which, according to the early sources, got people upset and enraged the local clergy. The sayings attributed to him as a child are significant, since they are found among the early *logia* of Jesus, some of which are

being accepted by scholars today as genuine utterances of
the Lord:[13] "My nature is not like yours. I existed before you
were born. . . . If you wish to become a father, be taught by
me. . . . No one else has seen the mark of the cross which I
have sworn to bear. . . . You do not know how you were
born or where you came from; I alone know that. . . . I
know where you were born, and I know it from my Father
who knows me."[14] When he heals the foot of a young man
who had injured himself with an ax, Jesus says, "Arise now,
split the wood and think of me!" This is very close to the
recently discovered logion, "When you split the wood, there
am I!" which scholars now accept as a genuine utterance of
Jesus.[15] Whether authentic or not, these childhood sayings of
Jesus do represent the oldest, pre-Synoptic, Christian record.
Also, all three references to Jesus' childhood in the New
Testament mention his phenomenal wisdom, even the greatest doctors at Jerusalem being "astonished at his understanding and answers" (Luke 2:47).

Another significant element in the "Infancy" stories is
their constant preoccupation with the temple. This again is a
mark of the earliest tradition, for as we have shown elsewhere, the church writers after the fall of Jerusalem become
definitely hostile to the temple as a purely Jewish institution.[16] The main theme is Mary's service in the temple, "behind
the veil of the altar," where she offered up sacrifices—a strange
thing for a woman to do. "Her tunic came down over her
seal, and her head-cloth came down over her eyes; she wore
a girdle round her tunic, and her tunic was never soiled or
torn."[17]

Of peculiar interest in the older stories are the accounts
of the family's sojourns in the desert. The Protoevangelium
of James tells how Jesus, when he was eight, walked with his
family from Jericho to the Jordan, that is, right through the
heart of the "Dead Sea Scrolls Country" at the very time
when the communities were going full blast. On the way, we
are told, young Jesus turned aside to inspect a cave where a

lioness had a pair of cubs. The rest of the company were terrified, but the lioness and her cubs first trotted along down to the Jordan and then on out into the desert.[18] Now this is just the sort of thing one would expect to happen: the country was indeed peppered with caves, and lions were being hunted there as late as the time of the Crusades. What Jesus did was just the sort of naive and foolhardy things that little boys do. The later legends, with the Pseudo-Matthew in the lead, make a great production of this: Jesus approaches a cave of dragons, who instantly obey him, while all the animals of the desert then accompany the family on their journey in a regular Dionysiac procession. Embellishing the sober old story of Anna, Jesus' grandmother, the same stories then have the trees of an oasis bowing down to Mary while a spring of water bursts forth at their feet, and so on.[19] The fact that the early version resists every temptation to tell a miracle story about the lions is a strong argument for its authenticity. But the thing to notice is that we have here the whole family going out beyond Jordan into John the Baptist's country.

A recently discovered Coptic fragment tells how Elizabeth took her son, John, and fled with him to Torinê, which can mean either "hill country" or "the desert of Torinê,"[20] the latter being favored in view of another Coptic source that says that Elizabeth and her son lived "in the desert of Torinê" for years.[21] They actually had a house there, and a Coptic bishop who tells how Mary went out there to see Elizabeth cries, "I marvel at thee, O virgin, how thou didst know where Torinê was, and who shewed thee the house of Zacharias."[22] When Elizabeth died, according to Serapion's Life of John the Baptist, Mary and Jesus came to spend a week with the seven-and-a-half-year-old John. When their visit was at an end, Mary had misgivings about leaving the boy: "Woe is me, O John, for thou art alone in the desert and hast no one." They did not leave, in fact, until they had instructed John "how to live in the desert," being themselves something of experts in desert lore. Jesus reassured them with the news that John would not be alone, but actually live in a community of prophets and angels, "as if it were a multitude of people."[23]

Now Serapion knew precious little about the desert Saints of Qumran who had disappeared 300 years before his day, and naturally thought as we do of one living in the desert as necessarily living *alone*. But today we know that those very deserts in Jesus' time housed large communities of pious Jews who had retired from Jerusalem by invitation, in the manner of Lehi. Jesus, as we know from the Bible, often retreated to the desert; and the practice seems to go back to his childhood. After the return from Egypt, according to the Pseudo-Thomas, Joseph took Jesus into the desert, where they lived until things quieted down in Jerusalem. Mary went to stay with her relatives in Capernaum, planning to join her husband later in Nazareth, where Joseph possessed the property of his father. Then when Jesus was seven years old and things were quiet in the realm, they returned to Bethlehem and lived there.[24] James confirms the picture: "I, James, who wrote this, went into the desert when there was rioting in Jerusalem at the death of Herod."[25] It was the natural and customary thing to do, as the Dead Sea Scrolls and the example of Lehi amply attest.

The Proto-Gospel of James begins by telling how the righteous and childless Joachim, desiring a blessing, went out in the desert and lived in a tent for forty days. It also tells that when doubts were expressed by some regarding the virginity of Mary, Joseph went out into the desert to be tested, after first submitting to the "water of testing"; and after he had returned, his honor vindicated, Mary went out next to undergo the same test.[26] The story is peculiar and awkward enough not to be anybody's invention, and indeed one is reminded of the great importance placed upon testing and examining the purity of all comers to the community of the Dead Sea Scrolls, and of their purging of defilements by baptisms and washings. If any doubts existed as to a person's sanctity, passing the tests of the holy covenanters of the desert would allay them.[27] A valuable apocryphal source first detected by this writer recounts that it was in one of the desert communities of priests by the banks of the Jordan that Mary became betrothed to Joseph.[28]

So we would suggest as a possible historical kernel of the stories about the childhood of Jesus certain basic propositions: (1) the family was poor and hard-working; (2) they moved about a good deal; (3) the youthful Jesus said things that astonished and disturbed people; (4) the local ministers stirred up trouble and spread scandalous reports about the family; and (5) they had connections with the pious heretics of the desert, whose writings are full of New Testament ideas and phraseology.

The Latter-day Saint reader cannot but note striking parallels between the early anti-Christian scandal stories and the Palmyra tales about the Joseph Smith family.

NOTES

1. The subject is discussed at length by Oscar Cullmann in *NA* 1:279, 303. See also the English translation in *NTA* 1:373, 405.

2. *NA* 1:303 and *NTA* 1:405.

3. These stories are found in the Pseudo-Gospel of Thomas, in *NA* 1:293–98 and *NTA* 1:392–99; Sylvain Grébaut, "Miracles of Jesus," in *PO* 12:636; the Pistis Sophia, and in later works, cited in *ANT* 66–70. The most important later work and the source of the "Golden Legend" stories is the Pseudo-Gospel of Matthew, in *ANT* 70–79.

4. Pseudo-Thomas, in *NA* 1:296–97 and *NTA* 1:397.

5. There is a complete discussion and translation of the text in *Protoevengelium Jacobi*, in *NA* 1:277–90 and *NTA* 1:370–88. H. Wall, "A Coptic Fragment Concerning the Childhood of John the Baptist," in *Revue d'Egyptologie* 8 (1951): 207–14, has a reproduction of the text.

6. Origen, *Contra Celsum* 1:27, 32, in *PG* 11:711–14, 719–23.

7. O. Cullman, "Infancy Gospels," in *NA* 1:278–79 and Wilson in *NTA* 1:372–74.

8. The quote is from "Demetrius on the Birth of Our Lord," in E. A. Wallis Budge, *Miscellaneous Coptic Texts in the Dialect of Upper Egypt* (London: British Museum, 1915), 656. See also the reprint in 2 vols. (New York: AMS Press, 1977), 656.

9. His particular enemy is the son of Annas the Scribe. See Pseudo-Thomas, in *NA* 1:294 and *NTA* 1:393. It is the Scribes who accuse the child Jesus of working miracles on the Sabbath and stir up the people against him (Pseudo-Matthew, in *ANT* 76) and it is to them that the people complain about Him. It is with the scribes at the local school that Jesus has the most trouble; see above note 4.

10. The quotation is from Budge, *Miscellaneous Coptic Texts in the Dialect of Upper Egypt*, 679–80.

11. Pseudo-Thomas, in *NA* 1:294 and *NTA* 1:393; the translation here is Wilson's.

12. Budge, *Miscellaneous Coptic Texts in the Dialect of Upper Egypt*, 680, 682.

13. We have treated the subject of the Logia in Hugh W. Nibley, "Since Cumorah," *Improvement Era* 67 (November 1964):924.

14. The fullest collections are in Grébaut, "Miracles of Jesus," in *PO* 12:630–31, and in the Syriac Pseudo-Thomas, in *NA* 1:298–99 and *NTA* 1:399–400.

15. Pseudo-Thomas, in *NA* 1:296 and *NTA* 1:396, and in the Gospel of Thomas, in *NHLE* 126 (Logion 77). Most of the childhood sayings here quoted are found in this work. Jesus' double in Pistis Sophia, ch. 61, and his passing "through the midst of the Archons," ibid., ch. 7, also belong to the oldest Christian traditions.

16. Hugh W. Nibley, "Christian Envy of the Temple," *Jewish Quarterly Review* 50 (1959): 97–123, 299–40; reprinted below in this volume, 390–432.

17. Budge, *Miscellaneous Coptic Texts in the Dialect of Upper Egypt*, 655; Protoevangelium Jacobi 4–7, in *NA* 1:281–83 and *NTA* 1:376–78.

18. Pseudo-Matthew, in *ANT* 78.

19. *NA* 1:306–08 and *NTA* 1:410–12.

20. Wall, "A Coptic Fragment Concerning the Childhood of John the Baptist," 209.

21. Budge, *Miscellaneous Coptic Texts in the Dialect of Upper Egypt*, 682.

22. Ibid., 667.

23. *NA* 1:311 and *NTA* 1:416.

24. *ANT* 59.

25. Colophon of the Protoevengelium Jacobi 25, in *NA* 1:290 and *NTA* 1:388.

26. Colophon of the Protoevengelium Jacobi 16, in *NA* 1:286 and *NTA* 1:382-83.

27. See, for example, the "Manual of Discipline," in G. Vermes, *The Dead Sea Scrolls in English* (New York: Penguin, 1975), 74-75, 79-80.

28. Tha'labī, *Kitāb Qiṣaṣ al-Anbiyā* (Cairo: Muṣṭafā al-Ḥalabī al-Bābī wa-Awlāduhu, 1354 A.H.), 260.

2

Evangelium Quadraginta Dierum: The Forty-day Mission of Christ—The Forgotten Heritage

While those who ponder the historical relevance of Acts 1:3 concern themselves almost exclusively with the evidence of the canonical writings, we now possess in the early apocryphal texts, both those recently discovered and those being reappraised in the light of new findings, an impressive body of evidence that has direct bearing on the problem of the historicity of the 40 days. It is the purpose of the present study to indicate briefly the nature of this evidence.

The theme of the 40 days has always been a disturbing one. For many scholars the possibility of such an event as that indicated in Acts 1:3 is not even to be discussed,[1] for others such things are tolerable only as myths,[2] while some are frank enough to admit that they simply don't like the story.[3] It is astonishing how many writers on the resurrection pass by the 40-day interval in studied silence,[4] and indeed churchmen since Clement and Origen have employed all the arts of rhetoric and logic to evade its crass literalism.[5] It is claimed that the story is insufficiently attested,[6] or that the language[7] or the thought-forms of the ancients elude us,[8] or

This article first appeared under the title "Evangelium Quadraginta Dierum," in Vigiliae Christianae 20 (1966): 1–24. The article was reprinted under the title "The Forty-day Mission of Christ—The Forgotten Heritage" in When the Lights Went Out (Salt Lake City: Deseret Book, 1970), 33–54.

that the writers themselves are confused—e.g., in maintaining that "flesh and blood cannot inherit the kingdom" while asserting "the very opposite" in the doctrine of the resurrection.[9] We are often reminded today that we are here dealing with prefigured types and images that need not be taken literally, 40 itself being a well-known symbolic number in sacred writings.[10]

But on the other hand, Luke may well have chosen the round number precisely because everybody knew of like 40-day periods of spiritual discipline and preparation;[11] ancient thought-forms can be checked by the words and behavior of an Ignatius, willing to give his life to show how *he* interpreted the 40 days;[12] and contradictions may well have their source in the minds of readers rather than writers—the "flesh and blood" issue, in fact, seems to be of our own making.[13]

Yet even those who accept the reality of the 40-day ministry are at a loss to explain it. Plainly the key is missing when serious commentators can describe the event as a mere "example of condescension and friendship" by one who had more urgent business elsewhere,[14] or as a magnanimous recompense for the 40 *hours* of anguish occasioned by the Lord's absence in the tomb,[15] or as a long lingering farewell,[16] or as "forty-odd days of frustration and inaction,"[17] or as a strategic and psychological holding back of forces for a more effective charge on the enemy.[18] It is often claimed that a full 40 days were necessary to demonstrate the reality of resurrected flesh,[19] and if that seems odd (40 seconds were sufficient to convince Thomas) we are told that the Apostles had to *over*-learn their lesson in order to persuade an over-skeptical world.[20] The 40 days are also described as a weaning process, to draw the disciples away from undue attachment to each other,[21] or to the person of the Lord—lest they be too upset by his departure,[22] or, strangest of all, to wean their minds away from corporeal concepts to the pure realms of disembodied intellect.[23] In short, if anything like "The Great Forty Days" occurred, the enormous portent of it, which Luke puts at the very root of the Christian faith, quite escapes the commentators, who view it as an odd and rather "interesting" interlude, [24] but admit that in the end we do *not* know what Christ did or said during the 40 days but can only conjecture. [25]

The argument most confidently put forth today for the post-resurrectional activity of Jesus is the behavior of the apostles, who before the resurrection were by all accounts unready not only to preach but even to hear "the things of the kingdom," and yet presently went forth into the world fully laden. [26] But is it not remarkable that *nothing* has come down to us from that wonderful time when the church is supposed to have received all its knowledge and training? Why have we only the opening words of the Lord's discourse, declaring how badly the disciples needed the instruction that followed (Luke 24:25–27), of which nothing is preserved in the canon (v. 45)? Those early apocryphal writings which purport to tell the rest of the story may not be ignored by the serious student. These writings take a position of conscious resistance to the rising tide of skepticism regarding the reality of the resurrection. [27] Luke had made it perfectly clear at the outset of his history that he was dealing with solid reality; like his other prologue, the story of Zacharias, this one is a forthright factual account that leaves no margin for speculation. Unlike the related themes of the resurrection and ascension, the 40 days has had no appeal to artists and orators, for it offers the imagination nothing to play with—it is not a subject for discussion but an end of discussion, not something to be proven but the proof itself, the unshakable cornerstone of the edifice Luke is about to construct. [28] In this spirit the bulk of the early apocryphal writings make of the 40 days the foundation of their own teachings, and when Ignatius wants an unanswerable argument for the resurrection of the flesh, he appeals not only to the 40 days but to a non-canonical witness for them. [29]

It is significant that the *favorite* theme of the early apocrypha happens to be "the teachings of the Lord to the Apostles after the Resurrection," often directly indicated as such,[30] and often indirectly.[31] This has often been interpreted as both a bid for prestige by the various authors and a claim to immunity from criticism.[32] But the tradition could only offer such security if it enjoyed unquestioned acceptance in the church, and if we examine the actual teachings purveyed under the frank of the 40 days it soon becomes apparent that they were never designed to be popular, but represent old and very unpopular doctrines in retreat. Even among the first disciples belief in a literal resurrection was only enforced after long resistance,[33] and it proved an *horrendum* to the churchmen ever after.[34] But the most conspicuous teaching of all in the 40-day repertoire is a picture of the future which cannot be surpassed for unrelieved pessimism and gloom. Here surely is no product of wishful thinking or sly invention.

In a standard 40-day situation the apostles, deeply worried, ask the Lord what lies ahead for them and their work,[35] and receive an appalling reply: They are to be rejected by all men and take their violent exit from the world,[36] what time corrupters and false shepherds will appear within the church, where a growing faction of the worldly-minded will soon overcome and annihilate what remains of the faithful saints.[37] The sheep turn into wolves as the Wintertime of the Just settles down;[38] the lights go out and the long age of darkness begins under the rule of the Cosmoplanes, disastrously usurping the authority of Christ.[39] There is indeed a promise of comfort and joy, but it is all on the other side and in the distant return of the Lord.[40] The apostles protest, as we do today: Is this a time for speaking of death and disaster?[41] Can all that has transpired be but for the salvation of a few and the condemnation of many? But Jesus remains unyielding: that is not for us to decide or to question.[42] The grim picture is confirmed by the Apostolic Fathers, who are

convinced that they are beholding the fulfillment of these
very prophecies, and are driven by a tragic sense of urgency
and finality. [43] After them the early patristic writers accept
the pattern with heavy reluctance, [44] and only the surprising
and unexpected victory of the church in the fourth century
enable Eusebius's generation to turn the tables and discredit
the whole pessimistic tradition. [45]

Nobody would willingly invent such a depressing
message or accept it without the highest credentials. The picture, though full of familiar elements from the earlier Jewish
apocalypses, is not derived from them. The actors are not
prophets and kings of other ages but the very men sitting
before the Master; the predictions are not for distant ages
but limited to a scope of two generations; [46] and what is
described is not the fate of the world or even of Israel, nor
titanic upheavals of nature, but the undoing of the Christian
society by perverters and corrupters in its midst. [47] The more
grandiose imagery is not missing, but it is kept distinct from
the story of the church, which is concrete, specific, and utterly
gloomy. [47]

All the 40-day teaching is described as very *secret*,
delivered to a closed cult group. [48] There is no desire to intrigue
and mystify, however, as with the Gnostics, but rather the
clearly stated policy that knowledge should be given always
but only to those who ask for it, [49] with the corollary that the
higher and holier a teaching the more carefully it should be
guarded. [50] As "the last and highest revelation," the teaching
of the 40 days was top secret, and has not come down to
us. [51] Since Irenaeus, churchmen have strenuously denied that
there ever was a secret teaching or that anything really important has ever been lost. [52] To profess otherwise would be per-
ilously close to an admission of bankruptcy; yet Christian
scholars do concede that the Apostles had information that
we do not have, [53] allow the existence of an unwritten Apostolic tradition in the church, [54] and grant that there was a
policy of secrecy in the early church—though insisting that it

began with the catechetical schools. [55] The catechists, however, appeal to a much earlier tradition of secrecy, [56] and when the Fathers attempt to reproduce the unwritten tradition which they claim for the church they have nothing to offer but the commonplaces of the schools. [57] Plainly things *have* been lost.

After the alarming gap in the record following the fall of Jerusalem, the curtain rises on a second-century church seething with conflict and split into factions hotly debating the reality of the Resurrection. [58] The Gnostic exploited both the ignorance and the knowledge of the time—the knowledge that the answers to the great questions of existence were known and treasured by "the Elders" of another day, and the ignorance of just what that knowledge was. The oldest definition of the Gnosis specifies that it was the knowledge imparted secretly by the Lord to the Apostles after the Resurrection. The Gnostics claimed to have that very knowledge, [59] and their tremendous initial success shows how hungry the Christian world was for it—the "main church," in fact, had to invent a counter-Gnosis of its own to meet the threat and ended up with a compromise that has left a Gnostic stamp on Christian thinking ever since. [60] The Gnostics did not invent the 40-day situation, as has been claimed, for they were the last people in the world to imagine a return of the Savior in the flesh, and any tinkering would have been readily exposed in a quarreling and hyper-critical society; but they did exploit it because it was there and they had to: at a time when everything else was being questioned, it is one of the few things that is never challenged. [61]

The apocryphal teachings of the 40 days taken together comprise an imposing doctrinal edifice, totally unlike the patchwork systems of the Gnostics. It begins with the most natural question to ask anyone returning to earth after being away: Where did you go and what did you see? The Lord's discourse in reply recalls the journeys to worlds above and below recounted by the prophets and patriarchs of the old

Jewish apocrypha.[62] And yet the picture is quite different: They go as observers and report what they have seen, while he goes as a missionary and reports what he has done. The central theme is the Descensus, a mission to the spirits below closely resembling the Lord's earthly calling.[63] He brings the *kerygma* to all, and those who accept it follow him out of the depths into the light,[64] receive baptism,[65] and hence mount up by degrees to realms of glory, for as in the Jewish apocrypha the picture of other worlds is not a simple one.[66] This mounting up is depicted as the return of the spirit to its heavenly home, where it existed in glory before coming to earth.[67] This is not the Gnostic idea of preexistence, however, for the soul is not sent down as punishment nor imprisoned in the flesh, nor does it fly directly to God after its release from physical confinement;[68] rather it is sent to be tried and tested in "the blessed vessel" of the flesh whose immortality is guaranteed by the resurrection.[69]

There is a strong emphasis in early Christian literature on the doctrine of the Two Ways, depicting life as a time of probation, a constant confrontation with good and evil and the obligation to choose between them.[70] This is conceived as part of a plan laid down "in the presence of the first angels" at the creation of the world,[71] according to which through Adam's fall the human race would be placed in the position, envied by the angels, of being perfectly free to choose good or evil and thereby fully merit whatever rewards would follow.[72] Satan rebelled against the plan, refused obeisance to Adam, and was cast down upon the earth with his cohorts, to fulfill divine purpose by providing, as "the serpent," the temptation necessary for an effectual testing of human beings.[73] Through inspired prophets men from time to time are taught the rules of the game, but are prone to cheat, fall away into darkness, and require painful correction before return to divine favor and a new dispensation of heavenly gifts and covenants.[74] The historical picture is a complicated one, culminating in the final return of the Lord, but not before he has made other appearances, notably to a few "righteous and pure souls and faithful," preparatory to the ultimate and glorious parousia.[75]

What gives substance to this peculiar doctrinal structure is the imposing body of rites and ordinances that goes with it.[76] Ritual and doctrinal elements are inextricably interwoven in a complex in which everything is oddly literal and all fit solidly together: The *kerygma*, whether above or below, is real and must have a "seal," which is baptism, though the word is also used to designate rites of washing and anointing that go with it;[77] after such rites the initiate receives a symbolic but real and tangible garment,[78] and then sits down to a sacral meal, a real repast celebrating the perfect unity of the participants with each other and with the Lord, who is present in spirit.[79] Recent findings indicate unusual emphasis placed on a perfect unity of the sexes in marriage ordinances which were real enough and secret enough to excite the scandalized speculations of outsiders[80] and the fantastic imitation of the Gnostics.[81] After all allowances have been made, there remains a definite residue of early Christian ritual that goes far beyond anything known to later Christianity, which admittedly got its liturgy from the synagogue and the Hellenistic world, while the rites just mentioned all look to the temple and belong to the instructions of the 40 days.[82]

While the schools have their methods for dealing with unwelcome doctrines and traditions, the populace also has ways of absorbing and adapting teachings it does not understand, and the 40-day tradition left a bold imprint on vulgar Christianity. The fact that the Christian liturgy has always allowed a 40-day interval, and an important one, between the Resurrection and the Ascension is not to be lightly explained away,[83] but it is the popular literature of the pseudo-Acts of the Apostles and the legends of the martyrs that most clearly indicate what was paramount in the teachings embraced by the newly converted masses of the age of Constantine.[84] Here we have the monotonous repetition as

one standard miracle, the raising of the dead, performed to
demonstrate to a skeptical world the reality of the resurrection of Jesus.[85] As the saint performs this miracle, or has it
performed on him, Jesus himself stands by, now in his own
person, now in that of the apostle, who is but his double or
understudy.[86] This, it is often explained, is what Jesus meant
when he said he would continue to be with the Apostles to
the end—it is a series of real appearances continuing the personal tutelage and supervision of the 40 days.[87] The secular
equivalent to this is the recurring legend of a youthful military hero and convert who is repeatedly put to death with
spectacular tortures, only to be visited by Christ or the angels
in the night and restored to health, ready to deliver a lecture
on the resurrection and renew his painful demonstrations on
the following day. His resuscitation is celebrated sometimes
with the Eucharist and often with a great public banquet.[88]
The saints Victor, Theodore, George, Mercurius, Sebastian[89]
and the Seven Sleepers,[90] as well as the first lady martyrs,
Thecla, Felicitas, and Perpetua,[91] belong to this illustrious
company to which the names of most of the Apostles were
added.[92]

Recurrent motifs in the legends, such as their strongly
erotic orientation and the prominence of feasting, games,
holy springs, horses and chariots, etc., point unmistakably
to popular pre-Christian hero-cults,[93] typical of which is the
cult of the chaste Hippolytus, impaled on a tree and restored
to life, whose "tragic death and triumphant resurrection made
him a favorite theme alike on Greek and Roman sarco-
phagi."[94] It is well-known that local heroes and their cults
were often converted to Christianity, but why the emphasis
on a particular type of hero to the neglect of others, and how
could the Christians bring themselves to make such concessions to the familiar ways of heathen idolatry? It was not
because the Christian tradition was derived from the other—
we know now that the two were quite different—but because
there were definite points of resemblance at which they could

fuse. Thus Puech and Quispel have recently pointed to the
pagan origin of the cloud and chariot of apotheosis, a conspicuous object in our 40-day accounts.[95] But their well-
known pagan affinities would have rendered them invincibly
repugnant to the Christians had they not something of their
own that closely matched the pagan version. And what that
was is apparent on every other page of the legends, where
Jesus himself breaks into the story to give his instructions
and then mount up to heaven "in great glory." Again, how
could the panegyrics and protocol of the Imperial cult, hailing the Christian emperor as *praesens et corporalis deus*,
appear as anything but blasphemous unless there was a Christian precedent for them?[96] We see that precedent in the constant intervention of Christ and his angels in the solemn
assemblies of the emperor and on the field of battle; the
clouds and angels that surround the august personage are the
familiar properties not of the schools but of the monks of the
desert, who sought to recapture the ancient order of the
church, and who still thought of Christ as paying frequent
and familiar visits to holy men.[97] In the safely theatrical displays of rhetoric and architecture, the 40-day idea of God
mingling with men and supervising their affairs in person
was carried over as a basic Christian concept into the new
popular Christianity.

The easiest way of disposing of the 40-day problem is to
point out the numerous parallels and prefigurements to it,
taking as evidence of fraud what the early Christians regarded
as the sure stamp of authenticity. Easter, Ascension, Pentecost, Transfiguration, and even Parousia are depicted today
as "one undifferentiated experience," or at least as "different
ways of describing the same occurrence," which naturally
leaves no room for the awkward interruption of the 40
days.[98]

But a process need not be instantaneous, indeed cannot
be, and gaps and delays are required if only to allow some
time for preaching to the human family, while the idea that

the Messiah can appear only once denies the fundamental thesis of Christianity and was, in fact, the principal obstacle to the acceptance of Jesus by the Jews.[99] Moreover, if uniqueness is the mark of a historical event, the 40 days commands the highest respect. It is recognized today that the very oddness of Jesus' teachings is strong proof of authenticity. No group of men, it is argued, would come together and of their own volition fashion doctrines that were "a slap in the face . . . to everything that healthy human understanding has viewed as sound thinking from that day to this."[100] What is more, no one would *accept* the incredible reports about the risen Lord unless "facts forced them to it."[101] The argument applies with particular force to the absolutely unparalleled situation of the 40 days, when Christ, "immortal and glorious," condescends "to come to the table of illiterate and poor Apostles, partake of their course fare while he sits chatting with them" in a middle-class tenement or beside a smoky fire on the beach.[102]

The one thing that has got a respectful hearing for the 40-day Ministry is the need for such an episode to explain the founding of the church. Catholic theologians especially favor it as a time for settling all doctrinal issues, establishing proper officials, and preparing the Apostles for a missionary activity which the world was to find irresistible.[103] But we have already noted that the progress of the church was but a triumphal process *"out* of the world,"[104] and that nothing was ever handed down from that great time of instruction, conventional Christianity having rejected all the traditions of the 40 days and turned elsewhere for its doctrine and liturgy.[105] The church can hardly claim the 40 days as its franchise while confessing total ignorance of what was done and taught them.[106]

To summarize, then, we have in the early apocryphal writings both direct and indirect evidence for the reality of the post-resurrectional activity of Jesus. (1) By uniformly supporting the clear and unequivocal language of Acts 1:3, and by making the 40-day teaching their principal concern, these writers serve notice that this subsequently despised and neglected theme had top priority among the early Christians. (2) Under the heading of the 40-day conversations the same writings convey to us a consistent and closely-knit body of doctrine, (3) accompanied by an equally organic structure of rites and ordinances—*not* a farrago of odds and ends in the Gnostic manner. [107] (4) The Gnostic phenomenon itself attests the universal awareness that such a teaching had formerly existed and been lost to the main church: the specific Gnostic claim to possess the secrets of the 40 days shows what it was that was missing. (5) Furthermore, the apocryphal writings themselves fully explain that loss in terms of both secrecy and apostasy, while (6) the great impact of the 40-day image on popular Christianity is clearly reflected in popular legends and cults.

As indirect evidence we must consider the extreme oddness and unpopularity of the 40-day proposition, logically and artistically disturbing and burdened with a view of the future which is negative and frightening. It is anything but a product of wishful thinking or a bid for popular support. Yet the only arguments against it have been arguments of interpretation. Over against a facile manipulation of tests stands a massive array of phenomena which deserves more than the wave of the hand which we have given it here. Why is there no *Evangelium quadraginta dierum*? Its absence confirms the unreality of the 40 days to those scholars who point out that the record speaks only of what Christ *taught* during that period rather than what he *did*. [108] But as Anselm observes, before the resurrection Christ was human—after it he was God. [109] As such he came to teach and to teach only—all are agreed that even the eating and drinking had no other purpose—communing with men on a wholly different level from the man of sorrows in the Gospels. The 40-day episode is indeed unique. If it never took place, what was it that produced the singular phenomena that have been attributed to it?

NOTES

1. "We are bound to conclude that such an occurrence is not only improbable but impossible," John G. Davies, *He Ascended into Heaven* (New York: Association Press, 1958), quote on 56; generally 54-60. Cf. E. Grässer, "Die Apostelgeschichte in der Forschung der Gegenwart," *Theologische Rundschau* 26 (1960): 101. "So hat die Gemeinde . . . gedichtet und gewoben," Wilhelm Bousset, *Kyrios Christos* (Göttingen: Vandenhoeck & Ruprecht, 1926), 74.

2. To be taken "seriously, but not literally," M. J. Suggs, quoting R. Niebuhr, in "Biblical Eschatology and the Message of the Church," *Encounter* 24 (1963): 18-19. "Das können wir zwar nicht zusammendenken, aber die Evangelisten konnten es," David F. Strauss, *Das Leben Jesu*, 9th ed., 2 vols. (Leipzig: Brockhaus, 1864), 2:151-52. "We can only know Jesus clad in the garb of myth," J. Jeremias, "The Present Position in the Controversy Concerning the Problem of the Historical Jesus," *Expository Times* 69 (1958): 334-35.

3. "Half of it I like, and half of it I don't," P. Scherer, "Then Came Jesus and Stood in the Midst: A Sermon," *Interpretation* 12 (1958): 56. "The point is, do we or do we not like the answers?" Murdoch E. Dahl, *The Resurrection of the Body* (London: SCM Press, 1962), 92.

4. E.g., Severus of Antioch fails to mention the 40 days in his exhaustive treatise on the Resurrection, in M.-A. Kugener & Edgar Triffaux, eds. and trs., "Les homilia cathedrales de Sevère d'Antioche: Homélie LXXVII," in *PO* 16:794-862, as does Bousset, *Kyrios Christos*, 74; and Dahl, *The Resurrection of the Body*, 92, also Frederick J. Foakes-Jackson and Kirsopp Lake, *Commentary on Acts* (London: Macmillan, 1939), and Grässer in his long survey "Apostelgeschichte in der Forschung der Gegenwart," 92-167. Even J. F. Walvoord's carefully prepared list of seventeen post-resurrection appearances of Jesus fails to mention the 40 days, "The Earthly Life of the Incarnate Christ," *Bibliotheca Sacra* 117 (1960): 298-300.

5. Discussed by Carl Schmidt, *Gespräche Jesu mit seinen Jüngern nach der Auferstehung* (Leipzig: Hinrich, 1919), 524-29.

6. Thus Davies, *He Ascended into Heaven*, 56–60; S. MacLean Gilmour, "Easter and Pentecost," *Journal of Biblical Literature* 81 (1962): 63–64.

7. Ed. Schweitzer, "Die hellenistichen Komponente im neutestamentlichen Sarx-Begriff," *Zeitschrift für die neutestamentliche Wissenschaft* 48 (1957): 250–53; B. Holt, "Realities of the Ascension," *Encounter* 24 (1963): 88, 90.

8. "It is unlikely that the Apostle's [Paul's] logic bore any resemblance to ours, whether deductive or inductive," Dahl, *The Resurrection of the Body*, 23; Rudolf Bultmann, *Das Verhältnis der urchristlichen Christusbotschaft zum historischen Jesus*, in *Sitzungsberichte der Heidelberger Akademie der Wissenschaften*, no. 3 (1960): 24; Davies, *He Ascended into Heaven*, 57; G. Lindeskog, "Christuskerygma und Jesustradition," *Novum Testamentum* 5 (1961–62): 144.

9. Kirsopp and Silva Lake, *An Introduction to the New Testament* (New York: Harper, 1937), 46–47. John and Paul were both confused about post-resurrectional realities, Gilmour, "Easter and Pentecost," 62–63.

10. Davies, *He Ascended into Heaven*, 52–53. On 40 days as a symbol, Frederick J. Foakes-Jackson, *Acts*, a volume in the Moffatt New Testament Commentary, 17 vols. (New York: Harper, 1931), 5:2; Pierre Miquel, "Christ's Ascension and Our Glorification," *Theology Digest* 9 (1961): 68. See below, note 98.

11. P. A. van Stempvoort, "The Interpretation of the Ascension in Luke and Acts," *New Testament Studies* 5 (1958): 33–34, 39–41, shows that for Luke the designation of 40 days signifies simply "that the appearances of Christ after Easter had a certain duration." Most commentators note that the *paréstēsen hēautón* of Acts 1:3 indicates occasional appearances over a period of time. Hence it would be impossible and foolish to calculate the exact length of the post-Resurrectional sojourn. Even Hilary, *Commentarius in Matthaeum* (*Commentary on Matthew*) 3, in *PL* 9:928, is quite aware of the symbolic propriety of the 40-day expression.

12. Ignatius, *Epistola ad Trallianos* (*Epistle to the Trallians*) 10, in *PG* 5:681; *Epistola ad Smyrnaeos* (*Epistle to the Smyrnaeans*) 2–3, in *PG* 5:708–9.

13. The contradictions are discussed by C. F. D. Moule, "The Ascension—Acts 1:9," *Expository Times* 68 (1957): 205–9. "The blood is the life," but specifically the earthly life, H. W. Robinson, "Blood," in James Hastings, ed., *Encyclopaedia of Religion and Ethics*, 13 vols. (New York: Scribner, 1908–26) 2:715–16, and mention of blood is

pointedly omitted in Luke 24:39, being nowhere ascribed to
resurrected beings. Cf. Hippolytus, *Sermonum sive Homiliarum
Fragmenta* (*Fragments of Sermons or Homilies*) 1, in *PG* 10:861.

14. Cornelius à Lapide [C. van den Steen], *Commentaria in
Scripturam Sacram*, 20 vols. (Paris: Coen, 1877), 18:51.

15. Hildebert, *Sermons on Time* 48, 11 (471), in *PL* 171:579; à
Lapide, *Commentaria in Scripturam Sacram*, 18:48–49, gives other
sources.

16. Lapide, *Commentaria in Scripturam Sacram*,18:50.

17. F. R. Hancock, "The Man of Galilee," *Hibbert Journal* 57
(1958–59): 223.

18. John Chrysostom, *Commentarius in Acta Apostolorum*
(*Commentary on the Acts of the Apostles*) 1, 4, in *PG* 60:9–20;
Theophylactus, *Expositio in Acta Apostolorum* (*Exposition of the Acts
of the Apostles*) 1, 8, in *PG* 125:508.

19. Leo Magnus, *Sermo* (*Discourse*) 73 [71], in *PL* 54:394–96;
Ernaldus, *De Carnalibus Operibus Christi* (*On the Mortal Works of
Christ*) 11, in *PL* 189:1667–68; à Lapide, *Commentaria in Scripturam
Sacram*, 18:51.

20. Chrysostom, *Commentary on the Acts of the Apostles* 1, 5, in
PG 60:19–20; and Frederick F. Bruce, *The Acts of the Apostles*
(London: Tyndale, 1962), 67–68.

21. Miquel, "Christ's Ascension and Our Glorification," 71.

22. William Jenks, ed., *Supplement to the Comprehensive
Commentary on the Holy Bible*, 6 parts (Brattleboro, Vt.: Fessenden,
1838), 5:4.

23. Ernaldus, *On the Mortal Works of Christ* 11, in *PL* 189:
1667–68; á Lapide, *Commentaria in Scripturam Sacram*, 18:49.

24. "The conversations of the Great Forty Days must have been of
intensest interest, yet . . . these things are wrapped about with
thickest darkness," M. Dods, R. Watson, F. Farrar, eds., *An
Exposition of the Bible*, 6 vols. (Hartford: Scranton, 1903–4), 5:302.
"A great deal more passed on those most interesting subjects . . . than
is anywhere recorded," Matthew Henry and Thomas Scott,
Commentary on the Holy Bible, 6 vols. (London: Religious Tract
Society, 1866), 5, at Acts 1:3.

25. "Just what does a spiritual body do? We do not know,"
Eugène Jacquier, *Les actes des apôtres*, 2nd ed. (Paris: Librairie Victor
Lecoffre, 1926), 7–8. "We can only reverently conjecture," Charles J.
Ellicott, *Commentary on the Whole Bible*, 8 vols. (Grand Rapids:
Zondervan, 1954), 7, at Acts 1:3. "Nowhere set forth in the

Scriptures . . . impertinent to inquire and over-bold to specify,"
Lapide, *Commentaria in Scripturam Sacram*, 18:49.

26. Discussed by J. Schneider, "Der Beitrag der Urgemeinde zur
Jesusüberlieferung im Lichte der neuesten Forschung," *Theologische
Literaturzeitung* 87 (1962): 401–12.

27. Michel Testuz, ed., *Papyrus Bodmer X: Correspondance
apocryphe des Corinthiens et de l'apôtre Paul* (Cologne/Geneva:
Bibliotheca Bodmeriana, 1959), 51, 11, 55–56, 24–35; the same in the
Acts of Paul 7 (see in Léon Vouaux, trans. & comm., *Les actes de Paul
et ses lettres apocryphes* [Paris: Letouzey et Ané, 1913], 158–59); cf.
Polycarp, *Epistola ad Philippenses* (*Epistle to the Philippians*) 7, 1, in
PG 5:1012; *Gospel of the Twelve Apostles* 13, 14, in *PO* 2:168–69;
Gospel of Philip 105:9–14 (=*NHLE* 57:9–14, p. 134); Clement,
Epistola I ad Corinthios (*First Epistle to the Corinthians*) 24–27, in
PG 1:260–69; Clement, *Epistola II ad Corinthios* (*Second Epistle to the
Corinthians*) 9, 12, in *PG* 1:341–47; Ignatius, *Epistola ad Magnesios*
(*Epistle to the Magnesians*) 11, in *PG* 5:670; *Epistle to the Trallians*
9–10, in *PG* 5:669–72; *Epistle to the Smyrnaeans* 2–3, in *PG* 5:708–9;
Barnabas, *Epistola Catholica* (*Catholic Epistle*) 5–6, in *PG* 2:733–44;
Hermae Pastor (*Shepherd of Hermas*), *Similitudo* (*Similitudes*) 5, 7, in
PG 2:961–62; *Constitutiones Apostolicae* (*Apostolic Constitutions*)
VI, 26, in *PG* 1:976–77; Revelation to Peter, in E. Verdapet, "The
Revelation of the Lord to Peter," *Zeitschrift für die neutestamentliche
Wissenschaft* 23 (1924): 14; Epistle of the Apostles 19 (30), 21 (32), 25
(36) (Copt. xii, xiv, xix), in *ANT*, 491–94; Apocalypse of Peter, in
ibid., 512–13; Apocalypse of Thomas, in ibid., 561; Apocryphon of
James 11:35–12:17 (=*NHLE*, p. 34); cf. Athenogoras, *De
Resurrectione Mortuorum* (*On the Resurrection of the Dead*), in
PG 6:973–1024; Odes of Solomon 22:9–10, in *OTP* 2:755.

28. "St. Luke . . . gives to his narrative something of the seal of a
medical statement," James J. J. Tissot, *Life of Our Lord Jesus Christ*, 4
vols. (New York: McClure-Tissot, 1899), 4:257. "No metaphysical or
psychological explanation can be given," Hugh V. White,
"Immortality and Resurrection in Recent Theology," *Encounter* 22
(1961): 56–57.

29. Ignatius, *Epistle to the Smyrnaeans* 3, 2, in *PG* 5:709, from an
old Gospel of the Hebrews, according to Jerome, *De Viris Illustribus*
(*On Noted Men*), prologue and chapter 16, in *PL* 23:633, 655, though
Eusebius, *HE* III, 36, 11, in *PG* 20:289, does not know the source.

30. The Testament in Galilee 1, 45 (the Ethiopian version of the
Epistola Apostolorum), in *PO* 9:177, 216, also in Schmidt, *Gespräche
Jesu*, 26–27; this work can also be found in *ANT*, 485–503, and in

NTA 1:189–226; Apocryphon of James 2:19–26, 8:1–4, discussed by H. Puech and G. Quispel, "Les écrits gnostiques du Codex Jung," *Vigiliae Christianae* 8 (1954): 8; Acts of Thomas 1; "Les écrits gnostiques du Codex Jung," in *Testamentum Domini Nostri Jesu Christi (Testament of Our Lord Jesus Christ)*, ed. Ignatius E. Rahmani (Moguntiae: Kircheim, 1899), 1, prologue; *Gospel of the Twelve Apostles* 14, in *PO* 2:169–70; *Gospel of Bartholomew*, in *PO* 2:190–91, 194; and fragments in André Wilmart and Eugene Tisserant, "Fragments grecs et latins de l'evangile de Barthélemy," *Revue Biblique* 22 = n.s. 10 (1913): 185; Oxyrhynchus Logia, no. 8 (1); Freer Logion, in *ANT*, 34; Book of the Resurrection of Christ, in *ANT*, 185.

31. It has been shown that the term "the Living Jesus" (and even "kyrios") refers specifically to the risen Lord, Schmidt, *Gespräche Jesu*, 264; cf. James Rendel Harris, *The Odes and Psalms of Solomon: Now First Published from the Syriac Version* (Cambridge: Cambridge University Press, 1909), 73. Thus the same value must be given to the opening line of the Gospel of Thomas 80:10 (=*NHLE* 32:10, p. 118), as to the Oxyrhynchus Logia, no. 8 (1): "sayings which Jesus who liveth *and was dead* spake to Judas Thomas"; cf. Gospel of Thomas 99:7–8 (=*NHLE* 51:7–8, p. 129). The conversational and questioning form of discourse is another clue, Schmidt, *Gespräche Jesu*, 206; Puech and Quispel, "Les écrits gnostiques du Codex Jung," 9, n. 3; Gospel of Thomas 81:14–17 (=*NHLE* 33:14–17, p. 118); Oxyrhynchus Logia, 4–5, 13 (6), 8 (1); a large number of the pseudo Acts in E.A. Wallis Budge, *Contendings of the Apostles* (Oxford: Oxford University Press, 1935), begin with the Apostles questioning Christ after the Resurrection. Where an account of the Resurrection or Descensus is included in the report the setting is naturally post-resurrectional: this refers to all the apocrypha mentioned below, notes 63–66. The 40-day situation is implied where the resurrection of others is described, as in the second Akhmim fragment of the Gospel of Peter, in *ANT*, 508; *Gospel of the Twelve Apostles* 2, in *PO* 2:135; and Acts of Thomas 54–55, in *ANT*, 390–91. The Prologue to the Discourse on Abbatôn purports to offer documentary evidence from the hands of the Apostles for the typical 40-day situation it describes, in E.A. Wallis Budge, *Coptic Martyrdoms* (London: British Museum, 1914; reprinted New York: AMS, 1977), 225–26, 474–75.

32. Schmidt, *Gespräche Jesu*, 201–6.

33. Matthew 28:17; Mark 16:8, 11–14; Luke 24:11, 21–35, 21–43; John 20:9, 25–29.

34. Schmidt, *Gespräche Jesu*, 346–47.

35. "Let us know what is the end of the aeon for we stand in the midst of scandals and offenses," *Gospel of the Twelve Apostles*, in *PO* 2:160; Apocryphon of James, see Puech and Quispel, "Les écrits gnostiques du Codex Jung," 12–15; Gospel of Thomas 82:25 (=*NHLE* 34:25, p. 119); The Testament in Galilee 1:4, 40, 43, 45, 47–48, 51, 61; Revelation to Peter, in Vardapet, "The Revelation of the Lord to Peter," 12; Epistle of the Apostles 17 (28); 19 (30); cf. Testament of Moses 11, in *OTP* 1:933–34; *Testament of Our Lord Jesus Christ*, 2; Apocalypse of Peter, in *ANT*, 510–11.

36. For a general treatment, Hugh Nibley, "The Passing of the Primitive Church," *Church History* 30 (1961): 132–35, reprinted below in this volume, 169–72.

37. The two parties are the righteous *thlibomenoi* and the wicked *thlibontes*, Herbert Braun, "Zur nachpaulinischen Herkunft des zweiten Thessalonischerbriefes," *Zeitschrift für die neutestamentliche Wissenschaft* 44 (1952–53): 152–54. "They will combine against those who love me, to hate them and push them aside as nothing," Epistle of the Apostles 50 (61), in *ANT*, 503; *Testament of Our Lord Jesus Christ* 1:13. "The idea that the just are going to be persecuted by the wicked" is found in The Testament in Galilee, and Clement, *First Epistle to the Corinthians* 1, 3–6, 45–47, 57, in *PG* 1:205–8, 213–21, 299–308, 324–25; see L. Guerrier, "Avant-Propos," in *PO* 9:145.

38. On the wolves, Ignatius, *Epistola ad Philadelphenses* (*Epistle to the Philadelphians*) 2, in *PG* 5:820; Clement, *Second Epistle to the Corinthians* 5, in *PG* 1:336; Didache 16, in Kirsopp Lake, *The Apostolic Fathers*, Loeb Classical Library, 2 vols. (Cambridge: Harvard University/London: Heinemann, 1912), 1:332; 1 Enoch 89:13–27, 51–75; 90, in *OTP* 1:65–72; cf. Epistle of the Apostles 50 (61), discussed by Schmidt, *Gespräche Jesu*, 197–98. On the Wintertime, *Shepherd of Hermas*, *Similitudes* 3–4, in *PG* 2:955–58, and Charles Wessely, ed. and tr., "Les plus anciens monuments du christianisme écrits sur papyrus," in *PO* 18:469–70; Barnabas, *Catholic Epistle* 15, 5, in *PG* 2:772; Apocalypse of Baruch (=2 Baruch) 21:22–24, in *OTP* 1:628; Gospel of Philip 100:25–35 (=*NHLE* 52:25–35, p. 132), cf. 112:5–10 (=*NHLE* 64:5–10, p. 138). The same imagery of the seasons in Eusebius, *De Laudibus Constantini* (*In Praise of Constantine*) 17, in *PG* 20:1432–33; Cyril of Alexandria, *Commentarius in Joannis Evangelium* (*Commentary on John*) IV, 14, in *PG* 73:617–18, 620; E. W. Brooks, "A Collection of Letters of Severus of Antioch," no. 81, in *PO* 14:130; Gospel of Thomas 84:22–23 (=*NHLE* 36:22–23, p. 120); 1QS (Manual of Discipline) 4:18–19; *TB, Pesaḥim* 2a.

28 MORMONISM AND EARLY CHRISTIANITY

39. This is the most conspicuous theme in all the Apocrypha: The Testament in Galilee 1:3-6; Michaël Asin de Palacios, ed. and tr., "Logia et Agrapha Domini Jesus apud Moslémicos Scriptores, Ascelicos Praesertion Usitata," no. 115, in *PO* 19:542; Sylvain Grébaut, "Les miracles de Jésus," in *PO* 17:827-29; Odes of Solomon 38:9-15, in *OTP* 2:767; Ascension of Isaiah 3:19-4:5 (=Testament of Hezekiah, a Christian work), in *OTP* 2:160-61; Clement, *First Epistle to the Corinthians* 2-5, in *PG* 1:209-20; Ignatius, *Epistola ad Ephesios* (*Epistle to the Ephesians*) 17, in *PG* 5:657; *Epistle to the Philadelphians* 2-3, in *PG* 5:697-700; Barnabas, *Catholic Epistle* 16:9-72, in *PG* 2:773; *Apostolic Constitutions* VII, 32, in *PG* 1:1021-24; Didache 16, in Lake, *The Apostolic Fathers* 1:332; 1 Enoch 89:10-27, in *OTP* 1:65-66; Sibylline Oracles III, and IV, 49, in ibid. 1:385; Secrets of Enoch ([Slavonic] 2 Enoch) 34, in ibid. 1:158-59; 2 Baruch 27-30; 48:32-43; 70, in ibid. 1:630-631, 637, 644-45; 4 Ezra (=2 Esdras) 5:1-13; 9:1-13; 10:1-54, in ibid. 1:531-32, 544-48; *Testament of Our Lord Jesus Christ*, 8; Testament of Moses 5:1-6, in ibid. 1:929-30; The Second Coming of Christ, in *PO*, 145; Epistle of the Apostles 36-45, in *ANT*, 498-502; Apocryphon of Thomas 1, in ibid., 556-58; Akhmim & Freer fragments, in ibid., 507-8; Book of John the Evangelist, in ibid., 191-93.

40. "To these afflictions on earth corresponds the song of triumph in Heaven," E. Fascher, "Gottes Königtum im Urchristentum," *Numen* 4 (1957): 113. "Through their faithfulness unto death they will attain to the glory of God, which is their true destiny," Willem C. van Unnik, *Newly Discovered Gnostic Writings* (Naperville, Ill.: Allenson, 1960), 84. "Joyeuses promesses mêlées de menaces affligeantes, trop de sentiments contradictoires," Puech and Quispel, "Les écrits gnostiques du Codex Jung," 15.

41. Puech and Quispel, "Les écrits gnostiques du Codex Jung," 12, 6, 10, on Apocryphon of James 5:28-16:11; Epistle of the Apostles 36 (47, Copt. viii-ix), in *ANT*, 498; Clement, *Second Epistle to the Corinthians* 5 (Peter protests), in *PG* 1:336, cf. 1 Enoch 89:68-71; Verdapet, "The Revelation of the Lord to Peter," 12.

42. The Testament in Galilee 51, 54, 56; 2 Baruch 55:2-8, in *OTP* 1:640; just so Moses in Apocalypse of Paul, in E.A. Wallis Budge, *Miscellaneous Coptic Texts* (London: British Museum, 1915; reprinted AMS, 1977), 553-54, 1074; 1 Enoch 89:69, 75-77, in *OTP* 1:68-69. There is a special treatment in 4 Ezra 5:28-40; 6:59; 7:46; 8:1-3, 14-15, in ibid., 1:533, 536, 538, 542. The answer is always the same: The Testament in Galilee 1:42-43, 56; 1 Enoch 89:75; 2 Baruch 69:2-4,

75; 4 Ezra 5:40; 7:60–61; 8:47, 55–56; Epistle of the Apostles 19 (30), in *ANT*, 491–92.

43. To the testimony of the Apostolic Fathers, Hugh Nibley, "The Passing of the Primitive Church," 4–5, add Asin de Palacios, "Logia et Agrapha," nos. 108, 115, in *PO* 19:539, 542; Psalms of Solomon 8 (Odes of Solomon 51/50), 15–17, in *OTP* 2:658–60, 664–69; Testuz, *Papyrus Bodmer X*, 52; Apocalypse of Paul, in Budge, *Miscellaneous Coptic Texts*, 540–42, 1060–61; Acts of Thecla (Acts of Paul), cit., Schmidt, *Gespräche Jesu*, 196; Testament of Hezekiah (=Ascension of Isaiah) describes "the worldliness and lawlessness which prevailed" in the church, R. H. Charles, *Apocrypha and Pseudepigrapha of the Old Testament*, 2 vols. (Oxford: Clarendon, 1913), 2:155; Ephraim, Asketikon, in Budge, *Coptic Martyrdoms*, 163–64, 415–16, is very close to the Clement, *First Epistle to the Corinthians*, and the *Shepherd of Hermas*; 127 Canons of the Apostles 12, in *PO* 8:582–83; The Testament in Galilee 1:3, 6–9; *Testament of Our Lord Jesus Christ*, 8.

44. So Justin, *Dialogus cum Tryphone* (*Dialogue with Trypho*) 110, in *PG* 6:493; Origen, *Commentaria in Evangelium secundum Matthaeum* (*Commentary on Matthew*) 36–38, in *PG* 13:1650–53; Hippolytus, *Fragmenta in Danielem* (*Fragments on Daniel*) 38–40, in *PG* 10:664–65; and idem *Scholia in Danielem* 12, 1, in *PG* 10:688; Lactantius, *Divinae Institutiones* (*Divine Institutes*) IV, 30, in *PL* 6:540–44; V, 6, in *PL* 6:567–69; VII, 17, in *PL* 6:793–95; Irenaeus, *Contra Haereses* (*Against Heresies*) V, 30, 1, in *PG* 7:1203; cf. ibid., IV, 34, 4, in *PG* 7:1086; Ephraim, Asketikon, in Budge, *Coptic Martyrdoms*, 163–64, 415–16. "It is as if the Main Church had a premonition of its demise which constantly and ceaselessly resounds through the early writings," R. Abramowski, "Der Christus der Salomooden," *Zeitschrift für die neutestamentliche Wissenschaft* 35 (1936): 69, n. 41.

45. Nibley, "The Passing of the Primitive Church," 135–36.

46. These things happen not to the Apostles but to the second generation after them. The Testament in Galilee 4; so *Shepherd of Hermas, Similitudes* 9, 14; 10, 4, in *PG* 2:979–80; cf. Asin de Palacios, "Logia et Agrapha," no. 224, in *PO* 19:601; Hegesippus in Eusebius, *HE* III, 32, in *PG* 20:281; Epistle of the Apostles 34 (45), in *ANT*, 497. Paul is "the last of the last who will preach to the heathen," Schmidt, *Gespräche Jesu*, 187; cf. 1 Corinthians 4:9–13, and Origen, *Contra Celsum* (*Against Celsum*) 4, 22, in *PG* 11:1056–57; W. Nestle, in *Zeitschrift für Religions- und Geistesgeschichte* 4 (1952): 118–19.

47. Schmidt, *Gespräche Jesu*, 385, notes that there is no mention whatever of the pagans as a source of danger or discomfort; it is the

believers themselves who turn into betrayers and "enemies of
righteousness," Epistle of the Apostles 35, 37, 44, in *ANT*, 497–98,
510. A clear distinction is made between the immediate end and the
end of the world, Epistle of the Apostles 34, in ibid., 497; 1 Enoch 1:2;
Schmidt, *Gespräche Jesu*, 102, 339, 484, comments on this.

48. E.g., "These are the secret sayings which the living Jesus
spoke," Gospel of Thomas 80:10 (=*NHLE* 32:10, p. 118). Since
Apocrypha are by definition secret writings, citations are not
necessary. Even the "canonical traditions record appearances only to
believers" during the 40 days, E. C. Rust, "Interpreting the
Resurrection," in *Journal of Bible and Religion* 29 (1961): 27–28.

49. Matthew 7:8 following 7:6; so Gospel of Truth 19:4–18
(=*NHLE*, p. 39); *Recognitiones Clementinae (Clementine
Recognitions)* III, 53, 58, in *PG* 1:1305, 1307; Gospel of Thomas
96:30–34 (=*NHLE* 48:30–34, p. 128); 80:12–19 (=*NHLE* 32:12–19,
p. 118); 81:10–14 (=*NHLE* 33:10–14, p. 118); 88:16–18 (=*NHLE*
40:16–18, p. 122); 91:34–92:1 (=*NHLE* 43:34–44:1, pp. 124–25);
Tatian, *Orationes (Orations)* 6, in *PG* 6:817. See next note.

50. It can only damage even Christians who are not prepared for
it, 1 Corinthians 3:2; Hebrews 5:12–13; Ignatius, *Epistle to the
Trallians* 5, in *PG* 5:781; *Clementine Recognitions* II, 60, in
PG 1:1276–77; Clement of Alexandria, *Stromata* I, 1, in *PG* 8:704.
The highest is achieved by the fewest: Gospel of Thomas 94:9–13
(=*NHLE* 46:9–13; p. 126); Gospel of Truth 21:3–6 (=*NHLE*, p. 40);
Gospel of Philip 105:32–106:10 (=*NHLE* 57:32–58:10, p. 135);
Clementine Recognitions I, 23, in *PG* 1:1219; I, 28, in *PG* 1:1222; I,
52, in *PG* 1:1236; III, 3, in *PG* 1:1283; III, 34, in *PG* 1:1297; IV, 25, in
PG 1:1324–25; 4 Ezra 14:44–46 in *OTP* 1:555; *Testament of Our Lord
Jesus Christ* 1:18; Clement of Alexandria, *Stromata* V, 10, in
PG 9:93–101; Gospel of Bartholomew 66–68, in *ANT*, 179–80;
Apocalypse of Peter, in ibid., 520; Apocryphon of James 1:8–25
(=*NHLE*, p. 30).

51. At this time the Apostles with some embarrassment ask
questions which they have never asked before, "The Testament in
Galilee," 31, 35 in *PO* 9:204–5, 207; Epistle of the Apostles 20 (31), 24
(35), 25 (36), in *ANT*, 492–95; Gospel of Bartholomew 4–5, in ibid.,
173–81; *Gospel of the Twelve Apostles*, in *PO* 2:135; cf. Jerome,
Dialogus contra Pelagianos (Dialogue against the Pelagians) II, 15, in
PL 23:576–77. They are chided for asking too much, Apocryphon of
James 2:33–39 (=*NHLE*, p. 30); Epistle of the Apostles 25 (36); but are
told "the last and highest teachings," Discourse on the Abbâton, in
Budge, *Coptic Martyrdoms*, 231–32, 480; *Gospel of the Twelve*

Apostles, in
PO 2:160–61; Epistle of the Apostles 12 (23): "great and amazing and
real things." Acts of Thomas 36, in ANT, 382; Gospel of
Bartholomew, fragment in Wilmart and Tisserant, "Fragmenta grecs et
latins," 185. On the ignorance of the Apostles before the Resurrection,
R. Latourelle, "Révélation, histoire et incarnation," Gregorianum 44
(1963): 257.

52. Irenaeus, Against Heresies, Introduction 2, in PG 7:440–44;
II, 27, in PG 7:802–4; III, 1, 1, in PG 7:844; III, 14, in PG 7:913–14. It
was all to be taught "from the housetops," H. Rahner, "The Christian
Mystery and the Pagan Mystery," in Joseph Campbell, ed., The
Mysteries (New York: Pantheon, 1955), 357–58; at least nothing
important has been lost, Latourelle, "Révélation, histoire et
incarnation," 258. Yet it is quite possible to publish some things while
withholding others, Gospel of Thomas 87:10–17 (=NHLE 39:10–17,
p. 122); 4 Ezra 14:6.

53. So Latourelle himself, "Révélation, histoire et incarnation,"
258, and A. de Bovis, "La fondation de l'Église," Nouvelle revue
théologique 85 (1963): 12–13. Clement of Alexandria, Stromata I, 1, in
PG 8:701, insists that his own teachings sound imbecile beside those of
the Apostles, as does Ignatius, Epistle to the Trallians 5, in PG 5:784
(long version); cf. Polycarp, Epistle to the Philippians 3, in PG 5:1009.
Clement of Alexandria tells how early teachings inevitably become
lost, Stromatum I, 1, in PG 8:704; and John Chrysostom, In Epistolam
I ad Corinthios Homilia (Homily on the First Epistle to the Corinthians) 7, in PG 61:58, and Basil, Epistolae (Letters) 8, in PG 32:257,
note that many sacred writings have been lost. Irenaeus, Against
Heresies, himself puts the knowledge of the Apostles in a special
category, I, 13, 6, in PG 7:588, and when pressed admits that the Bible
does not explain everything, and so falls back on tradition, III, 3, 1, in
PG 7:848, and when this fails him he appeals to the oldest churches,
III, 4, 1, in PG 7:851, and when these disagree to the most outlying
ones, III, 4, 2, in PG 7:855–56.

54. A favorite teaching of Basil, Gottfried Thomasius, Die
christliche Dogmengeschichte als Entwicklungsgeschichte des
kirchlichen Lehrbegriffs, 2nd ed. (Erlangen: Deichert, 1886–89), vol. 1,
Die Dogmengeschichte der alten Kirche (Erlangen: Deichert, 1886),
279–80. The greatest teachings were not trusted to writing, Clementine
Recognitions I, 21, in PG 1:1218; Epistles of Paul and Seneca 6, in
ANT, 482; John Chrysostom, De Laudibus Sancti Pauli Apostoli
Homilia (Homily on the Praise of St. Paul the Apostle) 5, in

PG 50:500, and *Homilia de Melchisedeco* (*Homily on Melchizedek*) 1, in *PG* 56:257–58.

55. Albert Schweitzer, *Geschichte der Leben-Jesu-Forschung* (Tübingen: Mohr, 1913) 1:396, admits the secrecy though at a loss to explain it (= *The Quest of the Historical Jesus* [New York: Macmillan, 1964]). An awkward attempt to explain the secrecy of the 40 days is made by John Chrysostom, *Commentary on the Acts of the Apostles* 1, in *PG* 60:19, and borrowed by Oecumenius, *Commentary on the Acts of the Apostles* 1, 2, in *PG* 118:45, and Theophylactus, *Exposition of the Acts of the Apostles* 1, 16, in *PG* 125:505. On the *doctrina arcana* and the catechetical schools, J. Baum, "Symbolic Representations of the Eucharist," in Campbell, ed., *The Mysteries*, 261; O. Chadwick, *From Bossuet to Newman* (Cambridge: Cambridge University Press, 1957), 68.

56. Discussed by A. Adam, "Ein vergessener Aspekt des frühchristlichen Herrenmahles," *Theologische Literaturzeitung* 88 (1963): 10–11, for Origen and Clement of Alexandria. Cf. Clement (dubia), *Homiliae* (*Homilies*) 19, 20, in *PG* 2:441; Lactantius, *Divine Institutes* VII, 26, in *PL* 6:815; *Clementine Recognitions* III, 74, in *PG* 1:1314. Baum himself is seeking to explain why representations of the Lord's supper in art are "shunned down to the fifth century," Baum, "Symbolic Representations of the Eucharist," 262.

57. Irenaeus can only use the feeble arguments of the Gnostics against them: *Against Heresies* II, 2, 4, in *PG* 7:714; II, 8, 3, in *PG* 7:733; II, 22, 6, in *PG* 7:785; II, 25, 3, in *PG* 7:799; II, 28, 2–3, in *PG* 7:804–7. "When, however, we come to inquire into the nature of this sublime knowledge, we find that it consists of subtle explanations . . . allegorical and mystical interpretations . . . and of moral precepts," John Kaye, *Ecclesiastical History of the Second and Third Centuries, Illustrated from the Writings of Tertullian* (London: Griffith, Farran & Browne, 1894), 16–17.

58. Justin, *Dialogue with Trypho* 80, 2–5, in *PG* 6:664–65. This remains the question of questions, to distinguish Christians from pagans and true Christians from false: Augustine, *Enarrationes in Psalmos* (*Expositions on the Psalms*) 88, in *PL* 37:1134; *Sermones* (*Sermons*) 109, in *PL* 39: 1961; *Questions from Both Sides* 114 (Against Pagans), in *PL* 35:2345 (Appendix).

59. Irenaeus, *Against Heresies* IV, 33, 8, in *PG* 7:1077–78; Eusebius, *HE* II, 1, 3–4, in *PG* 20:136; cf. III, 32, 8, in *PG* 20:284–86.

60. Gnosticism "left a mark upon the Christian Church which has persisted right up to the present day," van Unnik, *Newly Discovered Gnostic Writings*, 43. Even Irenaeus's rebuttal is but "a commonplace

presentation of ordinary Gnostic beliefs," A. S. Peake, quoted in Werner Förster, "Das System des Basilides," *New Testament Studies* 9 (1963): 235. The opening lines of the *Clementine Recognitions* pose the "great questions" as the legitimate object of all human search, to which, it is later explained, the Gnostics had the wrong answers and Peter the right ones.

61. The charge of Irenaeus against the Gnostics is not that they invent new absurdities, but that they misrepresent true and familiar doctrines; so also Polycarp, *Epistle to the Philippians* 7; Testuz, *Papyrus Bodmer X*, 52:3. Their teachings are very convincing to Christians, for they use *genuine logia* but give them a false twist, Irenaeus, *Against Heresies* I, Introduction 1; their teachings look perfectly orthodox, I, Introduction 2; their fault is not in appealing to noncanonical writings, but in counterfeiting such, I, 20; I, 8, 1; they imitate the sacrament, I, 13, 2; they fake prophecy, I, 13, 3-5; they counterfeit revelation with potions and drugs, I, 13, 5; they parody marriage rites, I, 21, 3, and baptism, I, 21, 3, and anointing, I, 21, 4-5; they feign miraculous healings, I, 23, 1. They do *not* (except for Marcus) change the scriptures but misinterpret them, I, 27, 4; their teachings are a patchwork taken from the schools, II, 14, 2-6, all in *PG* 7:437-754; Ignatius brings the same charges: they are bad interpreters of the good word, mixing poison with good wine, *Epistle to the Trallians* 6, in *PG* 5:668; as Irenaeus says, they mix chalk with milk, *Against Heresies* III, 17, 4, in *PG* 7:931-32.

62. Such cosmic tours are described in Jubilees, 1 Enoch, 2 Enoch, Apocalypse of Abraham, Odes of Solomon, Testament of Moses, Apocalypse of Isaiah, Ascension of Isaiah, 2 Baruch. In the Testaments of Abraham, Isaiah, Isaac, the XII Patriarchs, Adam, Enoch, the saint gives blessings and prophecies to his (12) descendants or disciples before mounting to heaven and immediately *after* his return from a cosmic tour: the parallel to the 40 days is obvious; see Marinus de Jonge, *The Testaments of the XII Patriarchs* (Assen: Van Gorcum, 1953), 120.

63. Schmidt, *Gespräche Jesu*, 481-86. On the present-day "rediscovery" of the Descensus, O. Rousseau, "La descente aux enfers, fondement sotériologique du baptême chrétien," *Recherches des sciences religieuses* 40 (1951-52): 273; Martin H. Scharlemann, "He Descended into Hell," *Concordia Theological Monthly* 27 (1956): 81. Bo Reicke, *The Disobedient Spirits and Christian Baptism* (Copenhagen: Munksgaard, 1946), 14-15, asks why the Descensus is not treated in the earliest literature even though it "was clearly developed already in the writings of the Apostolic Fathers." Obviously because it

was a secret teaching, though very popular in the early Church, A. Dell, "Matthew 16, 17–19," *Zeitschrift für die neutestamentliche Wissenschaft* 15 (1914): 31–33.

64. For a general treatment, John A. MacCulloch, *The Harrowing of Hell* (Edinburgh: Clark, 1930), chs. 15 & 16. On the Jewish background, Marc Philonenko, *Les interpolations chrétiennes des Testaments des XII Patriarches* (Paris: Presses Universitaires de France, 1960), 22–24. See note 65.

65. Rousseau, "La descente aux enfers, fondement sotériologique du baptême chrétien," 273–97, declares the Descensus to be nothing less than "the soteriological foundation of Christian baptism," and Bo Reicke, in *Archiv für Kirchengeschichte*, n.s. 27:2–3, notes that early Christian baptisms were consciously dramatized to represent a release from the underworld. Harris, *The Odes and Psalms of Solomon*, 123, identifies Christ's own baptism with the Descensus. On the baptism in the Acherusian Lake, J. B. Frey, "La vie de l'au-dela dans les conceptions juives au temps de Jésus-Christ," *Biblica* 13 (1932): 145–46; Erik Peterson, "Die Taufe im acherusischen See," *Vigiliae Christianae* 9 (1955): 1–20. Cf. John H. Bernard, "The Descent into Hades and Christian Baptism," *Studia Sacra* (London: Hodder & Stoughton, 1917), 1–50.

66. The doctrine by which "the soul mounts up continually from topos to topos was thoroughly orthodox, Carl Schmidt, *Gnostische Schriften in koptischer Sprache aus dem Codex Brucianus* (Leipzig: Hinrich, 1892), 193–94; Schmidt, *Gespräche Jesu*, 496–97, 512–13; cf. Origen, *Homiliae in Librum Jesu Nave* 25, in *PG* 12:944; cf. Gospel of Thomas 90:5–7 (=*NHLE* 42:5–7, p. 123); Gospel of Truth 21:23–34 (=NHLE 21:23–24, p. 40); Gospel of Philip 133:17–18 (=*NHLE* 85:17–18, p. 150); Apocalypse of Paul, in Budge, *Miscellaneous Coptic Texts*, 1027–28, 1055; Ignatius, *Epistle to the Trallians* 5, in *PG* 5:781–85; *Epistle to the Ephesians* 19, in *PG* 5:753; *Epistola ad Polycarpum* (*Epistle to Polycarp*) 7, in *PG* 5:869, calling Polycarp *theodromos*, "God runner," "Messenger of God"; Epistle of the Apostles 13–14; 19, in *ANT*, 489–92; 2 Enoch 61:2; Oxyrhynchus Logion 1, 2; Clement of Alexandria, *Stromata* II, 9, in *PG* 8:975–81; V, 14, 96, in *PG* 9:148–49. Cf. the doctrine of "stages of ascent," i.e., three levels of enlightenment to which the Christian can aspire even during this life, H. P. Owen, "The 'Stages of Ascent' in Hebrews 5:11–6:3," *New Testament Studies* 3 (1957): 243–53.

67. An old and orthodox idea. According to Wilhelm Bousset, *Jüdisch-christlicher Schulbetrieb in Alexandria und Rom* (Göttingen:

Vandenhoeck & Ruprecht, 1915), 269, Clement of Alexandria was the first to reject it. Though it was condemned by the Council of Constantinople in 553, A. Méhat, " 'Apocatastase' Origène, Clément d' Alexandrie, Acts 3, 21," *Vigiliae Christianae* 10 (1956): 196, Pius XII himself in *Mediator Dei* refers to this life as "an exile."

68. Irenaeus, *Against Heresies* I, 25, 4, in *PG* 7:676–78; *Clementine Recognitions* II, 57, in *PG* 1:1275. Augustine condemns the idea that the soul sinned in its pre-existence and is being punished on earth, without condemning the doctrine of pre-existence itself, M. Leusse, "Le probleme de la Préexistence des Ames chez Marius Victorinus Afer," *Recherches des sciences religieuses* 29 (1939): 236, n. 1; 237, n. 1. So also Cyril of Jerusalem, *Catechesis IV de Decem Dogmatibus* (*Catechetical Lecture on the Ten Doctrines*) 19, in *PG* 33:480; while Origen even suggests that earth-life is a reward rather than a punishment, *Peri Archon* (*On First Things*) I, 8, 4, in *PG* 11:179–82; II, 9, 6–8, in *PG* 11:230–33.

69. Quote is from Barnabas, *Catholic Epistle* 21, 7–8, in *PG* 2:780–81; cf. *The Testament in Galilee* 47, in *PO* 9:218–19; *Gospel of Philip* 124:32–36 (=*NHLE* 76, p. 146); *Psalms of Thomas*, in Alfred Adam, *Die Psalmen des Thomas und das Perlenlied als Zeugnisse vorchristlichen Gnosis*, in *Zeitschrift für die neutestamentliche Wissenschaft*, Supplement 24 (Berlin: Töpelmann, 1959), 9:1, 8–10; 2 Baruch 15:8, 16; 19:1; 21:13, 16; *Testament of Our Lord Jesus Christ* 1:13; Tertullian, *De Baptismo* (*On Baptism*) 20, 2, in *PL* 1:1332–34.

70. Sources listed in de Jonge, *The Testaments of the XII Patriarchs*, 119–20, to which add *127 Canons of the Apostles* 2, in *PO* 8:575; Asin de Palacios, "Logia et Agrapha," nos. 145, 193, in *PO* 19:562–63, 583; *Homiliae Clementinae* 7, in *PG* 2:221; Clement, *Second Epistle to the Corinthians* 6, in *PG* 1:336; Ignatius, *Epistle to the Magnesians* 5, in *PG* 5:761–64; Barnabas, *Catholic Epistle* 5, 19–20, in *PG* 2:733–37; *Clementine Recognitions* II, 24, in *PG* 1:1261; often in the *Manual of Discipline* (1QS) 3:2–4, 13–25; 4:1–26; cf. Psalm 1.

71. On the Council, Justin, *Dialogue with Trypho* 102, in *PG* 6:712–13; 141, in *PG* 6:797–800; 1 Enoch 48:2–6; 62:7; Ignatius, *Epistle to the Ephesians* 19, in *PG* 5:753; 4 Ezra 9:18; *The Hypostasis of the Archons* 135:23–25 (=*NHLE* 87:23–25, p. 153). A genuine biblical motif, H. Wheeler Robinson, "The Council of Yahweh," *Journal of Theological Studies* 45 (1944): 151–57; Frank M. Cross, "The Council of Yahweh in Second Isaiah," *Journal of Near Eastern Studies* 12 (1953): 274–77. Cf. N. A. Dahl, "Christ, Creation, and the Church," in William Davies & David Daube, *The Background of the*

New Testament and Its Eschatology (Cambridge: Cambridge University, 1956), ch. 22, on the importance of protology in early Christian thought; Masao Sekine, "Schöpfung und Erlösung im Buche Hiob," in J. Hempel and L. Rost, eds., *Von Ugarit nach Qumran*, in *Zeitschrift für die alttestamentliche Wissenschaft*, Supplement 77 (Berlin: Töpelmann, 1958): 220-21. That the Two Ways is part of the Plan is specified by *Clementine Recognitions* I, 24, in *PG* 1:1220; I, 28, in *PG* 1:1222; III, 26, in *PG* 1:1294-95; V, 9, in *PG* 1:1334; cf. *Odes of Solomon* 7:11-12; 31, and Harris' comment, p. 129; *Apocryphon of James* 4:27-5:6 (=*NHLE* 4:27-5:6, pp. 31-32); *Psalm of Thomas* 8:16-18 (the demons have a counterplan); Justin, *Dialogue with Trypho* 102, in *PG* 6:712-13; 141, in *PG* 6:797-800, and *Apologia pro Christianis* (*Apology*), 10, in *PG* 6:460-61.

72. Irenaeus calls this "the ancient law of liberty," *Against Heresies* IV, 37, 1-6, in *PG* 7:1099-1103; IV, 39, 3, in *PG* 7:1109-10. It is explained in *Clementine Recognitions* II, 23-25, in *PG* 1:1260-61; III, 26, in *PG* 1:1294; III, 49, in *PG* 1:1303; III, 59, in *PG* 1:1312; IV, 24, in *PG* 1324; IV, 34, in *PG* 1:1330; *Apocalypse of Paul*, in Budge, *Miscellaneous Coptic Texts*, 1066; *The Testament in Galilee* 50, in *PO* 9:221-23; *Apocryphon of James* 4:27-5:6 (=*NHLE* 4:27-5:6, p. 31-32); Clement, *Second Epistle to the Corinthians* 7, in *PG* 1:337; *Shepherd of Hermas, Similitudes* 10, 2, in *PG* 2:989; *Clementine Recognitions* I, 7-8, in *PG* 1:1210-11; I, 16, in *PG* 1:1215; I, 27, in *PG* 1:1222; I, 51, in *PG* 1:1236; II, 21, in *PG* 1:1259; IV, 14, in *PG* 1:1320-21; V, 5, in *PG* 1:1333; 1 Enoch 69:11; 2 Baruch 54:15; 4 Ezra 7:72; 8:55-56; 9:10-11; Tatian, *Orations* 7, in *PG* 6:820-21.

73. Testuz, *Papyrus Bodmer X*, 53-54; *Psalm of Thomas* 9:7-16; *The Pearl*, in Adam, *Die Psalmen des Thomas und das Perlenlied*, 9-15; Theodosius, *On St. Michael*, in Budge, *Miscellaneous Coptic Texts*, 339-40, 906-7; *Discourse on the Abbatôn*, in Budge, *Coptic Martyrdoms*, 240, 488; *Gospel of Philip* 102:29-31 (=*NHLE* 54:29-31, p. 133); 123:4-14 (=*NHLE* 75:4-14, p. 145); *Homiliae Clementinae* (*Clementine Homilies*) 9, in *PG* 2:241-58; Ignatius, *Epistle to the Ephesians* 13, 19, in *PG* 5:746-47; *Epistle to Polycarp* 3, in *PG* 5:709. Satan rules the earth, Barnabas, *Catholic Epistle* 2, in *PG* 2:729; 4, in *PG* 2:731-33; 18, in *PG* 2:776-77; *Psalm of Thomas* 1:17-37; 3:5-8; 1 Enoch 6:7; 44; 2 Enoch 18, 31:4; *Acts of Thomas* 32-33, 44-45, in *ANT*, 379-80, 386; Jerome, *Dialogue against Pelagians* II, 15, in *PL* 23:576-77, citing an old apocryphon. Cf. the "rule of Belial" in the Dead Sea Scrolls, *Zadokite fragment* 3:4; Jubilees 10:5-9; 11:5, etc. On the Origin of the World (=*NHLE* 98:27-99:28, p. 162-63).

74. The rules were first explained to Adam, 2 Enoch 30:14-15; it is the business of the true prophet to announce them, *Clementine Recognitions* V, 10, in *PG* 1:1334-35. The image of the games is familiar from the New Testament and the Apostolic Fathers, e.g., Clement, *Second Epistle to the Corinthians* 7, in *PG* 1:337-40; and 4 Ezra 7:57-61. The cycle of revelation—apostasy—punishment—restoration is well-known, de Jonge, *The Testaments of the XII Patriarchs*, 83-86.

75. Testament of Our Lord Jesus Christ 1:8; 12; 13; this is a 40-day teaching, according to Adolf von Harnack, in *TU* 9:16-17. Cf. The Testament in Galilee 7, in *PO* 9:184; 2 Baruch 29, 2-3; 70:7; Hippolytus, *On Daniel* 10, in *PG* 10:685; 12, in *PG* 10:688; *Clementine Recognitions* V, 11, in *PG* 1:1335. The preliminary coming is not to be confused with the later coming, M. Feuillet, "Le sens du mot Parousia dans l'Evangile de Matthieu," in Davies & Daube, *The Background of the New Testament and Its Eschatology*, 262-69, and L. Guerrier, "Les Tes Avant-Propos," in "The Testament in Galilee," in *PO* 9:151.

76. Abramowski, "Der Christus der Salomooden," 60: "die Formeln eschatologisch klingen . . . aber real kultisch gemeint." Albertus F.J. Klijn, *The Acts of Thomas* (Leiden: Brill, 1962), 54ff.

77. Types of "seals" are discussed by Harris, *The Odes and Psalms of Solomon*, 78-79, and Klijn, *The Acts of Thomas*, 56-59. In Odes of Solomon 42:20, the seal is a name, in 4:8 it is a garment, in 8:16 it is a mark, in 23:8-12 it is an actual seal on a letter. In *Shepherd of Hermas*, *Similitudes* 8, 1-2, in *PG* 2:971-73, all receive seals and garments; in *Similitudes* 9, 16, in *PG* 2:995, "the seal is the water"; in *Apostolic Constitutions* VII, 22, in *PG* 1:1012-13, it is an anointing; in Barnabas, *Catholic Epistle* 9, 23-27, in *PG* 2:749-52, it is circumcision; in The Pearl it is both on a letter, 48-49, and a garment, 80-85, in the Testament of Moses 12:9 God wears a seal or ring on his right hand, cf. *127 Canons of the Apostles* 10, in *PO* 8:580. As the soul mounts up "all these stations have their taxeis and their seals and their mysteries," Schmidt, *Gnostische Schriften in koptischer Sprache aus dem Codex Brucianus*, 193-94. Anointing is conspicuous in the Gospel of Philip; there is anointing after the baptism in *Apostolic Constitutions* VII, 22, in *PG* 1:1012-13; Acts of Thomas 27, in *ANT*, 376; 121, in *ANT*, 418; 132, in *ANT*, 422; 157-58, in *ANT*, 433-34; Testament of Our Lord Jesus Christ 2:9; Life of Adam and Eve 42; 2 Enoch 21-22; 56:2; 3 Baruch 15:1-2. The rites are often confused, Hans Achelis, *Die ältesten Quellen des orientalischen Kirchenrechtes* (Leipzig: Hinrich, 1891-1904), 96ff; *OTP* 1:138, note o; 677, ch. 15,

note, recommending Esther Quinn, *The Quest of Seth for the Oil of Life* (Chicago: University of Chicago Press, 1962).

78. Without the clothing the rite is invalid, *Shepherd of Hermas, Similitudes* 9, 13; cf. 8 2, in *PG* 977-79. The resurrection itself is conceived as the putting on of a new garment, Carl Clemen, *Primitive Christianity and Its Non-Jewish Sources* (Edinburg: Clark, 1912), 173-74. Beside the familiar white robe of baptism the sources speak of a garment of repentance, a skin coat worn by the prophets in the desert in the manner of John the Baptist, Robert Eisler, *Iesous Basileus ou Basileusas*, 2 vols. (Heidelberg: Winter, 1929-30) 2:33-38. Clement, *First Epistle to the Corinthians* 17, in *PG* 1:241-44: this advice was taken literally, Apocalypse of Peter 17, in *ANT*, 508, where the whole community on the Mount of Transfiguration are so clothed; cf. Ascension of Isaiah 4:16; 11:40; and Life of Onnophrius, in Budge, *Coptic Martyrdoms*, 219, 469. Adam lost his garment of holiness and put on a garment of humility, Irenaeus, *Against Heresies* III, 23, 5, in *PG* 7:963-64; Jubilees 3:31; while Enoch reversed the process, 2 Enoch 22:8; cf. Acts of Thomas 6-7, in *ANT*, 367-68; 146, in *ANT*, 428-29; Acts of Philip, in Constantin von Tischendorf, *Apocalypses Apocryphae Mosis, Esdrae, Pauli* (Leipzig: Mendelssohn, 1866; reprinted Hildesheim: Olms, 1966), 147.

79. The meal taking place after baptism marked the death and resurrection, *Apostolic Constitutions* VIII, 12, in *PG* 1:1092-1108; Oscar Cullmann, *Urchristentum und Gottesdienst* (Zürich: Zwingli, 1950), 18, notes that this consciously goes back to "those meals where Jesus after his Resurrection appeared to the disciples." The mystic unity is emphasized in *Gospel of the Twelve Apostles*, in *PO* 2:132-35; Gospel of Thomas 28:28-30 (=*NHLE* 50:28-30, p. 129); Gospel of Philip 106:11-14 (=*NHLE* 58:11-14, p. 135); Odes of Solomon 41:5-7; Ignatius, *Epistle to the Philadelphians* 4, in *PG* 5:821-28; Didache 9; Testament of Our Lord Jesus Christ 1:23, in Rahmani, *Testament of Our Lord Jesus Christ*, 44. The Jewish parallels are many, e.g., "the table of the community," in 1QSa 2:18; cf. Adam, "Ein vergessener Aspekt des frühchristlichen Herrenmahles," 9-20.

80. Aristides, *Apology* 17, 2; Minucius Felix, *Octavius* 8-10, in *PL* 3:266-76. The charges were "not altogether without foundation," R. M. Wilson, *The Gospel of Philip* (New York: Harper & Row, 1962), 21-22, though the nature of the rites cannot be surmised either from the anti-Christian scandal stories or from the Gnostic distortions. The famous passage about the "two becoming one," etc., is not the abolition of the sexes (the later Fathers often puzzle about the survival of the sexes in the resurrection), but the overcoming of all prurient

THE FORTY-DAY MISSION OF CHRIST

distinction and rivalry, the two becoming one "in the Lord" (1 Corinthians 11:11); Gospel of Thomas 85: 25-35 (=NHLE 37:25-35, p. 121); Gospel of Philip 113:1-26 (=NHLE 65:1-26, p. 139), 118:13-22 (=NHLE 70:13-22, p. 142); Acts of Thomas 14, in ANT, 370; Oxyrhynchus Frg. 655; Clement of Alexandria, Stromata III, 13, in PG 8:1192; III, 9, in PG 8:1165-69; Clement, Second Epistle to the Corinthians 12, in PG 1:345-48.

    81. Robert M. Grant, "The Mystery of Marriage in the Gospel of Philip," Vigiliae Christianae 15 (1961): 140, argues that this consisted in "literalizing" the orthodox ideas. But Irenaeus's stock charge against the Gnostics is that they de-literalize everything, their marriages of the Aeons being a good example, Against Heresies I, 28, 1, in PG 7:690-91; I, 21, 3, in PG 7:687. Tatian, Orations 8, in PG 6:821-25, maintains that marriage is defilement, as in the Acts of Thomas 12. In a conversation of the 40 days Salome wrongly "imagined that it is wrong to have children," Clement of Alexandria, Stromata III, 9, 66, in PG 8:1165-69.

    82. While in a sense the synagogue is a shadow of the temple and preserves or rather cherishes aspects of its rites and teachings, the essential qualities of the latter are lacking in the synagogue, as we indicated in Hugh Nibley, "Christian Envy of the temple," Jewish Quarterly Review 50 (1960): 230-33, 239. The temple's "rich cosmic symbolism which was largely lost in later Israelite and Jewish tradition," William F. Albright, Archaeology and the Religion of Israel (Baltimore: Johns Hopkins Press, 1942), 154-55, 88-89, 167, included, as Alfred Jeremias, Sigmund Mowinckel and others have shown, such elements as its cosmic orientation, its significance as a place of contact with other worlds above and below, the ritual drama of creation, fall, and victory over death, rites of initiation and purification, etc. These basic elements of Near Eastern "patternism" have been recently discussed with special reference to the Jerusalem cult by the authors of Samuel H. Hooke, ed., Myth, Ritual, and Kingship (Oxford: Clarendon, 1958). The relation of these things to early Christian thought and practice is discussed by N. Dahl, "Christ, Creation, and the Church," 422-43. Even the Christian sacral meal which Cullmann believes was meant to supplant the temple worship, Oscar Cullmann, "Le Temple de Jérusalem," New Testament Studies 5 (1959): 171, is now traced to the temple itself by Adam, "Ein vergessener Aspekt des frühchristlichen Herrenmahles," 9-20. The problem of just what went on in the temple at Jerusalem at various periods calls for extensive investigation.

83. Davies, *He Ascended into Heaven*, 55. The *length* of the interval is not the significant thing, as van Stempvoort notes, "The Interpretation of the Ascension in Luke and Acts," 34, but its existence is.

84. Though there is a trend in the legends away from history and doctrine towards "pure thaumaturgy," *ANT*, 474, the literature as a whole goes "back to standard themes in popular preaching and Apocryphal Acts," Klijn, *Acts of Thomas*, 25.

85. The raising of the dead is an actual demonstration of the Resurrection, *Apostolic Constitutions* V, 7, in *PG* 1:837–52; "Letters of Severus," 88, in *PO* 14:153; the dead are raised in response to the challenge, "How could . . . Jesus Christ rise from the dead?" Budge, *Contendings of the Apostles*, 177–21. Upon raising a dead man Peter cries, "Ye men of Rome, it is thus that the dead are raised up!" Acts of Peter 28–29, in *ANT*, 329; cf. Gospel of the Twelve Apostles 16, in *PO* 2:135; Budge, *Contendings of the Apostles*, 580–81; Acts of Paul (Martyrdom, 1–5), in *ANT*, 294–96.

86. "I saw (Jesus) standing by thee at the moment when thou didst raise me up from the dead," Budge, *Contendings of the Apostles*, 86. "He saw our Lord Jesus Christ in the form of Judas Thomas sitting on the bed," ibid., 343; Thecla in the arena "saw the Lord sitting, like unto Paul," in the audience, Acts of Paul 2:21, in *ANT*, 276. After Philip's death Jesus appears "at the end of 40 days . . . in the form of Philip," to teach his disciples, Acts of Philip 148, in ibid., 450. The post-burial appearances and the ascension of Thomas are exactly like Jesus', Acts of Thomas 169, in ibid., 437. The closest identity is with Mary who is inseparable from Jesus during the 40 days, and whose resurrection was "a greater miracle than the Resurrection of the Lord," Gospel of the Twelve Apostles 16, in *PO* 2:182. The 40 days must even follow *her* resurrection! Falling Asleep of Mary, in Forbes Robinson, *Coptic Apocryphal Gospels* (Cambridge: Cambridge University Press, 1896), 65.

87. Jesus "would appear to them in the form in which they used to know Him," give his instructions, and then "mount up into heaven in great glory," Story of Joseph of Arimathea 2–3, in *ANT*, 164–65; Acts of John 72–76, in ibid., 246; Acts of Peter 3:1, in ibid., 304; 5, in ibid., 307–9; 16, in ibid., 317; 35, in ibid., 333; Acts of Philip 20, in ibid., 441; Budge, *Contendings of the Apostles*, 154–56, 158–62, 171, 185, 230, 247, 265–68, etc. He could appear "in any form I please," ibid., 318; Acts of John, in Montague R. James, *Apocrypha Anecdota*, 2nd series (Cambridge: Cambridge University Press, 1897), ii, 5; iv.

88. During the feast of St. George the Saint himself appeared, multiplied the loaves and wine and brought all the sacrificed animals to life. Franz Cumont, "St. George and Mithra 'The Cattle-Thief,' " *Journal of Roman Studies* 27 (1937): 71. This multiplying of loaves and fishes is a theme of the post-resurrectional meals with the Lord, e.g., Gospel of the Twelve Apostles 2, in *PO* 2:132–34. Tha'labī, *Kitāb Qiṣaṣ al-Anbiyā* (Cairo: Muṣṭafā al-Halabī al-Bābī wa-Awlāduhu, 1354 A.H.), 272, 276–77, 280, cites a number of early Christian legends in which the raising of the dead is accompanied by a feast miraculously provided from heaven. The Apostles often celebrate a raising of the dead with a feast or the Eucharist, Acts of John 84, in *ANT*, 250; cf. Acts of Peter 5, in ibid., 308–9; Acts of Andrew 20, in ibid., 344; Budge, *Contendings of the Apostles*, 22.

89. For Victor, Budge, *Coptic Martyrdoms*, 1–101; for Theodore, Budge, *Miscellaneous Coptic Texts*, 1–48; the St. George cycle is in Tha'abī, *Kitāb Qiṣaṣ al-Anbiyā*, 299–304; for Mercurius, Budge, *Miscellaneous Coptic Texts*, 231–99; for Sebastian, Ambrose, *Acta Sancti Sebastiani* (*Acts of St. Sebastian*), in *PL* 17:1111–50, where after his final demise the saint still returns to give instructions, 1149–50.

90. "Toutes les versions des Sept Dormants servent à prouver la résurrection des morts," Bernhard Heller, "Eléments, Parallèlles et Origine de La Légende des Sept Dormants," *Revue des études Juives* 49 (1904): 215. The identity of the Seven Sleepers with the seven heroic brothers of 4 Maccabees 8:3–11 has long been recognized, Hippolyte Delehaye, "Hagiographie Napolitaine," *Analecta Bollandiana* 57 (1939): 30. Though the latter tale is in praise of philosophy, even there the resurrection motif occurs, as when the eldest brother appears "as if he were suffering a change by fire to incorruption," 4 Maccabees 9:22.

91. A friend of Thecla's embraces her after one of her resuscitations crying, "Now do I believe that the dead are raised up!" Acts of Paul 39 in *ANT*, 280. The seven sons of Felicitas repeat the story of 4 Maccabees 8; see Peter Chrysologus, *Sermones* (*Discourses*) 134, in *PL* 52:564–65; Gregory, *Homiliae* (*Homilies*) 3, in *PL* 76:107–8 treats the successive slayings as a repeated martyrdom of Felicitas herself. Perpetua's story is in *PL* 3:17–46.

92. Thomas, who is repeatedly martyred, is called the "Twin of Christ," Acts of Thomas 39, in *ANT*, 383–84; Philip and Paul are repeatedly executed, Budge, *Contendings of the Apostles*, 530, 466, 470, 472, and Andrew, ibid., 326–30, and Mark, ibid., 258, 261–63, and Matthew, *ANT*, 460–62; when Paul survived the fire "all the people believed," Budge, *Contendings of the Apostles*, 459–60, 524.

93. Many examples may be found in L. Radermacher, "Hippolytos und Thekla: Studien zur Geschichte von Legende und Kultus," in *Sitzungsberichte kaiserliche Akademie der Wissenschaften in Wien*, Philosophisch-historische Klasse 182:3 (1910): 1–111; R. Vallois, "Les origines des jeux olympiques," *Revue des études Anciennes* 31 (1929): 122, 128–30.

94. Arthur B. Cook, *Zeus*, 3 vols. (Cambridge: Cambridge University Press, 1914–40) 2:417, n. 2. The seven brothers motif in notes 90 and 91 above is close to the archaic legend and cult of Niobe.

95. Puech and Quispel, "Les écrits Gnostiques du Codex Jung," 15–19. The problem of such radical borrowings is treated by Erwin R. Goodenough, *Jewish Symbols in the Greco-Roman Period*, 13 vols. (Princeton: Princeton University Press, 1953), 1:3–32.

96. Hugh W. Nibley, "The Hierocentric State," *Western Political Quarterly* 4 (1951): 232, 249–51; "The Unsolved Loyalty Problem: Our Western Heritage," *Western Political Quarterly* 6 (1953): 641–46, for references.

97. Life of Apa Cyrus, in Budge, *Coptic Martyrdoms*, 128–36, 381–89, is typical. Far from being unworldly, all the monkish writers in these two volumes of Budge are intrigued and bedizened by the glory of the royal court, which is constantly brought into conjunction with the heavenly court. The heroes, military or clerical, are invariably of high birth, great wealth, and brilliant popularity. Regal pomp and circumstance are not decried but described with loving enthusiasm as the earthly counterpart of the heavenly order.

98. S. MacLean Gilmour, "The Christophany to More Than 500 Brethren," *Journal of Biblical Literature* 80 (1961): 251–52, citing John Knox; and "Easter and Pentecost," 62–66. For some recent studies identifying these events see Davies, *He Ascended into Heaven*, chs. 2, 3; Grässer, "Die Apostelgeschichte in der Forschung der Gegenwart," 155; W. von Loewenich, "Das Johannes-Verständnis im zweiten Jahrhundert," in *Zeitschrift für die neutestamentliche Wissenschaft* Supplement 13 (Giessen: Töpelmann, 1932): 16; Charles E. Carlston, "Transfiguration and Resurrection," *Journal of Biblical Literature* 80 (1961): 233–40; Joachim Jeremias, "Zwischen Karfreitag und Ostern," *Zeitschrift für die neutestamentliche Wissenschaft* 42 (1949): 194; Hans-Joachim Schulz, "Die 'Höllenfahrt' als 'Anastasis,' " *Zeitschrift für Katholische Theologie* 81 (1959): 1–66.

99. Justin, *Dialogue with Trypho* 2, 31–34, in *PG* 6: 476–77; 40, 4, in *PG* 6:561; 49, 2, in *PG* 6:581; 52, 1 and 4, in *PG* 6:589; 111, in *PG* 6:732–33; *Clementine Recognitions* I, 32–33, in *PG* 1:1226–27; III, 61, in *PG* 1:1306.

100. K. Holl, "Urchristentum und Religionsgeschichte," *Zeitschrift für systematische Theologie* 2 (1924): 403; cf. Joachim Jeremias, "The Present Position in the Controversy Concerning the Problem of the Historical Jesus," *Expository Times* 69 (1958): 337–38; Schneider, "Der Beitrag der Urgemeinde zur Jesusüberlieferung im Lichte der neuesten Forschung," 401–3. The argument has been skillfully pressed by C. S. Lewis.

101. Lindeskog, "Christuskerygma und Jesustradition," 145, 149–50.

102. "Ad rudium et pauperum Apostolorum mensam, escam et salinum vile et luteum se demittere, eis assidere, cum eis convivari," á Lapide, *Commentaria in Scripturam Sacram* 17:51. On the nature of the coarse food, Tissot, *Life of Our Lord Jesus Christ* 4:260.

103. So Jacques-Paul Migne, *Scripturae Sacrae Cursus Completus*, 28 vols. (Paris: Migne, 1840), 23:1130; Leo, *Discourse* 73, in *PL* 54:394–96; E. Jacquier, *Les actes des apôtres*, 9; J. Sint, "Die Auferstehung Jesu in der Verkündigung der Urgemeinde," *Zeitschrift für katholisches Theologie* 84 (1962): 149–51.

104. Clement, *Second Epistle to the Corinthians* 5–8, in *PG* 1:336–41; Didache 9; Epistle of the Apostles 36 (47), in *ANT*, 498; Gospel of the Twelve Apostles, in *PO* 2:154; Asin de Palacios, "Logia et Agrapha," no. 129, in *PO* 19:551; Justin *Dialogue with Trypho* 110, 6, in *PG* 6:729–32; 119, 5–6, in *PG* 6:752–53.

105. See note 25 above.

106. Some insist that because we know the *subject* of the 40-days' discourse we also know its *content*—which is far from being the case. J. Sint, "Die Auferstehung Jesu in der Verkündigung der Urgemeinde," 149–51; Frederick F. Bruce, *Commentary on the Book of Acts* (London: Marshall, Morgan & Scott, 1962), 34.

107. The same association of ideas meets us in such venerable documents as the so-called Shabako Stone, Kurt Sethe, *Dramatische Texte zur altägyptischen Mysterienspielen* 1 (Leipzig: Hinrichs, 1928), and the Enuma Elish, where we find the council and controversy in heaven, the creation of the world, the law of the Two Ways, the champion and redeemer of the race who overcomes the powers of death, and the obligation of the human race to participate in rites commemorating and dramatizing those cosmic events. The same motifs are conspicuous in the Dead Sea Scrolls, and form the foundation of what is sometimes designated today as "patternism." Whatever the significance of these resemblances, they do show that our apocryphal concepts are *not* the contrivances of undisciplined Oriental fantasy.

108. Thus Schmidt, *Gespräche Jesu*, 205.
109. Anselm, *Homiliae (Homilies)* 7, in *PL* 158:628–29.

3

The Early Christian
Prayer Circle

The nature of the early Christian prayer circle may be described by letting the oldest documents speak for themselves, beginning with the latest and moving backwards to the earliest. The rite was depicted for the last time in a document read to the assembled churchmen of the Second Council of Nicaea in A.D. 787 and condemned by them to the flames. Their objection was to parts of the text that proclaimed the Gnostic doctrine of the total immateriality of Christ; on the subject of the prayer circle, which was strange to them, they preserved a discreet silence.[1] Actually that part of it was an excerpt taken from a much older writing, the Acts of John, being the earliest apocryphal Christian Acta, dating at least to the early third century.

In reading this and other accounts of the prayer circles, we seem to enter, as Max Pulver expressed it, into "a strange space, a strange world—unlike ours—a world above the world that opens before us when we enter into the round dance of the disciples, led by Christ."[2] The passage from the Acts of John reads as follows, after a notice on the extreme secrecy in which these things were guarded:

> Before he was seized by wicked men and by the wicked serpent of the Jewish authorities (lawgivers, *nomothetoumenoi*), he called us all together and said: "Before I am given over to those men, let us sing a hymn (of praise) to

"The Early Christian Prayer Circle" first appeared in Brigham Young University Studies 19 (1978): 41-78.

the Father and so go forth ready to face whatever lies ahead." Then he commanded us to form a circle, taking hold of each other's hand; And he himself taking up a position in the middle uttered the Amen (formula) and "pay attention to me (*epakouete mou*—follow my instructions)." Then he began a hymn, saying,

"Praise (glory, *doxa*) to thee, Father," and we standing in the circle, followed him with the Amen.

"Glory to thee Logos, glory to thee grace (*charis*, love). Amen.

Glory to thee spirit, glory to thee Holy One; praise to thy glory. Amen (or be praised [*doxasou*] with glory. Amen).

We praise thee Father; we thank thee Light in which there is no darkness. Amen.

And while we (all) give thanks, I say (explain):

I wish to be saved and I wish to save. Amen.

I wish to be delivered, and I wish to deliver. Amen.

I wish to bear wounds (*titrōskō*) and I wish to inflict them. Amen.

I wish to be born and I wish to bring forth (bear). Amen.

I wish to eat and I wish to be eaten. Amen.

I want to hear and I want to be heard. Amen.

I want to comprehend (know), being all intelligence (*nous*). Amen.

I want to be washed, and I want to wash. Amen.

Charis (grace) (leads) dances in the chorus: I wish to pipe (Play the flute)—dance all of you! Amen.

I wish to mourn, all of you mourn (lit. *kopsasthe*—inflict blows [cuts] upon yourselves). Amen."

And after having led us in other things in the circle (chorus), beloved, the Lord went out. And we went forth like lost wanderers or like people in a dream, fleeing our several ways. [3]

St. Augustine in his 237th Epistle quotes a slightly different version, calling it "a hymn . . . commonly found in the apocryphal writings," which he gets from the Priscillians, who believed it to be "the hymn of the Lord which he recited in secret to his disciples, the holy Apostles, according as is written in the Gospel: After he recited a hymn, he ascended the mountain" (Matthew 26:30; Mark 14:26). Its absence from the New Testament, which was Augustine's argument for rejecting it as spurious, was explained by the sectaries by quoting Tobit 12:7: "The *ordinances* of the King it is well to conceal, though it is praiseworthy to reveal the *works* of God." Conventional Christianity, following Augustine, has always denied that there was any significant teaching of Christ not included in the New Testament, for to admit such would be to admit serious gaps in their own knowledge. Yet Augustine labors to show line by line that the hymn is not heretical (as the Bishops of Nicaea found it 350 years later) but that each statement can be duplicated somewhere in the scriptures.[4] The further back we go the more prominent becomes the rite in the church.

The actual performance of such a rite is described in a very old text, attributed to Clement of Rome and preserved in a seventh-century Syriac translation entitled "The Testament of our Lord Jesus Christ as delivered orally by him to us the Apostles after his Resurrection following his death."[5] In celebrating the sacrificial death of the Lord (Pulver calls his study "The Round Dance and the Crucifixion"), the bishop would

> make the sacrifice, the *veil* of the *gate* being drawn aside as a sign of the straying of the former people; he would make the offering within the veil along with priests, deacons, authorized widows, subdeacons, deaconesses, readers and such as were endowed with spiritual gifts. As leader the Bishop stands in the middle . . . [the men and women are assigned their places, north, south, east and west, around him]. Then all give each other the sign of peace. Next, when absolute silence is established, the deacon says: "Let your hearts be to heaven. If anyone has any ill feeling towards his neighbor, let him be reconciled. If anyone has

any hesitation or mental reservations [doubts] let him make
it known; if anyone finds any of the teachings incongenial,
let him withdraw [etc.]. For the Father of Lights is our witness with the Son and visiting angels. Take care lest you
have aught against your neighbor. . . . Lift up your hearts
for the sacrifice of redemption and eternal life. Let us be
grateful for the knowledge which God is giving us." The
Bishop . . . says in an awesome voice: "Our Lord be [or
is] with you!" And all the people respond: "And with thy
spirit."[6]

A sort of antiphonal follows with the people in the ring
responding to the words of the bishop. Then the bishop begins
the prayer proper, the people repeating these same things,
praying. He thanks God for the Plan of Salvation, by which
"thou hast fulfilled thy purposes by preparing a holy people,
hast stretched forth thy hands in suffering, that they who
have faith in thee might be freed from such suffering and
from the corruption of death."[7]

The identical idea is expressed in the prayer circle so
fully described by Bishop Cyril of Jerusalem (ca. A.D. 350)
which we have discussed elsewhere:

O strange and paradoxical thing! We did not die in
reality . . . after having been actually crucified. Rather it
was an imitation by a token. . . . O love of men overflow-
ing! Christ really received the nails in his blameless hands
and feet and suffered pain; while I, without any pain or
struggle, by his sharing of suffering the pain enjoy the
fruits of salvation![8]

Also in a long passage in the Acts of John:

You who dance, consider what I do, for yours is this passion
of Man which I am to suffer. For you could by no means
have understood what you suffer unless to you as Logos I
had been sent by the Father. . . . If you knew how to suffer you would be able not to suffer. Learn how to suffer
and you shall be able not to suffer.[9]

Plainly the rite is intimately involved with the suffering of the crucifixion.

The Syriac prayer ends: "Grant, therefore, O God, that all those be united with thee who participate in these sacred ordinances" And the people say amen. Bishop: "Give us unity of mind in the Holy Ghost, and heal our spirits . . . that we may live in thee throughout all eternity!" Then certain ordinances are explained to those in the circle: "It is he who gave Adam . . . a garment and the promise that after death he might live again and return to heaven." It is explained how Christ by the crucifixion reversed the blows of death, "according to the Plan of the Eternal Father laid down before the foundations of the earth."[10]

Still older are some documents designated as the Gospel of Bartholomew, belonging to that growing corpus of very early writings believed to contain instructions and teachings given to the Apostles in secret by the Lord after his resurrection. On one occasion when the apostles were met together, "Bartholomew . . . said to Peter, Andrew, and John, 'Let us ask [Mary] the favored one how she conceived the Lord and bore him.'" This was an embarrassing question, and no one was willing to approach Mary on the subject. "And Bartholomew said to Peter, 'You are the President and my teacher, you go and ask her!'" But Peter says Bartholomew himself should ask, and after much hesitation he approaches Mary on behalf of the other apostles, and she agrees to enlighten them.[11]

They form a prayer circle, "and Mary, standing before them, raised her hands to heaven" and began to call upon the Father in an unknown language, a number of versions of which are given.

> When she finished the prayer, she said, "Let us sit on the ground [or stand quietly, *kathisomen*, at the prepared place, *edaphos*—since it is plain that they remain standing]; come Peter, you are in charge. Stand at my right hand and place

> your left hand under my forearm; and you, Andrew, you
> do the same thing on my left side."[12]

John and Bartholomew are instructed to support or catch
Mary if she faints, "lest my bones fail me when I start to
speak." This mutual support in the circle is necessary where
some may be caught away in the Spirit and pass out.

In a variant version, when the brethren are met together
on the Mount of Olives, "Peter said to Mary, 'Blessed one,
please ask the Lord to tell us about the things that are in
heaven.' " But Mary reminds Peter that as Adam has prece-
dence over Eve, so it is his business to take the lead in such
things.[13] Having taken position in the circle, Mary begins to
speak:

> When I was in the Temple of God [a number of early
> sources report that Mary served in the Temple, like Samuel,
> as a child][14] . . . there appeared to me one day a manifes-
> tation like an angel of unfamiliar aspect. . . . And sud-
> denly the veil of the Temple was rent and there was a great
> earthquake and I fell on my face unable to bear the sight
> of him. But he stretched forth his hand and raised me up,
> and I looked up to heaven and a dewy cloud came and
> [lacuna] moistened me from head to foot; and he wiped
> me off with his stole (robe, shawl) and said to me, "Greet-
> ings, thou favored one, chosen vessel!" and he grasped my
> right hand. And there was bread in abundance and he set
> it out on the altar of the Temple [cf. the shewbread], and
> he ate first and then gave to me. And he put forth his hand
> from his garment and there was wine in abundance, and
> he drank first and then gave to me, and I beheld and saw a
> full cup and bread. And he said to me, "In three years'
> time I shall send to you my Logos and you will bear a son,
> and through him all the creation will be saved. . . . Peace
> to thee, my beloved, forever and ever." And suddenly he
> was gone from me, and the Temple was as it was before.

At this point the Lord himself appeared and commanded
Mary "to utter no more of this mystery," while "the Apostles

were sore afraid that the Lord would be angry with them."[15] The sacramental episode is close to the holy wedding in the temple described in the Story of Joseph and Asenath, giving some indication of the great age and wide ramifications of the motif.[16] The account continues with Jesus giving the apostles further instructions in the ordinances, but the text is badly damaged. In one version Andrew accuses Mary of teaching false doctrine (an authentic human touch is the occasional reference in the early documents to a slight but uncomfortable tension between Mary and some of the apostles), but Peter reminds him that the Lord confided in Mary more than any other, while Mary, upset, weeps and says, "Peter, do you think I am making all this up?"[17]

In the book of 2nd Jeu, considered by Carl Schmidt to be the most instructive of all early Christian texts, the apostles and their wives all form a circle around the Lord, who says he will lead them through all the secret ordinances that shall give them eternal progression.[18] Then "all the Apostles, clothed in their garments, . . . placing foot to foot, made a circle facing the four directions of the cosmos," and Jesus standing at the altar [shourē] proceeded to instruct them in all the signs and ordinances in which the Sons of Light must be perfect.[19]

Snatched at the last moment from the rising waters of the Aswan Dam in 1966 was the Kasr al-Wazz fragment, where we read,

> We made a circle and surrounded him and he said, "I am in your midst in the manner of these little children." When we finished the hymn they all said Amen. Then he said other things and each time they must all answer Amen. "Gather to me, O holy members of my body, and when I recite the hymn, you say Amen!"[20]

The Acts of John describes the circle as being in *motion*, a sort of dance, and earlier texts than the Nicaean version add a cosmic touch to the formula:

I would pipe: Dance all of you. I would mourn: mourn
all of you![21]
One Ogdoad sings praises with us. Amen.
The number 12 dances on high. Amen.
All that which is above participates in the circle. Amen."
[Or—(alternate version)] "He that danceth not knoweth
not what is being done. Amen. . . . "
"Now if you follow my dance
See yourself in Me who am speaking,
and when you have seen what I do,
keep silence about my mysteries."[22]

It is doubtless to this rite that Clement of Alexandria refers
in the second century when he writes, "Come to our mysteries and you shall dance with the angels around the Unbegotten
and Eternal one and only true God, while Logos of God
sings along with us . . . the great High Priest of God, who
prays for men and instructs them."[23]

Clergymen of every denomination have vied in fervor in
condemning all dancing as of the devil, yet strangely the
only passages they can find to use from early Christian writings never condemn it outright. The favorites are St.
Augustine's dictum: *"Melius est enim arare quam saltare"*
("It is better to plow than to dance"),[24] and Chrysostom's,
"Where there is dancing, there is the devil also," but the
churchmen who quote it never finish what Chrysostom has
to say, as he continues, "God gave us feet . . . not to cavort
shamefully . . . but that we may some day join in the dance
of the angels!"[25] To which angelic dancing the great Basil
also refers as part of the Christian tradition: "What is more
blessed than to imitate the dance of the angels here on
earth?"[26] Ritual dancing was condemned by the fathers not
because it was new, but because it was old in the church—it
smacked of the old Jewish heritage. Both Augustine and
Chrysostom condemn the old Jewish dancing as part of the
Sabbath rejoicing.[27]

Were it not for a violent prejudice against dancing, the long debates of the scholars as to whether the participants in the prayer circle really danced or not would be pointless, since the earliest texts clearly say they did dance. But what kind of a dance? In the classic work on the Therapeutae, Philo, writing at the time of Christ, tells how men and women in the circle, following the lead of an *exarchos* or choral instructor, would chant hymns with antiphonal responses in a manner resembling both the "rapt enthusiasm" and the circular motion of ancient choric dances, "hands and feet keeping time in accompaniment."[28] The Therapeutae were an Essene group related both to the Egyptian communities of desert sectaries and to the people of the Dead Sea Scrolls— one could hardly accuse them of frivolity.

The Greek and Russian Orthodox churches still preserve the ring dance around the altar in that most conservative of rites, the wedding ceremony, when bride, groom, and priest all join hands and circle the altar three times; H. Leisegang connects this definitely with the old prayer circle.[29] At the coronation of the Byzantine emperor, everyone danced around the emperor's table three times.[30] The most common representations of ritual dancing in early Christian art show pious damsels dancing around the throne of King David.[31] And the Jewish apocryphal writings often depict a situation best described at the opening of the Book of Mormon, where Lehi sees God on his throne "surrounded with numberless concourses of angels in the attitude of singing and praising their God" (1 Nephi 1:8). Surrounding concourses are concentric circles, and the singing and praising are never static: it is a dynamic picture with everything in motion, as Lehi sees it, and as the cosmic pattern of the thing requires. The prayer circle is often called the *chorus* of the apostles, and it is the meaning of *chorus* which can be a choir, but is originally a ring dance, as Pulver designates it in the title of his study. The prayer was a song such as Paul prayed and sang in the darkness of a prison: "About midnight they prayed a hymn to God" (see Acts 16:25). And if they sang in chorus, would they not dance? Philo says that the true initiate during the rites moves "in the circuit of heaven, and is borne around in a circle with the dances of the planets and stars in accordance with the laws of perfect music"—the music of the spheres. [32]

The most puzzling reference to the dance is also the oldest one, that in Matthew 11:16–17: "[This generation] . . . is like unto children sitting in the markets, and calling unto their fellows, and saying, We have piped unto you, and ye have not danced; we have mourned unto you, and ye have not lamented." It was taking liberties with this strange passage "as a pretext" that the early sectaries justified the dancing in their prayer circles, according to Gougaud. [33] In the text read at Nicaea the Lord says to the circle, "Amen! When grace comes I want to pipe and you all dance." But in a circle where they are already singing, the dancing is only to be expected in view of old Jewish customs—and this episode takes place in the upper room at the Last Supper, the Passover. Why should that playful game be introduced on that most solemn of occasions? In Matthew 11:7, Jesus is speaking about John the Baptist's followers and begins, "concerning John, What went ye out into the wilderness to see?" This is a challenge to the desert sectaries. They were out there, as the Manual of Discipline so clearly tells us, [34] to "prepare the way" (see Matthew 11:10). He speaks of John's great mission as the herald of a dispensation, an "Elias, which was for to come" (Matthew 11:14), and then addresses the initiates: "He that hath ears to hear, let him hear" (v. 15), describing the present generation as those rejecting John's message (v. 12)—they would accept neither John nor the Lord (vs. 18–19): they refused to dance to their playing, nor would they mourn with them for the sins of the world (vs. 16–17). The knowledge is properly guarded—"he that hath ears to hear, let him hear" (v. 15), a hint to the initiated that it is meant only for them. In the Acts of John, the Lord says, "Grace is dancing.

I would pipe: Dance all of you. I would mourn: mourn all of you!" The connection with Matthew is undeniable, and again the limitation of the real meaning to the inner circle: "He that does not move in the circle knows not what is happening. Amen." An important clue is the likening to little children in Matthew 11:16. The Kasr al-Qazz fragment says, "We made a circle and surrounded him and he said, 'I am in your midst in the manner of these little children,' he added, 'Gather to me, O holy members of my body, and when I recite the hymn, you say Amen.' "[35]

In both the Acts of John and the Apocryphon of John, Jesus appears at the same time as a grown man and a little child; and in a famous infancy account when he and John embrace as small children, they fuse into one.[36] Is it a mere coincidence that he repeatedly speaks of the little children and the dancing when declaring unity with John? The central act of the prayer circle was prayer, and it was "as he was praying in a certain place, when he ceased, one of his disciples said unto him, Lord, teach us to pray, as *John* also taught his disciples" (Luke 11:1–2; italics added). Again in close comparison with John, he teaches them the Lord's prayer. Jeremias in a recent study of that prayer notes the significant fact that in it Christ addresses the Father as *Abba*. And that, Jeremias observes, "was something new," using an Aramaic word "used by a small child when addressing his father. . . . Jesus' contemporaries," Jeremias writes, "never addressed God as Abba"[37]—that was little child's talk, addressing God as a real, intimate father, as a trusting little child would. Little children do not stand on their dignity when they are happy; their singing and dancing is spontaneous. Some of that spontaneity and simplicity carries over into the later cult of the Christ child; but in the early Christian texts it is the clue to an authentic situation. In the Testament of the Twelve Apostles, the Lord, appearing to the people after the resurrection just before producing bread and wine miraculously for the administering of the sacrament, has a conversation with a little child.[38] In exactly the same situation in the Book of Mormon the resurrected Lord blesses the little children "one by one," but he begins his discourse to the Nephites by telling them three times that no one can approach him except as a little child (see 3 Nephi 9:22, 11:37–38). The prayer circle is the nearest approach to the Lord that men make on earth—and they can approach him only "as little children."

The prayer spoken in the circle differs every time; it is not strictly prescribed. The one leading the prayer expresses himself as the Spirit moves him, and the others either repeat each line after him (which would not be necessary if they all knew it by heart) or add an "amen" at the end of each phrase, which is the equivalent of reciting the prayer for oneself. The most significant example of this freedom of composition is certainly the Lord's Prayer. "Originally," wrote Jeremias, "the doxology, 'For thine is the kingdom, and the power, and the glory, for ever,' was absent," yet it is found in the oldest church order, the "Teaching of the Twelve Apostles." Has someone taken liberties with the sacred canon, then? No, "the absence of the doxology from the original text," Jeremias explains, "does not mean that Jesus intended his prayer to be recited without a word of praise at the end. But in the very earliest times, the doxology had *no fixed form* and its precise wording was left to those who prayed." Only "later on . . . it was felt necessary to establish the doxology in a fixed form,"[39] which explains why the prayer has different forms in Matthew 6:13 and Luke 11:4. Also, the older Aramaic form of the prayer required forgive "our debts," which the Greek of Luke changes to forgive "our *sins*."[40] This vindicates both the inclusion of the doxology in the Lord's prayer in 3 Nephi 13:9–13 and the reading there of "debts" instead of "sins."

Almost all accounts mention the introduction of the prayer as being in a *strange language*, a triple formula of words resembling each other. Thus in 1 Jeu after they form the circle, Jesus begins a hymn which appears to be meaningless, a speaking in tongues, a glossolalia. [41] In the Pistis Sophia also, the Lord, having formed the apostles and their wives in a circle around him and "taking the place of Adam at the altar, called upon the Father three times in an unknown tongue." [42] Elsewhere the text explains how while they stood "all in white, each with the cipher of the name of the Father in his hand," Jesus prayed in a strange language, beginning with the words *Iaō, aōi, ōia!* which, we are told, meant "Hear me Father, the Father of all fatherhood, boundless light!" According to our source, "This is the interpretation: Iota, because everything came out of (began with) it; Alpha because everything will return to it; Omega because everything is process (lit. the fulfilling of all fulfilling)." [43]

In another version, when the Lord "ordered the Twelve to make a prayer circle and join him in a triple Amen and hymn to the Father and Creator of all treasure," he began by saying "iē, iē, iē, [calling upon the Father] . . . to create beings to be the Lords of every treasure, and as such to bear the name of their Father Jeu, who has replenished the treasuries with countless spirits and degrees of glory." [44] When Abraham, according to an old and highly respected source, "rebuilt the altar of Adam in order to bring a sacrifice to the Eternal One," as he had been instructed by an angel, he raised his voice in prayer, saying: "El, El, El! El Jaoel! [the last meaning Jehovah] . . . receive the words of my prayer! Receive the sacrifice which I have made at thy command! Have mercy, show me, teach me, give to thy servant the light and knowledge thou hast promised to send him!" [45] Abraham was following the example of Adam, who prayed to God for three days, repeating three times the prayer: "May the words of my mouth be heard! God, do not withdraw thyself from my supplication! . . . Then an angel of the Lord came with a book, and comforted Adam and taught him." [46] When Adam and Eve found themselves cut off from the glory of the Lord, according to the intriguing Combat of Adam, they stood with upstretched hands calling upon the Lord, as "Adam began to pray in a language which is unintelligible to us."[47] The so-called Coptic Gnostic Writing purports to give us Adam's words on the occasion as being composed of the elements *lō-i-a* and *i-oy-ēl*, meaning "God is with us forever and ever," and "through the power of revelation."[48] The Jewish traditions indicate that the story is no Gnostic invention, though of course mysterious names and cryptograms are the stuff on which human vanity feeds, and every ambitious sectary would come up with his own words and interpretations. Yet, though none of these writings may be taken as binding or authentic, taken all together they contain common elements which go back as far as the church of the apostles. When Mary asks the Lord, "Tell me your highest name!" "He, standing in the midst of a cloud of light, said, 'He, Elohe, Elohe, Elohe; Eran, Eran, Eran; Rafon, Rafon, Rafon; Raqon, Raqon, Raqon,' " etc.[49] Such mysteries are just the sort of thing unqualified persons love to play around with, and various Gnostic groups took fullest advantage of them. But again, the Jews are way ahead of them, as we see in the huge catalogues of mysterious angelic names in such works as 3 Enoch.

What H. Leclercq calls "that magnificent gesture" of raising both hands high above the head with which those in the prayer circle began their prayer was, as he notes, a natural gesture both of supplication and submission.[50] It was specifically a conscious imitation of the crucifixion,[51] and that brings to mind the significant detail, mentioned by the Synoptic writers, that the Lord on the cross called upon the Father in a strange tongue: those who were standing by, though Aramaic was supposed to be their native tongue, disagreed as to the meaning (see Mark 15:33–36), and indeed the manuscripts give many variant readings of an utterance which the writers of the Gospels left untranslated, plainly because there was some doubt as to the meaning. It recalls the cry of distress of David in Psalms 54:2: "Hear my prayer, O God; give ear to the words of my mouth,"[52] and in Psalms

55:1–4: "Give ear to my prayer, O God. . . . Attend unto me, and hear me. . . . My heart is sore pained within me: and the terrors of death are fallen upon me."

F. Preisigke, studying the same gesture among the Egyptians (it is none other than the famous "ka" gesture), notes that it represents submission (the "hands up" position of one surrendering on the battlefield) while at the same time calling the attention of heaven to an offering one has brought in supplication. He also points out that the early Christians used the same gesture in anticipation of a visitation from heaven, to which they added the idea of the upraised arms of the Savior on the cross.[53] We have already mentioned the prayers of Adam and Abraham calling upon God in a strange tongue in the midst of darkness and distress. Abraham, says the Zohar, received no message until he built an altar and brought an offering, "for there is no stirring above until there is a stirring below . . . we do not say grace over an empty table"—or altar.[54] Enoch was another who as he prayed "stretched forth his arms, and his heart swelled wide as eternity," and to comfort him God sent him the vision of Noah's salvation (see Moses 7:41–67). Noah also cried out in his distress, "calling upon Enoch three times and saying, Hear me! hear me! hear me!"[55] Let us also recall that when Mary led the prayer circle of the apostles "she raised her hands to heaven, and began to call upon the Father in an unknown tongue."[56]

Suffering is an important theme of the ancient prayer circle. The rite is always related to the crucifixion, according to Pulver, which was anticipated by it in the upper room, for "the core of the Lord's Supper is the idea of sacrifice."[57] In the rites "the believer must incur the same sufferings as his god, and therefore he must mourn with him"—hence the peculiar passage in Matthew 11:16–17.[58] Ignatius' Letter to the Romans shows that "real suffering . . . alone enables one to become a disciple, to learn and gain experience. . . . For Ignatius, the believer must repeat the destiny of his God, he must become an imitator of God, *mimētēs tou Theou.*"[59] This is done ritually as is plainly stated by Cyril of Jerusalem and the author of the Testament of Jesus Christ, cited above: "and thou hast stretched forth thy hands in suffering, that they might be freed from such suffering" by an act of imitation.[60]

The clearest expression of the idea is given in that archetype and model of all initiates and suppliants, Adam. As he and Eve were sacrificing on an altar "with arms upraised," an angel came down to accept the sacrifice, but Satan intervened and smote Adam in the side with the sacrificial weapon. Adam fell upon the altar and would have died were it not that God intervened and healed him on the spot, declaring that what Adam had suffered so far was acceptable to him as a true sacrifice, being in the similitude of his own offering: "Even so will I be wounded!"[61]

The prayer asks for light and knowledge as well as other aid, and the answer is a teaching situation. Thus the angels who came down in answer to Adam's three-fold appeal, "May the words of my mouth be heard!" etc., came with a book, and comforted Adam and taught him.[62] Or, in another version, when Adam and Eve prayed at their altar three messengers were sent down to instruct them.[63] The Lord himself appears to teach Abraham as he is studying the heavens, according to Clement,[64] and the valuable Testament of Abraham begins with his receiving instruction at an altar on a holy mountain, surrounded "by men whom I will show you, how they will form a circle around you, being on the mountain of the altars."[65] Indeed, the main theme of those many ancient writings called "Testaments," and attributed to almost every patriarch, prophet, and apostle of old, is the journey of the purported author to heaven, during which he receives lessons in the most advanced theology, history, and astronomy.

Of particular interest is the Testament of Job, whose age has been vindicated by the recent discovery of fifth-century

Coptic fragments of it.[66] "Make a circle around me, my children, form a circle around me that I may show you what the Lord and I did" (lit., what the Lord did *met'emou*—along with me). Thus he begins with what seems no more than admonition to gather round. But when he begins explaining things to his daughters, strange ordinances emerge. When the famous three daughters of Job complain to him that their seven brothers received a greater inheritance than they, he assures them that he has reserved for them a better heritage.[67] He then tells one of the girls to go to the "celle" and fetch three golden caskets containing their inheritances. In each one is a mysterious article of clothing designated as a *chorda*—a string or thread, but of such cunning design as to defy description, being of no earthly design, but of heaven "giving off lightning-like emissions like sunbeams."[68] The girls are told to put them on like shawls "so that it would be with them throughout the days of this earthly life."[69] One of the women asks, disappointed, "Is this the heritage you told us about?" In reply Job tells her that these *chordai* will not only preserve them in this life "but will also lead you into a better world, even the heavens."[70] He explains that the Lord gave him the three bands "on the day when he decided to show me mercy," healing him of the afflictions of the flesh, and placing the item before him saying: "Arise, gird up thy loins like a man! I shall ask you certain questions, and you shall give me certain answers!"[71] When Job tied them on, all sickness left him and his body became strong and his mind at ease.[72] "And the Lord spoke to me in power, showing me things past and future."[73] He tells the girls that they will have nothing to fear in this life from the Adversary, because these things they wear are a "power and a protection (*phylaktērion*) of the Lord."[74] Then he tells them to arise and gird themselves to prepare for heavenly visitants.[75]

> Thus it was that when one of the three daughters . . .
> arose and clothed herself (*periezōsen*—showing that this

was a garment and more than a string) according to her
father's instructions, she received another heart and no
longer thought about earthly things. And she began to
utter words (*apephthenxato*—make a clear and important
statement) in the angelic sounds (*phōne*), and sent up a
hymn to God using the manner of praising of the angels.
And as she recited the hymns, she let the spirit be marked
(*kecharagmenon*) on her garment.[76]

Here the "string" or chord is definitely called a garment—
stolē. The next girl girded herself likewise and recited the
hymn of the creation of the heavens speaking "in the dialect
of the Archons," making her a true Muse.[77] The third girl
"chanted verses in the dialect of those on high . . . and she
spoke in the dialect of the Cherubim," her words being preserved as The Prayers of Amaltheiaskeras—a most significant
name.[78]

In the opening lines of the Testament, Job tells his three
daughters and seven sons to form a circle around him (the
second son is called Choros). "Make a circle around me
(*perikyklōsate me*—he repeats the word) and I will demonstrate (*hypodeixō*, a very explicit word) to you the things
which the Lord did with me (*epoiesen met'emou*, i.e., which
we did together. It does not mean what he did to or for me!).
For I am your father Job who was faithful in all things (*en
pasei hypomonei*) and you are of the chosen and honored
lineage (*genos*) of the seed of Jacob"; i.e., he gives them a
patriarchal blessing—his "Testament."[79]

Then Job recounts an adventure quite like that of Moses
in the first chapter of the Book of Moses, after which Job
suddenly appears as the humiliated King who regains his
glory, the "Job who ruled over all of Egypt," no less![80] He
shows his royal visitors his real throne, which is in heaven,[81]
and they become upset and angry about his illusive "eternal
kingdom," which he assures them is the *only* stable state of
existence.[82] "If you do not understand the functions of the
body," he asks them, "how can you hope to understand

heavenly matters?" [83] In the midst of his terrible afflictions he calls upon the Lord with upraised hands: "They lifted me up, supporting my arms on each side, and standing thus I first of all gave thanks, and then after a great praying I said to them: Lift up your eyes to the East" and there they saw Job's dead children crowned in the presence of the Heavenly One [84] and his wife who had just joined them: she having died of sorrow and exhaustion. According to an old legend, Satan had appeared to her as a baker, and when she asked for a scrap of bread to feed herself and her ailing husband, reminding him of his former generosity to one and all, Satan coolly replied that he would give her bread when she gave him money, piously assuring her—"You can have anything in this world for money!"[85] Eliphaz and the other friends were forgiven by God for resenting Job's claim (which is also Enoch's) that God had given him a right "to his own throne in the heavens,"[86] and in his joy Eliphaz led *another* prayer circle: "He began a hymn, the other friends repeating after him along with their supporters (troops) near the altar." He began by casting out Satan.[87] "Behold, the Lord has drawn near, the Saints now stand prepared, their crowns of glory awaiting them in advance (*proēgoumenōn*)."[88] "After Eliphaz finished with the hymn, all the others repeating after him (*epiphōnountōn*) while moving in a circle (Kraft: 'and circling about'), we arose and went into the city to the house where we live and carried on festivities rejoicing in the Lord."[89] Thus the story ends as it were in the upper room where it began (cf. Matthew 26:30 and Mark 14:26).

In 2 Jeu the apostles and their wives form a circle around Jesus specifically "so that he can *teach* them the ordinances of the treasury of light, they being conducted by him through all the ordinances and thereby learning to progress in the hereafter."[90] At Mary's request on behalf of the apostles the Lord specifies the progressive order of "all ordinances (*mystēria*), all knowledge (instructions—*sooun*), seals (*sphragidēs*), tokens (*psephoi*), supplications (or forms of

address—*epikalesthai*), degrees (or positions—*topoi*)."[91] And
in the Acts of John he tells those in the circle, "What you do
not know, I myself will teach you."[92] The whole situation
centers around the Last Supper and belongs to the church
from the beginning.[93]

In a Bartholomew text, the Lord takes the Twelve up into
the mountain and standing in their midst gives them certain
signs and tokens and then departs.[94] The Gnostics exploit
and distort this situation in their usual way: Thus when an
angel comes to rescue Norea in response to her prayer he
says, "I am El-El-Eth . . . who stands before the Holy Ghost
(obviously a Hebrew source—the Shekhina). I have been
sent to converse with you and to save you from the Adversary. I will instruct you concerning what you should
know."[95]

Indeed, in various accounts Satan tries to get in on the
act. We have seen how he smote Adam, interrupting his lessons at the altar. And when Abraham prayed at his altar,
"Have mercy, show me, teach me, give to thy servant light
and knowledge thou hast promised to send him!" Satan
promptly appears on the scene with an insolent "Here I am!"
And as he began to teach Abraham, a true messenger from
God arrived and cast Satan out and proceeded with the proper
instructions.[96] In 2 Jeu the Lord warns the men and women
in the circle that the ordinances in question are very secret,
because Satan wants them distorted and misrepresented, as
they surely will be if they go abroad in the world.[97] Divulging those very things, it will be recalled, was the sin for
which the Watchers in Enoch's day were destroyed.[98] According to Rabbi Eleaser, Abraham built three altars in order to
instruct his children and fortify them against apostasy.[99]

As to the teacher, sometimes it is Jaoel or Jehovah as "the
heavenly choirmaster," and sometimes it is Michael or Gabriel.
As often as not it is three Sent Ones.[100] But of course all the
knowledge is sent down from God. "Abraham . . . would

utter prayers on certain occasions while sacrificing, thus invoking the 'One God.' "[101] This was the beginning of Jewish liturgy. Clement, however, takes it back a step farther: "Adam finding he needed help, solicited divine assistance with prayers and sacrifices. . . . That was the beginning of the ordinances of God."[102] According to the Moslem commentators, all creatures form in circles around God to be taught, suggesting the gathering of all the beasts at life-giving water holes in the desert.[103] H. Leisegang finds that throughout the ancient world the prayer circle is for the instruction of initiates.[104] We may even go beyond his range to the medicine circles of Indians all over America. Among the Plains Indians, as described by H. Storm,

> the people all sit quietly together and learn the four harmonies of balance. Each of the people can now perceive the others, and they realize that they are all *Teachers*. They put their arms around each other and care for each other. Then they begin to dance towards the Flowering Tree together in a Great Circle.[105]

The "four harmonies" mentioned in the last quotation appear throughout the world in the ring dance. The number of those forming the circle is among the pagans almost always sixteen, as Leisegang shows; with the Christian circle it is twelve, combining the three levels and the four cardinal points.[106] In the Jewish 3 Enoch the three levels of the twelve produce rings of thirty-six. In 1 Jeu, "At every station (or step, *topos*) there are twelve springs of reason . . . and in each every father has three faces, so that the fathers that encircle Setheus have 36 faces. . . . At every level (*taxis*) there is a treasure containing 12 heads . . . and in each *topos* there are always three Watchers to instruct."[107] As might be expected, the number 360 is constantly mentioned and pedants and mystics had a field day shuffling and rearranging their cosmic circles, as did mathematicians and astronomers— our circles still have 360 degrees. If the Gnostic can tell us in

a typical text that "the Nous of the universe has 12 faces and
the prayer of each one is directed solely towards Him," while
in the midst stands an altar upon which is the Only Begotten
Word,[108] that is not so far from the impeccably orthodox
Ignatius of Antioch, for whom the dance of twelve "is in imitation of God."[109]

Monuments of great age and imposing majesty in many
parts of the world suggest the prevalence of the main ideas.
Thus when Heliodorus went far up the Nile to Meroe, describing conditions during the Persian occupation of the fourth
century B.C., he saw a council of holy men sitting in a circle
of twelve with three altars in their midst.[110] As an eyewit-
ness to the operation and as a personal friend to the emperor,
Eusebius was able to describe the arrangement of Constantine's
tomb and the mystique behind it. "He built a martyrium in
memory of the 12 Apostles in the city bearing his name." It
was a golden superdome, open to the sky and utterly dazzling. A ring of twelve columns with relics of an apostle
deposited at the foot of each represented the holy chorus.
Then Constantine had a happy afterthought: He had twelve
reliquaries in honor and memory of the sacred chorus of the
apostles placed in the circle of the rotunda, each at the foot
of a column; and in the center of this he put his own cas-
ket . . . so that, as he explained it, by a clever calculation
any honor shown to an apostle would be automatically
focused—as if by a burning glass, on the object in the center—the remains of the emperor. Thus that smart man characteristically "utilized the intercession of the Apostles to his
own advantage."[111]

The plan was carried out in the still-surviving mausoleum
of Constantine's daughter Constantia, with its twelve double
columns in a circle around the sarcophagus or altar,[112] and
from the same period in the Tomb of Diocletian at Split and
many other imposing monuments dedicated to harnessing
the power of the heavens through the prayer circle. There is
a definite cosmic connection here. " 'What is eternal . . . is

circular, and what is circular is eternal,' " write Giorgio de
Santillana and Hertha von Dechend, quoting Aristotle with
the comment, "That was the mature conclusion of human
thought over millennia. It was . . . an obsession with
circularity."[113] If Plato bids us behold "immortal souls standing outside of heaven (as) the revolution of the spheres carries them round, and they behold all things beyond,"[114] 1
Clement, among the oldest and most esteemed of Christian
writings, declares that "the sun and the moon and the chorus
of stars according to his decree in harmony and without any
deviation circle in their appointed orbits."[115] The life of the
soul is related to the motions of the heavenly bodies in the
Twelfth Thanksgiving Hymn of the Dead Sea Scrolls, and
the remarkable tenth page of the Manual of Discipline is an
ecstatic song with instrumental accompaniment and dance in
the temple attuned to the circling of the spheres and the revolutions of the times, seasons, and festivals. It begins:

> At the beginning of the rule of light in its circling, at the
> gathering to the appointed place, at the beginning of the
> watches of darkness, when its treasury is opened and poured
> out upon the earth, and in its revolving and drawing
> together from its source of [or for the sake of] light, when
> the outpouring of the light shines forth from the holy abode,
> etc. . . . I will sing what I learn and all my harping is for
> the glory of El, and all the sound of my harp shall be
> attuned to his holiness while the flute of my lips shall
> strictly conform to [lit. be laid to the line of] his instruc-
> tion. . . . I will prescribe the limits from which I will not
> depart (11) . . . I will gladly receive what he teaches me. . . .
> As soon as my hand and feet are stretched forth I will call
> upon (abarekh) his name at the beginning both of the
> going out and the coming in [line 13].[116]

Here the singer compares his solitary song to the strict
discipline and instruction of the prayer circle in the temple,
e.g., "I will make the heave-offering with my lips" (line 6),
that being a temple ordinance.

With the Fall, according to a Hebrew Enoch fragment,
Adam tried his best to behold again the glory of the Shekhina,
but had to settle in his fallen state for "the circle of the Sun
which all behold in glory as the sign of the Shekhina with
6000 prophets circling around it."[117] In the various "ascension"
texts we are taken again and again through the various levels
of concentric rings, "the order [taxis] of holy angels in their
ring-dances [chorostasian, lit. standing properly in a ring]."
Isaiah is instructed in his Ascension not to worship at any of
the six central thrones at any of the chorostasias or singing
praise-circles, circles he must pass on the way up, since all
the others are simply focusing their praise on "him who
sitteth in the Seventh Heaven."[118] Such a mounting up is
described by Philo:

> The soul . . . is borne ever higher to the ether and the cir-
> cuit of heaven, and is carried around with the dances of
> the planets and fixed stars in accordance with the laws of
> perfect music, reaching out after . . . the patterns of the
> originals of things of the senses which it saw here (on
> earth, while) longing to see the Great King himself.[119]

Philo is attempting to combine Jewish lore with the
mysteries of Egypt. Pulver notes that the eight-circle is com-
moner than the twelve and "occurs also in early Christianity
whenever it discloses an *Egyptian* influence."[120] Certainly
what is purportedly the first and oldest shrine in Egypt, the
Abaton, tomb of Osiris and first place of settlement with its
great ring of 365 altars and its three levels, etc.,[121] suggests
the circle of 365 aeons that marks the place of the Adam of
light with its three sides or directions,[122] and even more does
the arrangement of the ideal temple in the newly published
Temple Scroll from the Qumran Cave I.[123] Plutarch explains
certain mysteries on the authority of the Egyptians in a combination of earthly and heavenly geography which is typically Egyptian: The worlds are so ordered that "one always
touches the other in a circle, moving as it were in a stately

ring-dance," which takes place surprisingly within a triangle, "the foundation and common altar of all these worlds, which is called the Plain of Truth, in which lie the designs, moulds, ideas, and permanent examples or samples of all things that ever were or shall be."[124] Some have suggested that the three-cornered plain in question is the Nile Delta,[125] and it is not surprising that Plutarch's image of things was Christianized by an Egyptian, Clement of Alexandria: "That which Christ brings forth (is) transformed into an Ogdoad . . . and through three names is liberated as a triad. . . . When you bear the image of the terrestrial world then you also bear the image of the celestial."[126]

It is because each prayer circle is a faithful reproduction of the celestial pattern that impulses can be transmitted from one to the other by all who are in a receptive state; the thoughts of those in the circle are concentrated as in a burning glass, or, since the thing most emphasized as the indispensable requirement of the circle is the absolute purity of mind, concentration of thought devoid of any reservations or distractions, and since the communication is beamed from one Treasury of Light to others, the analogy of the laser is quite striking.[127] The three who were sent to teach Adam and Eve the order of prayer gave them the pattern "after the manner of what is done above in the Treasury of Light."[128] If that sounds too Gnostic, the same image meets us in the above-mentioned tenth page of the Manual of Discipline. In the Book of Adam, Adam is endowed

> with the image and likeness of the Lords (above), while Eve is the Queen of this world. . . . I (God) provided [sent] the three visitors (genies) for their protection, and taught them the holy mysteries . . . and the prayers which they must recite . . . and I told them further, "I have provided for you this earth, in a dwelling-place fit for eternity. And then sitting near them I taught them the manner of calling upon the Lords to bless them."[129]

According to the Hasidic teaching, "the order of prayer is in accordance with the emanation of the Worlds," since through prayer we become "attached . . . to Him Who is blessed"[130] and rules the worlds. In orthodox Judaism "the Talmud represents the Beth Din or Tribunal of Heaven, as a circle, in the centre of which, God is seated," and the earthly Sanhedrin as a reflection of it.[131] The sympathetic vibration makes the individual also a microcosm responding to the cosmic forms, as we see in the Odes of Solomon, which echo the Dead Sea Scrolls with the ecstatic declaration, "The Lord is the Crown upon my head, I will not be shaken. Even though the universe is shaken, I will remain standing. . . . As I strike the chords of the lyre the Spirit of the Lord speaks in my members."[132]

In forming the prayer circle one excludes the outer world, as families holding the Passover feast form closed circles with their backs all turned on the outer world, or as the true initiates form the inner or "esoteric" circle, leaving all the rest to the outer or "exoteric" world. The Lord explains this to the apostles, telling them of higher prayer circles as he takes each by the hand and introduces him into "the First Mystery," explaining, "That is why I said to you that you were chosen out of the world."[133] It was from such a circle in heaven that God at the creation of this earth chose those who would be his rulers in it, according to 1 Jeu, the Apocalypse of Abraham and the Book of Abraham 3:23: "And God . . . stood in the *midst* of them, and he said: These I will make my rulers; for he stood among those that were spirits."[134]

The special object of Leisegang's study, an alabaster Orphic bowl depicting a prayer circle, bears an inscription beginning with "a:. invocation of the celestial force which moves the outermost sphere, encompassing all the other spheres of heaven";[135] the third line reads, " ' . . . because thou movest in a circle,' " and "exhorts the readers to invoke the divine cosmic power, the sun which rules the infinite cosmic space over the heaven of fixed stars . . . [carrying] the reader's thoughts back to the primordial age before the birth of the cosmos."[136] For the rites in the circle "take place in the supercelestial space beyond the starry heavens."[137] Leisegang concludes that the many pagan versions of the thing "all bear witness to the mysteries, to the diverse yet always interrelated forms of the original Orphic-Dionysian cult . . . that extended deep into the Christian world."[138] His final word is that "all these rites were in some way related, though today the nature of the connection can only be surmised."[139] They go much farther back than the Orphic-Dionysian tradition, however, since the old Babylonian hymn of creation, the Enuma Elish, tells how at the Creation God drew "the universal figure," the quartered circle, which is repeated at every level of existence,[140] with the idea that whatever is done on one level or world is done in heaven also.[141]

The only proper place for such activities is the temple, since that edifice is expressly designed for taking one's bearings on the universe in every sense. "The Temple is the center from which light goes forth, and which at the same time draws everything to itself and brings all things together."[142] Its ordinances are those prescribed after the heavenly pattern (see Hebrews 8:5). We have written extensively elsewhere on the "hierocentric" layout of ancient temples, cities, camps, and other ritual complexes—of their universality and antiquity there can be no doubt.[143] Nor is there any shortage of early writings to tell us what they signified to their builders.

In 3 Enoch, the Rabbi Ishmael mounting up to heaven must pass through six *hekaloth*, " 'chamber within chamber,' the Halls being arranged in concentric circles." The word *hekal* usually means simply *temple* (it is the Arabic word for shrine or temple), but in the Enoch literature it regularly refers to the chambers or rooms of the temple representing various steps of initiation.[144] "Arriving at the entrance of the seventh *hekal*," Rabbi Ishmael reports, in the opening lines of his epic:

> I stood still in prayer before the Holy One, blessed be He,
> and, lifting up my eyes on high (i.e. toward the Divine
> Majesty), I said: "Lord of the Universe, I pray thee that
> the merit of Aaron . . . who received the crown of priest-
> hood from [in the presence of] Thy Glory on the mount of
> Sinai be valid for me in this hour" [no unclean thing can
> take this step otherwise].

One thinks of Moses also "clothed upon with glory" on the
mountain (Moses 7:3; 1:2, 9). Rabbi Ishmael having reached
the door to the presence of God must become a crowned
king and a priest before he can enter. He asks for this because,
like others who make this supreme prayer, he seeks to be
delivered from his lower condition, that Satan (Qafsiel) "may
not get power over me nor throw me down from the
heavens,"[145] i.e., even as they were, for on meeting Adam in
the dark and dreary world, Satan boasts and taunts him,
that he has caused him to be cast out of Paradise even as
Adam had caused his expulsion from heaven at the time of
the Creation.[146] In short, Ishmael utters the classic prayer of
Adam, Moses, Abraham, and others, and receives the proper
reply when God immediately sends "Metatron, his Servant
the angel, the Prince of the Presence" to instruct him and
bring him farther on the way:

"Forthwith the Holy One . . . sent to me Metatron, his
Servant the angel, the Prince (sar) of the Presence," who
came joyfully to Ishmael, grasped him firmly by the right
hand in the sight of all, and said, " 'Enter in peace before the
high and exalted King and behold [comprehend] the picture
[likeness] of the Merkabah.' " The use of special words
(hitsaqel, "comprehend" for "see," demuth, "likeness" or
"picture" instead of simply saying God, and Merkabah [that
elaborate circumlocution]) all save the writer from further
obligation to say just what it was Rabbi Ishmael saw—since
it cannot be described to those mortals who have seen nothing like it. The same caution is expressed in Lehi's report that

"he was carried away in a vision, even that he saw the heavens open, and he *thought* he saw God sitting upon his throne" (1 Nephi 1:8; italics added). Rabbi Ishmael also reports, like Enoch (and he is reporting all this to explain what it was that *Enoch* experienced), that God had given him a throne "similar to the Throne of Glory [cf. Moses 7:59]. And He spread over me [before me, on my account—'*ali*] a curtain [veil] of splendour and brilliant appearance, of beauty, grace and mercy, similar to the curtain of the Throne of Glory; and on it were fixed all kinds of lights in the universe."[147] "The Curtain," comments Odeberg on this, "regularly represents the recording of the Divine decrees with regard to the world, the secrets of the world's creation and sustenance, etc., in short, the innermost Divine Secrets"[148]—the secrets, that is, of this earth and of all other "lights in the universe." We pointed out in the *Egyptian Endowment* that ancient temple veils represented the point or act of transition between man's sublunary life and the vast open reaches of the immensity of space beyond, into which one passes by passing through that veil.[149] They were cosmic veils, appropriately adorned, as Rabbi Ishmael reports, with astronomical marks and emblems.

Such a veil was discovered in a cemetery of Astana in central Asia by Sir Aurel Stein and has been hailed by de Santillana and von Dechend as done "in true archaic spirit (which means that only hints are given, and the spectator has to work out for himself the significance of the details)."[150] It dates from the seventh century, was found in position suspended from pegs on a north wall; it was found near the body of a man dressed in Sassanian style. "Near the head lay also the crown-shaped paper hat." An accompanying document says "that several sutras were copied and recited by monks" at the funeral of the man's wife: she was buried A.D. in 8 December 667, her husband in 689.[151] A mixture of cultures is apparent—the Sutras, Sassanian art and Chinese elements (the Chinese having moved in quite recently—A.D.

640)—and the ritual with which the parties are so much concerned may have been somewhat eclectic, with a foundation of Nestorian Christianity. In the veil in question, what first catches the eye are the signs of the square and the compass, boldly drawn as they are held up in the right and left hands respectively of the lady and her husband. To quote the official description: "Silk . . . perhaps originally white. Subject the legendary Emperor Fu-hsi with his consort Nuwas facing each other" about three-quarters life-size. "The bodies rise from a continuous flounce-like short white skirt"—an apron, "their two inner arms stretched stiffly and horizontally towards each other . . . the hand of each appearing under the opposite armpit of the other shows that they are embracing . . . Fuhsi holds in his uplifted left hand a mason's square. . . . Nuwas holds in her right hand a pair of compasses. . . . From below issue two intertwined serpentine bodies which coil around each other "—the well-known caduceus, of life and death, signifying that all things have their opposites (cf. John 3:14, etc.). The whole design is completely surrounded with diagrams of the constellations, while above the heads of the two figures "is the sun disc, white with red spokes," surrounded by twelve smaller circles, each connected to the next by a straight line to form an unbroken circle except at the very top where it is left open—plainly the circle of the months of the year.[152] Fu-hsi is not only the first king but also the patron of artisans, the creator-god. As de Santillana and von Dechend explain it, "The two characters surrounded by constellations are Fu Hsi and Nu Kua, i.e., this craftsman god and his paredra, who measure the 'squareness of the earth' and 'the roundness of heaven' with their implements, the square with the plumb bob hanging from it, and the compass,"[153] as they lay the foundations of the world. So the Pharaoh would go out by night with the Lady Seshat to lay out the foundation of a new temple by taking direct bearing on the stars with the proper instruments. The Lady was his one indispensable assistant on the occasion.[154] Let us recollect that in the creation hymn of the Manual of Discipline the singer promises to gauge all his doings and mark the course of his ring-dance to the music of the spheres with the plumb-bob and line.[155] The constellations on the Astana veil are dominated by the Great Bear, indicating the center of the universe, the *omphalos* or *umbilicus mundi*, the navelof the cosmos.[156] Thus square, compass, and Pole-star designate the veil as the cosmic gate, curtain, or barrier to worlds beyond.

Rabbi Ishmael recited his prayer just before passing through to the throne which was behind a curtain, and he also informs us that God "made for me a garment of glory,"[157] bearing the same markings as the veil and having the same cosmic significance, which reminds one of the close affinity between robe and veil in the very early Christian Hymn of the Pearl[158] and also recalls how the bishop leading the prayer circle in the Syriac Testament of Our Lord "stands with upraised hands and offers a prayer at the veil," after which he proceeds "to make the sacrifice, the veil of the gate being drawn aside."[159] St. Augustine's version of the Priscillian prayer circle ends with the apparently incongruous statement, "I am the Gate for whoever knocks on me," which Augustine explains in terms of Psalms 24:7, referring to the veil of the temple.[160]

The fullest expression of that altruism by which one saves oneself in saving others is a simple but ingenious device employed in the prayer circle; it was the "diptych," a sort of looseleaf notebook or folded parchment placed on the altar during the prayer. It contained the names of persons whom the people in the circle wished to remember. The diptychs are among the oldest treasures preserved in the oldest churches. The name means "folded double," though the documents could be folded triple or quadruple as well if the list of names was very long.[161] The prayer for the people on the list was never part of the later mass but was always a *litany*, a special appeal for certain persons: "By litanies one intercedes

for certain classes of persons."[162] The original diptychs were
the consular diptychs, carried around by top Roman officials—the mark of the busy pagan executive in high office.
According to Leclercq, when bishops became important figures in city politics, high government officials would present
them with diptychs "as flattering presents."[163] As notebooks
they were convenient and practical—just the thing for keeping and handling important lists of names, and to such a use
the Christians gladly put them.[164] "In the place of the diptychs
properly so designated [those used in government business]
there were substituted at an early time notebooks or leaves
of parchment which one would place on the altar during the
celebration of the Mass. . . . Gradually that practice [the
reading of the names (out loud)] was given up, [and] the
priest merely referred to all the faithful whose names were
written down on the diptychs or the leaves taking the place
of diptychs."[165] The practice of laying names on the altar is
of unknown origin though it is very old and, it is agreed,
may well go back to the days of the apostles.[166] Confusion
with the old Roman pagan custom of reading off the names
of donors from such lists caused it to be repeatedly denounced
by the early fathers in the West;[167] but the problem never
arose in the East, and "the laying of a small tablet containing
the names is to this day the practice in the Western Syrian
rite."[168]

   At first the list of names was read aloud before being
placed on the altar, but as that took up too much time (one
of the surviving lists has over 350 names) the reading was
phased out; "the list could be placed on the altar without
any vocal reading of the names."[169] The common practice of
scratching one's name on the altar to assure inclusion in the
prayers forever after may go back to old Jewish practice, for
in 3 Enoch when the ministering angels utter the prayer (the

Qaddish) "all the explicit names that are graven with a flaming style on the Throne of Glory fly off. . . . And they surround and compass the Holy One . . . on the four sides of the place of His Shekhina."[170]

Since the purpose of the prayer circle was to achieve total unity of minds and hearts, "keeping in mind the absent ones," it was natural to include the dead as well as the living in remembrance. One prayed for himself "and also for all my relatives and close associates (consanguinitate vel familiaritate) and for all the Saints of the Church of God, as well as for those who died in the faith, who are recorded in my Book of Remembrance."[171] "We pray for ourselves, our brothers and sisters . . . and for those who have paid their due to death, whose names we have written down or whose names appear on the holy altar, and all who stand in the circle whose faith and devotion are known to thee." [172] But in the earliest times the lists of the living and the dead were kept strictly separate "in two separate books."[173] For the work for the dead was something special and apart. "We remember the dead," wrote Epiphanius in the fourth century, "(1) by performing ritual prayers, (2) by carrying out certain ordinances, and (3) by making certain special arrangements (oikonomias)."[174] In the Clementine Recognitions when Clement asks Peter, "Shall those be wholly deprived of the kingdom of heaven who died before Christ's coming?" he receives a cautious answer: "You force me, Clement, to make public things that are not to be discussed. But I see no objection to telling you as much as we are allowed to." He tells him of the spirits of the dead "retained in good and happy places" but refuses to explain how they are to be redeemed. [175] Likewise when Mary asks the Lord on behalf of the apostles how "a good man who has completed all the ordinances" may save an undeserving relative who has died, she is told that the good man must repeat all the same ordinances again while naming "the soul of such-and-such a person, on whom I am thinking my heart (mind)," whom he thus mentally accompanies through "the proper number of circles (*kykloi*) in the transformations (*metaboliai*), as he becomes baptized and sealed with the signs (*psēphoi*) of the kingdom . . . and so advances."[176] What these circles are the reader may decide for himself. "We remember not only the saints," writes the Areopagite, "but our parents and friends, rejoicing in their condition in the *refrigerium* and praying that we too may finish this life worthily. We all join together in this."[177] The *refrigerium* referred to by the Areopagite means those "good and happy places" spoken of by Peter and Alma. The Greek name for it is *anapausis*, a place where you rest for a time, and the famous Stowe Missal says the members pray for all who are in the *anapausis*, "from Adam down to the present day, whose names are known to God . . . and also for us (the living) sinners."[178]

Lists beginning with Adam smack of genealogy, and we have already noted one person who prayed for all those "even including the faithful dead who are recorded in my Book of Remembrance"[179] In the fierce contentions between churches, from the second century (the Age of Heresy) on, in which each sought to establish its priority in authority and doctrine, the lists of bishops were brought forth as the strongest proofs of rival claims tracing the line of each church down from Adam, Abel, Seth, etc., thus combining the idea of dispensation with that of genealogy. The idea of keeping such bishop lists was inspired in the first place, Stegmüller maintains, by the general practice of keeping family records and genealogies among the Romans and Greeks; indeed it may go back to what Mommsen called "the genealogical mania" of the Hellenistic world.[180] In one of the earliest of all orthodox Christian writings, the *Pastor of Hermas*, when the angel asks the writer if he knows the names of the elect, he replies, "I cannot keep them in my memory; give me a book and I will write them down."[181] In his *Confessions*, St. Augustine requests, "Whoever reads this, please remember my mother and father at the altar," for which purpose he gives their full names.[182]

St. Augustine makes a sharp "distinction between the martyrs *to* whom one prays and the living *for whom one prays*." [183] Typically Roman, Innocent I condemned the old Gallic and Celtic practices of praying "for all the faithful of this place as well as our kinsmen and servants in this place" and limited the prayer to the official dead and recognized saints of the Roman church though the order was not enforced outside of Italy until Charlemagne cracked down.[184] In the Eastern churches the lists and the prayers were always separate; it is specifically for the living, Chrysostom says, "that we pray standing with upraised hands."[185] As Cyril of Jerusalem explains it, "In the circle we pray for those who are sick and afflicted; in short, we pray for whoever is in need of help."[186] Cyril does not mention the list of names on the altar in this account, but he does elsewhere, referring to this very custom and specifying separate lists for the living and the dead.[187] In the Eastern churches "they prayed mentally for the living," while the memento for the dead was something else, requiring, of course, the actual speaking of their names at some time. The prayer uttered for those whose names were on the altar was not a fixed formula, to judge by one old rubric giving instructions: "He (the leader) joins hands and prays for a while (no set limit); then he proceeds with his hands stretched out (*extensis*, extended): and all those standing in the circle join in."[188]

The physicist Fritjof Capra in his "Reflections on the Cosmic Dance"[189] calls attention to that "system of archetypal symbols, the so-called hexagrams," formed of trigrams which were "considered to represent all possible cosmic and human situations," in the religious philosophy of the Far East. To convey their message "the eight trigrams [are] grouped around a circle to the 'natural order,' " the circle among other things "associated with the cardinal points and with the seasons of the year." These rings, based on multiples of six and eight, he compares with the latest schemes and formulas of advanced physics for interpreting the universe. Not only is the basic circle of eight hexagrams in the *I Ching* "vaguely similar" to the way in which "the eight mesons . . . fall into a neat hexagonal pattern known as the 'meson octet,' " but also the great ring dance, "the sixty-four hexagrams . . . the cosmic arch-types on which the use of the *I Ching* as an oracle book is based," presents "perhaps the closest analogy to the S-matrix theory in Eastern thought," both being as near as the mind of man can get to explaining reality and matter.[190]

The various patterns and designs produced by ancient Oriental religion and modern Western science do look a lot alike, and this is no accident, according to Capra, because they both represent the same reality, though why that should be so, and exactly what the reality is, and how the two systems of thought are related is beyond human comprehension at present and may remain so forever. What bids us take both systems seriously, however, is that each is not only perfectly consistent within itself, but that without any collusion both turn up the same series of answers. So there must be something behind it. This reminds us of Leisegang's discovery that "all these rites were in some way related, though today the nature of the connection can only be surmised."[191] The many ring dances to which he refers were also cosmic circles and must somehow fit into the same picture.

Yet one closes Capra's book, and a lot of others, with a feeling of disappointment. Somehow this Mayahana fails to get off the ground. What is wrong? In giving us a picture of the entire universe, including ourselves, both the Eastern sages and modern physics, covering the same ground in different ways, seem to leave out something very important. They give us the stage without the play. Granted it is a magnificent stage, a universal stage with self-operating scene-shifts providing constant display of ever-changing light, color, and sound, filling the beholder with genuine religious awe; still the more we see of it the more restless and disturbed we become. We are taken on a tour of the studio, but that is all. The sets are overpowering, they include the most dazzling space-science spectaculars, but our tour group becomes restive. Where are the actors, where is the show, what is the play? What is supposed to be *going on* here? The cosmic dance of particles whose nature we can never hope to grasp is not ultimately satisfying, even after we are convinced that that is all there is. "The divine *lila* is a rhythmic, dynamic play," Capra tells us.[192] Yet "ultimately there is nothing to explain," and "as long as we try to explain things we are bound by *Karma*." What you have seen is the whole show, for "every part 'contains' all the others. . . . Every particle consists of all other particles."[193] The "bootstrap principle" would quiet all complaints with its neat circular argument; e.g., one hadron (particle) produces other hadrons and they produce *it*—don't ask how, because the process cannot be grasped in terms of anything in our own experience. So the only solution is to stop worrying or looking for explanations; you must settle for that because that is all there is. Learn to live with it: "Don't expect more and you will not be disappointed"; that is the sum and substance of the wisdom of the East.

The whole thing rests in the end not on reason or experience, we are repeatedly told; nothing can be described or defined, but all depends on feeling and intuition. But if that is so, must we not have respect for our own deep-seated feelings in the matter? The fact is that we cannot escape that haunting discontent; there is surely more to the play than the properties. The prayer circles, Christian and Jewish, give us assurance of that.

The old Christian prayer circle does not pretend, as the Orientals do, to embrace the whole universe and to sum up all knowledge; it is merely a timid knocking at the door in the hopes of being let into what goes on in the real world.

82   Mormonism and Early Christianity

Mr. Capra completely ignores the Near Eastern and old European schemes and patterns in his survey, and they are quite as rich and ingenious and probably more ancient than their Far Eastern derivatives. The Jewish and Christian systems are late and confused as we get them; they wander in an apocalyptic mist that cannot distinguish between revelation and speculation, but the dominant idea is that there is more, much more, going on than we have yet dreamed of, but that it is all on the other side of the door. The Oriental shuts his eyes in mystic resignation and with infinite humility makes sure that we are aware of his quiet omniscience. He knows all there is to know, and that is the message.

It is Joseph Smith's prayer circle that puts it all together. Not only did he produce an awesome mass of purportedly ancient writings of perfect inner consistency, but at every point where his contribution is tested—and since he affects to give us concrete historical material as well as theology and cosmology it can be tested at countless points—it is found to agree with other ancient records, most of which are now coming to light for the first time. The prayer circle is one example of that; we may not discuss his version too freely, but we have seen enough of the early Christian prayer circle to justify some important conclusions:

1. It always appears as a solemn ordinance, a guarded secret and a "mystery" for initiates only. This does not express a desire to mystify but the complete concentration and unity of the participants that requires the shutting out of the trivial and distractions of the external world.

2. It always takes place in a special setting—the temple. Even in Christian churches of later time there is a conscious attempt to reproduce as nearly as possible the original temple situation.

3. The words and gestures do not always make sense to outsiders—only "he who has ears to hear" may hear, and only "he who joins in the circle knows what is going on." This because the prayer circles are integral parts of a longer

series of ordinances that proceed and follow them; taken out of that context they necessarily seem puzzling.

4. Though private prayer circles would seem to be out of the question (quackery, magic, and witchcraft made use of them), the members of the circle are never those of a special social rank, family, guild, or profession—they are ordinary men and women of the church, with a high priest presiding.

ADDENDUM

In the Cairo Museum, written on a huge shard of red pottery, is an ancient Coptic liturgical text which provides a remarkable link between ancient Egyptian and early Christian beliefs. It is a Christian "Book of Breathings" with the name of Osiris (representing the initiate) replaced by that of Adam, as if the "Egyptian Endowment" were organically linked to the Christian. Equally instructive is the predominance of the prayer circle in the text and the cosmic significance given it. As its modern editor, L. Saint-Paul Girard, notes, it has eight main divisions. [194]

A. *Calling upon God*

Line 1. (The Tau-Rho sign). [195] Hail El! Fathouriel, [196] who giveth

2. strength (comfort?), who gives replies [*antiphonei*] to the angels! [197]

3. Hail Adonai (My Lord), Hail Eloi (My God), Hail

4. Abrasax! Hail Iothael! [198] Hail

5. Mistrael (for Mizrael) who has looked upon the face of the Father [199]

6. in the power of Iao! [200] KHOK. [201]

B. *Solemn adjurations. Adam as the type of initiate.*

I adjure you (i.e. put you under covenant). [202]

7. by the first seal placed upon the bo-

8. dy of Adam. I adjure you (a different word: "give the hand to," "make to swear") [203] by the second

9. [seal] which is upon the members of Adam. I covenant with you

10. by the third seal which marked the vitals (bowels) [204]

11. and also the breast (heart, mind)[205] of Adam, when
he was brought low (cast down) to become dust (earth)

C. *The healing of the man Adam*
12. until Jesus Christ stands bail for him (lit. takes
him by the hand) in the embrace
13. of his Father.[206] The Father hath raised him up (or
met him).[207]

D. *The breathing (Resurrection) motif*
He hath breathed in
14. his face and filled him with the breath of life. Send
to me
15. thy breath of life, (even) to this true and faithful
one (or, to this vessel)[208] Amen, amen, amen!

E. *A type of the Crucifixion*
16. Sousa, sousa, sousa![209] I covenant with you by
the three cries (of distress) which
17. The Son uttered on the cross, namely: *Eloi, Eloi,
A-*
18. *hlebaks atōnē*[210] That is to say, God, my God,
why *(djou)* hast thou forsaken me?

F. *The hymn*
19. Holy, Holy, Holy! Hail David the father (ancestor)
20. of Christ! He who sings praises (psalms) in the
Church of the First-born (pl.) of heaven, Hail
21. David, theopa [tor?] (ancestor of the Lord), of the
joyful ten-stringed lyre[211] who sings
22. within (the veil of) the altar[212]
23. the joyful one (either David or the altar). Hail
Hormosiel, who sings within the veil

G. *Prayer circle*
24. of the Father![213] They repeat after him, those who
are at the entrances (gates,
25. doors) and those who are upon the towers (i.e. the
watchmen at the gates). And when they hear what he says,
namely the tribes (or gates?) who

26. are within the Twelve Worlds, they joyfully

27. repeat it after him:[214] Holy, Holy, One (or Jesus) Holy Father.[215] Amen,

28. Amen, Amen. Hail Arebrais in heaven and earth!

29. Then you (pl.) bless (praise God, pray), KOK (meaning that at this point certain actions are performed). Hail O Sun! hail ye twelve little children

30. who overshadow (protect?) the body of the Sun![216] Hail ye twelve phials

31. filled with water. They have filled their hands, they have scattered abroad

32. the rays of the Sun, lest they burn up the fruits

33. of the field[217] Fill thy hands, pronounce blessing upon this

34. cup. KOK [another ordinance]

H. *Entering the Presence*

Hail ye four winds of heaven!

35. Hail ye four corners of the earth! (the inhabited earth, *oikoumenē*)[218]

36. Hail ye hosts (*stratia*) of heaven (i.e., the stars)! Hail

37. thou earth (land) of the inheritance

38. Hail O garden (or power, authority) of the Holy Ones (saints)

39. [of] the Father![219] One holy Father

40. Holy [Son] Holy Ghost

41. Amen.

NOTES

1. Johannes D. Mansi, *Sacrorum Conciliorum Nova et Amplissima Collectio*, 54 vols. (Graz: Akademischer Verlag, 1960), 13:169–75. The minutes of the meeting are instructive, beginning with col. 172:

"Tarasius, the most holy Patriarch, said: Let us view the document as a whole as contrary to the Gospel.

"The Holy Synod said: Aye, sir: and it says that the human nature was only an appearance. . . .

"Constantine the most holy bishop of Constantia in Cyprus said: This book is the basis of their unauthorized assemblies.

"Tarasius the m. h. Patriarch said: These things are simply ridiculous.

"Theodore the most God-beloved Bishop of Catana said: Yes, but this book has been undermining the authority [lit. wrenching the vestments] of the Holy Church of God!

"Euthymius the most holy Bishop of Sardis said: Their false sects [parasynagogai] had to have this book to back them up [lit., as witnesses].

"The Entire Synod declared: All heresy depends on this book.

"Tarasius the most honorable Bishop said: Alas, how many heretical books support their false teachings!

"Gregory the most holy bishop of Neocaesarea said: But this book is worthy of all vile infection [miasma] and a disgrace.

"[On a motion by Tarasius] the Holy Synod said: Let it be condemned [anathema] from the first letter to the last.

"John a most revered monk and vicar to the Eastern Patriarchs said: Behold, blessed Fathers, it is most clearly demonstrated herewith that the leaders of the heresy which criticizes true Christianity are really the companions and fellow travelers of Nebuchadnezzar and the Samaritans, to say nothing of the Jews and Gentiles (Greeks), and also of those cursed atheists the Manichaeans, whose testimony they cite. . . . Let them all be anathemized along with their writings!

"The Holy Synod said: Anathema! . . .

"John the Reverend Monk . . . then made a motion: May it please the Most Holy and Oecumenical Synod to vote that no further copies be made of this pestilential book.

"The Holy Synod voted: Let no copies of it be made; furthermore we herewith declare it worthy to be consigned to the flames.

"[Here Peter, the secretary of the meeting, signs his name to the minutes.]"

Conventional Christianity views the ancient prayer circle as a sort of Gnostic aberration. L. Gougaud, "Danse," in DACL 4:248–58. It is never mentioned again in orthodox sources. See Henri Leclercq, "Agape," in DACL 1:787–92.

2. Max Pulver, "Jesus' Round Dance and Crucifixion according to the Acts of John," in Joseph Campbell, ed., The Mysteries (New York: Pantheon, 1955), 169.

3. Texts of this part of the Acts of John, taken from a number of sources, may be found in Mansi, Sacrorum Conciliorum Acta; Leclercq, "Agape," 787–92; ANT 253–70; NTA 2:227–32.

4. Augustine, *Epistolae (Letters)* 237, in *PL* 33:1034–38; quoted partially by Leclercq, "Agape," 786, and *NTA* 2:227–28, n. 5.

5. Ignatius Ephraem II Rahmani, ed., *Testamentum Domini Nostri Jesu Christi* (Moguntiae: Kirchheim, 1899). The age of the work is discussed on pp. ix-xiv.

6. Ibid., 36–37.

7. Ibid., 38, 40–42.

8. Cyril of Jerusalem, *Catechesis XX, Mystagogica II, de Baptismi Caeremoniis (Catechetical Lecture on the Rites of Baptism)*, in *PG* 33:1081; also in Hugh W. Nibley, *The Message of the Joseph Smith Papyri* (Salt Lake City: Deseret, 1976) 282.

9. *NTA* 2:230–31, lines 31–42.

10. Rahmani, *Testamentum Domini Nostri* , 44, 60.

11. A. Wilmart and E. Tisserant, "Fragments grecs et latins de l'évangile de Barthélemy," *Revue Biblique* 22 (n.s. 10) (1913): 321.

12. Ibid., 324.

13. Ibid., 327.

14. Some references to this are found in Hugh W. Nibley, "Qumran and 'The Companions of the Cave,' " *Revue de Qumran* 5 (April 1965): 186; reprinted in *Collected Works of Hugh Nibley* 1:261–62.

15. Wilmart and Tisserant, "Fragments grecs et latins," 324–25.

16. Joseph and Asenath, chs. 14–17.

17. Evangelium Mariae 17–18, ed. W.C. Till, *Gnostische Schriften des koptischen Papyrus Berolinensis 8502*, (Berlin: Akademie, 1955), 74–76.

18. 2 Jeu, 54 (40), text in Carl Schmidt, *Gnostische Schriften in koptischer Sprache aus dem Codex Brucianus* (Leipzig: Hinrich, 1892), 99. Cf. German tr., 193.

19. Ibid., 66–67 (53g), in Schmidt, *Gnostische Schriften in koptischer Sprache*, 114–17, quote from p. 114; cf. tr., 204. Both First and Second Jeu contain sketches showing various arrangements of prayer circles. Other texts, e.g., the Gospel of Bartholomew and Pistis Sophia, p. 358, make it clear that the facing in four directions denotes standing in a circle.

20. Kasr al-Wazz fragment, p. ii-end, from photographs kindly lent to the author by Professor Hughes at the University of Chicago at the time of their discovery in 1966.

21. Pulver, "Jesus' Round Dance and Crucifixion," 186, notes that mourning here denotes that the initiate is expected to suffer after the

manner of the leader. The word for "mourn" in Matthew 11:17 is *koptomai*, literally, to inflict wounds upon oneself.

22. Variants in Montague R. James, *Apocrypha Anecdota*, second series, *Texts and Studies* 5:1 (Cambridge: University Press, 1897), 3:10–16.

23. Clement of Alexandria, *Cohortatio ad Gentes (Exhortation to the Nations)* 12, in *PG* 8:241.

24. Augustine, *Enarrationes in Psalmos (Expositions on the Psalms)* 111, 2, in *PL* 37:1172; quoted differently along with other texts on the same subject, by Gougaud, "Danse," 250.

25. John Chrysostom, *Commentarius in Sanctum Matthaeum Evangelistam (Commentary on Matthew)* 48, in *PG* 58:491, and Gougaud, "Danse," 248.

26. Basil the Great, *Epistolae (Letters)* I, 2, in *PG* 32:225–26.

27. Augustine, *Expositions on the Psalms* 91, in *PL* 37:1171–81; Chrysostom, *Contra Judaeos et Gentiles, quod Christus Sit Deus (Against the Jews and the Gentiles that Christ Is God)*, in *PG* 48:845–46.

28. Philo, *On the Contemplative Life* xi. The passage as rendered by F. H. Colson in the Loeb Classical Library edition (Cambridge, Mass.: Harvard University Press, 1967), Philo series, 9:165–69, reads: "After the supper . . . they rise up all together and standing in the middle of the refectory [cf. Qumran!] form themselves first into two choirs [*choroi*, circles], one of men and one of women, the leader and precentor [*exarchos*] . . . being the most honored amongst them. . . . Then they sing hymns to God . . . sometimes chanting together, sometimes . . . antiphonally. . . . Then . . . they mix and both together become a single choir, a copy of the choir set up of old beside the Red Sea." This is the way Augustine and Chrysostom describe the Sabbath dancing of the Jews (see preceding note), but Philo being himself a Jew found nothing shocking in it.

29. Gougaud, "Danse," 250, giving these and other examples of ancient dances surviving in the Christian church. Hans Leisegang, "The Mystery of the Serpent," in Campbell, *The Mysteries*, 244.

30. Constantine Porphyrogenitus, *De Caeremoniis Aulae Byzantinae (On the Ritual of the Byzantine Court)* 1, 65, in *PG* 112:568; 1, 83, in *PG* 112:689.

31. Many illustrations from early Christian art published in Gougaud, "Danse," 253–58.

32. Philo, *De Opificio Mundi (On the Creation)* 70–71, tr. Colson (as cited in Leisegang, "The Mystery of the Serpent," 234), modified.

33. Gougaud, "Danse," 248.

34. *1QS* 8:12–16.

35. See notes 20 and 21 above.

36. Acts of John 88, in *NTA* 2:225; Apocryphon of John, in ibid., 1:322; cf. the Life of John according to Serapion, in ibid., 1:415; Pistis Sophia, p. 77 (Schmidt), in *ANT*, 66.

37. Joachim Jeremias, "The Lord's Prayer in Modern Research," *Christian News from Israel* 14 (April 1963): 12–13. Cf. Joachim Jeremias, *The Prayers of Jesus* (London: SCM Press, 1967), 1–29.

38. *Gospel of the Twelve Apostles* 2, in *PO* 2:133.

39. Jeremias, "Lord's Prayer in Modern Research," 10; italics added.

40. Ibid., 11.

41. Pulver, "Jesus' Round Dance and Crucifixion," 175.

42. Pistis Sophia, p. 358; tr. Mead, 295.

43. Ibid., 375; tr. Mead, 310; 357–58; tr. Mead, 295.

44. 1 Jeu, in Schmidt, *Gnostische Schriften in koptischer Sprache*, 326, 370.

45. Apocalypse of Abraham 12:8–9; 17:11–17; cf. *OTP* 1:697.

46. M. J. Bin Gorion, *Die Sagen der Juden*, 5 vols. (Frankfurt: Rutten & Loening, 1913), 1:260–62; cf. Ginzberg, *Legends of the Jews* 1:91.

47. G. B., "Le Combat d'Adam et Eve," text in *DA* 1:329–32.

48. Coptic Gnostic Work, 37–38, in Schmidt, *Gnostische Schriften in koptischer Sprache*, 253; cf. tr., 300.

49. Sebastian Euringer, "Die Binde der Rechtfertigung," *Orientalia*, 2nd ser., 9 (1940): 249.

50. Henri Leclercq, "Main," in *DACL* 10:1212.

51. Pulver, "Jesus' Round Dance and Crucifixion," 175–78, 193.

52. Psalms 54:2: 'Elohīm shma^c 't^{e}phillati ha^{ca}zina l^e-'imrei-phi.

53. Friedrich Preisigke, *Vom göttlichem Fluidum nach ägyptischer Anschauung* (Berlin: de Gruyter, 1920), p. 41, note 3; p. 42.

54. *Zohar*, Lech Lecha, 88a.

55. 1 Enoch 65:2.

56. See above n. 17.

57. Pulver, "Jesus' Round Dance and Crucifixion," 174–76.

58. Ibid., 186.

59. Ibid., 176.

60. Rahmani, *Testamentum Domini Nostri*, 40, 44; cf. Nibley, *Message*, 282.

61. "Combat d'Adam," in *DA* 1:329–32.

62. Bin Gorion, *Sagen der Juden* 1:260–62.

63. F. Tempestini, trans., "Livre d'Adam," in *DA* 1:87.

64. *Recognitiones Clementinae* (*Clementine Recognitions*) I, 32–33, in *PG* 1:226–27.

65. Apocalypse of Abraham, ch. 12; cf. *OTP* 1:695.

66. Robert A. Kraft, *The Testament of Job according to the SV Text* (Missoula, Mt.: Scholars Press, 1974), 3–111 on the various texts. Part of the Greek version is also reproduced by F. C. Conybeare, "The Testament of Job and the Testaments of the XII Patriarchs," *Jewish Quarterly Review* 13 (October 1901): 111–13.

67. The Testament of Job 46:1–5.

68. Ibid., 46:8.

69. Ibid., 46:9.

70. Ibid., 47:3.

71. Ibid., 47:4–6

72. Ibid., 47:7–10.

73. Ibid., 47:10–11.

74. Ibid., 47:11–12.

75. Ibid., 47:12

76. Ibid., 48:1–8.

77. Ibid., 49:1–3.

78. Ibid., 50:1–3.

79. Ibid., 1:1–5.

80. Ibid., 28:7–8.

81. Ibid., 33:1–9.

82. Ibid., 36:1–6.

83. Ibid., 38:5.

84. Ibid., 40:1–3

85. Cf. Ibid., 24:6–8.

86. Ibid., 43:1.

87. Ibid., 43:1–17.

88. Ibid., 43:14.

89. Ibid., 44:1.

90. 2 Jeu, 54 (40), in Schmidt, *Gnostische Schriften in koptischer Sprache*, 99; tr., 193.

91. Pistis Sophia, pp. 358–60 (363–66), (Mead, 300).

92. Acts of John 1:43, in *NTA* 2:231.

93. Even those Gnostic versions defending the proposition that Jesus did not really suffer on the cross celebrate "a pseudo passion and

a pseudo death of Christ," according to Pulver, "Jesus' Round Dance and Crucifixion," 176–78.

94. Gospel of Bartholomew, fol. 14b-15a, in E. A. Wallis Budge, *Coptic Apocrypha* (London: British Museum, 1913).

95. Hypostasis of the Archons 140:3, translated into German by Hans-Martin Schenke, " 'Das Wesen der Archonten': Eine gnostische Originalschrift aus dem Funde von Nag-Hamadi," *Theologische Literaturzeitung* 83 (1958): 667.

96. Apocalypse of Abraham 12:8–10; 17:11–17.

97. 2 Jeu, 54–55, in Schmidt, *Gnostische Schriften in koptischer Sprache*, 100–109.

98. August Wünsche, *Der Midrasch Bemidbar Rabbah* (Leipzig: Schulze, 1882), 11 (101).

99. G. H. Box, *The Apocalypse of Abraham* (London: Society for Promoting Christian Knowledge, 1919), xxv.

100. See the important discussion of Three Men in White, in Erwin Goodenough, *Jewish Symbols in the Greco-Roman Period*, 13 vols. (New York: Pantheon, 1953), 1:25–28.

101. A. Z. Idelsohn, *Jewish Liturgy and Its Development* (New York: Holt, 1932), 3.

102. *Clementine Recognitions* IV, 11, in *PG* 1:1319–20.

103. F. Dieterici, ed., *Thier und Mensch vor dem König der Genien* (Leipzig: Hinrich, 1881), 2–4; cf. Clement, *Epistola I ad Corinthios* (*First Epistle to the Corinthians*) 20, in *PG* 1:249.

104. Leisegang, "The Mystery of the Serpent," 244.

105. Hyemeyohsts Storm, *Seven Arrows* (New York: Harper & Row, 1979), 20.

106. Especially instructive on the circles of eight and twelve, etc., is the Coptic *Sophia Christi*, 95–96, 107–17, 123–24, in Till, *Gnostische Schriften*, 230–33, 254–75, 286–89.

107. 1 Jeu 10–11, in Schmidt, *Gnostische Schriften in koptischer Sprache*, 52–53; cf. tr. 151; cf. Second Coptic-Gnostic Work, 10–11, in ibid., 233–34, cf tr. 284.

108. Second Coptic Gnostic Work, 8a, in Schmidt, *Gnostische Schriften in koptischer Sprache*, 231–32.

109. Pulver, "Jesus' Round Dance and Crucifixion," 175–77.

110. Heliodorus, *Aethiopica* 10, 5–6.

111. Eusebius, *De Vita Constantini* (*On the Life of Constantine*) 58–60, in *PG* 20:1209–11.

112. Photo in Moses Hadas, *Imperial Rome* (New York: New York Times, 1965), 175.

113. Giorgio de Santillana and Hertha von Dechend, *Hamlet's Mill* (Boston: Godine, 1977), 48-49.

114. Plato, *Phaedrus* 247.

115. Clement, *First Epistle to the Corinthians* 20, in *PG* 1:249.

116. 1QS (Manual of Discipline) 10:1-3, 9; cf. Theodor Gaster, *The Dead Sea Scriptures*, 3rd ed. (Garden City, N.Y.: Doubleday, 1976), 136-43; 121.

117. Adolf Jellinek, *Bet ha-Midrasch*, 6 vols. (Jerusalem: Wahrmann, 1967), 5:172 (Book of Enoch).

118. Ascension of Isaiah 4:15-17, in *OTP* 2:162.

119. Philo, *On the Creation* 70-71.

120. Pulver, "Jesus' Round Dance and Crucifixion," 187.

121. See Hugh W. Nibley, *Abraham in Egypt* (Salt Lake City: Deseret, 1981), 186, 166-67.

122. Second Gnostic Work, 6a, text, in Schmidt, *Gnostische Schriften in koptischer Sprache*, 230; cf. tr., 282.

123. Yigael Yadin, *The Temple Scroll*, 3 vols. (Jerusalem: Israel Exploration Society, 1978), 34, 39-42.

124. Plutarch, *De Defectu Oracularum* 22.

125. I.e., the so-called Pyramidologists. A hypocephalus like that of Facsimile No. 2 of the Book of Abraham depicts the geography of the earth as a reflection of that heaven, with the Delta in the center.

126. Clement of Alexandria (dubia), *Excerpta ex Scriptis Theodoti* (*The Teachings of Theodotus*) 80, in *PG* 9:696.

127. Second Gnostic Work, 8a, in Schmidt, *Gnostische Schriften in koptischer Sprache*, 231-32.

128. Pistis Sophia, 10-11.

129. "Livre d'Adam," in *DA* 1:87-88.

130. *Or ha-Meir*, ii, 109b, cited in J. G. Weiss, "The Kavvanoth of Prayer in Early Hasidism," *Journal of Jewish Studies* 9 (1958): 182-83.

131. Isaac Myer, *Qabbalah* (Philadelphia: Myer, 1888), 306.

132. Odes of Solomon 5 and 6.

133. Pistis Sophia, 10-11.

134. Cf. 1 Jeu 10, in Schmidt, *Gnostische Schriften in koptischer Sprache*, 53-54; Apocalypse of Abraham 21-22. Italics added.

135. Leisegang, "The Mystery of the Serpent," 201; cf. 241.

136. Ibid., 211, 215.

137. Ibid., 233.

138. Ibid., 259.

139. Ibid., 240.

140. Enuma Elish 1:60-80; 6:51-73 (esp. 69, 73); 4:136-46. Cf. translations by Speiser, in James Pritchard, *Ancient Near Eastern*

Texts Relating to the Old Testament, 60–72, and Alexander Heidel, *The Babylonian Genesis* (Chicago: University of Chicago Press, 1942). See Heidel, *The Babylonian Genesis,* 43, n. 96 for further bibliography.

141. Enuma Elish 6:113. It is the circle of time divided into 12 lunar positions, 5:1–4, 9–14.

142. Cf. Second Coptic Gnostic Work, 1, in Schmidt, *Gnostische Schriften in koptischer Sprache,* 226; Pistis Sophia, ch. 65, p. 134.

143. Hugh W. Nibley, "The Hierocentric State," *Western Political Quarterly* 4 (1951): 226–53.

144. Hugo Odeberg, *3 Enoch or the Hebrew Book of Enoch* (New York: KTAV, reprint, 1973), 3.

145. Ibid., 3–4; cf. *OTP* 1:255.

146. Life of Adam and Eve xii–xvii, in R. H. Charles, *Apocrypha and Pseudepigrapha of the Old Testament,* 2 vols. (Oxford: Clarendon, 1964), 2:137. Cf. *OTP* 1:262–64.

147. Odeberg, *3 Enoch or the Hebrew Book of Enoch,* ch. 1, p. 4; ch. 10, pp. 27–28. Cf. *OTP* 1:263.

148. Odeberg, *3 Enoch or the Hebrew Book of Enoch,* ch. 1, p. 28.

149. Nibley, *Message,* 245–49.

150. de Santillana and von Dechend, *Hamlet's Mill* 273, with reproduction.

151. Sir Mark Aurel Stein, *Innermost Asia,* 3 vols. (Oxford: Clarendon, 1930), 2:665–67.

152. Ibid., 707.

153. de Santillana and von Dechend, *Hamlet's Mill,* 273, with reproduction.

154. Haus Bonnet, *Reallexikon der ägyptischen Religionsgeschichte* (Berlin: De Gruyter, 1952), 700.

155. *1QS* 10.

156. Another veil was found by Stein, sloppily executed by an artist to whom the details were a puzzle. His constellations are unrecognizable save for the Great Bear, which is identical on both veils. Stein, *Innermost Asia* 2:708.

157. This is made perfectly clear in Odeberg, *3 Enoch or the Hebrew Book of Enoch,* chs. 10 and 12.

158. Nibley, *Message,* 271; cf. 246.

159. Notes 5 and 6 above.

160. Augustine, *Letters* 237, in *PL* 33:1037–38.

161. O. Stegmüller, "Diptychon," in *Reallexikon für Antike und Christentum* (Stuttgart: Hiersemann, 1957) 3:1138.

162. F. Cabrol, "Diptyques (Liturgie)," in *DACL* 4:1050.

163. Ibid., 1095–96.

164. Ibid., 1046–47; Stegmüller, "Diptychon," 1140.

165. Cabrol, "Diptyques," 1061.

166. Stegmüller, "Diptychon," 1138, 1147; Cabrol, "Diptyques," 1051, citing Bona.

167. Stegmüller, "Diptychon," 1143; Cabrol, "Diptyques," 1059, noting that the donor lists were unknown in the East until Constantine introduced them from Rome.

168. Stegmüller, "Diptychon," 1147; cf. 1144–46.

169. Ibid., 3:1147, citing the famous Bobbio Missal.

170. Odeberg, *3 Enoch or the Hebrew Book of Enoch*, ch. 39.

171. Quote is from Cabrol, "Diptyques," 1061; cf. Stegmüller, "Diptychon," 1140. The names in the diptych show "by this meeting of individuals the close bond of communion and love which united all the members of the church." Cabrol, "Diptyques," 1049.

172. Ibid., 1061–62.

173. Stegmüller, "Diptychon," 1146; cf. 1144–45.

174. Epiphanius, *Adversus Haereses* (*Against Heresies*) 3, 77; 7, 21, in *PG* 42:649–52.

175. *Clementine Recognitions* I, 52, in *PG* 1:1236; also in Hugh W. Nibley, *The World and the Prophets* (Salt Lake City: Deseret, 1962), 153; 3rd ed. (1987), 168.

176. Pistis Sophia, pp. 325–26 (322–23).

177. Anonymous (attributed to Origen), *Commentarius in Job* (*Commentary on Job*), 3, in *PG* 17:517.

178. Cabrol, "Diptyques," 1073.

179. See above n. 171.

180. Stegmüller, "Diptychon," 146–47.

181. *Hermae Pastor* (*Shepherd of Hermas*), Visio (Vision) 2, in *PG* 2:895.

182. Augustine, *Confessiones* (*Confessions*) IX, 8, in *PL* 32:770–72.

183. Cabrol, "Diptyques," 1051.

184. Ibid., 4:1071–74, 1073. Alcuin introduced the names of the dead into the regular prayer-lists of our ancestors, where they first appear in an Irish canon of circa A.D. 700, Stegmüller, "Diptychon," 1144.

185. Chrysostom, *Commentary on Matthew* 48, in *PG* 58:491.

186. "Dissertatio de Vita Sancti Cyrilli," 1, 16, in *PG* 33:116.

187. Ibid.; Nicephoros Callistus, *HE* XIV, 26–27, in *PG* 146:1137–49.

188. Cabrol, "Diptyques," 1067.

189. Fritjof Capra, "The Tao of Physics: Reflections on the Cosmic Dance," *Saturday Review* 5 (10 December 1977): 21–23, 28, being a summary of his book *The Tao of Physics* (New York: Bantam, 1977), to which following page references refer. These quotations occur between pp. 268 and 272; 2nd ed., 278–83.

190. Ibid., 270.

191. Note 139 above.

192. Capra, *The Tao of Physics*, 78; 2nd ed., 88.

193. Ibid., 28; 2nd ed., 291; 285; 2nd ed., 295.

194. L. Saint Paul Girard, "Un Fragment de liturgie magique copte sur ostrakon," *Annales du Service des Antiquités de l'Egypte* 27 (1927): 62–68.

195. The earliest signs of the cross were formed by a Greek Chi (X) with the vertical shaft of a Greek Rho (P) or Iota (I) through the middle, or by a Rho with a horizontal bar below the loop (☧ ⳩ ⳨). They were interchangeable and are found in varying combinations, being closely associated also with the "Crux Ansata," the famous Egyptian ankh or life symbol: ☥ . For many examples, see Henri Leclercq, "Chrisme," in *DACL* 3:1481–1534. The classic Latin cross does not appear in the West until the fourth century and like the others seems to have come from Egypt, ibid., 1485–89, and Leclercq is puzzled "that the Christians adopted a sign which ran a serious risk of being misunderstood," ibid., 1483. Not to worry: these symbols had conveyed for centuries the very ideas which the Christians wished them to represent in a new context, just as they borrowed current alphabets and other symbols of general acceptance to convey their own peculiar ideas. The symbol prefacing this note is both the monogram of Christ and the earliest symbol of the crucifixion; as such, it also designates the victory of light over darkness as represented in the performance of the mysteries.

196. Phathouriel for Bathuriel, from Hebrew Bait-tsuri-el, "the house of my strength is God," or "My God My Rock." Girard, "Fragment de Liturgie," 66, n. 1, citing Moise Schwab, *Vocabulaire de l'angelologie*, (Paris: Klincksieck, 1897) s.v.; cf. Souri-el, "My Rock Is God." Henri Leclercq, "Abrasax," in *DACL* 1:145. Since the names El, Adonai, Eloi, and Abrasax invoked together at the opening of the rites are all designations of the supreme God, Bathuriel, as second on the list, must be another epithet for El. Tsur is properly a stone and a foundation; coming at the beginning of the rites it strongly suggests the Stone of Truth in the Egyptian initiation rites and the Eben Shetiyah of Hebrew tradition. Nibley, *Message*, 120–24.

197. Girard alters *eb-ti phonē nenankelōs* ("who gives a voice to the angels") to *ef [an]tiphōnei nenangelos,* "whose voice replies to the angels," because he cannot imagine the meaning of the former. Girard, "Fragment de Liturgie," 66, n. 2. The first suggests the Creation Hymn, the second the exchange of expressions at the conclusion of the rites (lines 24–27 below).

198. The names of Adonai, Eloi, and Abraxas are the most common found on those carved Gnostic gems called "Abraxas" or "Abrasax." Henri Leclercq, "Anges," in in *DACL* 1:2087–88. Such gems representing "the world of Alexandria and the Egyptian-Greek magical papyri" consist of "stones which figure in superstition as well." Reiss, "Abrasax," in *RE* 1:110; Augustine writes, "Basilides gives to the Almighty God the portentous name of ABRAXAS, and says it contains the number of the course of the year in the Sun's circuit, while the Gentiles designate the same number by the name of Meithra." *Commentarius in Amos (Commentary on Amos)* 1, 3, in *PL* 25:1080–89. In our text, Abrasax is an epithet of God as the ruler of all and the director and guide of Mysteries: The most common type of Abrasax gem (of Egyptian origin, though their meanings have never been explained—Reiss, "Abrasax," 109–10) depicts the god as Anubis with the staff of office that shows him to be the psychopomp, conductor of souls or *paralemptor* (guide) through the mysteries; as such, he is identified with the classic Mercury and the Christian Michael. Leclercq, "Abrasax," 134–37. He is often shown as the mummified Osiris, with or without a crown; cf. Leclercq, "Anges," 2127, fig. 653.

199. Mizrael is the angelic embodiment of divine authority, which enables him to see behind the veil. Girard, "Fragment de liturgie," 66, n. 5, cit. Schwab, *Vocabulaire de l'Angelologie.*

200. Iao is the common equivalent for Jehovah and God. Leclercq, "Abrasax," 147, 141.

201. KHOK occurs in lines 29 and 32 as KOK. It introduces a new phase or change of scene and indicates that at this point certain actions take place. Our text, in the manner of a prompting sheet, contains only words recited, without describing acts or rites performed but only the point at which they take place. The Coptic word KOK is the common word for "disrobe" and related concepts, and may indicate changes in costume.

202. *Ti-ōřk erō-tn̄,* the erō- indicating "the person adjured," here in the plural, while the n̄- is the thing sworn by; see W. F. Crum, *Coptic Dictionary* (Oxford: Clarendon, 1939), 529. To adjure is to place another under solemn obligation by entering a covenant with him.

203. *Titarko* means literally "give the hand to" in token of covenant. Wilhelm Spiegelberg, *Koptisches Handwörterbuch* (Heidelberg: Winter, 1921); "make to swear, adjure, entreat." Crum, *Coptic Dictionary*, 430.

204. *Tōōbe e-* as here means to set a mark or stamp upon, to impress upon, to leave a mark on. For vitals the original has *t-tchot*, meaning size, age, form, which Girard emends to *tchlot*, meaning "Kidney, also other internal organs" (possibly from the root *tschlodj*, bend, be interlaced). It is the Hebrew *kliyot*, "the reins, kidneys, inward parts." Crum, *Coptic Dictionary*, 813.

205. *P-het*, heart mind, thought reason; cf. the Greek, *stēthos*, the breast as the receptacle of principles of thought, and Hebrew *lēb*, the heart "as the seat of the various feelings, affections and emotions . . . and of the moral sentiments." Benjamin Davies, ed., *A Compendious and Complete Hebrew and Chaldee Lexicon to the Old Testament* (Boston: Bradley, 1875), 315.

206. The verb for covenant is here *sh(e)p tōre*, vb. intr., "grasp the hand, be surety for, undertake;" Crum, *Coptic Dictionary*, 425; with the object *m̄mof* (as here) it means "be surety for." *Hñ ñ-tchidj m̄-pef-iot* Girard renders "entre les mains de son Pere," i.e., "in his embrace."

207. *Tahof erat.f* can mean either "set up," "establish," "cause to stand," or "meet with," "reach another."

208. The Coptic word *pites* Girard reads as Greek *pithos*, vessel, though he finds the idea "bizarre." Early Christian and Jewish writers, however, speak of the living body (which is the subject of this passage) as a vessel *(angeion)*. Barnabas calls the living body "the blessed vessel" *(to kalon skeuos)*, Barnabas, *Epistola Catholica* (*Catholic Epistle*) 21, in *PG* 2:727–82. On the other hand, *pithos* is an alternative spelling for *peithos*, a Greek equivalent for *pithanos*, "obedient," "receptive," a fit epithet for an initiate.

209. Girard makes no attempt to translate *sousa*, but since this is a cry for help, one thinks of the Greek imperative *sōze* (mid. *sōzou*, aorist *sōson*) or aorist mid. *sōsai*, meaning "to rescue." Some maintain that the name of *Abrasax* is derived from *Habros* and *Sao*, "gentle Savior" or "le magnifique sauveur." Leclercq, "Abrasax," 129.

210. Is the unfamiliar Aramaic the subject of mystic speculation or just confusion? Girard restores it to *elema sabaktani*. The trouble seems to be the scribe's insistence on reading the last three syllables as the familiar *Adonai* (*atōnē*).

211. Girard alters *thea* to *theo* and borrows the *pat-* from the next word to get *theopator*, "l'ancêtre du Christ," an epithet of David in

Byzantine liturgy. *Pa.ti.tshittharashē* is divided into *[pa] ti-kithara [ñn] rashe tamēt ñkap*, the harp of joy of ten strings. The ten-stringed harp is a cosmic concept, ten being the perfect number of the Pythagoreans.

212. After writing "veil of the altar" the scribe erased the "veil." The expression *m.pethesasterion* is for the Greek formula *entos tou thysiastēeriou*, meaning "inside the sanctuary." Walter Bauer, *A Greek English Lexicon of the New Testament and other Early Christian Literature*, tr. William F. Arndt and F. Wilbur Gingrich (Chicago: University of Chicago Press, 1957), s.v. *thysiastērion*, 366; though *thysiastērion* properly means altar.

213. Harmosiel is the exalted angel who sounds the trumpet and shares with Mizrael the privilege of beholding the Lord behind the veil. The Priscillianists were accused of worshipping him.

214. Harmosiel instructs them? Girard: "Ceux qui sont sur les portes et les tours font écho à sa voix" is quite specific.

215. *Is per hakios* for the Greek formula *Heis Pater Hagios*, though *Is* is the common writing for Jesus, and such an identity is monophysite, making Jesus identical with the Father. As it is, Girard must insert another *hagios* to make a proper *trishagion*.

216. Girard: "Salut, o douze petits enfants qui protegez (?) le corps du soleil." Though this can also be read "minor servants," the reference to the little children in our prayer circle situation recommends the former. Also the preposition *m̄mof* would justify "screen from him the body of the Sun." Walter Till, *Koptische Grammatik* (Leipzig: VEB Verlag Enzyklopädie, 1970), #258. See the following note.

217. The twelve water jugs and reference to the watering of vegetation recall the peculiar arrangements of the prayer circles in 1 and 2 Jeu. According to Pistis Sophia, p. 84, the earth must be shielded from the rays of the sun by veils or curtains lest all life be consumed. Today, the filtering of the sun's rays by layers of atmosphere of various particles is held to be essential to sorting out life-giving rays from deadly ones and thus making vegetation and other life possible upon the earth.

218. The imagery of the closing passage belongs to the coronation rites. The four corners of the earth motif is basic. See Hugh W. Nibley, "Facsimile No. 1, by the Figures, A New Look at the Pearl of Great Price: Part 8," *Improvement Era* 72 (August 1969): 82–85. Paulinus of Nola associated the coronation and universal rule with the types of crosses discussed above, note 1; *Poema* (*Poem*) XIX, 638–41, in *PL* 61:546; a teaching confirmed by Ambrose and Jerome.

219. *P-tchom* means either garden or authority; both are appropriate, the garden as the sanctified inheritance of the Saints, the authority being that with which the exalted "Holy Ones of the Father" are invested. The original text, however, has *p-shom*, which also makes sense, since it means "summertime," i.e., the "Summertime of the Just" when the Saints receive their celestial inheritance, e.g., the *Shepherd of Hermas*.

4

Baptism for the Dead
in Ancient Times

In 1895 there was found in Egypt a Coptic papyrus purporting to contain an account of the teaching of Christ to his apostles after the resurrection. The most learned church historian of modern times, Adolf von Harnack, was prompted to point out that this document was neither "a provincial production of the Egyptian Church" nor a brainchild of the Gnostics, but an authentic statement of certain important doctrines of salvation and resurrection common to the whole Christian church at a very early date. Shortly after, Carl Schmidt, second only to Harnack in his knowledge of early Christian documents, produced a number of ancient fragments, matching the Coptic text word for word in a half dozen languages and showing it to be derived from the Greek original of an apostolic general epistle which had enjoyed widespread authority and popularity in the church at least as early as the second century. The subject of this epistle was salvation for the dead, a doctrine which, as Schmidt demonstrated, was believed in the early church to have been the main theme of Christ's teaching after the resurrection.

"Baptism for the Dead in Ancient Times" first appeared as a series of articles in the Improvement Era *51 (1948): 786–88, 836–38; 52 (1949): 24–26, 60, 90–91, 109–10, 112, 146–48, 180–83, 212–14. Discussed by Bernard M. Foschini, "Those who are Baptized for the Dead; I Cor. 15:29,"* Catholic Biblical Quarterly *13 (1951): 51–53, 70–73. This study was also published as a pamphlet,* Dap for de dode i Oldtidere, Forithz of Fluge, *trans. (Oslo: Drammdnsveren, 1957).*

As the early texts were compared with each other and with the testimony of the oldest church writers, it became apparent that the main weight of early Christian doctrine was not on the cross (the *Blut und Kreuztheologie* of later times) but on the work of the Lord as a teacher, marking the way of eternal progress for the living and the dead according to a pattern first followed by Adam, to whom the texts attribute an importance out of all proportion to the teachings of the later church. This new light on the early Christian teachings was not hailed with enthusiasm by some people, who for obvious reasons preserve a discreet silence regarding the many discoveries of recent years which call for a complete readjustment of accepted patterns and concepts. For Latter-day Saints, however, the new findings should be thrice welcome, proving as they do the keen interest among the Saints of the primitive church in the subject of work for the dead. The purpose of the present paper is to pass in review those passages from early Christian sources which can shed some light on beliefs and practices connected with baptism for the dead in ancient times. We shall see how the early Saints answered the question "What is to become of the righteous dead who have never been baptized?" a question that sorely perplexed the doctors of the medieval church who, lacking the knowledge of earlier times, were forced to choose between a weak law that allowed the unbaptized to enter heaven, and a cruel God who damned the innocent.

The Moral Question

When the Jew, Trypho, discussing the New Jerusalem with Justin, a Christian convert, asked, "Do you actually believe that you people will be gathered together and made joyful with Christ and the patriarchs and prophets, both those of our race and those who became proselytes *before* the coming of that Christ of yours?" the latter answered emphatically in the affirmative, [1] having shortly before pointed out that those who have done that which is naturally, universally, and eternally good are pleasing to God, and shall be saved through this Christ in the resurrection just as much as those righteous men who were before them—Noah, Enoch, Jacob, and the like—or even as those who have actually known this Christ, the Son of God, who was before the morning star.[2]

Says Clement of Alexandria:

It is not *right* to condemn some without trial, and only give credit for righteousness to others who lived after the coming of the Lord.[3]

For, he observes:

Certainly one righteous man is not different from another as far as righteousness goes. . . . For God is not the God of the Jew alone but of all men. . . . Those who live righteously before the law are to be counted as faithful and reckoned among the just. . . . God is good and Christ is mighty to save, according to principles of justice and equality, those who turn to him, whether here or in the next world.[4]

Peter, in the straightforward and convincing Clementine account, has only contempt for Simon Magus' doctrine of limited salvation:

He saves adulterers and murderers if they know him; but good and sober and merciful people who don't happen to know him, simply because they have received no information concerning him, he does not save! A great and good god, forsooth, whom you proclaim, not only saving the wicked but showing no mercy to the good![5]

Wrote Irenaeus in the second century:

Christ did not come for the sole benefit of those who believed in him at the time of Tiberius Caesar, nor has the Father a plan for those only who happen to be living today; but it is for all the human family (*propter omnes omnino homines*) who from the beginning by righteousness pleased God and feared him in their generations, and dealt justly and religiously with their neighbors, and yearned to see Christ and hear his voice. [6]

This doctrine of universal salvation of the righteous is matched by the contemporary teaching of the Jews that "all who die hoping for the Messiah will be resurrected to eternal life." [7]

The most conspicuous pre-Christian candidates for salvation were, of course, the prophets of old. Says Ignatius:

> They too have proclaimed the gospel, and hoped for him [Christ] and waited for him. Believing in him they were saved, through union with Jesus Christ, being worthy of love and admiration, holy men [or saints], borne witness to by Jesus Christ and counted among those who share our common hope in the gospel. [8]

While it would be hard indeed to deny salvation to God's chosen men of old, it was another class of the dead whose redemption concerned the Christian convert most closely: what about his own friends and family who had never heard the gospel? That is the natural and inevitable question. [9] One of the first questions that Clement, the ardent investigator, puts to Peter is, "shall those be wholly deprived of the kingdom of heaven who died before Christ's coming?" To this the apostle gives a most significant answer: he assures Clement that the people in question are not damned and never will be, and explains that provision has been made for their salvation, but this, he says, is "as far as we are allowed to declare these things," excusing himself from telling more: "you compel me, O Clement, to touch upon things which we are forbidden to discuss." [10]

The Reticence of the Apostles

Why was Peter forbidden to discuss salvation for the dead with an investigator? If this text is called in question, we need only point to the New Testament, where on a number of occasions Peter and other apostles are forbidden to talk about certain things. That work for the dead is one of these will appear from a brief examination of one of the best-known episodes in the book, the promising of the keys to Peter.

Being alone with the apostles, the Lord began to sound them out with the question, "Whom do people say that I am?" The ensuing discussion led to the next question, "But whom do you say that I am?" To this Peter gave the right answer and was assured by Jesus that that knowledge had come to him by a revelation from the Father.[11] Having passed the test, the disciples were ready for more knowledge, but the momentous teaching to which they were introduced is merely hinted at in three short verses of Matthew,[12] and passed over in complete silence by Mark and Luke.[13] Plainly the apostles had no intention of publishing this thing to the world at large, and all three of them emphasize the Lord's insistence on secrecy, Luke[14] employing a remarkable formula which has puzzled all translators and which rendered literally reads: "But he, having pronounced a penalty (*epitimesas*), instructed them not to tell it to any man." The word for "instructed" used here is a military term meaning "to give a watchword" and has an air of great solemnity and secrecy.

Now whereas Matthew has the discussion end with Christ's admonition to secrecy, Luke and Mark tell only what he said *after* that warning, that is, after the great things had been revealed, and in both these accounts the words of the Savior are almost exclusively confined[15] to the strangely negative announcement that the work is to be utterly rejected by the world, and that only suffering and death can be expected by the apostles themselves, who are charged, moreover, not to be ashamed of Jesus and his doctrine. Why ashamed? It was

certainly no conventional teaching that the Lord was imparting, and he certainly predicted no rosy future for it in that
dispensation.

The extremely abbreviated nature of this account (Mark
and Luke do not even mention the "rock," though Eusebius
tells us that Mark, Peter's own secretary, omitted nothing of
importance from his gospel)[16] has led to much misunderstanding regarding the awkward and ungrammatical passage found
in Matthew 16:18. But it may be assumed that if we do not
understand everything, at least the apostles did. And that is
exactly the point: they heard everything, but of what they
heard they have left us but a few terse sentences which run
no danger of divulging "the mystery of the kingdom" to the
uninitiated. If we are to believe Eusebius or the Apostolic
Fathers, the New Testament scriptures are little more than a
sketchy outline which without a special interpreter are as a
code-message without a key.[17]

But why this emphasis on secrecy? The great Migne was
hard put to it to explain how Christ could order his disciples
to be silent on a matter which he wished divulged to the
world.[18] The only possible answer is that he did *not* wish it
divulged to the world, so Migne remains hesitant and vague,
eschewing any positive answer, for to admit the obvious
would be to admit that we have in Matthew 16:17-19 not the
public proclamation which later ages made it out to be, but
reference to a special doctrine. And that we have here the
teaching of a very special doctrine indeed is sufficiently indicated by the significant association of "the keys," the sealing,
and "the gates of hell."

The Gates of Hell

To the Jews "the gates of hell" meant something very
specific. Both Jews and Christians thought of the world of
the dead as a prison—*carcer, phylake, phroura*—in which
the dead were detained but not necessarily made to suffer
any other discomfort.[19] In the Jewish tradition the righteous

dead are described as sitting impatiently in their place of
detention awaiting their final release and reunion with their
resurrected bodies and asking, "How much longer must we
stay here?"[20] The Christians talked of "the prison of death"
to which baptism held the key of release[21]—a significant
thought, as we shall see.

It is the proper function of a gate to shut creatures in or
out of a place;[22] when a gate "prevails," it succeeds in this
purpose; when it does not "prevail," someone succeeds in
getting past it. But *prevail* is a rather free English rendering
of the far more specific Greek *katischyo*, meaning to over-
power in the sense of holding back, holding down, detain-
ing, suppressing, etc. Moreover, the thing which is held back,
is not the church,[23] for the object is not in the accusative but
in the partitive genitive: it is "hers," part of her, that which
belongs to her, that the gates will not be able to contain.
Since all have fallen, all are confined in death which it is the
Savior's mission to overcome; their release is to be accomplished through the work of the church, to which the Lord
promises that at some future time he will give the apostles
the keys. In one of the very earliest Christian poems Christ is
described as going to the underworld to preach to the dead,
"And the dead say to him, . . . 'Open the gate to us!' " where-
upon the Lord, "heeding their faith," gives them the seal of
baptism.[24] Baptism for the dead, then, was the key to the
gates of hell which no church claimed to possess until the
nineteenth century, the gates remaining inexorably closed
against those very dead of whose salvation the early Christians had been so morally certain. In passing it should be
noted that this poem in its conclusion definitely associated
the release of the dead with the "rock."

Thus thy Rock became the foundation of all; upon it
didst thou build thy kingdom, that it might become a
dwelling place for the saints.[25]

The same idea is even more obviously expressed by Ignatius in what is perhaps the earliest extant mention of the rock after New Testament times, making it equivalent to

> the high priest . . . to whom alone the secrets of God have been confided. . . . This is the Way which leads to the Father, the Rock . . . the Key . . . the Gate of Knowledge, through which have entered Abraham, and Isaac, and Jacob, Moses and all the host of prophets.[26]

From which it is clear that Matthew 16:17–19, with its combination of gates, keys, and rock, definitely hinges on the subject of salvation for the dead, and the work by which they are admitted to the presence of the Father.

Those who fondly suppose that "the gates of hell shall not prevail" is a guarantee of the security of the church on *this* earth[27] are inventing a doctrine diametrically opposed to the belief of the early church. If there was one point on which the primitive saints and their Jewish contemporaries saw eye to eye, it was the belief that Satan is "the prince of *this* world,"[28] nay, "the god of this world."[29] It is here that men are under his power, and here that he overcomes the kingdom of God by violence.[30] "The days are evil," says the Epistle of Barnabas, "and Satan possesses the power of this world."[31] Beyond this earth his power does not extend: Jehovah alone rules in the spirit world, according to the Jewish doctrine, and *his* angels stand guard over the wicked ones.[32] It is on this earth that the devil is to be conquered and his power finally broken—he has no other stronghold to which to flee.[33] When he goes to hell, it will not be in triumph, but to be bound and imprisoned there.[34] His bonds are the "snares and deceptions" that "bind the *flesh* of men with lust," and which will be meaningless after the judgment, when none may enjoy the prerogative of being deceived.[35] When the devil rules hereafter it will be only over those "sons of perdition" who willingly follow his example.

The medieval idea that the devil is the proper ruler of the dead is a borrowing from obvious pagan sources, popular and literary.[36] In the *earliest* versions of what eventually became the medieval Easter drama, the *Harrowing of Hell*, Satan and Death appear as rulers of different spheres: in the dialogue between them Death begs Satan to retain Christ in his realm, which is the earth, so that he might not descend and cause havoc in the underworld.[37] This idea appears in the very old pseudo-gospel of Nicodemus, wherein Satan, boasting that he has overcome Christ on earth, asks Death to make sure that the Lord's mission is likewise frustrated in his kingdom below.[38] No less a scholar than Harnack after prolonged searching declares that he knows of no passage in which "the Gates of Hell" signifies the realm of Satan, or is used to refer to the devil himself or to his hosts.[39]

"The gates of hell," then, does not refer to the devil at all; though his snares and wiles might lead men sooner or later to their death, delivering them "to the destruction of the flesh,"[40] his power ends there. The gates of hell are the gates of hell—the "holding back" of those who are in the spirit world from attaining the object of their desire.

There is a great wealth of oriental legend and liturgy recalling how a divine hero overcame Death in a knock-down and drag-out contest—the central episode of the famous Year-drama.[41] Sometimes the hero smashes the door of the underworld as part of his campaign. Contamination from these sources was sure to occur in the Christian interpretation of Christ's mission to the "underworld," but as Schmidt has shown at length, the *early* Christians never connect the two traditions: there is no fight when Christ goes to open the way for the release of the dead; he meets absolutely no opposition, and does not have to smash the gates, since he has the key.[42] How incompatible the two versions are is apparent in those early accounts which, characteristically, attempt to combine them. Thus when Prudentius, the first great Christian poet, tells of Christ's visit to the underworld, he includes the gate-smashing episode, derived not from any Christian source, however, but borrowed from the tragedy *Hercules Furens* of the pagan Seneca. [43]

Thus in the Odes of Solomon:

> And I opened the doors that were closed; I rent asunder the iron bolts . . . and nothing appeared closed to me, since I myself was the gate of everything; and I went to all my imprisoned ones to free them, so that I left none in bonds; and I imparted my knowledge without stint . . . sowing my seed in their hearts and turning them to me. [44]

Christ would hardly smash the gate if he himself were the gate.

The Restoration of All Things and the End of All Things

The unfolding of the great plan of salvation with "the mysteries of the kingdom of heaven" was continued a week after the "gates of hell" discussion, when the Lord took Peter, James, and John with him up onto the mount. [45] The two events are remarkably alike: there is the same great care to insure privacy, the same limited and selected number of participants, the same mention of a long and important conversation, with the same reluctance to reveal what was said; in each case there is an outburst by Peter, mention of a direct revelation from the Father regarding his Son, the same strict admonition to secrecy, and the same full and explicit declaration that the message is not going to be accepted by the world at that time. [46] The whole thing reminds one strikingly of the restoration of the gospel in the latter-days, when the great key revelations came in just such quick, wonderful succession to just such a selected few and by the ministrations of the same heavenly beings. Could Joseph Smith have worked that all out?

The Apostles awoke from sleep to find Jesus conversing with "two men," Moses and Elias. Of this consummately

important discussion not a word is given. The first utterance
reported on the mount is Peter's ecstatic reaction to what he
had heard, and the apostle is described as *answering* someone: no mere Hebraism, as the churchmen would have it, for
we are told that a conversation was already in progress. [47]
On the mountain the three apostles saw Moses and Elias not
as essences, historic allegories, or lovely old legends, but
simply as "two men." They also saw Jesus glorified, and he
did not dissolve into an ocean of being; "The fashion of his
countenance was altered," as was his raiment, but he still
had a countenance and wore raiment, and the apostles, though
they had been sleeping, recognized who he was. He did *not*
see the Father, however, because, we are explicitly told, a
cloud came and "screened" or "shielded" them from the sight,
as was indeed necessary, since they had already had as much
as they could stand and "were sore afraid." [48] Even if one
renders *episkiazo* "overshadow," as the King James version
of the Bible does, one has but to consider that a cloud can
overshadow an object only when it is between that object
and something brighter than itself: if it "overshadowed" the
apostles, the cloud, brilliant though we are told it was, must
have shut off a still greater light. It was by just such a cloud
that Jesus at the Ascension was "caught up away from their
eyes." [49] Is God the Father a cloud? If not, then this was
either a gross misrepresentation, or else the cloud was provided to screen a presence so glorious that the apostles could
not support the sight. The voice they heard through the cloud
was not an inner voice or a rational conclusion or the clink
of a chain of syllogisms, but something that actually came
"out of the cloud"; the voice of the Father did not come, as it
might have, from any other direction but from the same
direction as the light, for in this revelation when the most
privileged of the apostles were seeing Moses, Elias, and Christ
in their glory as they really are, they were also allowed to
experience as great a proximity to the real person of the
Father as they could stand.

Is it not strange that in the endless philosophical speculation that has gone into forming the creeds of Christendom from Nicaea to the present day almost no mention is ever made of the one instance in which the true nature of the Godhead was plainly revealed? Until the days of Joseph Smith it apparently never occurred to anyone to take the scripture at its face value. Why has this most illuminating passage of scripture been consistently ignored? Plainly because the whole episode has not been understood. The whole story of the transfiguration passes for little more than a theatrical interlude—something for plasterers and painters to work on. Yet as the four descend from the mountain, their talk is of "the restoration of all things." That explains why Moses was there, for to him had been entrusted the covenant of the Old Testament, while the mission of Elias, the Lord explains, was "to restore all things." As in their former conversation, Jesus warned the apostles to tell no man what they had seen and heard, and announced again with the greatest emphasis that the work was to be completely rejected by the world, even as Elias had been rejected.[50] It is hardly surprising, then, to find these same apostles announcing a few years later that "the end of *all things* is at hand" (Peter), that "it is the last time" (John), and that the Saints should be "an example of suffering affliction" with no hope of rescue save in the world to come (James).[51] What was meant by "all things" coming to an end? The universe and heaven and hell were not coming to an end, and neither was the world itself, for John states that the antichrist is just beginning to take over the church, "whereby we know that it is the last time."[52] For the apostles, the beginning of the antichrist's rule is the sign that something else has reached its end, and what can that be? "The restoration of all things" and "the end of all things" obviously refer to the same thing—the fulness of the gospel. What Elias restored, the antichrist, as the Lord predicted, put an end to, "until the times of restitution of *all things*" predicted by Peter[53] as a future event, when the fulness of the gospel would *again* be brought to the earth (Peter speaks of "restitution" and "refreshment") as it had been in the days of the transfiguration.

Here it is time to mention a third instance in which Christ insisted on secrecy. No more obvious allegory could be imagined on the face of it than the parable of the sower; and yet the gospels treat it as one of the greatest of mysteries, as "the mystery of the kingdom of heaven" itself, whose meaning the Lord divulged only to the Twelve when he was alone with them.[54] In every gospel version the challenge, "he who hath ears let him hear!" announcing that something of great import has been said, follows immediately upon mention of the three degrees, thirty, sixty, and one hundred. They are "the three degrees of glory," referring not to the world at all, but only to those who have heard the gospel, understood it, accepted it, brought forth fruit, and persisted in patience."[55] This is the gradation and arrangement of those who are *saved*," says Irenaeus, citing a doctrine which he attributes to "the elders," i.e., those who had been actual hearers of the apostles:

> The Elders say that those who are deemed worthy of an abode in heaven shall go there, others shall enjoy the delights of Paradise, and others shall possess the splendor of the City; for everywhere the Savior will be seen, according as they shall be worthy to see him. But that there is a distinction between the habitation of those who produce one-hundred-fold, and that of those who produce sixty-fold, and that of those who produce thirty-fold; for the first will be taken up into the heavens, the second class will dwell in Paradise, and the last will inhabit the City; and that on this account the Lord said, "In my Father's house are many mansions."[56]

Clement reports that the Lord ordered the apostles to preach to the world "for the time being" no doctrine beyond that of baptism, of which Peter says:

Be this therefore the first step to you of thirty
commands, and the second sixty, and the third a hundred,
as we shall expound more fully to you at another time.[57]

The fuller exposition, if it was ever written down, has
never reached us, and the whole doctrine, certainly an important one, has no place in the teachings of the later churches,
ignorant as they were of the great plan of universal salvation.[58]

The Teaching of the Lord After His Resurrection

The Lord admonished the disciples to preserve secrecy
regarding what they had seen, heard, and discussed *only*
until his resurrection. Until that time they were "to tell no
man." But whom were they to tell after the resurrection?
Certainly not everyone, if Paul's deliberate reticence toward
the Hebrews and Corinthians means anything.[59] In what
they write after the departure of Christ, the apostles, like the
apostolic fathers, seem extremely reluctant to impart knowledge of higher things.[60] This is painfully evident in the gospels
themselves. The real nature of the Lord's work escaped the
apostles while he was with them before the crucifixion.[61]
Such being the case, can a modern or medieval reader of
their fragmentary reports be expected to draw any wiser
conclusions from the events they describe than the apostles
themselves did? A full understanding *first* came to the disciples after the resurrection, when the risen Lord in a great
sermon, "beginning at Moses and all the prophets, . . .
expounded unto them in all the scriptures the things concerning himself."[62] Of this wonderful discourse which at last
opened the eyes of the apostles, *we* are only given the opening words: "O fools and slow of heart!"[63] It was what the
Lord said and did *after* the resurrection that established his
doctrine,[64] yet we are told only what he said and did *before*.
If the New Testament, written some time after the resurrection, is silent on those things, we can only assume that they

are being deliberately withheld. A goodly part of the Sermon on the Mount has been transmitted to the world, showing that, had the apostles so intended, the infinitely more important sermons after the resurrection might also have reached us. But the Sermon on the Mount is a social discourse, containing nothing that any honest man could fail to comprehend: this is not the sort of thing which needs to be concealed from the world at any time. We may be sure that it was a very different sort of matter which could only be imparted to a few in private with strict admonitions of secrecy, warnings of danger, and injunctions not to be "ashamed."

What lends weight to these considerations is the fact that it was the common belief in the early church that the subject of that last great discourse was nothing less than salvation for the dead: indeed, that was only to be expected, the Lord having just returned from his own mission to the spirit world.[65] While it was a favorite device of the Gnostics to gain a following in the church by claiming to possess written accounts of the secret teachings of Christ after the resurrection[66] the rest of the church was not backward in producing scriptures dealing with salvation for the dead and bearing such titles as *"The testament which our Lord Jesus Christ made with his Apostles after his resurrection from the dead and the instructions which he gave them,"* some of these texts being of great antiquity and held to be authentic by the strictest Christians.[67] The mere existence of these works is indicative of the keen interest which the saints still felt in a subject which the later church ignored. The fact that the Gnostics were able to gain an immense and immediate success in the church by spurious versions of these "last and highest revelations,"[68] shows that they were exploiting a genuine hunger which the central church could no longer satisfy. We shall deal with this problem later.

Christ's Mission to the Dead

The early Christians believed that Christ after the crucifixion descended to the spirit world.[69] They had no special term for the place but designated it very loosely by a variety of vague and general expressions as, the lower regions (*infera*), those below (*ad* or *apud inferos*), the place of detention, the guardhouse (*phylake, phroura*), the lowest places (*katotata*), hades, the place of Lazarus, the regions beneath the ground (*katachthonia*—because the dead were buried there), the land of the dead, etc. Such freedom shows that no definite locale is insisted on, all the expressions making it clear that Christ was to be thought of as being among the dead but not in heaven, while any attempt to specify the location of the place is deliberately avoided.[70] The early Christians were so averse to a geographical hell (wishing to describe only a condition) that they did not hesitate to use pagan terms which if taken literally would have been very misleading, implying belief in all sorts of outlandish things. Having no understanding of these things, however, the Middle Age could only take them in the literal heathen sense, with the result that Dante's hell is a faithful reproduction of well-known pagan originals.

As to the purpose of Christ's visit to the spirits in prison, the early sources are in perfect agreement. "What I have promised you," he tells the Twelve in the "Discourse to the Apostles,"[71]

> I shall give to them also, that when they have come out of the prison and when they have left their bonds . . . I shall lead them up into heaven, to the place which my Father has prepared for the elect, and I will give you the kingdom, and rest [*anapausis*, i.e. rest in the midst of work or on a journey, *not* a permanent stand-still], and eternal life.[72]

Elsewhere he says:

I have received all authority from my Father, so that I
might lead out into light those who sit in darkness, [73]

telling the apostles:

> You shall become fellow-heirs with me. . . . Such a
> joy has the Father prepared for you that the angels and the
> powers long to behold it. . . . yet it is not granted them. . . .
> [Cf. D&C 132.] You shall partake of the immortality of
> my Father, and as I am in him, so you will be in me.

And when they ask in what form they shall enjoy this
blessedness, the answer is:

> [As resurrected beings] even as my Father raised me
> from the dead, so you, too, will rise again and be received
> into the highest heaven. [74]

Irenaeus says that Christ came "to destroy death, point
the way of life, and set up a common way of life between
God and man." [75] "He himself opens to us who were enslaved
by death the doors of the temple," says the Epistle of Barnabas,
"and introduces us into the incorruptible . . . spiritual temple builded for the Lord." [76] "Until Christ came and opened
the door, no one, no matter how righteous, could enter the
presence of the Father. Only after the resurrection was a
common existence with the Father and Jesus Christ possible."
Thus Ignatius. [77] The dead were to be liberated that they
might reach eventually the highest state of exaltation, the
presence of the Father, in a word, the celestial kingdom.

Eventually, we say, for the highest glory is not bestowed
in an instant, but must be achieved through a definite course
of action. Christ opens the gates and points the way; the
spirits themselves must do the rest. " 'Come out of bonds,'
he cries 'all ye who *will*,' calling those willingly bound who
sit in darkness," writes Clement of Alexandria. [78] "Descending to the other world," says one of the oldest Christian
hymns, Christ "prepared a road, and led . . . all those whom
he shall ransom." [79] And Irenaeus: "The Lord destroyed death

and . . . showed us life, pointing the way of truth and imparting incorruptibility."[80] He is the way, the gate, the key and instrument of salvation, providing the *means* of passing from one state to another.

Through the door there is a definite order of exit from the lower world, says Origen, each biding his time: first "the prophets, then all the rest of the just . . . and finally the gentiles."[81] Justin states a belief common to Christian and Jew that there are stages or waiting-places along the way from the world of the dead to final judgment,[82] an idea expressed likewise in a logion attributed to Jeremiah and quoted by Irenaeus,[83] who further informs us of a teaching of "the elders," that all spirits released from confinement had to progress through a definite "order of promotion," the whole process of salvation for the dead taking place "in separate and definite steps."[84] All spirits must pass through various *prokopai*, according to Clement of Alexandria, a *prokope* being literally a stage or station on a journey: "everyone is in a particular station at any given time, depending on his knowledge of God."[85] He compares this progress toward exaltation with advancement in the priesthood on earth:

> For even on this earth, following the order of the Church, there are definite stages of progress: that of bishop, priest, and deacon. Such also, I believe are the steps of angelic glory in the economy of the other world, according to which, so the scriptures tell us, those are temporarily detained who are following in the footsteps of the Apostles towards a fulfilling of all righteousness in accordance with the precepts of the gospel.[86]

Anselm is thus not without authority (though suspiciously reminiscent of Philo the Jew)[87] when he writes:

> For whoever is baptized in Christ, to him heaven is opened and God above is ready to receive him [note that it is baptism that opens the gate]; but he must ascend by the steps of a ladder, which reaches from baptism up to

God. . . . Even so the children of Israel . . . reached the
promised land only by a long journey. So let no one who
is baptized be lazy, but let him strive to reach his promised celestial home by the road of God's commandments,
and by the steps of the ladder of generation let him ascend
if he desires to reach God.[88]

Christ Preached to the Dead

Following 1 Peter 4:6, it was believed in the early church
that Christ preached "to them that are dead." "For this reason,"
says the Lord in the "Discourse to the Apostles," "have I
gone below and spoken to Abraham, Isaac, and Jacob, to
your fathers, the prophets, and preached to them, that they
might enjoy their rest in heaven."[89] To quote more fully a
passage already cited from the Epistle of Barnabas, "He opens
to us, who were enslaved by death, the doors of the temple,
that is the mouth; and by giving us repentance introduced us
into the . . . spiritual temple builded for the Lord."[90] Christ
is the king "of those beneath the earth," says Hippolytus,
"since he also was reckoned among the dead, while he was
preaching the gospel to the spirits of the saints [or holy or
righteous ones]."[91] The same writer says Jesus "became the
evangelist of the dead, the liberator of spirits and the resurrection of those who had died."[92] The idea is thus expressed
by the author of the Sibylline Discourses: "He will come to
Hades with tidings of hope to all the saints, and [tidings] of
the end of time and the last day."[93] Clement of Alexandria is
thus following the accepted doctrine when he says: "Christ
went down to Hades for no other purpose than to preach the
gospel."[94]

A great favorite with the early Christians was a passage
from the apocryphal Book of Sirach: "I shall go through all
the regions deep beneath the earth, and I shall visit all those
who sleep, and I shall enlighten all those who hope on the
Lord; I shall let my teaching shine forth as a guiding light
and cause it to shine afar off."[95] Schmidt distrusts the claims

that this was a genuine Hebrew scripture, since it is found only in Christian translations;[96] but for our purpose that fact only enhances its value. Whatever its source, the ancient church received it gladly, as it did another Jewish text attributed to Jeremiah and quoted by Justin and (no less than five times) by Irenaeus: "The Lord God hath remembered his dead among those of Israel who have been laid in the place of burial, and has gone down to announce to them the tidings of his salvation."[97] The Christians angrily accused the Jews of having expunged this passage from their scripture in order to damage the Christian cause, from which it would appear that the doctrine of salvation for the dead was a major issue in those early times, and a most precious possession of the church.[98]

In all these texts we are told that Jesus did not simply "harrow" hell and empty it with a single clap of thunder, as was later imagined. The whole emphasis in the *Descensus* was on the *Kerygma*, or the Lord's preaching of the gospel.[99] He preached the gospel in the spirit world exactly as he had done in this one. Our informants insist, in fact, that Christ's mission below was simply a continuation of his earthly mission, which it resembles in detail. The spirits there join his church exactly like their mortal descendants, and by the same ordinances.

"Descending into the other world," says the old hymn, Christ "prepared a road, and led in his footsteps all those whom he shall ransom, leading them into his flock, there to become indistinguishably mingled with the rest of his sheep."[100] "I made a congregation of the living in the realm of the dead," says the Lord in the Odes of Solomon, "I spake to them with living lips . . . and sealed my name upon their heads, because they are free and belong to me."[101] Another Ode says: "I went to all my imprisoned ones to free them . . . and they gathered themselves together to me and were rescued; because they were members of me and I was their head."[102] "He went down alone," writes Eusebius, citing a popular formula, "but mounted up again with a great host towards the Father."[103] Tertullian is more specific: "Christ . . . did not ascend to the higher heavens until he had descended to the lower regions [lit. lower parts of the worlds], there to make the patriarchs and prophets his *compotes*."[104] The word *compos* [singular form] in Tertullian always denotes "one who shares secret knowledge;"[105] he made them his disciples in the other world.

Though rejected at his first coming, says Irenaeus, Christ nonetheless "gathers together his dispersed sons from the ends of the earth into the Father's sheepfold, mindful likewise of his dead ones who fell asleep before him; to them also he descends that he may awaken and save them."[106] The philosopher Celsus, making fun of the strange doctrine, asks Origen: "Don't you people actually tell about him, that when he had failed to convert the people on this earth he went down to the underworld to try to convert the people down there?" It is significant that Origen answers the question, for all its mocking tone, in the affirmative: "We assert that Jesus not only converted no small number of persons while he was in the body . . . but also, that when he became a spirit, without the covering of the body, he dwelt among those spirits which were without bodily covering, converting such of them as were willing to Himself."[107] According to this the dead not only have the gospel preached to them, but are free to accept or reject it, exactly like the living.

The resemblance between Christ's earthly and other-worldly missions leads one to conclude with Clement: "What then, does not the same economy prevail in hades, so that there, too, all the spirits might hear the gospel, repent and admit that their punishment, in the light of what they have learned, is just?"[108] A much older fragment offers a parallel to this: "I have become all in all that I might [establish?] the economy of the Father. . . . I have become an angel among angels."[109] In both cases the Savior fulfills the Father's "economy" in other worlds even as he had in this one.

The parallel between the Lord's earthly and post-mortal missions is preserved even to the extent of having his coming in the spirit world heralded by John the Baptist. Origen says John "died before him, so that he might descend to the lower regions and announce [preach] his coming."[110] And again: "For everywhere the witness and forerunner of Jesus is John, being born before and dying shortly before the Son of God, so that not only to those of his generation but likewise to those who lived before Christ should liberation from death be preached, and that he might everywhere prepare a people trained to receive the Lord."[111] "John the Baptist died first," wrote Hippolytus, "being dispatched by Herod, that he might prepare those in hades for the gospel; he became the forerunner there, announcing even as he did on this earth, that the Savior was about to come to ransom the spirits of the saints from the hand of death."[112] Even in the medieval Easter drama, the "Harrowing of Hell," the arrival of Christ in hell is heralded by John the Baptist.[113]

How the Dead Received Baptism

John's function in the spirit world, like the Savior's, was identical with his mission on this earth. Yet his very special mission here was to baptize. Likewise the worldly preaching of the Lord and the apostles was to prepare their hearers for baptism. It is not surprising then to read in the *Pastor of Hermas*, one of the most trustworthy guides to the established beliefs of the early church, that not only Christ and John but also "these Apostles, and the teachers who had proclaimed the name of the Son of God, after they had fallen asleep in [the] power and faith of the Son of God preached likewise to the dead; and they gave them the seal of the preaching. They accordingly went down with them into the water and came out again. But although they went down while they were alive and came up alive, those who had fallen asleep before them (*prokekoimemenoi*) went down dead, but came out again living; for it was through these that they were made alive, and learned the name of the Son of God."[114] The Latin version reads: "These Apostles and teachers who had preached the name of the Son of God, when they died in possession of his faith and power, preached to those who had died before, and themselves gave them this seal. Hence [igitur] they went down into the water with them; but they who had died before went down dead, of course, but ascended living, since it was through them that they received life and knew the Son of God."[115]

Needless to say, this text has caused a great deal of embarrassment to interpreters, ancient and modern. The source of the trouble is obvious: there are *two* classes of living persons referred to, those who enjoy eternal life, and those who have not yet died on this earth. The apostles (or whoever "they" were) belonged to the latter class when they went down *living* to be baptized for those who had gone *before*; a sharp contrast is made between their state—they being alive both before and after the ordinance—and that of those who were actually dead and yet received eternal life through the ministrations of baptism. What is perfectly clear is that the apostles while they were still living performed an ordinance—the earthly ordinance of baptism in water—which concerned the welfare of those who had already died. That it was an earthly baptism which could only be performed with water is emphatically stated in the sentences immediately preceding those cited: "It is necessary, he said, for them to come up through the water in order to be made alive; for otherwise none can enter the Kingdom of God . . . therefore even the dead receive the seal. . . . The seal is of course, the water."[116]

"I think," says Clement of Alexandria, commenting on this passage, "that it was necessary for the best of the Apostles to be imitators of their Master on the other side as well as here, that they might convert the gentile dead as he did the Hebrew."[117] Elsewhere he says: "Christ visited, preached to, and baptized the just men of old, both gentiles and Jews, not only those who lived before the coming of the Lord, but also those who were before the coming of the Law . . . such as Abel, Noah, or any such righteous man."[118] In the "Discourses to the Apostles" Jesus says:

> I went down and spoke to Abraham, Isaac, and Jacob, your fathers, and declared unto them how they might rise, and with my right hand I gave them the baptism of life and release and forgiveness of all evil, even as I do to you here and to all who believe on me from this time on.[119]

In hotly denying that the Hebrew prophets and patriarchs received the seal of baptism in the other world, the Marcionites only add to our evidence that the early church did believe.[120]

Are we to believe on the strength of these passages that the primitive church held that the Christ *personally* baptized all the disciples? That would make Jesus the only baptizer, and such in fact St. Augustine repeatedly insists he is: though acting through various ministers, it is always and only Christ himself who is baptizing.[121] How is that possible? Long before the days of Augustine the "Discourses to the Apostles" gives us the explanation, telling how the Lord promised his apostles that they would become "fathers, and masters, and servants," which he elucidates thus:

> Servants [*diakonoi*] because they [the dead] will receive the baptism of life and the forgiveness of your sins *from my hand through you*, . . . and so have part in the heavenly kingdom.[122]

As the Apostles in all their work are simply acting for their Lord, so all the ordinances they perform in his name are to be regarded as his own but done vicariously.

This principle of vicarious work, running through the whole economy of the church, also unties another knot which has no other solution. Were the spirits of the dead actually baptized with water? There is indeed a baptism of the spirit, but as Cyril,[123] Tertullian,[124] and others[125] point out, one simply cannot escape the physical element in baptism: indeed, Paul cites baptism for the dead as definite argument for belief in a physical resurrection. [126] How then can the incorporeal dead be baptized? As we have seen, the *Shepherd of Hermas* describes the living as performing the rite of baptism in the interest of the dead, without saying exactly how it was done. [127] One alternative was to explain the rite as the actual baptism of dead bodies—a counsel of desperation. [128] Quite unsatisfactory also is the theory that "before the righteous can enter Paradise, Christ must lead them through a fiery river to receive baptism," since our source (Origen) specifies that no one can be baptized in this river who has not been "*first* baptized with water and the Holy Ghost on this earth." [129] Quite as inadequate as this were theories of a sort of heavenly baptism to take the place of the missing earthly one; thus Albertus Magnus:

> He to whom baptism has been denied not through contempt of religion, but by necessity, does not lose the fruits of baptism, but is to be considered as baptized by the baptism of the flame of the Holy Spirit. [130]

The early church, however, was not obliged to seek such vague consolations, for it had the solution.

Speaking of 1 Corinthians 15:29, Tertullian expostulates:

> Now if some of them are "baptized for the dead," can we not assume that they have a reason for it? Certainly he [Paul] is maintaining that they practised this in the belief that the ordinance would be a vicarious baptism and as such be advantageous to the flesh of others, which they assumed would be resurrected, for unless this referred to a physical resurrection there would be no point in carrying out a physical baptism. [131]

But later Tertullian has doubts (how far they already seem to be from the Primitive Church!):

I don't believe that the Apostle was giving his approval to the practice, but rather signifying that those who practised it thereby indicated their belief in a physical resurrection, being foolishly [vane] baptized for the dead. . . . For elsewhere he speaks of only one baptism. Therefore to baptize "for the dead" means to baptize for bodies; for the body, as we have demonstrated, is really dead.[132]

All subsequent interpreters display the same perplexity and follow the same violent and arbitrary method of explaining how St. Paul said one thing while meaning something totally different. Because there is only *one* baptism, we are to be told forever henceforward, there can be no baptism for the dead. But that is the very reason why there *must* be baptism for the dead, which is not another baptism or another kind of baptism but in every detail the identical ordinance which is administered to the living and to them only, and therefore can profit the dead (who must have it if they are to be saved) only when done for them by proxy. Later writers, such as St. Ambrose, are not disturbed by the types and varieties of baptism practiced in their day because, they explain, there is after all really only one baptism, which is the baptism of Christ.[133] By the same token the argument of *one* baptism would be worthless as a refutation of baptism for the dead, which is also the baptism of Christ. The Bishop of Bristol observed that Tertullian in changing his opinion on the subject apparently concluded that baptism for the dead was "an idle fancy, on which it was unlikely that St. Paul should found an argument."[134] How then do we explain the perfectly obvious fact that St. Paul *did* found an argument on it?

At the beginning of the fifth century Epiphanius reports:

From Asia and Gaul has reached us the account [tradition] of a certain practice, namely that when any die without baptism among them, they baptize others in their place and in their name, so that, rising in the resurrection, they will not have to pay the penalty of having failed to receive baptism, but rather will become subject to the authority of the Creator of the World. For this reason this tradition which has reached us is said to be the very thing to which the Apostle himself refers when he says, "If the dead rise not at all, what shall they do who are baptized for the dead?"[135]

It is significant to find this practice surviving in those outlying places where, as Irenaeus points out, the pure old Christian doctrine was best preserved.[136] As to the rest of the church, Epiphanius explains:

> Others interpret the saying [1 Corinthians 15:29] finely [kalos], claiming that those who are on the point of death if they are catechumens [candidates for baptism] are to be considered worthy, in view of the expectation of baptism which they had before their death. They point out that he who has died shall also rise again, and hence will stand in need of that forgiveness of sins that comes through baptism.[137]

In the fourth century, St. Ambrose recalled, but did not approve, the practice:

> Fearing that a dead person who had never been baptized would be resurrected badly [male] or not at all, a living person would be baptized in the name of the dead one. Hence he [Paul] adds: "Else why are they baptized for them?" According to this he does not approve of what is done but shows the firm faith in the resurrection [that it implies].[138]

Ambrose is following Tertullian: Paul doesn't approve. Where does he disapprove? It is true that he wishes to emphasize the intention in this case, and not discuss the practice, which like Ignatius he takes for granted [139] (in fact, his casual mention of it without explanation indicates perfect familiarity with it on the part of the saints), but only as a last resort would one pounce on that as proof that he disapproved the

custom. He certainly does not cite a practice which he condemns, for that, of course, would weaken his argument: if
baptism for the dead is *wrong*, why should it be cited to
strengthen that faith in the resurrection which it illustrates?
Oecumenius even suggests that Paul says "why do *they* baptize for the dead" instead of "why do *you*" for fear of offending his hearers and possibly causing them to give up the
practice.[140] Attempts to find in Paul's words a condemnation
of baptism for the dead were carried to their ultimate conclusion by Peter the Venerable in the twelfth century. His
argument deserves to be quoted at length as an example of
where this sort of thing leads to.

> They were baptized at that time for the unbaptized
> dead, with good intention but not wisely, supposing that
> since they had not received baptism while alive, they could
> help out the dead by baptizing living persons for them.
> Speaking of which work the Apostle temporizes, praising
> the intention of the baptizers while not approving the bap-
> tism. For as far as baptism is concerned he does not approve
> of the baptism of one person for another, living or dead,
> but he obviously approves and seconds the intention of
> those who are baptizing, who by the works of the living
> were able to help out the dead by such means as bap-
> tism. . . . But he recognizes that it is *not* the work of bap-
> tism (for there is only *one* baptism) but by various *other*
> works (and there are many) that the living are able to help
> the dead.[141]

St. Paul wants to say that the living can help the dead
not by being baptized for them but by certain other works,
so of course instead of mentioning any of those many other
works he specifies only baptism. Word-juggling, the avoca-
tion of the Middle Ages, could hardly go further. Note that
the stubborn Paul can only be handled if *he* is charged with
temporizing! "Living *or* dead" is pure sophistry, since of
course the living should not be baptized for the living, and

by that very token must be baptized for the dead, who cannot (as the living can) be baptized for themselves. We have seen that the "one baptism" argument, far from condemning it, is in fact one of the strongest arguments in favor of vicarious baptizing for the dead. Elsewhere the Venerable Peter says: " 'They were being baptized for the dead' refers to the good works which the living were doing for the dead," *except*, that is, baptism, "for it is *not* by baptism but by *other* good works of the living; . . . it is to these and *not* to baptism that the Apostle refers."[142] Which is precisely why he says baptism, for by strange logic when the Apostle says black he really means white, and that is why he says black.

To such extremes of wresting the scripture were the medieval churchmen driven in their determination to discredit an ordinance which the church had lost. Thus Oecumenius decides that "for the dead" really means "for those whom you falsely suppose to be dead;" falsely, because "dead" necessarily means perpetually dead, and if they are going to rise again, they cannot be that, so that Paul when he said "the dead" does not mean the dead at all.[143] Just as when he said "baptize," he of course meant anything but baptize. Chrysostom and Photius, following Tertullian, tried to show that "for the dead" dies not mean "for the dead" but for the *body* which, since it dies, must be considered as dead.[144] Others (Theodoret, Zonaras, Balsamer, etc.) argued that it means "to be baptized for the dead *works* of sin."[145] It may mean that, according to St. Bruno, or else "the dead" may refer to "those who are to perish because of sin." He even suggests that Paul is shaming the Corinthians by showing them that even people who are so *wicked* as to baptize for the dead have faith in the resurrection, so why shouldn't they? He does not fail to mention, as all our other sources do, that baptism for the dead was actually practiced in the early church by certain members who "would baptize themselves in the place of a dead parent who had never had the gospel, thereby securing the salvation of a father or a mother in the resurrection."[146]

St. John Damascene suggests that "the dead" means either the body or the works of sin,[147] while Lanfranc was for its signifying "the works of death," but goes on to point out that there are people who believe that the passage is to be understood literally, "but it is not to be believed on the authority of the stupid that the Apostle intended to approve a thing *which has been a subject of so much uncertainty among the highest authorities*."[148]

By the seventeenth century a German savant was able to produce from the writings of the churchmen no fewer than seventeen different interpretations of 1 Corinthians 15:29.[149]

To return to early practices, an interesting aberration of the rite is found among the Marcionites. When a catechumen died, they would lay a living person under his bed; then they would ask the corpse if he wished to receive baptism, to which the living person under the bed would reply in the affirmative; then the living person would be baptized for the dead one.[150] Theophylactus, commenting on this in the eleventh century, says that when the Marcionites were upbraided for this practice, they would cite 1 Corinthians 15:29 in their defense; but they were wrong, he insists, since what Paul *really* meant to say (here we go again!) was, what should they do who were baptized expecting their own dead bodies to rise again,[151] i.e., who were baptized for themselves!

The Marcionite practice is a half-way point between baptism for the dead and the later rite of baptism *of* the dead. "Why do we not baptize the dead?" asks Fulgentius, and rightly points out that baptism is a rite requiring both body and spirit; if a disembodied spirit is not a fit candidate, neither is an inanimate piece of flesh.[152] "Even though one should have displayed his will and intention in life," he explains, "and shown faith and devotion, yet once dead, even though it means that he is to be without the sacrament of baptism, he may not be baptized; because the will, faith, and devotion which justify such a baptism belong to the spirit which has departed."[153] Nothing could be more reasonable; baptism may only be performed on a living person. This of course is an unanswerable argument for baptism by proxy: if the dead may not be baptized and yet are to enjoy salvation, there is no other way out. Baptism *of* the dead misses the whole point: it is the exact opposite of baptism *for* the dead, the one rendering the other perfectly useless. Yet in their need to find some official condemnation of baptism for the dead, churchmen have had to resort to citing those instances which deal with condemnation of its opposite, namely baptism of the dead.[154] This deliberate confusion (the Latter-day Saints have been accused of baptizing the dead) is natural enough and seems to have been an early one, for Philastrius includes "baptizing the dead" among a number of false and exaggerated charges against the Cataphrygians in the fourth century.[155]

Who in the church performed the actual ordinance of baptizing for the dead? It was "those apostles and teachers" of the first generation, according to the *Shepherd of Hermas*, who "went down living into the water" in behalf of those who had died[156] and in speaking of the whole affair as a thing of the past that source implies that the work was confined to those men and their generation. This is clearly borne out in our other accounts.

To begin with, it was not all Christians who baptized for the dead, for Paul reminds the Corinthians that "they," namely someone else and not the Corinthians (who were "but babes") did the work. But who were "they"? A very large class of believers is eliminated by confining the doctrine to the teachings of Christ's *second* ministry, which were only received by a limited number of people. It will be recalled that in his discussion with the Apostles, the Lord promised them the keys at some future time; since this conversation took place shortly before the crucifixion, and since Jesus himself *postponed* any discussion of the mysteries of the kingdom "till the Son of Man be risen from the dead,"[157] we can believe that nothing much was done in the matter during his first mission. In a passage of impeccable authority Eusebius quotes Clement as saying: "To James the Just, and to John and to Peter *after* the resurrection the Lord transmitted the gnosis; these passed it on to the other Apostles, and they in turn to the Seventy, of whom Barnabas was one."[158] Note the careful limitation of this teaching: Peter did not announce it to the whole church, nor the Apostles to all the world, nor is there mention of "the gnosis" being handed down any further than to the Seventy, though that would certainly be Eusebius' main interest in the passage if it were so.[159] "The gnosis" is that fulness of knowledge, which Paul always speaks of as the highest and holiest of God's gifts, a rare, choice, and hidden thing, reserved for but a few.[160] Just how few were eligible to receive the risen Lord is painfully clear in all the gospel accounts of his second mission.

Christ's second mission caught everyone, from weeping Mary to doubting Thomas, completely by surprise, "for as yet they knew not the scripture, that he must rise again from the dead."[161] The news of the Lord's return was heard by everyone, within the church and without, then as now, with incredulity, and Matthew can end his gospel with the discouraging words: "And when they saw him, they worshiped him; but some doubted," while the closing scenes in Mark and Luke show the Savior rebuking the apostles with great severity for "their unbelief and hardness of heart." The Gospels duly note the peculiar circumstance that it was apparently possible for some to doubt even in the presence of those who were actually beholding the risen Lord. One is forcibly reminded of the appearance of resurrected beings to witnesses in modern times, and by all accounts we must recognize that Jesus' second mission was not a public preaching but a series of revelations, "not to all the people, but unto witnesses chosen."[162] In fact it soon became common in the church to doubt that this second mission had ever taken place: the phrases "they deny the resurrection," "they say that he was only a man," meet us from the very first in the writings of apostolic times, where they recur with the regularity of set formulas. Ignatius describes this attitude when he says that he hears people in the church saying, "If I don't find it in the archives, I won't believe it."[163] As Eisler has shown, the records in question were the *Acta Passionis Jesu Christi*, the official court transcript of the trial and sentence of Jesus, which did not extend, of course, beyond his death.[164] To say that one would only believe what was in the archives was to say that one would only believe in the Savior's first mission.

"If I have told you earthly things, and ye believe not," the Master had said, "how shall ye believe, if I tell you of heavenly things?"[165] It is not necessary here to labor the point of "milk and not meat," "pearls before swine," "to you it is given to know . . . but to them it is not given," etc., to show that knowledge of the gospel was anciently imparted only to that degree in which people could receive it.[166] But if only a few could receive it at first, did it not in time spread to many? Far from it.[167] Eusebius explains the situation in a citation from Hegesippus: "When the holy chorus of the Apostles ended their lives in various ways, and that generation passed away of those who had heard the divine wisdom with their own ears, at that very time the conspiracy of godless error took its beginning through the deception of false teachers who, when the last remaining Apostle had gone, first came out into the open and opposed the preaching of the truth with what was *falsely* styled the gnosis."[168] The last expression is the identical term used by Paul when he warns Timothy to beware of the very class of people here described.[169] With the passing of the apostles the teachers of false doctrine, as if they had been awaiting a signal, "sprang up like mushrooms," to use Irenaeus' expression, each claiming to *the* gnosis that Christ had given the apostles after his resurrection.

This outbreak of gnostic pretenders, which was no passing flurry but lasted for over a hundred years, never could have occurred had apostolic authority remained in the church to overawe the upstarts, or had the true "gnosis" been available to oppose their false ones. In taking the gnosis away from them, the apostles had left the field free to swarms of impostors; which is exactly what the apostles themselves had predicted would happen.[170] As for the gnosis, Paul tells the Corinthians unequivocally: "the gnosis shall be taken away."[171] He explains that the three great gifts of prophecy, tongues, and the gnosis are all to be removed from the church, and in their place be left only the more general gifts of faith, hope, and love, "these three." To soften or justify the loss of such great things he explains that at the time those gifts are only partial anyway: "We only know [possess gnosis] in part, and only prophesy in part" (or, "in proportion to our lot, or dispensation"), but he looks forward to the time "when the fulness shall come," and things partial be done away with. "For the present moment," he states significantly, "we see in a mirror [as] in an enigma. . . . For the time being there remain faith, hope, and love—these three."[172] To Paul's hearers an enigma was a concealed teaching, not to be understood without a key: Jesus, it will be recalled, accused the Jewish experts in the law of hiding[173] "the key of the gnosis," while Paul charged that the law itself had become a mere parody of the gnosis.[174]

If nothing was lost of Christ's teachings, why do the apostolic fathers, the immediate successors of the apostles, regard themselves as immeasurably beneath the latter in the knowledge of heavenly things? At the very beginning Polycarp protests: "Neither I nor any other such one can come up to the wisdom of the blessed and glorified Paul,"[175] while Clement tells the Corinthians of his day that they are no longer under the direction of proven apostles or men appointed by such,[176] and Ignatius tells the Romans: "I do not as Peter and Paul issue commandments to you; they were Apostles of

Jesus Christ; I am but a condemned man."[177] This is no special deference to the Roman Church, as Catholic theologians
claim, for the Trallians no less he says, "I cannot use a high
manner in writing to you. . . . I do not issue orders like an
Apostle," and he adds significantly:

> I would like to write to you of heavenly things [in
> some versions, "things more full of mystery"], but I fear to
> do so, lest I should inflict injury on you who are but
> babes. You would be strangled by such things. . . . For
> though I am able to understand heavenly things . . . yet I
> am not perfect, nor am I a disciple such as Paul or
> Peter.[178]

Yet Ignatius was perhaps the greatest living authority on
doctrine. When soon after writing this he was put to death,
what became of that knowledge of "heavenly things" which
he refused to divulge to one of the oldest branches of the
church? The Romans and Trallians had the Gospels, which
thus cannot have contained the information he was holding
back.

The bankruptcy of the church after the passing of the
apostles became glaringly apparent in her struggle with the
"Gnostics so-called." In the first place, the sudden and immense
success of the Gnostics showed only too plainly, as Neander
has observed, that people were looking for something which
the church could no longer supply.[179] Then, too, the fact
that the church yielded to the Gnostics on point after point,
adopting many of their more popular practices and beliefs,
shows that she had nothing to put in their place.[180] The fact
that the church finally denied that there ever *was* a gnosis,
and defined the heresy of Gnosticism not as a false claim to
possess higher revelations (the early writers are always careful to give it this meaning), but the mere belief that such
revelations had ever existed—that shows clearly enough that
the church no longer possessed "the gnosis" to which the
New Testament repeatedly refers.[181] When the church fights

shy of the very word and is alarmed at the mere suggestion that there could be such a thing, it needs no argument to show how little of it she still possessed.

The Gnostic pretenders bear important witness to the nature of the thing they were copying. Just as they recognized that the name of Christ was essential to the work and accordingly "went about bearing the name of Christ," so they recognized also that they should not be without the gifts of the Spirit, or baptism for the dead, of which they devised various spurious versions, as we have seen. More significant are those purist cults of the second century, striving to return to the original order of the church, who included baptism for the dead among their practices. Such were the Cataphrygian branch of the Montanists, mentioned above. It was the Montanists whom Tertullian joined when he left the big church in his vain search for the lost gifts and blessings of the church of Jesus Christ.

It should now be fairly obvious that work for the dead did not outlast that generation for which the "end" had been predicted, nor spread beyond the circle of those possessing what the ancient church called "the gnosis," that is (to follow Eusebius) beyond those who shared the knowledge of those "many hidden things" which are not set forth in our present scripture. [182]

Early Disappearance of the Doctrine

It is immediately after mentioning the preaching of the gospel "to them that are dead" that Peter ominously adds, "But the end of all things is at hand." [183] In the "Discourse to the Apostles" the Lord thus describes the fate of the great teachings he has given them:

> Another doctrine will arise and with it confusion; for they will seek their own advancement and bring forth a useless doctrine. And it will cause vexation even unto death;

and they will teach and turn away those who believed on
me and lead them away from eternal life.[184]

This constant refrain of a complete falling away runs
through all the apostolic writings, where the saints are repeatedly warned against assuming (as many modern Christians
do)[185] that such a falling away is impossible.[186] This is not
the place to examine the disappearance of the true church as
a whole, but it is in order to point out that the saints had
from the first been taught to expect it.

That the people of the primitive church were looking forward to an immediate end is granted by all students of church
history, who usually interpret this as a mistaken and starry-
eyed expectation of the second coming of Christ.[187] It was
nothing of the sort. While the apostles and apostolic Fathers
all keep repeating that *"the end"* is at hand, they not only
refuse to commit themselves on any time, soon or late, for
the coming of Christ, but denounce as deceivers those who
do. Peter warns emphatically that "the end of all things is at
hand," yet when it comes to the question of "the promise of
his coming" he counsels the saints to allow a possible margin
of at least a thousand years.[188] He is speaking of *two* events,
the one immediate, the other absolutely indeterminate, as is
Paul when he addresses the Corinthians as at the last extrem-
ity of a great emergency, with the time desperately short,[189]
only to speak in a totally different tone when discussing the
return of the Lord: "be not soon shaken in mind, or be troubled . . . as that the day of Christ is at hand," going on to
explain that there must be a falling away first, and that that
has just begun.[190] In all their troubles the release that the
saints expect is *not* that Christ shall presently come down to
them, but that they shall presently go to him. Paul's attitude
is typical: the Lord is not coming down to rescue him, but
rather he himself shall quickly depart, and *after* that departure things shall go ill with the world and the church; there
are to be wolves on earth, not angels; love shall wax cold,

error abound, the church turn away from sound doctrine; and the mystery of iniquity which "doth already work" shall come to its own. He describes himself as a man working against time:

> . . . three years I ceased not to warn every one night and day with tears.[191]

Why the terrible urgency, and why the tears, if the church was to win in the end? It is *not* the coming of Christ that leads John to observe, "little children, it is the last time," but rather the coming of the antichrist—the very opposite![192] "It is the wintertime of the just," the *Shepherd of Hermas* proclaims, and it will be a long one, for the Lord "is as one taking a far journey"; at some future time is to burst upon the world "the summertime of the just."[193] Meantime the people of the early church were as likely to confuse winter and summer as to identify "the end of all things" with "the restoration of all things." A clear and authentic statement of the situation is given in the closing section of the famous Didaché:

> For in the last days the false prophets and the corrupters shall be multiplied, and the sheep shall be turned into wolves, and love shall change to hate; for as lawlessness increases they shall hate one another and persecute and betray, and *then* shall appear the one who leads the world astray as [the] Son of God, and he shall do signs and wonders and the earth shall be given over into his hands and he shall commit iniquities which have never been since the world began. . . . 5. Then shall the creation of mankind come to the fiery trial. . . . 6. and then shall appear the signs of the truth. First the sign spread out in heaven, then the sign of the sound of the trumpet, and thirdly the resurrection of the dead, but not of all the dead. . . . 8. *Then* shall the world "see the Lord coming on the clouds of Heaven."[194]

He who is to come forthwith is not the Christ but a
deceiver, and before the Lord can come again very special
manifestations, "the signs of truth," must precede him.

All this, of course, goes back to the Savior's own teaching: "Many shall come in my name . . . and shall deceive
many . . . but the end is not yet . . . these are the beginning
of sorrows," etc., with the promise, "he that shall endure
unto the end, the same shall be saved."[195] Repeatedly the
saints are told that they will be hated of all men, persecuted,
and slain, and always a comforting promise is given. That
promise is *never*, either in the New Testament or in the apostolic fathers, that the church will be victorious in the end,
but always and only that a reward awaits the individual on
the other side. Summarizing his career, Paul says, "I have
fought a good fight; I have finished my course; I have kept
the faith. Henceforth. . . ."[196] What is to be henceforth? One
expects the natural and heartening announcement that henceforth the church is secure, the work established, the devil
overcome. But one looks in vain in any apostolic writer for
such a hopeful declaration. Instead we are given the frightening promise that

> the time will come when they will not endure sound doc-
> trine. . . . And they shall turn away their ears from the
> truth . . . [197]

as the Galatians[198] and "all they which are in Asia"[199] had
already begun to do.

It is highly significant that the hope of final triumph for
the cause, that vision of the church filling and dominating
the entire world which is the perpetual boast and comfort of
the writers of the fourth and fifth centuries, is never so much
as hinted at in apostolic times, even when the saints are most
hard pressed and that would be their natural comfort.[200]
Were those people so self-engrossed that they could never

find any cause for consolation or congratulation in the pleasing thought that others would some day benefit by their sufferings? Why this perfect silence regarding the ultimate
triumph of the church? Simply because there was to be no
such triumph.[201]

Astonishing as it seems, then, the immediate second
coming of Christ, which everyone seems to take for granted
as the basic doctrine of the early church, is not only not proclaimed among its writings, but is definitely precluded by
the expected rule of evil, which also rules out completely any
belief in an immediate end of the world. There was to be an
end, and that end was at hand, with the winter and the
wolves closing in: "the night cometh, when no man can
work."[202] The modern Christian theory is that such a night
never came, but the Apostles knew better.

Three things will be taken away, says Paul, and three
remain; the former are prophecy, tongues, and the gnosis,
the knowledge of Jesus Christ, compared with which, he tells
us elsewhere, all other things are but dross. Now it is interesting that almost all Christians admit, nay insist, that prophecy and tongues were lost, but will not allow for a moment
that the "higher knowledge" that went with them has disappeared. They claim in other words, that they still have that
gnosis—which makes them Gnostics! False Gnostics, that is,
since they profess to have the full teaching of Christ while
admitting that they lack the gifts which the Lord promised
would surely follow those who had his doctrine. The reason
for claiming the knowledge without the power thereof is obvious: tongues and prophecies are not easily come by, while
doctrines can be produced to order. But the doctrine without
the other gifts is not valid; Irenaeus confounded the Gnostics
by showing that they lacked those other gifts while claiming
the gnosis—and then he gave himself away by conspicuously
failing to produce any convincing evidence for those gifts in
his branch of the church.[203] After him the great Tertullian
argued that the lack of spiritual gifts in the main church of

his day invalidated the claims of that church to possess divine authority.[204]

If church members were doubting the resurrection itself even in New Testament times and quite generally in the days of the Apostolic Fathers, is it surprising that the doctrine of salvation for the dead, so closely bound with the economy of the resurrection, should also be a matter of doubt and confusion? Or is it hard to believe that baptism for the dead should soon become a lost doctrine when from early times baptism for the *living* was a subject of the widest disagreement? The greatest fathers and doctors of the church profess a bewildering variety of opinions as to the proper time, place, manner, authority, subject, validity, durability, efficacy, and scope of the Christian baptism.[205] One who would ask, therefore, what became of baptism for the dead need only contemplate the doctrinal shambles of baptism for the living to have an answer.

As early as the time of Justin the doctrine of salvation for the dead, though still preached, was a subject of serious uncertainty that can only reflect a general lack of information. When asked whether he really believes in the salvation of all the righteous Jews of the Old Covenant as well as the Christians Justin states:

> I and others are of this opinion. . . . But on the other hand there are many who belong to the pure and pious faith, and are true Christians, who think otherwise.[206]

Where is the uncompromising stand of the early church? A few years later we find both Tertullian and Irenaeus hedging on the question of whether Christ ever visited the spirits in prison—a doctrine repugnant to philosophy.[207] Typical is Irenaeus' statement that though he does not believe it himself, he will not condemn as heretics those who do,[208] and he sounds a sinister note when he observes that in the church "there are some who even try to turn these things into allegories."[209] There was a period of hesitation after this when some versions of the Apostles' Creed contained the phrase, "He descended into hades," or "He descended to the inhabitants of the spirit-world," while others did not, but in time this annoying fragment of antique arcana came to be generally condemned.[210] With Origen and Clement "wavering between the old faith and Plato,"[211] we are well on the way to the medieval church, where we presently arrive with St. Augustine .

In his younger days St. Augustine

> dared promise not only paradise but also the kingdom of the heavens to unbaptized children, since he could find *no other escape* from being forced to say that God damns innocent spirits to eternal death. . . . But when he realized that he had spoken ill in saying that the spirits of children would be redeemed without the grace of Christ into eternal life and the kingdom of heaven, and that they could be delivered from the original sin without the baptism of Christ by which comes remission of sins—realizing into what a deep and tumultuous shipwreck he had thrown himself . . . he saw that there was *no other escape* than to repent of what he had said.[212]

The saint was in a trap, with escape blocked at both ends—a terrible dilemma, the only refuge from a cruel God leading straight to a weak law, which is no escape at all, but "shipwreck." Only baptism for the dead can avoid these catastrophic extremes, but that is out. The Pelagians tried to dodge the issue by putting a soft seat, *quasi medium locum*, between the horns, positing a colorless limbo which satisfied no one and which Augustine brushes aside with the declaration that there is no middle region, and that the unbaptized will go to hell and nowhere else.[213] Only this does not satisfy Augustine either; he characteristically tries to eat his cake and have it too with the declaration that unbaptized children must be damned, completely damned, and be with the devil in hell, only, he explains, they will be damned "most gently" (*mitissime*)![214] In such a liberal spirit, Bottom, the weaver, in order not to frighten the ladies while playing the role of a most terrible lion, promised to "roar you as gently as any sucking dove."[215] A "gentle" damnation, indeed!

It is interesting that Augustine can still report that there actually are

> a few who believe that that custom was part of the gospel according to which the work of substitutes for the dead was effective, and the members of the dead were laved with the waters of baptism,[216]

thus confusing baptism for the dead (use of substitutes) with baptism of the dead. The universal opinion after Augustine is that there is no hope whatever for the unbaptized dead. Typical is the statement of his famous contemporary, St. Ambrose, that to die without baptism is to go to eternal misery,[217] while another contemporary, St. Basil, says simply, "It is damnation to die without baptism,"[218] and yet another, Gregory of Nyssen, draws the shocking but logical conclusion that

> It is better to be found among the number of the wicked who have reverted to sin after baptism than to end one's life without having received baptism.[219]

This immoral doctrine that places ritual conformity before good works is simply one of the unavoidable consequences of denying baptism for the dead. "We cannot believe that any catechumen, even though he dies in the midst of his good works, will have eternal life," wrote Gennadius, to whom the catechumen's ardent desire for baptism counts for nothing.[220] Compare this to the teaching of the Shepherd of Hermas, who concludes the passage referred to above with the words:

> They died in righteous and great purity, and this seal was the only thing they lacked.

Gennadius and his church would damn them for that, but not so the early church. The Shepherd explains:

> For this reason they [the Apostles] went down living with them into the water . . . and gave them life . . . and came up out again with them, and were gathered up together with them,

that all might share eternal life.[221] The contrast is instructive.

And how about "the gates of hell"? They seem to be "prevailing" in fine style. Augustine wished "would that God had saved from hell" those good and great schoolmen of ancient times who from their chairs proclaimed the divine unity, but stern reason forbids it.[222] Not long after him Ennodius

> in his *Libellus* in defence of Pope Symmachus . . . pictures the Imperial City lamenting the fate of her famous and mighty sons . . . who, unredeemed by the Church, were doomed to hell, because they had lived before the coming of Christ.[223]

A famous poem of the Middle Ages tells how the apostle Paul was led to the grave of the poet Vergil, who had died just too soon to hear the gospel preached; the saint stands beside the tomb shedding tears of bitter frustration, the picture of helplessness: "What I could have made of you, O greatest of poets," he cries, "had I only found you alive!"[224] As it is, there is nothing the church can do about it, and poor Vergil is forever damned. If you doubt it, behold him in the fourth canto of the *Inferno*, conducting the dejected Dante into an horrible region "of infinite woes . . . deep darkness and mist . . . a blind world," at the sight of which Vergil himself turns pale. "You ask what spirits these are that you see?" he asks the younger poet:

They are not here because of sin, and if they lack a
sufficient boon of mercy, it is for not having been baptized. . . . Having lived before the days of Christianity
they did not duly worship God; and I am one of them—
we are lost for that one failing and not for any sin; for that
offence alone we live in hopeless longing![225]

He then tells indeed of Christ's visit to that world, and of
the release of the great patriarchs of the Old Testament, but
adds, "Aside from them not another human spirit was
saved!"[226] One cannot resist saying with Peter in the
Clementine account:

A good and great god indeed, who . . . damns the good . . .
simply because they do not know him!

So much for those unfortunates "who lived before his
coming." As for those who came after, a writing to Peter the
Deacon states that

from that time when our Savior said, "Except a man be
born of water," etc., no one lacking the sacrament of baptism can either enter the kingdom of heaven or receive
eternal life.[227]

"O grave where is thy victory, O death where is thy
sting?" Where indeed! By a conservative estimate, the unbaptized should represent at the very least ninety percent of the
human family—a substantial victory for the grave and a
most effective stinging of God's children. Says Fulgentius:

You are to believe with the utmost firmness that
all . . . who end this present life outside the Catholic Church
are to go to the eternal fire which is prepared for the devil
and his angels.[228]

It is cold comfort for any church to claim that the gates
of hell do not prevail against its small minority, but only

against those who do not belong to it; that is the very doctrine which, as we saw at the outset of this study, the Christians of an earlier day found simply unthinkable and immoral. Even the stern St. Bernard when faced with the cruel logic that would damn "good persons, who meant to be baptized but were prohibited by death," balks at it; "God forgive me!" he cries, but he cannot admit they are damned, though his church offers him no alternative. [229]

Some divines have maintained that the human race was brought into existence for the express purpose of filling the void left in heaven by the fall of the angels, a doctrine impressively set forth by the preacher in Joyce's *Portrait of the Artist as a Young Man;* yet we are to believe that the overwhelming majority of human spirits were condemned even before their creation never to see heaven at all, but to spend eternity in those nether regions which, so far from having any vacancies to fill, are, to follow the same enlightened guide, indescribably overcrowded! And they defend their inhuman doctrines in the name of "reason"!

When Christ "went down and preached . . . overcoming death by death," [230] he delivered those who were in bondage because they had never completely fulfilled the law of obedience, including baptism in particular. Yet that is the very class of dead whom the later Christian churches regard as beyond saving. When the Roman Church, to the loud dismay of Paul, Ennodius, Dante, St. Augustine, etc., is absolutely helpless to open the gates of hell—and hence of heaven—to her beloved Vergil she fails to fill in the most important qualification of the church of Jesus Christ; and that very verse of scripture upon which she rests the full weight of her vast pretentions, letting the world think against all knowledge that "the gates of hell" is but a poetic generalization, that verse condemns her utterly. [231]

At present the justification of the Christian churches for denying baptism for the dead may be found in the statement that "the church believes that baptism operates only on the

person who receives it."[232] To be sure, and is there anything
wrong with receiving it by proxy? Is it not a far more extrav-
agant arrangement to have an infant at baptism accept the
gospel by proxy, as most churches do? Those offering the
child for baptism, we are told, *answer for it*, [233] and the little
one believes "through another" (*in altero*) "because he sinned
through another."[234] Not only is the purely spiritual act of
believing (instead of the physical act of immersion) done by
proxy, but the baptism itself is administered vicariously. How
is it possible, St. Augustine asks, that Jesus baptizes and yet
does not baptize?[235] The explanation is that "it is not the
minister but Christ himself who baptizes,"[236] for "the authority [*potestas*] of baptism the Lord always keeps to himself,
but the ministry of it he *transfers* to anyone, good or
bad."[237]

     In a like manner the vicarious principle runs through the
whole economy of the church: through Christ's vicarious
sacrifice every member is thought to have paid the penalty
for sin and satisfied the demands of justice, while the Lord's
own work is carried out by his earthly delegates. If it is possible for the Father and Son to be presently represented through
the ministrations of men in the flesh, is it outrageous presumption for men to stand proxy for their own kin in the
spirit world? Do not Christian churches today require that
every candidate for baptism be "according to most ancient
usage" accompanied by a vicarious parent?[238] All that men
can do for themselves they must do, the gospel preaches, but
whatever they cannot possibly do for themselves must be
done for them; hence the great atonement.

     Can there be any serious objection then to a vicarious
baptism which makes it possible to satisfy all the demands of
the law, enjoy the mercy of God without qualification, and
retain the ordinance in its purity, intact and unaltered? It
should be remembered that in the very matter of baptism the
Christian churches will waive all their careful rules in an
emergency, and allow anyone to baptize anyone else at any

time or place and in almost any manner, lest some poor soul *in extremis* be eternally damned.[239] Thus the churches are willing to distort the rite of baptism beyond recognition for the laudable purpose of making it as universal as possible; but as the price of being universal it ceases to be a baptism at all. And so the dilemma remains, with only one escape: baptism for the dead.

In summing up the data at hand, we note three aspects of the documentary remains: their adequacy, their paucity, and their distribution. The three support and explain each other and lead to certain obvious conclusions.

In the first place, the evidence is more than sufficient to establish the presence and prominence in the early church of belief in the salvation of the dead through ministrations that included preaching and baptism. The actual practice of vicarious baptism for the dead in the ancient church is equally certain, even the hostile commentators, with their seventeen different interpretations, agreeing on that one thing alone.

Yet if they are clear and specific, references to baptism for the dead are nonetheless few. How is that to be explained in view of the extreme importance of the subject and the obvious popularity of the doctrine with the saints? For one thing the apostolic literature is not extensive; one volume could easily contain it all. Yet it is in these fragments of the earliest church writings that virtually all our references are to be found: the earlier a work is, the more it has to say about baptism for the dead. After the third century no one wants to touch the subject, all commentators confining themselves to repeating the same arguments against baptism for the dead and supplying the same far-fetched and hair-splitting explanations of what Paul really meant. After the second century the vast barns of the *Patrologia* are virtually empty, and the fathers who love nothing so much as spinning out their long commentaries on every syllable of scripture pass by those passages of hope for the dead in peculiar silence. As

Lanfranc put it, how can one presume to cope with a problem which has baffled the greatest minds of the church? It
was the early church that preached and practiced work for
the dead, that no one denies; [240] the later church, condemning the work, confesses at the same time that she does not
understand it.

It has not been the purpose of this discussion to treat
baptism for the dead as practiced by the Latter-day Saints.
No one having any acquaintance with that system, however,
can fail to notice the essential identity of the ancient with the
modern usage and doctrine. This close resemblance poses a
problem. Where did Joseph Smith get his knowledge? Few if
any of the sources cited in this discussion were available to
him; the best of these have been discovered only in recent
years, while the citations from the others are only to be
found scattered at wide intervals through works so voluminous that even had they been available to the Prophet he
would, lacking modern aids, have had to spend a lifetime
running them down. And even had he found such passages,
how could they have meant more to him than they did to the
most celebrated divines of a thousand years, who could make
nothing of them?

This is a region in which great theologians are lost and
bemused; to have established a rational and satisfying doctrine and practice on grounds so dubious is indeed a tremendous achievement. Yet we are asked to believe that Joseph
Smith produced out of a shallow and scheming head the
whole great structure of work for the dead that for over a
century has engaged thousands of quite sane people in an
activity which has been the chief joy of their lives. To design
such a work would more than tax the powers of the greatest
religious leaders of the past, but to have made it conform at
the same time to the patterns of the primitive church (not
brought to light until the last seventy years) is asking far too

much of genius and luck. Compared with such an accomplishment the massive and repetitious productions of the ecclesiastical mind from St. Augustine to the present are but the mechanized output of the schools, requiring little more than "patience and a body."

Work for the dead is an all-important phase of Mormonism about which the world knows virtually nothing. Not even the most zealous anti-Mormon has even begun to offer an explanation for its discovery, which in its way is quite as remarkable as the Book of Mormon. The critics will have to go far to explain this one.

NOTES

1. Justin Martyr, *Dialogus cum Tryphone (Dialogue with Trypho)* 80, in *PG* 6:664.

2. Ibid. 45, in *PG* 6:572.

3. Clement of Alexandria, *Stromata* VI, 6, in *PG* 9:272.

4. Ibid. VI, 6, in *PG* 9:269.

5. *Recognitiones Clementinae (Clementine Recognitions)* II, 58, in *PG* 1:1276.

6. Irenaeus, *Contra Haereses (Against Heresies)* IV, 22, 2, in *PG* 7:1047, 259.

7. 2 Baruch 30:1; 85:15. A treatment of the Jewish doctrine may be found in August F. von Gall, *Basileia tou Theou* (Heidelberg: Winter, 1926), 303–8.

8. Ignatius, *Epistola ad Philadelphenses (Epistle to the Philadelphians)* 5, in *PG* 5:701.

9. St. Bruno notes the eagerness of the primitive Christians "to secure the salvation of a father or mother" who had died without hearing the gospel; *Expositio in Epistolam I ad Corinthios (Commentary on the First Epistle to the Corinthians)* 15, in *PL* 153:209.

10. *Clementine Recognitions* I, 52, in *PG* 1:1236.

11. Matthew 16:13–17; Mark 8:27–30; Luke 9:18–21.

12. Matthew 16:17–19; also R. V. G. Tasker, "An Introduction to the Mss. of the New Testament," *Harvard Theological Review*, 41 (1948): 77. Such an obscure and puzzling text as Matthew 16:17–19 would be just the one to receive such helpful treatment.

13. See Adolf von Harnack, "Der Spruch über Petrus als den Felsen der Kirche," in *Sitzungsberichte der preussischen Akademie der Wissenschaften*, Philologisch-Historische Klasse (1918), 637.

14. Luke 9:21.

15. As also in Matthew 16:21-28.

16. Eusebius, *HE* III, 39, 15; V, 8, 3, in *PG* 20:300, 449.

17. Eusebius, *HE* III, 24, 3-7, in *PG* 20:264-65; cf. *Clementine Recognitions* I, 21, in *PG* 1:1218: "Which things were indeed plainly spoken by Christ but are not plainly written; so much so that when they are read, they cannot be understood without an expounder."

18. Jacques-Paul Migne, ed., *Scripturae Sacrae Cursus Completus*, 25 vols. (Paris: Migne, 1840) 21:823-24; cf. 22:795-96, 106-7, suggests that the Lord commanded secrecy as to his true nature lest men afterwards beholding his death, "being offended by the infirmity of his flesh should lose their faith." As if all the disciples did not do that very thing, the lesson of the resurrection receiving particular force when it came as a rebuke to the doubters. Migne also gives his *opinion* only, that Christ withheld this information "lest people be offended at his calling himself the Son of God"—the last motive in the world to attribute to Jesus, whom the world hated because he made no concessions to its prejudices, the whole gospel being a "rock of offense."

19. 1 Peter 3:19; Tertullian, *De Anima (On the Soul)* VII, 35, 55, in *PL* 2:697-98, 753-54, 787-90; The Wisdom of Solomon 17:15; Book of Enoch (1 Enoch) 10:13; 69:28; Jerome, *Commentarius in Osee (Commentary on Hosea)* 1, 13, in *PL* 25:938: "a lower place in which the spirits are confined, either in rest or punishment, according to their deserts."

20. 4 Esdras 4:35-36; 7:75-99; cf. Josephus, *Jewish Antiquities* XVIII, 1, 3.

21. Tertullian, *On the Soul* 55, in *PL* 2:790: "From the prison of death, thy blood is the key of admission to all paradise." He is speaking of the blood of the martyrs, with which they are baptized. It has been common at all periods of the church to speak of baptism as "the gate."

22. Isaiah 45:1.

23. Matthew 16:18.

24. Odes of Solomon 42:15-20.

25. Odes of Solomon 22:12, quoted at length in Carl Schmidt, *Gespräche Jesu mit seinen Jüngern nach der Auferstehung: Ein katholisch-apostolisches Sendschreiben des 2. Jarhhunderts* (Leipzig: Hinrich, 1908), 565-66.

26. Ignatius, *Epistle to the Philadelphians* 9, in *PG* 5:836; the same combination as in *Hermae Pastor (Shepherd of Hermas)*, *Similitudo (Similitude)* 9, 12, and 16, in *PG* 2:992, 996; cf. Clement of Alexandria, *Stromata* VI, 6, 46, in *PG* 9:269.

27. Thus Migne, *Scripturae Sacrae Cursus Completus* 21:814: "There is no doubt that 'the gates of hell' refers to all the power of the devil." He then proceeds to cite in support of this only the following: Psalm 147:13; Genesis 22:17; 24:60; Judges 5:8; 1 Kings 8:37; and Psalm 107:16, *none* of which refers to "all the powers of the devil," but every one of which refers to the real *gates* and the functions of gates.

28. Matthew 12:26-29; Luke 10:18; 11:18; 13:16; 22:31; Mark 3:23-27; John 12:34; 14:30; 16:11; 1 John 2:13; John 14:4-6; 5:19; Ignatius, *Epistola ad Ephesios (Epistle to the Ephesians)*, chs. 9, 17, 19, in *PG* 5:656, 657, 660, 745, 752-53.

29. 2 Corinthians 4:4.

30. John 12:31; 16:11.

31. Barnabas, *Epistola Catholica (Catholic Epistle)* 2, in *PG* 2:729-30.

32. 1 Enoch 20:2. This subject is fully treated by Schmidt, *Gespräche Jesu*, 547-48, 507, cf. 285-87.

33. John 12:31; 16:11; Schmidt, *Gespräche Jesu*, 549-50, 556, 573, 462, 571; Gall, *Basileia tou Theou*, 290-301, treats the subject at length.

34. Matthew 25:41; Schmidt, *Gespräche Jesu*, 548, 550, 576.

35. Romans 2:16; Psalm 44:21; Jeremiah 23:24; 49:10; Ezekiel 28:2, etc.

36. The literary motif is frankly pagan, as in Dante. In folklore it is no less of popular pagan origin, cf. Stith Thompson, *Motif-Index of Folk-Literature* (Bloomington, Ind.: Indiana University Press, 1934) G 303.25.19. Cf. Gall, *Basileia tou Theou*, 290-301.

37. Schmidt, *Gespräche Jesu*, 572 cites a text of this in use in the Syrian Church as early as A.D. 340.

38. Gospel of Nicodemus 15; virtually the same dialogue is found in Ephraim and in a *Descensus* of the 2nd or 3rd century, K. von Tischendorf, *Evangelia* (Leipzig, 1876; reprinted Hildesheim: Olms, 1966), 394-97.

39. Harnack, "Der Spruch über Petrus als den Felsen der Kirche," 638-39.

40. 1 Corinthians 5:5; Luke 13:16.

41. For the best general treatment of this much-handled subject, see Samuel H. Hooke, ed., *The Labyrinth* (London: Society for Promoting Christian Knowledge, 1935).

42. Ignatius, *Epistle to the Philadelphians* 9, in *PG* 5:836; the "keys of the kingdom of the heavens" of Matthew 16:19 would be useless unless "the gates of hell" of the preceding verse were opened to give up their dead. Indeed, the first words of verse 19 show a wide variety of readings in the manuscripts, with a strong indication that Christ said, "I shall *also* give you the keys to the kingdom of the heavens."

43. The references to Prudentius and Seneca are given by F. J. E. Raby, *A History of Christian-Latin Poetry* (Oxford: Clarendon, 1937), 70.

44. Odes of Solomon 17:8–15.

45. Constantin von Tischendorf, *Synopsis Evangelica* (Leipzig: Mendelssohn, 1864), xxxvi-xxxv, calls attention to the significant emphasis of the gospels of the time of this event as a continuation of the former.

46. Matthew 17:1–13; Mark 9:2–13; Luke 28–36.

47. Migne, *Scripturae Sacrae Cursus Completus* 21:837 explains that this is a Hebraism, simply the equivalent of "Peter said." Only he fails to note that verse 4 is an *immediate* continuation of verse 3. Even the Hebrew never uses "answered" for "spoke" with the first utterance in a story; of course, if Peter answered, he spoke—"answered" necessarily means "spoke," but it also necessarily means something more.

48. Matthew 17:5–6; Mark 9:7; Luke 9:34.

49. Acts 1:9 following the Bezae (D) manuscript.

50. Matthew 17:9–13; Mark 9:9–13; Luke 9:36.

51. 1 Peter 4:7; 1 John 2:18; James 5:7–11.

52. 1 John 2:18.

53. Acts 3:21.

54. Matthew 13:10–15; Mark 4:10–13; Luke 8:9–10.

55. Matthew 13:23; Mark 4:20; Luke 8:15.

56. Irenaeus, *Against Heresies* V, 36, in *PG* 7:1221–23.

57. *Clementine Recognitions* IV, 35–36, in *PG* 1:1330–32.

58. Thus St. Augustine doubts the idea of "many mansions," noting that there is but one house of God and but one salvation: there are no degrees of salvation, *De Anima et Eius Origine (On the Soul and Its Origin)* II, 10; III, 11, 13, in *PL* 44:503, 518, 520.

59. 1 Corinthians 3:2; Hebrews 5:12.

60. John 16:12: "I have yet many things to say unto you, but you cannot bear them now." Acts 10:41: "Not unto all the people, but unto witnesses chosen." Acts 15:28: "For it seemed good . . . to lay upon you no greater burden than these necessary things." *Clementine*

Recognitions I, 21, in *PG* 1:1218: "Which things were plainly spoken but are *not* plainly written." *Clementine Recognitions* I, 23, 52, in *PG* 1:1236, 1282; III, 1: "I [Peter] . . . endeavor to avoid publishing the chief knowledge concerning the Supreme Divinity to unworthy ears," Clement of Alexandria, *Stromata* VI, 7, 61, in *PG* 9:284; Eusebius, *HE* II, 1, 4–5 (citing Clement), in *PG* 20:136. Innumerable passages on this head might be cited.

61. Matthew 15:16; 28:17 (even *after* the resurrection, "some doubted"); Mark 9:32; 16:14; Luke 8:25; 9:45; 18:34; 24:16; John 2:22–24; 3:32; 6:36; 6:60–67; 7:5; 11:13; 12:16; 13:7; 16:25–33. This last is another lost teaching: in verse 25 the Lord promises that the time will come when he will speak plainly to the apostles; after three short verses, announcing nothing new, they declare: "*now* speakest thou plainly. . . . Now are we sure that thou knowest all things." What brought on such a change? What was it he told them? That *we* are not told.

62. Luke 24:27.

63. Luke 24:25.

64. Acts 1:3.

65. Schmidt, *Gespräche Jesu*, 304–36.

66. Ibid., 201–8.

67. Ibid., 156–68, gives an extensive list of these; they were strictly orthodox, ibid., 168–72, 190, 204–5.

68. Ibid., 205: It was universally believed in the early church that "the last and highest revelations" were those given by the Lord after his resurrection, and that these dealt with "the kingdom of God."

69. For references, *PL* 2:787–88, n. 70.

70. On various terms designating the spirit world, see Philip Schaff, *The Creeds of Christendom*, 3 vols. (New York: Harper, 1919), 1:21, n. 6; 2:46, n. 2. Others may be found scattered throughout Schmidt, *Gespräche Jesu*. The geographical hell first appears in Tertullian, *On the Soul* 55, in *PL* 2:787–88; in *On the Soul* 7, in *PL* 2:998, he notes that since suffering must be physical, the spirits in prison must have corporeal bodies; a true African, he cannot believe that mere detention of the spirit could cause suffering: it is *matter* alone that suffers, he says.

71. By this title we shall henceforth refer to the second-century Coptic manuscript found in 1895 and eked out by later texts, the whole edited and published by Carl Schmidt and Isaak Wajnberg, under the title *Gespräche Jesu mit seinen Jüngern nach der Auferstehung: Ein katholisch-apostolisches Sendschreiben des 2.*

154   MORMONISM AND EARLY CHRISTIANITY

Jahrhunderts, see above note 25. The passage cited is from pp. 89,
84–85 (xxii, xxi of the Coptic text).

72. See lexicons. In Plato's *Timaeus* XXIV (59) *anapausis* is an
agreeable activity, devoid of any coercion.

73. Schmidt, *Gespräche Jesu,* 74–75.

74. Ibid., 63, 66, 71–73.

75. Irenaeus, *Epideixis (Proof of the Apostolic Preaching)* 6, in
PO 12:664; cf. Irenaeus, *Against Heresies* II, 20, 3, in *PG* 7:778.

76. Barnabas, *Catholic Epistle* 16, in *PG* 2:776.

77. Ignatius, *Epistola ad Magnesios (Epistle to the Magnesians)* 8,
1; 9, 2, in *PG* 5:765–66; Ignatius, *Epistola ad Trallianos (Epistle to the
Trallians)* 8, in *PG* 5:788.

78. Clement of Alexandria, *Stromata* VI, 6, in *PG* 9:265.

79. Acta Thomae, 265, cited in Schmidt, *Gespräche Jesu,* 557–58.

80. Irenaeus, *Against Heresies* II, 20, 3, in *PG* 7:778.

81. Origen, *Contra Celsum (Against Celsus)* II, 56, in *PG* 11:885-
88.

82. Justin, *Dialogue with Trypho* 5, in *PG* 6:488; 45, in *PG* 6:573.

83. Cited in Schmidt, *Gespräche Jesu,* 489: The logion states that
the Lord visited the dead and brought the Fathers and prophets of old
from a lower to a higher *anapausis.*

84. "Ordo promotionis, ordo resurrectionis." Irenaeus, *Against
Heresies* V, 30, 1; V, 31, 1, in *PG* 7:1203–5, 1208; cf. Irenaeus, *Proof
of the Apostolic Preaching* 56 and 78, in *PO* 12:702, 717.

85. Clement of Alexandria, *Ex Scripturis Profeticis Eclogae
(Selections from the Prophetic Writings)* 56–57, in *PG* 9:725. Prokope
expresses the idea of a temporary rest even better than *anapausis,* cf.
above note 72.

86. Clement of Alexandria, *Stromata* VI, 107, 2, in *PG* 9:328–29.

87. Philo, *On Dreams* 1, 23 (643).

88. Anselm, *Homiliae (Homilies)* 8, in *PL* 158:637.

89. Schmidt, *Gespräche Jesu,* 86–87, 315.

90. Barnabas, *Catholic Epistle* 16, in *PG* 2:776. It was extremely
common in the second and especially third centuries to "spiritualize"
actual practices, e.g., baptism, marriage, feasting, etc., without in any
way implying that the real thing was done away with.

91. Hippolytus, *Demonstratio de Christo et Antichristo (On
Christ and the Antichrist)* 26, in *PG* 10:740.

92. *De Elcanam et Annam* fragment 4 (Hippolytus I, 2) quoted at
length in Schmidt, *Gespräche Jesu,* 509.

93. Sibylline Oracles 8:310–11.

94. Clement of Alexandria, *Stromata* VI, 6, in *PG* 9:268.

95. Sirach 24:32, in Schmidt, *Gespräche Jesu*, 473.

96. Schmidt, *Gespräche Jesu*, 473.

97. Justin, *Dialogue with Trypho* 4, 6, in *PG* 6:645; Irenaeus, *Against Heresies* III, 20, 4, in *PG* 7:945; IV, 22, in *PG* 7:1046; IV, 33, 1, in *PG* 7:1208; it is also cited by Jerome, *Commentarius in Evangelium Mattheum* (*Commentary on Matthew*) 4, 27, in *PL* 26: 213.

98. Justin, *Dialogue with Trypho* 4, 6, in *PG* 6:645; cf. Jerome, *Commentary on Matthew* 4, 27, in *PL* 26:213.

99. Though he is inclined to separate the two traditions, Schmidt must nonetheless admit that the *decensus* and the *kerygma* are found inseparably joined from the first.

100. Acta Thomae, p. 265, in Schmidt, *Gespräche Jesu*, 558.

101. Odes of Solomon 42:14, 20.

102. Odes of Solomon 17:12, 15–16.

103. "And he was crucified, and went down to Hades, and broke through the barrier which till then had never been breached; and he awoke the dead, and went down alone, but came up with a great host toward his Father." Eusebius, *HE* I, 13, 19, citing the letter of Thaddeus to Abgar, one of the most ancient of all Christian documents.

104. Tertullian, *On the Soul* 55, in *PL* 2:788.

105. References in "Index Latinitatis," in *PL* 2:1372, s.v. "*compos.*"

106. Irenaeus, *Against Heresies* IV, 33, in *PG* 7:1081.

107. Origen, *Against Celsus* II, 43, in *PG* 11:864–65.

108. Clement of Alexandria, *Stromata* VI, 6, in *PG* 9:272.

109. Schmidt, *Gespräche Jesu*, 49, 51.

110. Origen, *In Lucam Homiliae* (*Homily on Luke*) 4, in *PG* 12:1811.

111. Origen, *Commentaria in Evangelium Joannis* (*Commentary on John*) 2, 30, in *PG* 14:181.

112. Hippolytus, *On Christ and the Antichrist* 5, 45, in *PG* 10:764.

113. Thus in the Anglo-Saxon version, "Höllenfahrt Christi," in Richard Paul Wülker, *Bibliothek der Angelsächsischen Poesie*, 3 vols. (Leipzig: Wigands, 1897), 3.1:177.

114. *Shepherd of Hermas*, Similitudes III, 9, 16; we are following the various texts given in Max Dressel, *Patrum Apostolicorum Opera* (Leipzig, 1863), 548–49, 631.

115. Codex Vaticanus 3848.

116. See note 114.

117. Clement of Alexandria, *Stromata* III, 6, in *PG* 9:268.

118. Ibid. II, 9, in *PG* 8:980; Clement cites the entire passage from *Shepherd of Hermas, Similitudes* 9, 16; he also quotes Deuteronomy 32:21; Isaiah 65:1–2; Romans 10:20–21; 2:14.

119. Schmidt, *Gespräche Jesu*, 315; cf. 317–18: "Christ not only appears as a preacher in the lower world, but also as one administering baptism; and here, too, his activity runs parallel to his earthly mission." Cf. John 3:22–26; 4:1.

120. The Gnostics would not tolerate the idea that any who lived under the Old Law could be saved, but instead they insisted that Christ went to the lower world and liberated only the enemies of the ancient prophets and patriarchs! Thus Theodoretus, *Haereticae Fabulae (Heretical Tales)* 1, 24, in *PG* 83:373, 376; Epiphanius, *Adversus Haereses (Against Heresies)* 42, 4, in *PG* 41:700–701; Irenaeus, *Against Heresies* I, 27, 3, in *PG* 7:689.

121. Augustine, *Epistolae (Letters)* III, 89, 5, in *PL* 33:312; "Minister . . . non iste sed . . . ipse Christus qui baptizat." So likewise in Augustine, *Contra Epistolam Parmeniani (Against the Letter of Parmenienus)* II, 16, 35, in *PL* 43:77; *Contra Litteras Petiliani Donatistae (Against the Writings of Petilianus the Donatist)* III, 35, 40, in *PL* 43:368–69; *Against the Donatists* I, 18, 47, in *PL* 43:427; I, 21, 58, in *PL* 43:435.

122. Schmidt, *Gespräche Jesu*, 133–35.

123. Cyril of Jerusalem, *Catechesis 3 de Baptismo (Catechetical Lecture on Baptism)* 4, in *PG* 33:429: "For since a man is two-fold, consisting of body and spirit, so must be the purification. . . . The water cleans the body, the spirit seals the soul." See also 418, in *PG* 33:432, 440, and *Catechesis 13 de Christo Crucifixo et Sepulto (Catechetical Lecture on the Crucifixion and Burial of Christ)* 21, in *PG* 33:797–800.

124. Tertullian, *De Baptismo (On Baptism)* 4, 7, in *PL* 1:1312, 1315–16.

125. Thus Fulgentius, *Epistolae (Letters)* 11, 4, in *PL* 65:379; *Letters* 12, 9, in *PL* 65:388: "Once one has died without the sacrament of baptism, he may not be baptized, because the spirit, to which belonged that will and faithful devotion (which justify baptism) has departed." Cf. Crisconius, *Breviarium Canonicum (Canonical Epitome)* 247, in *PL* 88:925.

126. 1 Corinthians 15:29; see below note 138.

127. Catholic commentators regard the status of living and dead as referring only to spiritual or eternal life. This completely ignores the fact that the dead receive a real baptism in water, no explanation being

offered as to how the "mortui baptizandi erant [dead were to be baptized]."
128. See below notes 157–60.
129. Origen, *Homily on Luke* 24, in *PG* 13:1864–65.
130. Albertus Magnus Ratisboneus, *De Sacramento Eucharistiae (On the Eucharist)* 6, 2, 1, cited by Elmhorst, in *PL* 58:1042, who gives a list of medieval writers holding the same opinion, *PL* 58:1043.
131. Tertullian, *De Resurrectione (On the Resurrection)* 48, in *PL* 2:864.
132. Tertullian, *Adversus Marcionem (Against Marcion)* 5, 10, in *PL* 2:495.
133. Ambrose, *Epistolae (Letters)* I, 72, 18, in *PL* 16:1302; Ambrose (dubia), *De Sacramentis (On the Sacrament)*, in *PL* 16:443; on the same subject, St. Peter Chrysologus, *Sermones (Discourses)* 171, in *PL* 52:647.
134. Tertullian, *Against Marcion*, 5, 10, in *PL* 2:526–27, cited in John Kaye, *The Ecclesiastical History of the Second and Third Centuries Illustrated from the Writings of Tertullian* (London: Farran, 1894), 272.
135. Epiphanius, *Against Heresies* I, 28, 6, in *PG* 41:384.
136. Irenaeus, *Against Heresies* III, 4, 2, in *PG* 7:855–56.
137. Epiphanius, *Against Heresies* I, 28, 6, in *PG* 41:384–85.
138. Ambrose, *Commentaria in Epistolam I ad Corinthios (Commentary on the First Epistle to the Corinthians)*, in *PL* 17:280.
139. Ignatius, *Epistle to the Magnesians* 8, 1 and 9, 2, in *PG* 5:699, 765, 768, assumes like Paul that his readers know all about the work of baptism for the dead, as Schmidt demonstrates, Schmidt, *Gespräche Jesu*, 476.
140. Oecumenius, *Commentaria in Epistolam I ad Corinthios (Commentary on the First Epistle to the Corinthians)* 15, 29, in *PG* 118:877.
141. Peter the Venerable, *Adversus Patrobrusianos Haereticos (Against the Patrobrusian Heretics)*, in *PL* 189:831–32.
142. Ibid., in *PL* 189:832.
143. Oecumenius, *Commentary on the First Epistle to the Corinthians* 15, 29, in *PG* 118:876–77.
144. W. Henry, "Baptême des morts (Le)," in *DACL* 2:380.
145. Ibid.
146. St. Bruno, *Commentary on the First Epistle to the Corinthians* 15, 29, in *PL* 153:209.
147. John of Damascene, *In Epistolas ad Corinthios (Commentary on the Epistles to the Corinthians)* 116, in *PG* 95:693.

148. Lanfranc, *Commentarius in Epistolam B. Pauli Apostoli ad Corinthios Primam (Commentary on the First Epistle to the Corinthians)* 15, 29, in *PL* 150:210.

149. It was Henri Müller, in 1656; see Henry, "Baptême des morts," 380.

150. John Chrysostom, *In Epistolam I ad Corinthios Homilia (Homily on the First Epistle to the Corinthians)* 40, in *PG* 61:347.

151. Theophylactus, *Expositio in Epistolam I ad Corinthios (Commentary on the First Epistle to the Corinthians)* 15, 29, in *PG* 124:768.

152. Fulgentius, *Letters* 12, 9 (20), in *PL* 65:388.

153. Ibid., cf. *PL* 65:379.

154. Henry, "Baptême des morts," 381, produces no laws or regulations against baptism for the dead, but cites as having the same force those specifically directed against baptism of the dead, e.g., Third Council of Carthage, in *PL* 140:734; Canon law 19, in *PL* 96:1049; cf. Theodoretus, *Heretical Tales* 1, 111, in *PG* 83:361, which they also cite.

155. Philastrius, *Liber de Haeresibus (On Heresies)* 49, in *PL* 12:1166; the Cataphrygians were a branch of the Montanists, noted, if nothing else, for their sobriety. Yet Philastrius mentions *rumors* of savage and bloody sacramental rites.

156. See above note 114.

157. It is precisely in ordering the apostles "to tell no man that thing" that the Lord tells them how he is presently to be put to death. Mark 8:30-31; Luke 9:21-22; Matthew 16:20-21. The injunction to secrecy is the same in the "gates of hell" discussion as on the Mount, when "they kept it close and told no man *in those days*," Luke 10:36, since they were commanded to "tell the vision to no man, until the Son of man be risen again from the dead." Matthew 17:9; the same in Mark 9:9.

158. Eusebius, *HE* II, 1, 4-5, in *PG* 20:136.

159. Eusebius describes as the purpose of his history "to record the successions of the holy apostles . . . down to the present, and to tell . . . what individuals in the most prominent positions eminently governed and presided over the church." *HE* I, 1, 1. The "most prominent" offices in the church of his own day he regards as four great bishoprics of Jerusalem, Rome, Antioch, and Alexandria, which are the main lines of succession from the apostles, yet he is unable to furnish an instance in which "the gnosis" is given to one of these. Tertullian is very clear and specific in this matter: "You are reversing and altering the manifest intention of the Lord in endowing Peter

personally . . . for he says . . . 'I shall give to *thee* the keys,' not to the Church, and: 'Whatsoever *thou* shalt loosen or *thou* shalt bind,' not whatsoever *they* shall loosen or *they* shall bind." He then goes on to show that Peter's authority was not "handed down," but if it still exists in the church must come by direct revelation and not through the mere episcopal office (sed Ecclesia Spiritus per spiritalem hominem, non ecclesia numerus episcoporum). Tertullian, *De Pudicitia (On Modesty)* 21, in *PL* 2:1078–80.

160. Thus Romans 11:33, noting Romans 2:17–20 that the Jewish law preserves but a shadow *(morphosis)* of the gnosis; 1 Corinthians 8:7: "Not in everyone is the gnosis" which is (12:8) "given through the spirit" to particular individuals; in 1 Corinthians 13:2 it is described as the most rare and wonderful of attainments, in 1 Corinthians 13:8 it is predicted that "it shall vanish away." It is an inspired thing, 1 Corinthians 14:6, known to the world only very indirectly by its effect on the lives of the Saints. God "making known the odor *(osmēn)* of the gnosis of Him through us in every place," 2 Corinthians 2:14. It is the gnosis that sets Paul apart from other teachers, 2 Corinthians 11:6. The love of Christ is the greatest of all things, since it excels *even* the gnosis, he tells the Ephesians (3:19); and to the Philippians (3:8) he says that all earthly things are as nothing compared to the value of the gnosis of Jesus Christ. The gnosis is again described, Colossians 2:2–3, as a treasure and a mystery, hidden in Christ, and a thing which must be carefully guarded and not exposed to "that which is *falsely* called the gnosis," 1 Timothy 6:20.

161. John 20:9.

162. Acts 10:41.

163. Ignatius, *Epistle to the Philadelphians* 8, in *PG* 5:833.

164. Robert Eisler, *Iesous Basileus ou Basileusas* (Heidelberg: Winter, 1930) 1: xxix–xxxiv, 298, 353.

165. John 3:12.

166. Instances in which an actual limitation is placed on the preaching of the gospel are very numerous in the scriptures, e.g., Matthew 7:6–7; 11:14–15, 25–28; 13:11–16; 13:34–36; 19:11; 24:3; Mark 4:9–12; 9:33–34; 11:33; Luke 8:10; 9:36, 43–45; 10:21–23; 12:41; 18:34; 22:67–71; John 1:11–12; 3:11–12; 6:60–66; 8:43–44; 10:24–27; 16:12–18, 25, 29–30; Acts 10:41; 15:28; 19:2; 20:20; 28:26–27; Romans 6:19; 11:30–34; 1 Corinthians 2:14; 3:1–3; 7:25; 14:2, 9–10; 14:22; 15:34; 2 Corinthians 1:13; 3:3; 12:2–5; Galatians 2:2; Ephesians 3:1–5; Colossians 1:26; 1 Peter 2:2; 2 Peter 3:16; 2 John 1:12.

167. In this connection should be cited the much-discussed remark of Jesus to the Pharisees (Luke 17:20–21) that the kingdom of God was in their midst, but that it was not for them to see. The word rendered "observation" in the King James version has in all contexts the meaning of an intense, expectant watch, a spying out *(parateresis)*— much stronger than mere observation, so Christ tells the Pharisees that no matter how *hard* they look *(paratereo* always means to look very *hard)* they will not see the kingdom, which in fact *(idou gar)* is already among them. The word "within" *(entos)* can only be rendered so when used with a singular noun; here it is used with the plural and must of course be read "among" or (literally) "in the midst of." This has often been pointed out by scholars ever since the Renaissance. But the more philosophical and sentimental, if less accurate, King James version is usually preferred as avoiding embarrassing questions of doctrine.

168. Eusebius, *HE* III, 32, 7–8, in *PG* 20:284.

169. 1 Timothy 6:20.

170. First the apostles themselves should depart ("God hath sent forth us the apostles last, as it were appointed to death"), and then would come the wolves, against whom the flock is denied immunity, 1 Corinthians 4:9–15; Acts 20:29–31, God himself sending "a strong delusion" (2 Thessalonians 2:11, the "falling away" of verse 3 shows that this applies to the church), since they would not endure sound doctrine, 2 Timothy 4:3–4.

171. 1 Corinthians 13:8; the King James version correctly preserves the future indicative; the independent "whether" *(eite)* implies, "to whatever degree they exist," i.e., it is indefinite; but there is nothing indefinite about the result clause: whatever their present status these three *are* to be taken away.

172. 1 Corinthians 13:9–13. The King James "and now abideth" is very weak in comparison to the Greek *nuni de menei*, etc.: "but now these three remain." "These" is the proper subject of the verb, which, since the subject is neuter, should be translated in the plural.

173. Luke 11:52.

174. Romans 2:20.

175. Polycarp, *Epistle to the Philippians 3*, in *PG* 5:1008.

176. Clement, *Epistola I ad Corinthios (First Epistle to the Corinthians)* 47, in *PG* 1:308; neither are they under Clement's authority, as the Roman Catholics claim, for we learn in the introduction that this letter is written at the request of the Corinthians, and we know from the other apostolic letters that it was common for bishops to communicate with other congregations than their own *if* those congregations requested letters. Decisive in this matter is the

remark at the end of section 46 of this epistle in *PG* 1:305: "Your
falling out has turned many aside, has plunged many into despair,
caused many to vacillate, and brought sorrow to us all, and your
disorder *(statis)* is chronic *(epimonos)*." From this and other sections
(3, 14, 16, 46, in *PG* 1:213–16, 236–37, 240–41, 305) it is clear that the
evil is far advanced and has been going on for some time; yet it is not
until he receives a request from the Corinthians themselves that
Clement presumes to give them words of advice, which would not
possibly be the case had he the right and duty to intervene in
Corinthian affairs. When like crises arose in Rome, Polycarp, Bishop
of Smyrna, and Irenaeus, Bishop of Lyons, laid down the law to the
Roman congregation even more emphatically than Clement spoke to
the Corinthians, Irenaeus, *Against Heresies* III, 3, 4, in *PG* 7:85–88;
Eusebius, *HE* V, 24–28, in *PG* 20:493–517.

177. Ignatius, *Epistola ad Romanos (Epistle to the Romans)* 4, in
PG 5:689.

178. Ignatius, *Epistle to the Trallians* 5, in *PG* 5:781; cf. 3, in
PG 5:780: "Shall I . . . reach such a pitch of presumption . . . as to
issue commands to you as if I were an Apostle?" Here is a man who
obviously knows the difference between a bishop and an apostle; for
Ignatius was "the third Bishop of Antioch after Peter."

179. August Neander, *Antignostikus, Geist des Tertullians und
Einleitung in dessen Schriften* (Berlin: Dümmler, 1849), 3–14.

180. Among Gnostic teachings condemned by Irenaeus and later
adopted by the Catholic church are celibacy, *Against Heresies* I, 24, 2,
in *PG* 7:675; veneration of images, ibid., I, 25, 6, in *PG* 7:685–86;
allegorical interpretation of the scriptures, ibid., II, 27, 1, in *PG*
7:802–3; proof by demonstration, ibid., II, 22, 6, in *PG* 7:785; appeal
to philosophy and use of philosophic terms, ibid., II, 14, 2 and 7, in
PG 7: 750, 754; transubstantiation of water into blood, ibid., I, 13, 2,
in *PG* 7:579; extreme unction, ibid., I, 11, 5, in *PG* 7:665; use of
chrism, ibid., I, 13, 2, in *PG* 7:644; vileness of the flesh, ibid., I, 15, 4,
in *PG* 7: 683–84; irresistible Grace, ibid., I, 25, 5, in *PG* 7:685; the
incomprehensibility of God, ibid., II, 2, 4, in *PG* 7:714. This is not to
say that these were all taken over *from* the Gnostics, but rather from
the same source that supplied the Gnostics: the popular teachings of
the day.

181. Irenaeus expresses this idea: "Even if the Apostles had
possessed hidden mysteries . . . they would certainly have transmitted
them to those to whom they committed the churches." *Against
Heresies* III, 3, 1, in *PG* 7:848. Against this we have the word of those
men themselves, given in our preceding paragraph, that they did *not*

162   MORMONISM AND EARLY CHRISTIANITY

share all the knowledge of the apostles and that they did *not* pass on
what knowledge they did share.

182. Eusebius, *HE* III, 24, 5, in *PG* 20:264–65: Besides Paul "the
other disciples of our Savior were not ignorant of the same things,
both the twelve Apostles and the Seventy, and besides them a great
many others. Nevertheless out of all the things the Lord did, only
Matthew and John left records, and they only wrote down what they
were forced to, according to the report. . . . The three evangelists [the
Synoptics] only wrote an account of his doings for one year."

183. 1 Peter 4:6–7.

184. Schmidt, *Gespräche Jesu*, 116–18.

185. Thus Bishop John Kaye of Lincoln, *Ecclesiastical History*, 276:
"The promise of the Holy Spirit, made by Christ to the Church,
precludes the possibility of an universal defection from the true faith."
Apparently the good bishop is oblivious to the fact that the promise of
the spiritual gifts to accompany the Holy Spirit—prophecy, tongues,
etc.—precludes the possibility of any modern church possessing it.
The fact that the scripture is the *sole* source of "revelation" in all the
synods and councils of the Christian church cancels any claim it might
make to being the recipient of the promised Paraclete.

186. Both Apostles and Apostolic Fathers are careful to point out
to the church that even the angels "kept not their first estate." 2 Peter
2:4–22; Jude 1:5–19; Clement, *First Epistle to the Corinthians* 39, in
PG 1:285; Ignatius, *Epistola ad Smyrnaeos (Epistle to the Smyrnaeans)*
6, in *PG* 5:847; as a warning that no one is ever out of danger, typical
is the statement of Clement, *Epistola II ad Corinthios (Second Epistle
to the Corinthians)* 4, in *PG* 1:336: "For the Lord said, 'Even though ye
were gathered together to my very bosom, should you fail to keep my
commandments I would cast you away.' " The Jews, the covenant
people who lost the covenant, are repeatedly mentioned as an object
lesson to the Christians: thus Barnabas, *Catholic Epistle* 4, in *PG* 2:
734: "Beware lest resting at ease as being God's chosen ones, we fall
asleep in our sins. . . . And especially take heed when you observe
what marvelous signs and wonders were had among the Jews, in spite
of which God deserted."

187. As an authoritative statement of this point of view we may
cite Alfred Fawkes, "The Development of Christian Institutions and
Beliefs," *Harvard Theological Review* 10 (1917): 144: "The belief in the
literal and immediate Coming of Christ is the key to the Church of the
First Age." He discusses the subject at length.

188. 1 Peter 1:5–6, 20; 4:7, 12 speaks of an immediate end. 2 Peter
4:4–12: They say, "Where is the promise of his coming? . . . all things

continue as they were. . . . But, beloved, be not ignorant of this, that one day is with the Lord as a thousand years. . . . The Lord is not slack concerning his promise."

189. 1 Corinthians 7:29–31.

190. 2 Thessalonians 2:1–7.

191. Acts 20:31.

192. 1 John 2:18: "Even now are there many antichrists; whereby we know that it is the last time."

193. *Shepherd of Hermas, Similitudes* 3 and 4, in *PG* 2:955–56. As to Mark 13:34, "the absence of the Lord of the vineyard is the time that must pass until his coming." *Shepherd of Hermas, Similitudes* 5, 5, in *PG* 2:961–62.

194. Didache 16:3–8.

195. Matthew 24:5, 6, 8, 13.

196. 2 Timothy 4:7–8.

197. 2 Timothy 4:3–4.

198. Galatians 1:6.

199. 2 Timothy 1:15.

200. In Clement, *Second Epistle to the Corinthians* 5, in *PG* 1:335, the Lord tells the Apostles: " 'Ye shall be as lambs in the midst of wolves.' And Peter answered him and said unto him, 'What then if the wolves shall tear the lambs to pieces?' Jesus said to Peter: 'The lambs have no cause after they are dead to fear the wolves; and in like manner fear ye not them that kill you.' " This passage is typical in its absolute refusal to grant the church the slightest glimmer of hope in the matter of earthly success. Ignatius' entire *Epistle to the Romans* is a document of profoundest pessimism. He takes no comfort in the church and expresses no interest in her future, but wishes only to die; a less helpful attitude could not be imagined, but the saint explains that he is sick of living "among men" and seeks joy and illumination that come from the presence of the Lord: was it living "among men" to live in the church? and was there no joy or illumination to be enjoyed any longer in the church on this earth? Ignatius answers in the negative.

201. It is easy looking backward to claim that the blood of the martyrs was meant to guarantee the integrity of the church for all time; but the evidence is exhaustive that the martyrs themselves never thought of their sufferings in such terms. It cannot be too emphatically repeated that the survival of the Christian *name*, far from proving the survival of the church and the gospel, may be taken for evidence of the very opposite, since the Lord and the apostles repeatedly pointed out that the "deceiver of the world" would come in Christ's name. All

apostolic writers describe the great danger to the church as coming from within it, and never express the slightest concern about the activities of those outside. That victory of the church over paganism, in which the ministry are wont to glory, is thus seen to be a hollow victory indeed, since paganism as such presented no danger. Such pagan writings as Cicero's *De Divinatione* are far more devastating attacks upon the old state religion than anything ever produced by a Christian writer.

202. John 9:4.

203. Irenaeus, *Against Heresies* II, 32, 4, in *PG* 7:828–29.

204. Tertullian, *On Modesty* 21, in *PL* 2:1077–82, noting that the power to do miracles and that of forgiving sins have the same source, observes, "If the blessed Apostles enjoyed such power it was by a special gift of God, . . . and not by virtue of any special training. . . . Show me then some examples of such power today, and I will concede your right to forgive sins. But if you claim your authority simply by virtue of your office . . . and cannot show the power of Apostle or Prophet, you must be lacking in the authority you claim." On Matthew 9:4: "If the Lord himself took such pains to put his power to the proof, not presuming to forgive sins without a power great enough to heal the sick, certainly I may not claim power to forgive sins without at least an equivalent demonstration of divine power."

205. For evidence we refer the reader to the extensive indices of the *Patrologiae*, wherein few subjects are more extensively treated than baptism.

206. Justin, *Dialogue with Trypho* 80, in *PG* 6:664.

207. Their doubts are discussed by Schmidt, *Gespräche Jesu*, 519–20.

208. Irenaeus, *Against Heresies* V, 32, 1, in *PG* 7:1210.

209. Ibid. V, 35, 3, in *PG* 7:1220.

210. The Aquileian, Athanasian, and some Eastern versions of the Apostles' Creed contain the phrase which is further defended by Augustine and (in the late sixth century) by Venatius Fortunatus, according to Philip Schaff, *Creeds of Christendom* 1:21, n. 6; even the Roman creed adopted the clause, 1:19. Rufinus (Bishop of Aquileia A.D. 410–415) interprets the phrase as being simply equivalent to "he was buried," *Commentarius in Symbolum Apostolorum (Commentary on the Creed of the Apostles)*, in *PL* 21:356, but then cites a number of scripture passages which he regards as supporting a literal interpretation, ibid., in *PL* 21:363–64. The Arminensian and Acacian versions of the creed both contain the phrase "descended to the regions beneath the earth," Socrates, *HE* II, 37, and II, 41, in *PG* 67: 305, 348.

As late as the twelfth century the anonymous writer of a *Symboli Apostolici Explanatio (Explanation of the Apostolic Creed)*, in *PL* 213:734, includes the clause and the comment: "He descended to the lower regions that he might liberate the saints who were there by the first penalties *(debita)* of death."

211. Schmidt, *Gespräche Jesu*, 25–27; 521, 541. Origen is the first to conclude that *no* one who lived before Christ can possibly enjoy full salvation, a doctrine in which the persuasion of pagan philosophy is stronger than scripture, *Homiliae in Librum Regum (Homilies on the Book of Kings)* 2, in *PL* 12:1013–28.

212. Augustine, *On the Soul and Its Origin* 9, in *PL* 44:480–81.

213. Ibid., in *PL* 44:188–89, 503, 518, 520.

214. Ibid., in *PL* 44:120, 140, 188–89.

215. William Shakespeare, *A Midsummer Night's Dream*, act 1, scene 2, 82–83.

216. Augustine, *Contra Julianum Pelagianum (Against Julian the Pelagian)* 57, in *PL* 45:1596–97.

217. Ambrose, in *PL* 55:235.

218. Basilius, *Liber de Spiritu Sancto (Writings on the Holy Spirit)* 10, 26, in *PG* 32:113.

219. Gregory of Nyssen, *On Baptism*, in *PG* 46:424.

220. Gennadius, *De Ecclesiasticis Dogmatibus (On Church Doctrines)* 74, in *PL* 58:997. This doctrine precludes any belief in the "baptism of desire," a vague device by which modern Catholics attempt to provide baptism for the unbaptized. No one could be more eligible for such a baptism than the pure and desirous catechumen, whom Gennadius describes as lost.

221. *Shepherd of Hermas, Similitudes* IX, 16, 6–7.

222. Augustine, *Epistolae (Letters)* III, 164, in *PL* 33:708–18. Augustine finds it "absurd" to believe that one who lacked faith in life can "believe on Christ in hell," ibid., in *PL* 33:714. As to those who were disobedient in the time of Noah, 1 Peter 3:20, the scripture does not say that they ever lived in the flesh! Ibid., in *PL* 33:713. By such rationalizations Augustine upholds a doctrine which he describes as "hard" *(durum)*, ibid., in *PL* 33:712.

223. Raby, *Christian-Latin Poetry*, 117.

224. *Ad Maronis mausoleum*
   ductus fudit super eum
   piae rorem lacrimae

   Quem te, dixit, rededissem
   si te vivum invenissem,
   poetarum maxime!

166 MORMONISM AND EARLY CHRISTIANITY

("When brought to Vergil's tomb he shed the dew of a tender tear over him, saying, 'If I had found you alive, of all poets I would have restored you.' ") See Domenico Comparetti, *Vergil in the Middle Ages*, tr. E. F. M. Benecke (New York: Macmillan, 1895), 98.

225. Dante Alighieri, *The Divine Comedy, Inferno*, Canto IV, 7-12, 31-45. The poet says (43-45) that "great sorrow seized his heart" at the sight, for he knew many of the sufferers to be "people of great worth."

226. Ibid., 52-63.

227. Gennadius Massiliensis, *De Fide ad Petrum Diaconum (To Peter the Deacon on Faith)* 3, folio 159, cited in *PL* 58:1043.

228. Fulgentius, *De Fide (On Faith)* 38 (Reg. 35), in *PL* 65:704.

229. Cited by Elmhurst, *Notae in Librum de Ecclesiasticis Dogmatibus (Notes on the Book of Church Doctrines)*, in *PL* 58:1043.

230. A common formula, thus Hippolytus, *On Christ and the Antichrist* 26, in *PG* 10:748.

231. Prof. Sidney B. Sperry brings to my attention the Coptic rendering of "gates of hell" as "the gates of Amente," *The Coptic Version of the New Testament in the Southern Dialect*, 7 vols. (Oxford: Clarendon, 1911), 1:172-73. This is the well-known Egyptian word meaning "the West" and hence "the realm of the dead," Kurt H. Sethe, "Untersuchungen über die ägyptischen Zahlwörter," *Zeitschrift für ägyptische Sprache und Altertumskunde* 47 (1910): 31; it retains both meanings also in Coptic, see William Speigelberg, *Koptisches Handwörterbuch* (Heidelberg: Winter, 1921), 5, 25; also in Spiegelberg, "The God Panepi," *Journal of Egyptian Archaeology* 12 (1926): 35, where it has nothing to do with Satan or the devil. It is a fact of decisive importance that the earliest translators of the New Testament, and those nearest to the primitive church in time and in knowledge, chose this word instead of those expressions (such as *te* or *noun*) which mean "hell" in the bad tyrannical sense. *Amente* is simply the land of the dead, and regularly a word of good omen.

232. Henry, "Baptême des morts," 381.

233. Augustine, *De Baptismo contra Donatistas (Against the Donatists on Baptism)* 4, 24, in *PL* 43:175.

234. Augustine, *Sermones (Sermons)* 294, 11 and 18, in *PL* 38:1342, 1346.

235. Augustine, *In Johannis Evangelium (On the Gospel of John)*, in *PL* 35:1511.

236. "Minister . . . non iste sed . . . ipse Christus qui baptizat," Augustine, *Letters* II, 89, in *PL* 33:311-12.

237. Augustine, *On the Gospel of John*, in *PL* 35:1419, 1428, 1437; Augustine, *Against the Writings of Petilianus the Donatist* III, 35, 40, in *PL* 43:368–69; III, 40, 46, in *PL* 43:371–72.

238. Pius X, *Codex Juris Canonici* (Rome: Typis Polyglottis Vaticanis, 1918), can. 793.

239. Ibid., can. 742, 746, 747, 758, 762; these rules allow for *two* types of baptism which differ widely in their manner of being carried out.

240. As an example which we failed to include in the preceding article, a belated citation from the ninth century Bishop Almon (Haymon) of Halberstadt may be allowed at this point. Speaking of the primitive church, he says: "If their loved ones (friend or relative: *propinquus*) happened to depart this life without the grace of baptism, some living person would be baptized in his name: and they believed that the baptism of the living would profit the dead." The bishop must deny, of course, that Paul approved the practice, and has the usual difficulty explaining why the apostle chose an improper practice to illustrate and support (ut suadeat et ostendat) his doctrine. Haymon Halberstatensis, *Expositio Sancti Pauli in Epistolam I ad Corinthios (Commentary on the First Epistle to the Corinthians)*, in *PL* 117:598.

5

The Passing of the Primitive Church: Forty Variations on an Unpopular Theme

A Somber Theme: Ever since Eusebius sought with dedicated zeal to prove the survival of the church by blazing a trail back to the apostles, the program of church history has been the same: "To give a clear and comprehensive, scientifically established view of the development of the visible institution of salvation founded by Christ."[1] To describe it—not to question it. By its very definition church history requires unquestioning acceptance of the basic proposition that the church did survive. One may write endlessly about *The Infant Church, l'Eglise naissante, die Pflanzung der Kirche,* etc., but one may not ask why the early Christians themselves described their church not as a lusty infant but as an old and failing woman; one may trace the triumphant spread of *The Unquenchable Light* through storm and shadow, but one may not ask why Jesus himself insisted that the Light was to be taken away.[2] Church history seems to be resolved never to raise the fundamental question of survival as the only way of avoiding a disastrous answer, and the normal reaction to the question—did the church remain on earth?—has not been serious inquiry in a richly documented field, but shocked

"The Passing of the Church: Forty Variations on an Unpopular Theme" first appeared in Church History, *20 (June 1961): 131–154. It was reprinted under the title "The Passing of the Primitive Church" in* When the Lights Went Out *(Salt Lake City: Deseret 1970): 1–32. This article also appeared in BYU Studies 16 (1975): 139–64.*

recoil from the edge of an abyss into which few can look without a shudder.[3]

Yet today that question is being asked again, as it has been in other times of stress and crisis, not with the journalistic flourish of Soltau's *Sind wir noch Christen*? but with the cautious historical appraisal of an H. J. Schoeps, contemplating the age-old tension between eschatology and church with their conflicting ideas about the church's future. Can it be that the repugnance of churchmen to eschatology and their coolness toward the authentic writings of the early Fathers are due in no small part to the dim view which the primitive Christians took of the prospects of the church?[4] The purpose of this paper is to list briefly the principal arguments supporting the thesis that the church founded by Jesus and the apostles did not survive and was not expected to. We shall consider the fate of the church under three heads: (1) the declarations of the early Christians concerning what was to befall it; (2) their strange behavior in the light of those declarations; (3) the affirmations and denials, doubts and misgivings of the church leaders of a later day. Our *theme* is the Passing of the Church, our *variations*, designated below by Roman numerals, are a number of striking and often neglected facets of church history.

The Early Christian View: Christian apologists had a ready answer to those shallow-minded critics who made merry over Christ's failure to convert the world and God's failure to protect his saints from persecution and death: God does not work that way, it was explained, his rewards are on the other side, and his overwhelming intervention is reserved for the *eschaton*, until which all sorts of reverses can be expected— *nihil enim est nobis promissum ad hanc vitam*; the prospect of failure and defeat in the world, far from being incompatible with the gospel message, is an integral part of it.[5]

(I) Jesus announced in no uncertain terms that his message would be rejected by all men, as the message of the prophets had been before,[6] and that he would soon leave the world to die in its sins and seek after him in vain.[7] The Light was soon to depart, leaving a great darkness "in which no man can work" while "the prince of this world" would remain, as usual, in possession of the field.[8] (II) In their turn the disciples were to succeed no better than their Lord: "If they have called the master of the house Beelzebub, how much more shall they call them of his household?"[9] Like him they were to be "hated of all men," going forth as sheep among wolves, "sent last as it were appointed unto death,"[10] with the promise that as soon as they completed their mission the end would come.[11]

(III) But what of the church? Those who accepted the teaching were to suffer exactly the same fate as the Lord and the apostles; they were advised to "take the prophets for an example of suffering affliction and patience," and to "think it not strange concerning the fiery trial which is to try" them, but rejoice rather to suffer as Christ did "in the flesh . . . that we may also be glorified together."[12] After them too the prince of this world was waiting to take over; they too were to be lambs among wolves, rejected as were the Master and the disciples: "The world knoweth us not because it knew him not."[13] Knowing that "whosoever will save his life must lose it," they openly disavowed any expectation of success, individual or collective, in this world.[14] (IV) As for the doctrine, it was to receive the same rough treatment, soon falling into the hands of worldly men who would "pervert the gospel of Christ" from a thing the world found highly obnoxious to something it was willing to embrace, for such has always been the fate of God's revelations to men.[15]

(V) All this bodes ill for the "interval" between the Ascension and the Parousia; the *Zwischenzeit* was to be a bad time and a long one.[16] What is more, it begins almost immediately, the apostles themselves calling attention to all the fatal signs, and marveling only that it has come so soon.[17] As soon as the Lord departs there comes "the lord of this world, and hath nothing in me"; in the very act of casting out the Lord of the vineyard the usurpers seize it for themselves, to remain in possession until his return;[18] no sooner does he sow his wheat than the adversary sows tares, and only when the Lord returns again can the grain be "gathered together," i.e., into a church, the ruined field itself being not the church but specifically "the world."[19] After the sheep come the wolves, "not sparing the flock," which enjoys no immunity (Acts 20:29); after sound doctrine come fables;[20] after the charismatic gifts only human virtues (1 Corinthians 13:8, 13). The list is a grim one, but it is no more impressive than (VI) the repeated insistence that *there is to be an end*, not the end of the world, but "the consummation of the age."[21] It is to come with the completion of the missionary activities of the apostles, and there is no more firmly rooted tradition in Christendom than the teaching that the apostles completed the assigned preaching to the nations in their own persons and in their own time, so that the end could come in their generation.[22]

(VII) It was no imaginary end. When the saints were asked to "endure to the end," that meant just one thing, as Tertullian observes—to suffer death.[23] When the sorely pressed Christians need "a strong comfort," the only comfort forthcoming is the promise of the resurrection and the assurance of salvation "whether we live or die."[24] Never is there any mention of relief on the way, of happy times ahead, of final victory for the cause, or of the consoling thought that generations yet unborn will call one blessed. Such assurances belong to a later age; the only encouragement the first Christians ever got is that given to soldiers making a last-ditch stand: they are ordered not to attack but "to have long patience," grimly hanging on "to the end," because only by so doing can they show their worthiness to inherit eternal life.[25]

But we are told not only of one but explicitly of *two* ways in which the ancient church was to make its exit. (VIII) For far more numerous than those true saints who were to give their lives as witnesses were those who were to succumb to the blandishments of false teachers. The fate of the vast majority of Christians was not to be overcome by a frontal attack—true martyrs were relatively few—but to be led astray by perverters.[26] The spoilers do not destroy the vineyard, but "seize the inheritance" for themselves; we read of betrayal, disobedience, corruptions; of deceivers, perverters, traitors; of wresting the scriptures, denying the gifts, quenching the Spirit, turning love into hate, truth to fables, sheep to wolves; of embracing "another gospel," and so forth. The offenders are not pagans but loudly professing Christians.[27] As, once the prophets are dead, everyone paints their tombs with pro-testations of devotion, so "when the master of the house has risen up and shut the door," shall the eager host apply for admission to his company—too late.[28] The apostasy described in the New Testament is not *desertion* of the cause, but *per-version* of it, a process by which "the righteous are removed, and none perceives it."[29] The Christian masses do not realize what is happening to them; they are "bewitched" by a thing that comes as softly and insidiously as the slinging of a noose.[30] It is an old familiar story, as Bultmann notes: "The preaching of Jesus does not hold out any prospect for the future of the people. . . . The present people does not behave otherwise than its predecessors who had persecuted and killed the prophets. . . . The message of Jesus does not contain any promise of the splendid future of Israel."[31] (IX) As is well known, the early Christians viewed the future with a mix-ture of fear and longing, of longing for the triumphant return of the Lord, but of deadly fear of the long and terrible rule of the *Cosmoplanes* that had to come first. So great is the dread of what they know lies ahead, that devout fathers of the church pray for the indefinite postponement of the Day of the Lord itself as the price of delaying the rule of dark-ness.[32]

(X) The Apostolic Fathers denounce with feeling the all too popular doctrine that God's church simply cannot fail.

All past triumphs, tribulations, and promises, they insist, will count for nothing unless the people now repent and stand firm in a final test that lies just ahead; God's past blessings and covenants, far from being a guarantee of immunity (as many fondly believe) are the very opposite, for "the greater the knowledge we have received, the greater rather is the danger in which we lie."[33] The case of the Jews, to say nothing of the fallen angels, should prove that we are never safe.[34] God will surely allow his people to perish if they continue in the way they are going—he will hasten their dissolution: "Since I called and ye hearkened not . . . therefore I in my turn will laugh at your destruction. . . . For there will come a time when you will call upon me and I shall not hear you."[35] The Apostolic Fathers compare the church to fallen Israel, and confirm their solemn warnings by citing the most lurid and uncompromising passages of scripture.[36] (XI) They see the church running full speed in the wrong direction, and in great distress of mind plead with it to do an about-face "before it is too late," as it soon will be.[37] For their whole concern is not to make new converts, but rather "to save from perishing a soul that has already known Christ," seeing to it that as many as possible pass "the fiery test ahead," keep the faith that most are losing, and so reach the goal of glory beyond.[38] They know that the names of Christ and Christian carry on, but find no comfort in that, since those names are being freely used by impostors and corrupters,[39] whom "the many" are gladly following.[40]

(XII) The call to repentance of the Apostolic Fathers is a last call; they labor the doctrine of the Two Ways as offering to Christian society a last chance to choose between saving its soul by dying in the faith or saving its skin by coming to terms with the world.[41] They have no illusions as to the way things are going: the church has lost the gains it once made, the people are being led by false teachers,[42] there is little to hinder the fulfillment of the dread (and oft-quoted) prophecy, "the Lord shall deliver the sheep of his pasture and their fold and their tower to destructions."[43] The original tower with its perfectly cut and well-fitted stones is soon to be taken from the earth, and in its place will remain only a second-class tower of defective stones which could not pass the test.[44] In the *Visions* of the *Pastor of Hermas* the church is represented as an old and failing lady—"because your spirit is old and already fading away"—who is carried out of the world; only in the world beyond does she appear as a blooming and ageless maiden.[45] The Apostolic Fathers take their leave of a church not busily engaged in realizing the kingdom, but fast falling asleep; the lights are going out, the Master has departed on his long journey, and until he returns all shall sleep. What lies ahead is the "Wintertime of the Just," the time of mourning for the Bridegroom, when men shall seek the Lord and not find him, and "seek to do good, but no longer be able to."[46]

*Strange Behavior:*What the strangely negative behavior of the first Christians suggests is less the expectation of an immediate Parousia than the shutting up of the shop until a distant reopening. (XIII) It has often been noted that their public relations were the world's worst, that they "could not and did not court publicity outside the movement."[47] In sharp contrast to the later church, they were convinced, as Hilary observes, that the church "could not be Christ's unless the world hated it."[48] The disciples, following the example and precept of their Master, made no effort to win public sympathy and support.[49] This hard and uncompromising attitude has puzzled observers in every age, and indeed it makes little sense in an institution seeking either to convert the world or to survive in it.[50] None knew better than the Christians themselves that their intransigence had no survival value, and yet they went right on "turning the world upside down" and mortally offending respectable people.

(XIV) The first Christians maintained a strange and stubborn reticence on certain matters (including their beliefs about the Second Coming), even when their silence led to serious misunderstanding and persecution.[51] Even among the members the teaching was carefully rationed, for it was not the trivia but the high and holy mysteries, the most prized things of the kingdom, that were carefully kept out of circulation,[52] so that Origen can report no clear official teaching in his day "not only regarding minor matters, but on the very first principles of the gospel."[53] Critics and scholars since Celsus have been puzzled by this early Christian reticence on matters which, if the church was to carry on, should have been highly publicized.[54] And while Christians since Irenaeus have categorically denied that any teachings of the apostolic church were withheld, they have done so only to avoid the alarming implications of the primitive Christian reticence.[55]

(XV) Consistent with the policy of reticence is the strict limitation placed on the missionary activities of Jesus and his disciples, both in time and place, and their firm rejection of the highly successful proselytizing methods of the Jews. In his recent study of this anomaly, Joachim Jeremias has concluded that while Jesus did indeed envisage a universal call to the nations, he thought of it as coming only at the *eschaton* and not at the time of his mortal mission, which clearly did not have world conversion as its objective.[56]

(XVI) No less striking is the conspicuous absence of any missionary organization in the apostolic church, and the complete indifference of the Apostolic Fathers to the great business of converting the world.[57] Their prayer for the church is to be gathered *out* of the world, not spread abroad in it, and to be caught up into the kingdom, not to build it here.[58]

(XVII) Instead of settling down as the later Christians sensibly did to long-term projects of conversion, the early Christians were driven by the "keen sense of urgency and stress" that fills their writings. "The time is short" was the refrain, and the missionaries had only time to give a hasty warning message and be on their way. It seems, according to

K. Holl, that the apostles went about their business *ohne für die Zukunft zu sorgen*—without a thought for the future.[59] What strange missionaries! They never speak of the bright future ahead nor glory in its prospects, but seem quite prepared to accept the assurance that they would preach to a generation that would not hear them and that, as in the days of Noah, the end would follow hard upon their preaching.[60]

(XVIII) But if the early saints mention no glorious future for the church, when that should be their strongest comfort, they do shed abundant tears when they look ahead. If the fall of Jerusalem and the temple was to be the great opportunity for the church that later theologians insist it was, Christ and the early saints were not aware of it, for they give no indication of regarding the event as anything but tragic.[61] Paul viewed the future of the church "with tears" as, according to early accounts, did other leaders.[62] Apocryphal writings describe the apostles as weeping inconsolably when Jesus leaves them to their fates, and in turn the church shedding bitter tears for the loss of the apostles, that leaves it without guidance and counsel.[63] Whatever their historical value, such accounts convincingly convey a mood, and Kirsopp Lake recommended Browning's terrible *Death in the Desert* as the best background reading for understanding the state of mind of the church at the passing of the apostles—all is lost.[64]

(XIX) The failure of the apostles to leave behind them written instructions for the future guidance of the church has often been noted and sadly regretted. It is hard to conceive of such a colossal oversight if the founders had actually envisaged a long future for the church. The awkwardness of the situation is apparent from R. M. Grant's explanation of it, namely, that the apostles "did not live to see the Church fully organized and at work."[65] As if they should wait until the work was completed before giving instructions for completing it! Actually the most tragic disorganization and confusion followed hard upon the passing of the apostles, according to Hegesippus, and as a direct result of it.[66] Plainly the early leaders made no careful provision for the future, even as they "failed to compose anything that could properly be described as 'church-history' " in spite of their great interest in times, seasons and dispensations, and the imperative need and accepted use of sacred history in the economy of religious organizations. [67]

(XX) Then there is the total neglect of education in the early church, which G. Bardy would justify with desperate logic, arguing that education for the young was neglected because the church got its membership from converts among the adult population—*fiunt, non nascuntur Christiani.*[68] And were all those converts childless, and were there no children in the church for those three long centuries during which it was without schools? In view of the great emphasis placed on education by the church in the fourth century, its total neglect in the preceding centuries can only have been deliberate. Well might E. de Faye find it strange that Jesus "ne songe nullement à former une école de jeunes hommes qui . . . seraient les hérétiers de sa doctrine" ("does not think to form a school of young men who would be the heirs of his teaching"), for if there were to be heirs of the teaching such a provision was indispensable.[69] Why no education, then? Actually the Apostolic Fathers were greatly concerned about education, warning their people against the bad education of the world, and chiding them for their neglect of the only education that counted—that which prepared the young for the next life.[70]

(XXI) Neglect of standard education was matched by an equally disturbing indifference to the social and political problems which would necessarily be of vital concern to any enduring social institution. For years liberal scholars sought to discover a social gospel where none was to be found, and it is indeed hard to believe that a religion of brotherly love could so persistently ignore the crying social ills of the day.[71] But the Christians excused themselves with the explanation that more urgent business had priority—they had no *time* for such things.[72] Why not, if the church was to continue? (XXII) And why should a permanent and growing church refuse to invest in lands and buildings? For a long time eminent churchmen endorsed the old Christian prejudice against the construction of sorely needed church buildings.[73] But what could have been the original objection to anything as innocent and salutary as the building of a church? The early Christians tell us: the church cannot own real estate (they explain) because it is only here temporarily, and must never be allowed to forget that fact.[74] (XXIII) Hans Lietzmann has shown that when "the Church sojourning at Rome" or elsewhere writes to "the Church sojourning at Corinth" or elsewhere it means that both churches are thought of only as temporary visitors in their cities; collectively and individually the church was here only on a brief pilgrimage. They were *das wandernde Gottesvolk*, strangers and pilgrims all, destined for but a short time upon the earth.[75]

Planned Martyrdom: The strongest argument for the survival of the church is the natural reluctance of men to accept defeat—even temporary defeat—for the work of God: *"tot denique martyria in vacuum coronata?"* cries Tertullian, ignoring Polycarp's assurance that "all of these ran not in vain, because they are with the Lord in the place which is their due, with whom they also suffered. For they did not love this present world."[76] (XXIV) The loudly proclaimed objectives of the first martyrs do not include the future prosperity of the church. In bidding farewell to Jews and Gentiles Paul announces that his missions to them have been successful, not in terms of converts, but of clearing himself of a terrible responsibility: henceforth their blood is on their own heads; he has fulfilled his assignment successfully, for a crown awaits him—on the other side.[77] "Thus it appears," writes O. Cullmann, "that the coming of the Kingdom does not depend upon the success of this 'preaching' but only on the fact of the proclamation itself."[78] What does depend on the preaching is (1) the salvation of the preacher, who is under condemnation unless he bears witness and frees himself of "the blood of this generation," and (2) the convicting of a wicked world which must be "without excuse" in the day of judgment.[79] The preaching is not to convert the world but "for a witness"—*martyria* occurs more than six times as frequently as *kerygma* in the New Testament—and it has long been recognized that the primary qualification and calling of an apostle was to be an eye witness.[80] The calling of a witness is to preach to an unbelieving generation ripe for destruction, with the usual expectation (as the name "martyr" indicates) of being rejected and put to death.

(XXV) The strange indifference of the early martyrs to the future of a church for which later ages fondly believed they gave their lives has not received the comment it deserves. In a world in which a noble altruism was constantly on the lips of orators, in a society whose model citizen was that Pius Aeneas who promised his afflicted followers that grateful generations to come would call them blessed, and in a sect which placed brotherly love before all else, the Christian martyrs, unlike the pagan martyrs or Christian heroes of later times, never take comfort in the thought that others will profit by their sufferings, or that their deeds will be remembered and their names revered in ages to come. Ignatius, Andrew, and Perpetua will neither live nor die for the church, but talk of nothing but their personal glory with Christ hereafter, "for while he suffered for us, we suffer for ourselves."[81] This concept of martyrdom is the opposite of that which later prevailed, as Dionysius of Alexandria points out in a letter to Novatus, noting that whereas the early martyr was concerned "for his own soul alone . . . today the martyr thinks in terms of the whole Church."[82] Since the latter is the more humane and natural view, there must have been a very good reason for ignoring it. It could not have been that primitive Christians enjoyed suffering, for they did not;[83]

nor were they as self-centered even as the later Christians, who found in martyrdom the solace of matchless public acclaim and undying earthly renown.[84] The very tears of the early leaders show plainly enough (as Chrysostom often observes) that they were genuinely concerned about the future. If, then, the martyrs refuse to think and speak in terms of a continuing church, it is not because they are peculiarly self-centered people, but simply because they see no future for the church.

(XXVI) So firmly fixed in the Christian mind is the conviction that every true Christian, every saint, is by very definition a martyr, that when persecutions ceased devout souls felt themselves cheated, and new ways and means of achieving martyrdom had to be devised, though they were never more than substitutes for the real thing.[85] A telling argument for any sect seeking to prove its authenticity has ever been the claim to have more martyrs than the others,[86] while the largest church of all at the peak of its power must needs describe itself in pathetic terms as a persecuted little band of saints—for tradition will not allow any other kind of church to be the true one.[87] From the beginning the church is a community of martyrs, whose proper business is "nothing else than to study how to die";[88] and though "the final note is of the victory of God," as C. T. Craig observes, before that happy culmination John "seems to have anticipated a universal martyrdom for the Church."[89]

The Great Gap: That ominous gap in the records which comes just at the moment of transition from a world-hostile to a world-conditioned Christianity has recently received growing attention and a number of interesting labels, such as the lacuna, the eclipse, the void, the great vacuum, the narrows, the period of oblivion, etc.[90] Brandon compares it to a tunnel "from which we emerge to find a situation which is unexpected in terms of the situation which went before."[91] (XXVII) The church, that is, which comes out of the tunnel is *not* the church that went into it. The great gap is more than a mere absence of documents; it is an abrupt break in the continuity of the church, so complete as to prove to Theodore Brandt that "the living faith cannot be transmitted from past ages," which is at least an admission that it has not been.[92] The early Christians knew they were approaching a tunnel; they were acutely aware of "the terrible possibility of apostasy for the church"—not merely of apostasy *from* it,[93] and never doubted "the general apostasy which would precede the coming of the Messiah."[94] And the church of the next age is just as aware of having passed through the tunnel, and losing its more precious possessions in the process. (XXVIII) For after the passing of the apostles "le vide est immense" ("The void is immense"), since it was the presence of living witnesses that had made the original church what it was.[95] Henceforth the "Elders" of old are referred to as a fabulous race of beings endowed with gifts, powers, and knowledge far exceeding anything found on earth any more, and mere proximity to the apostles and the elders becomes a special mark of sanctity and authority.[96] As "the great lights went out" the most devoted Christians engaged in a wistful "Operation Salvage" to rescue what might still be saved of "those things which came by the living voices that yet remained."[97] What more eloquent commentary on the passing of the church?

(XXIX) At the same time a horde of deceivers "who up until then had been lurking in dark corners," as soon as they saw that there were no more apostles left to call them to account, came boldly forth, each claiming that he alone had the gnosis which the Lord had secretly imparted to the apostles after the resurrection.[98] Strangely, they met with no official opposition: the Fathers who oppose them emphatically disclaim any apostolic authority and, what is more, know of no one else who might have it.[99] "Nous sommes incapable", writes D. Busy, "d'expliquer comment, la terre entière se trouvant évangélisée, les prédicateurs de l'Evangile ont l'air de disparaître et laissent le champ libre aux faux méssies et aux faux prophètes; comme . . . la bête de la mer ne rencontre

plus la moindre résistance."[100] ("We are unable to explain
how, while the whole was being evangelized, the preachers
of the gospel seem to disappear and leave the field free for
false messiahs and false prophets; how . . . the beast of the
sea does not meet the least resistance".) The prophecy (2
Thessalonians 2:22) is no more puzzling than the event; for
the second century, the great moment of transition, is no age
of faith but "par excellence the age of Heresy."[101]

It was not a case of reformers or schismatics attacking
the main church—the problem was, since the Christians had
always rejected with contempt the argument of mere numbers,
to find the true church among a great number of sects, each
claiming to be the one true original article and displaying
facsimiles of ancient spiritual gifts, rites, and officers to prove
it.[102] Justin knows of no certain norm for distinguishing true
Christians from false, and Irenaeus struggles manfully but
vainly to discover one.[103] While the perplexed masses asked
embarrassing questions and flocked to the banner of any
quack who gave promise of possessing the gifts and powers,
especially prophecy, which it was commonly felt the church
should have inherited,[104] even the greatest churchmen hesi-
tated and wavered, unable to resist the appeal of the old
charismatic Christianity or to decide just where it was to be
found.[105] In the end, in Harnack's words, "Gnosticism won
half a victory," for if the "Gnostics-so-called" had to default
on electrifying promises which they could not fulfill, neither
was any found to match their false claims with the genuine
article, and the great surge of hope and enthusiasm that had
carried the Gnostics on its crest subsided in disillusionment
and compromise.[106]

(XXX) Still, the constant revival through the centuries of
the old stock Gnostic claim that the one true apostolic church
has by some miracle of survival come down to the possession of this or that group, is a perpetual reminder of the failure of subsequent Christianity to come up to the expectations
of the first church.[107] (XXXI) For the chronic discontent which

haunts the Christian churches is by no means limited to the lunatic fringe. The vigorous beginnings of monasticism and pilgrimage were frankly attempts to return to the first order of the church, with its unworldly austerities and its spiritual manifestations, and as such were viewed by official Christianity as a clear vote of no-confidence—a rebuke and repudiation of the system.[108]

(XXXII) Modern students have agreed in describing the second generation of the church as a time of spiritual decline and low vitality, of torpor and exhaustion, "a dull period of feeble originality and a dearth of great personalities."[109] "Enfin," writes G. Bardy, "c'est le tiedeur que domine."[110] Doctrinally it was a definite "Abfall vom Evangelium," with the basic teachings altered and denatured beyond recognition.[111] As "the understanding of the Spirit . . . became lost . . . and the Christian had to rely on his own powers," that Christian became calculating, complacent, and respectable, in a word, all that the first Christian was not.[112] The overall impression, Goguel reports, is "definitely one of decadence."[113]

Yet the same voices that bring these charges against the second generation unanimously approve the new mentality as a necessary coming down out of the clouds, a new-found sobriety and maturity, a sensible acceptance of the facts of life, as "uplifted eyes . . . [turned back] to earth . . . to find their assurance in hard facts."[114] At last, we are told, the Christian could enjoy "what he had been missing so long, the consideration and respect of the outside world."[115] Only by scrapping the old "evangelical eschatology," according to one Catholic authority, could "Christian morality and the Church itself . . . take on larger dimensions," this being (according to another) a necessary step "towards wider horizons than those to which the Galilean nucleus had chosen to confine itself."[116] One may well ask how wider horizons and larger dimensions could be achieved by a Christianity admittedly "more hard and fast, less spontaneous, and in a sense, more cramped" than what had gone before; J. de Zwaan, who describes it thus, marvels "that the main stream of Gospel-tradition could pass through these narrows."[117] But the larger dimensions were the intellectual splendors of Hellenism, toward which the Gnostic agitation had hurried the feet of the church, the new Christian culture substituting erudition for inspiration, the rhetoric of the schools for the gift of tongues, a *numerus episcoporum* for the *Spiritus per spiritalem hominem*,[118] and the orderly mechanics of ritual for the unpredictable operation of the spiritual gifts as "eschatological consciousness changed into sacramental piety."[119] "Christianity," wrote Wilhelm Christ, "was squeezed into a system congenial to pagan-Greek-rationalist thought, and in that safe protective suit of armor was able to face up to the world; but in the process it had to sacrifice its noblest moral and spiritual forces."[120] In paying the stipulated price for survival, the church of the second century proved what the early church knew so well, that whosoever would save his life must lose it.[121]

(XXXIII) The sensational change from the first to the second generation of the church was not, as it is usually depicted, a normal and necessary step in a long steady process of evolution. It was radical and abrupt, giving the old Christianity when set beside the new "tout l'aspect d'une anomalie," as Duchesne puts it—an anomaly so extreme that many scholars have doubted that the primitive church ever existed.[122] "Rapidity of evolution explains the difference between the gospels and the second century," we are assured.[123] But rapidity is the sign not of evolution but of revolution, and the second-century upheaval was no part of a continuing trend at all, for after that one tremendous shift there are no more such changes of course in the way of the church: henceforward fundamental attitudes and concepts remain substantially unchanged.[124] Eduard Norden has noted that early Christian literature had no literary predecessors

and no successors, but appears as a completely alien intru-
sion into the classical tradition, an incongruous and unwelcome interruption, an indigestible lump which, however, disappears as suddenly as it came, leaving the schoolmen to
resume operations as if nothing had happened. [125] The march
of civilization continued, but it was not the march of the
church.

Arguments for Survival: The arguments put forth by
those who would prove the survival of the church are enough
in themselves to cast serious doubts upon it. (XXXIV) The
first thing that strikes one is the failure of the ingenuity of
scholarship to discover any serious scriptural support for the
thesis. There are remarkably few passages in the Bible that
yield encouragement even to the most determined exegesis,
and it is not until centuries of discussion have passed that we
meet with the now familiar interpretations of the "mustard
seed" and "gates-of-hell" imagery, which some now hold to
be eschatological teachings having no reference whatever to
the success of the church on earth. [126]

The most effective assertions of survival are the rhetorical
ones. We have already referred to the subtle use of such
loaded terms as "the Infant Church," "the Unquenchable
Light," etc., which merely beg the question. Equally effective
is the "quand même" ("even though") argument, which frankly
admits the exceedingly dim prospects of the early church
and the scant possibility of survival and then, without further explanation, announces in awed and triumphant tones:
"But in spite of everything it *did* survive!" (XXXV) Survival
is admittedly a miracle and a paradox; its very incredibility
is what makes it so wonderful. [127] Ecstatic assertion alone
carries the day where any serious discussion of evidence would
mark one a cavilling cynic. For this argument comes right
out of the schools of rhetoric; its favorite image, that of the
storm-tossed ship which somehow never sinks because it bears
virtuous souls, is already a commonplace in the Roman schools
of declamation. [128] The thrilling voices that assure us that all

the powers of evil rage in vain are not those of the early Fathers, but of imperial panegyrists and spell-binding bishops of another day, with their comforting pronouncements that God has, as it were, invested so heavily in his church that he simply would not think of letting it fail at this late date. [129]

The strongest support of this "facile and dangerous optimism" has always been the decisive fact of survival itself, as proven by the undiminished eminence of the Christian name; only, in fact, if one defines apostasy as "a more or less express renunciation" of that name can the survival of the church be taken for granted, as it generally is. [130] But what is the authority of the Christian label when early apologists can declare that it has become meaningless in their time, being as freely employed by false as by true Christians? [131] Or when the Apostolic Fathers protest that vast numbers "bear the name deceitfully"? Or when Jesus himself warns that "many shall come in *my* name," and all of them falsely: "Believe none of them!" [132]

A favorite theme of fiction and drama has ever been the stirring victory of Christianity over all the powers and blandishments of paganism. But this was victory over a strawman, a papier-mâché dragon brought onto the stage to prove to a confused and doubting world that the right had been victorious after all. [133] The early leaders worried constantly, and only, about the enemy within; paganism, long dead on its feet, the butt of the schoolmen for centuries, was not the real enemy at all. (XXXVI) There were, to be sure, areas of doctrine and ritual in which paganism did present a real threat, but precisely there the church chose to surrender to the heathen, the pious economy of whose splendid festivals and the proud preeminence of whose venerated schools became an integral part of the Christian heritage. [134]

Christians have often taken comfort in the axiom that it is perfectly unthinkable that God should allow his church to suffer annihilation, that he would certainly draw the line somewhere. This is the very doctrine of ultimate immunity against which the Apostolic Fathers thunder, and later fathers remind us that we may not reject the appalling possibility simply because it is appalling.[135] (XXXVII) If wicked men can "kill the Prince of Peace," and Belial enjoy free reign as "the prince of this world;" where is one to draw the line at what is unthinkable? For Hilary the suggestion that Jesus actually wept is baffling, paradoxical, and unthinkable—"yet he wept!"[136] If "after the prophets came the false prophets, and after the Apostles the false apostles, and after the Christ the Antichrist," is it unthinkable that the church should likewise have a dubious successor?[137] After all, Christians like Jerome found it quite unthinkable that Rome could ever fall, and used identical arguments to affirm the ultimate impregnability of the church and the empire.[138] The hollowness of the rhetorical arguments for sure survival has become apparent in times of world-calamity, when the orators themselves have, like Basil and Chrysostom, suddenly reverted to the all-but-forgotten idiom of apocalyptic and eschatology, and asked, "Is it not possible that the Lord has already deserted us entirely?"[139] The question is the more revealing for being uttered with heavy reluctance and in times of deepest soul-searching.

(XXXVIII) How deeply rooted in Christian thinking was the belief that the church would pass away is seen in the remarkable insistence of the orators of the fourth century that the great victory of the church which at that time took everyone by surprise was actually a *restoration* of the church, which had passed away entirely: "We of the church were not half-dead but wholly dead and buried in our graves," the apostasy and the age of darkness had actually come as predicted, and were now being followed, as prophesied, by a new day of restoration.[140] Here was an explanation that fitted the traditional view of the future: the church, it was explained, is like the moon, a thing that disappears and reappears from time to time.[141] But if the fourth-century triumph was really that "restitution of all things" foretold by the apostle (Acts 3:21), it could only betoken the arrival of the *eschaton*, and so the orators duly proclaimed the dawn of the millennial day and the coming of the New Jerusalem. [142]

(XXXIX) One of the most significant things about "the glorious and unexpected triumph of the Church" was precisely that it *was* unexpected; everybody was surprised and puzzled by it. [143] It was not what people had been taught to expect, and the remedy for their perplexity was a bold revamping of the story: "The facts speak for themselves," is Chrysostom's appeal, [144] and Eusebius sets his hand to a new kind of church history, with success—easy, inevitable success—as his theme. [145] Traditional concepts were quickly and radically overhauled. The familiar Two Ways were no longer the ways of light and darkness lying before Israel or the church, but the way of the church itself, Our church, *versus* the way of the opposition, whoever they might be. [146] "To endure to the end" no longer meant to suffer death but the opposite—to outlive one's persecutors and enjoy one's revenge. [147] The old warnings and admonitions were given a new and optimistic twist: "As it was in the days of Noah" now meant that all was well, since "the rains did not come until Noah was safely in the Ark"; [148] "No man knows the hour" becomes a *cura solicitudinis*, a comforting assurance that there was plenty of time and no need to worry; [149] "this generation shall not pass away" really meant that the generations of the church would *never* pass away. [150] It did not disturb a generation bred on rhetoric to be told that Peter heard with amazement that one should forgive seventy times seven, that being an announcement of the future generations that should believe. [151] Nor did it seem overbold to explain the prediction that the apostles should be hated of all men as a rhetorical exaggeration; [152] or to interpret the Lord's prediction that men would seek him in vain as proof of his presence in the church, which would render any searching a waste of time, i.e., vain;[153] for it is *not* the Lord but the devil who comes "as a thief in the night."[154]

One might fill a book with examples of such bold and clever rhetoric: the presence of wolves in the church simply fulfills the millennial promise that the wolf and the lamb shall graze together;[155] tares in the church are a sign of its divinity, since it must embrace all men, good and bad, to be God's church.[156] What really happened was that the sheep promptly routed the wolves and the wheat overcame the tares—not the other way around![157] It was easy to show that all the bad predictions were duly fulfilled—on the heads of the Jews—while all the good promises made to *them* were properly meant for the Christians. The tears of the apostles were actually the happiest of omens for the church, exciting in all beholders, by a familiar rhetorical trick, those feelings of pity and devotion which would guarantee unflinching loyalty to the cause forever.[158] It is fascinating to see how Chrysostom can turn even the most gloomy and depressing reference to the future of the church into a welcome promise of survival: the very fact that the ancient saints *worried* about things to come proves that there was to be a future, and so—delightful paradox!—they had nothing to worry about![159] If it can be said of the orating bishops that "the true size and color of every object is falsified by the exaggerations of their corrupt eloquence,"[160] it must also be noted that these were not wanton or irresponsible men, but devoted leaders desperately desirous of assuring themselves and their people of the unassailable integrity of the church: John Chrysostom repeatedly declares that the church is higher, holier, and (above all) more enduring than heaven itself.[161] He could do that (on the authority of Luke 21:33) without a blush because rhetoric had transferred the church into a glorious abstraction, a noble allegory, and as such an eternal, spiritual, indestructible entity.[162] On the other hand he *had* to do it to meet the importunities of those who beset him

night and day "unceasingly and everlastingly" with searching and embarrassing questions as to whether the church still
possessed those things which in the beginning certified its
divinity.[163]

(XL) Where no rhetorical cunning could bridge the gap
between the views of the fourth century and those of the
early church, the latter were frankly discounted as suitable
to a state of immaturity beyond which the church had hap-
pily progressed, emancipated from the "childish tales and
vaporings of old grandmothers."[164] The learned fathers of
the fourth and fifth centuries boast that the wise and noble
who shunned the primitive church are now safe in a bosom
of a Christian society which preaches and practices things
that would have frightened off the rude converts of an earlier
day,[165] and invoke the eloquence of Demosthenes against the
simplicitatem rusticam of the literal minded.[166] This has been
the official line ever since, and modern churchmen duly shudder at the thought of being "at the mercy of the primitive
Church, *its* teachings, *its* life, *its* understanding,"[167] and con-
gratulate themselves on having outgrown the "fond imaginings
of the Apostles."[168]

The Dilemma: Ever since the recent "rediscovery of the
importance of eschatology within the New Testament"[169] scholars have been faced, we are told, with a choice between
eschatology and history—*tertium non datur*. ("there is no
third choice")[170] Actually there has always been a third choice,
namely to accept the passing of the church as the fulfillment
of prophecy in history. But that, of course, is exactly what
church history will not allow: "Modern New Testament
critics," writes R. M. Grant, "insist on the priority of the
Church to its written records."[171] The church must be rescued at all price. For that reason it has been necessary to
ignore Jeremias' simple and obvious solution to the
"vollendeter Widerspruch" ("complete contradiction") between
the conflicting missionary policies of the early church: the
limited preaching belongs to one act of the play, the world

preaching to another.[172] This is a thing that Christians will not concede, for if the church is to remain on the scene, the drama must be one act or none.[173]

To preserve this hypothetical unity students have ascribed to the first Christians a fantastic one-package view of the future in which all the culminating events of prophecy are fulfilled at a single stupendous blow, "gathering up into one great climax the many judgments the . . . prophets had foretold."[174] When the great event failed to transpire, the great delay turned the great expectation into the great fiasco (the terms are not ours!), the church passing through the great disappointment to the real fulfillment, the great triumphal procession of the kingdom through the world. Such an unflattering view of the founders' foresight is forced on the experts by a constitutional inability to think of the church as anything but a permanent and growing institution.[175] It was this very attitude, it will be recalled, toward his own church that made it impossible for Trypho the Jew to accept Justin's complicated Messianic history.

But though the "great misunderstanding" theory has the merit of preserving the integrity of the church, it gravely jeopardizes the integrity of its founders while failing to give due consideration to certain peculiar and significant facts, viz., that the early Christians did not predict an immediate culmination of everything, but viewed the future down a long vista of prophetic events having more than one "end";[176] that not a single verse of scripture calls for an immediate Parousia or end of the world;[177] that there is a notable lack of evidence for any early Christian disappointment or surprise at the failure of the Parousia.[178] While the enemies of the church exploited every absurdity and inconsistency in its position and made merry over "Jesus the King who never ruled," they never played up what should have been the biggest joke of all—the feverish, hourly expectation of the Lord who never came. For R. Eisler this strange silence is nothing less than "the most astonishing of all historical

paradoxes."[179] But what makes it such is only the refusal of
the evidence to match the conventional pattern of church
history: if there are no signs whatever of blasted hopes and
expectations, we can only conclude that there were no such
expectations. There *were* indeed Christians who looked for
an immediate coming of the Lord and asked, "Where are the
signs of his coming?" but they are expressly branded by the
early leaders as false Christians, just as the virgins who
expected the quick return of the Master, who "delayed his
coming," were the foolish ones.[180]

Students of church history have long been taught that
whereas the primitive saints, living in an atmosphere of feverish expectation, looked forward momentarily to the end of
everything, the later Christians gradually sobered up and
learned to be more realistic. Exactly the opposite was the
case, for while there is no evidence that the sober first Christians thought the end of the world was at hand, there is
hardly a later theologian who does not think so: "From the
days of the early church, through the vicissitudes of the
lengthening middle centuries, into the twilight of the medieval day, the conviction of the world's end . . . was part and
parcel of Christian thought."[181] It had to be the end of the
world, because the end of the church was inadmissible. Yet
such was not the case with the first Christians, thoroughly at
home with the idea that divine things, while they are preexistent and eternal, are taken away from the earth and restored
again from time to time.[182] If the church comes and goes like
the moon, it is only with reference to this temporal world
where all things are necessarily temporary.[183] A great deal of
attention has been given in recent years to early Christian
and Jewish concepts of time and history. The present tendency is to treat the church as existing *"sub specie aeternitatis,
et pourtant dans le temps"* (*"sub specie aeternitatis,* and yet
in time") as a supernatural and eschatological entity, "eine
Schöpfung von oben her" ("a creation from above").[184] This

releases it from earthly bonds, as does Ambrose's declaration that the *civitas* "which lives forever, because it cannot die," desires only to leave the earth in all possible haste and be caught up, literally as Elijah was, into heaven.[185]

To escape the dark interval between the apostles and the Parousia, scholars have bored two exits. The one recognizes a catastrophe ahead but postpones it to a vague and distant future,[186] while the other admits that it was near at hand but insists that the damage was not so bad after all.[187] Thus both convictions of the early church, that the end was *near* and that it was to be *disastrous*, receive reluctant confirmation— for no one suggests that only a distant *and* partial disruption was expected. There is a third escape hatch, around which there has been much milling and crowding in recent years, but it seems to be only a false door, a semantic exercise in which the conflicting claims of eschatology and history are simply placed side by side and declared reconciled in various ingenious and symbolic ways. If this vast literature of double-talk, "bewildering in its variety,"[188] shows any perceptible trend, it is an inclination to have eschatology, since it can no longer be brushed aside, swallowed alive by the church: "The Church is an 'eschatological community,' since she is the New Testament, the ultimate and final. . . . The doctrine of Christ finds its fulness and completion in the doctrine of the Church, i.e. of 'the Whole Christ.' "[189] Such language actually seeks to de-eschatologize eschatology by making "mythical and timeless what they [the early Christians] regarded to be real and temporal."[190]

More to the point is the searching question of Schoep with which we began this survey, whether after all the real church may not have been left behind in the march of history: "Waren sie am Ende doch die wahren Erben, auch wenn sie untergingen?" ("at the end were they the real heirs, even if they perished?")[191] We have indicated above some of the reasons for suggesting that the church, like its founder, his apostles, and the prophets before them, came into the world, did the works of the Father, *and then went out of the world*, albeit with a promise of return. Some aspects of the problem, at least, deserve closer attention than students have hitherto been willing to give them.

NOTES

1. Karl Bihlmeyer, *Kirchengeschichte* (Paderborn: Schönigh, 1951), 1. Teil, 1–2.

2. "There is always danger of a metaphor once adopted becoming the master instead of the servant," writes E. A. Payne, commenting on K. S. Latourette's "Unquenchable Light" in "The Modern Expansion of the Church: Some Reflections on Dr. Latourette's Conclusions," *Journal of Theological Studies* 47 (1946): 151.

3. While suspecting the worst, the Fathers could not bring themselves to admit it, according to John Kaye, *Ecclesiastical History of the Second and Third Centuries, Illustrated from the Writings of Tertullian* (London: Farran, 1894), 48–51. See note 139 below.

4. The tension is discussed by René Marlé, "Le Christ de la foi et le Jésus de l'Histoire," *Études* 302 (1959): 67–76. Cf. Robert M. Grant, "The Appeal to the Early Fathers," *Journal of Theological Studies*, n.s. 11 (1960): 14, 23.

5. Arnobius, *Adversus Gentes (Against the Heathen)* 2, 76, in *PL* 5:934a; 2 Corinthians 4:8–18; Tertullian, *Ad Scapulam (To Scapula)* 1, in *PL* 1:775–80; Cyprian, *Epistolae (Letters)* 56, in *PL* 4:362.

6. Matthew 17:12; 21:37–39; 23:31–37; Mark 12:6–8; Luke 17:25; John 1:5, 10–11; 3:11–12, 19, 32; 5:38, 40–47; 7:7; 8:19, 23–24, 37–38, 40–47; 15:22–25; cf. Acts 3:13–15.

7. Matthew 9:15; Luke 9:41; 13:25–27; 17:22; John 12:33–34; 12:35–36; 13:33; 14:30; 16:16; cf. Acts 3:21.

8. John 9:4–5; 14:30. Evil triumphs from Abel to the *eschaton*: Matthew 23:35–39; 17:12; Luke 11:51; *Recognitiones Clementinae (Clementine Recognitions)* 3, 61, in *PG* 1:1208.

9. Matthew 10:24–25; Mark 13:13; Luke 10:16; John 15:18–21; 17:14; Acts 28:26–27; Frederick C. Grant, "The Mission of the Disciples," *Journal of Biblical Literature* 35 (1916): 293–314.

10. Matthew 10:16–22, 28; 24:9; Mark 3:9; Luke 10:3; John 16:1, 2, 33; 1 Corinthians 4:9; Clement, *Epistola I ad Corinthios (First Epistle to the Corinthians)* 5, in *PG* 1:217–20.

11. Matthew 24:14; 28:20; Mark 13:10. Notes 17 and 21 below.

12. James 5:10–11; 1 Peter 1:6–7, 24; 4:12–14; Romans 8.

13. 1 John 3:1; 1 Peter 5:1; John 17:25.

14. Matthew 16:24–26; 2 Corinthians 4:8–16; Philippians 3:1–21; Luke 12:22–34.

15. Jude 4–11, 16–19; Matthew 13:13–30; Romans 1:16–32; 2 Corinthians 11:3–4; 2 Thessalonians 2:7–12; 1 Timothy 4:1–3; 6:20–21; 2 Timothy 4:3–4; 2 Peter 2:1–22.

16. It ends only with the second coming, Matthew 13:30, 39–43; Mark 12:9; 2 Thessalonians 2:8; Didache 16; Justin Martyr, *Dialogus cum Tryphone (Dialogue with Trypho)* 51, 2, in *PG* 6:588–89.

17. 1 John 3:1; John 17:25; 1 Peter 5:8.

18. John 14:30; Matthew 21:38; Mark 12:7; Luke 20:14.

19. Matthew 13:24–30, 38. Both *syllegein* and *synagogein* are used.

20. 2 Timothy 4:2–4; 2 Thessalonians 2:9–12; Romans 1:21–31.

21. Matthew 24:14; cf. 10:23; 28:20, where *aeon* refers to that particular age, Oscar Cullmann, "Eschatology and Missions in the New Testament," in William D. Davies & D. Daube, eds., *The Background of the New Testament and Its Eschatology* (Cambridge: Cambridge University Press, 1956), 417; cf. Niels Wilhelm Messel, *Die Einheitlichkeit der jüdischen Eschatologie* (Giessen: Töpelmann, 1915), 61–69, 44–50. See note 182 below.

22. Mark 13:9–10; Acts 2:16–17, 33; Origen, *Commentaria in Evangelium Secundum Matthaeum (Commentary on Matthew)* 39, in *PG* 13:1655B, concludes that, strictly speaking, *jam finem venisse*; so also John Chrysostom, *In Epistolam ad Hebraeos (On the Epistle to the Hebrews)* 21, 3, in *PG* 63:152.

23. Tertullian, *Adversus Gnosticos Scorpiace (Scorpiace)* 9–10, in *PL* 2:162–67; 13–15, in *PL* 2:171–75; Ignatius, *Epistola ad Polycarpum (Epistle to Polycarp)* 3, in *PL* 5:709; *Epistola ad Ephesios (Epistle to the Ephesians)* 9, in *PL* 5:652.

24. Hebrews 6:11; Philippians 3:8–10; 1 Peter 1:4–6, 9; Clement, *Epistola II ad Corinthios (Second Epistle to the Corinthians)* 5, 2–4 in *PG* 1:336; Barnabas, *Epistola Catholica (Catholic Epistle)* 8, 6, in *PG* 2:748; Justin, *Apologia pro Christianis (Apology)* I, 57, in *PG* 6:413–16.

25. Mark 13:34–37; 1 Peter 4:12–13. Like soldiers, each to remain at his post, Clement, *First Epistle to the Corinthians* 37, in *PG* 1:281–84; 21, in *PG* 1:256; Tertullian, *Liber ad Martyres (To the Martyrs)* 3, in *PL* 1:707–9; cf. Clement, *First Epistle to the Corinthians* 5, in *PG* 1:217–20; Ignatius, *Epistle to Polycarp* 3, in *PL* 5:709–10;

196   MORMONISM AND EARLY CHRISTIANITY

Epistola ad Magnesios (Epistle to the Magnesians) 5, in *PG* 5:761-64; Barnabas, *Catholic Epistle* 2, 1, in *PG* 2:729-30.

26. "Ita ut pauci remaneant certantes pro veritate usque ad finem, qui et salvandi sunt soli." Origen, *Commentary on Matthew* 24, in *PG* 13:1654D. There were few martyrs; G. de Ste. Croix, "Aspects of the 'Great' Persecution," *Harvard Theological Review* 47 (1954): 104, and countless betrayers, W. H. Frend, "Failure of the Persecutions in the Roman Empire," *Past and Present* 16 (November 1959): 15-16.

27. Early sources speak of two factions within the church, and of the "seducers" completely exterminating the righteous party, Carl Schmidt, *Gespräche Jesu mit seinen Jüngern* (Leipzig: Hinrich, 1919), in *TU* 43: 196-98; cf. Samuel G. F. Brandon, *The Fall of Jerusalem and the Christian Church* (London: Society for the Promotion of Christian Knowledge, 1951), 54.

28. Luke 13:25-30; Matthew 23:29. There is a time limit to the promise, Hebrews 12:17, and "when the tower is finished, you will wish to do good, and will have no opportunity," *Pastor Hermae (Shepherd of Hermas)*, *Visio (Visions)* 3, 9, in *PG* 2:907.

29. Justin, *Dialogue with Trypho* 110, in *PG* 6:729; Hilary, *Contra Constantium Imperatorem (Against the Emperor Constantius)* 4, in *PL* 10:581B.

30. Galatians 3:1-4. Ignatius describes the corruption with striking imagery as of pleasing and plausible wolves, *Epistola ad Philadelphenses (Epistle to the Philadelphians)* 2, in *PG* 5:697-708, a goodly label on a bottle of poison, a deadly drug mixed with sweet wine, *Epistola ad Trallianos (Epistle to the Trallians)* 6, in *PG* 5: 679-80, counterfeit coin, *Epistle to the Magnesians* 5, in *PG* 5:647-48, cleverly baited hooks, ibid., 11, in *PG* 5:653-56, etc.

31. Bultmann, "History and Eschatology in the New Testament," *New Testament Studies* 1 (1954): 7-8.

32. A mixture of "Freude, Sehnsucht, und bange Furcht," Rudolf Knopf, *Die Zukunftshoffnungen des Urchristentums* (Tübingen: Mohr, 1907), 7-11. Cf. Didache 16.

33. Clement, *First Epistle to the Corinthians* 41, 4, in *PG* 1: 289-92; "The last stumbling-block approaches," Barnabas, *Catholic Epistle* 4, 3 and 9, in *PG* 2:731-34; Clement, *First Epistle to the Corinthians* 7, 1, in *PG* 1:221-25; Clement, *Second Epistle to the Corinthians* 7-8, in *PG* 1:337-41; *Shepherd of Hermas*, Visions 2, 2, in *PG* 2:897; 4, 1, in *PG* 2:909.

34. Clement, *First Epistle to the Corinthians* 15, 4-6, in *PG* 1: 237-40; 8, in *PG* 1:225-28; 39, in *PG* 1:285-88; 57, in *PG* 1:324-26; Clement, *Second Epistle to the Corinthians* 6, in *PG* 1:336-37;

Barnabas, *Catholic Epistle* 4–5, in *PG* 2:731–37; 13–14, in *PG* 2:765–69.

35. Clement, *First Epistle to the Corinthians* 57–58, in *PG* 1:324–28. The promise of the Paraclete is no guarantee, Clement, *Second Epistle to the Corinthians* 6, 9, in *PG* 1:336–37.

36. So Clement, *First Epistle to the Corinthians* 3–7, in *PG* 1:213–25; Barnabas, *Catholic Epistle* 2–6, in *PG* 2:729–44; 16, in *PG* 2:773–76; *Constitutiones Apostolicae (Apostolic Constitutions)* 7, 32, in *PG* 1:1621; Lactantius, *Divinae Institutiones (Divine Institutes)* VII, 17, in *PL* 6:1008–9.

37. Clement, *First Epistle to the Corinthians* 1, in *PG* 1:201; 3, in *PG* 1:213; 19, in *PG* 1:248; 41, in *PG* 1:289; 47, in *PG* 1:305–8; 52, in *PG* 1:316; Barnabas, *Catholic Epistle* 2, in *PG* 2:729; Ignatius, *Epistle to the Ephesians* 17, in *PG* 5:749–52; *Epistle to the Philadelphians* 2, in *PG* 5:820; *Shepherd of Hermas, Visions* 2, 2, in *PG* 2:897; 3, 9, in *PG* 2:907; *Similitudo (Similitudes)* 7, in *PG* 2:969–72; 9, 21 and 25–26, in *PG* 2:999–1002; 10, 1, in *PG* 2:1009.

38. *Didache* 10:5; Ignatius, *Epistle to Polycarp* 1, 2, in *PG* 5:861–64; *Epistle to the Ephesians* 17, in *PG* 5:749–52; *Epistle to the Philadelphians* 1, in *PG* 5:820; *Shepherd of Hermas, Similitudes* 9, 14, in *PG* 2:917; Barnabas, *Catholic Epistle* 2, 1, in *PG* 2:729; 21, in *PG* 2:779–81.

39. Clement, *First Epistle to the Corinthians* 15, in *PG* 1:237; 30, in *PG* 1:269–72; Clement, *Second Epistle to the Corinthians* 3–4, in *PG* 1:333–36; Barnabas, *Catholic Epistle* 10, 4, in *PG* 2:752–56; Ignatius, *Epistle to the Ephesians* 15, in *PG* 5:657; 7, in *PG* 5:649; *Epistle to the Magnesians* 4, in *PG* 5:648; *Epistle to the Trallians* 6, in *PG* 5:680; Polycarp, *Epistola ad Philippenses (Epistle to the Philippians)* 10, in *PG* 5:1013; *Shepherd of Hermas, Visions* 1, 3, in *PG* 2:893–96; *Similitudes* 9, 13, in *PG* 2:991; 9, 21, in *PG* 2:999.

40. Polycarp, *Epistle to the Philippians* 7, in *PG* 5:1012; *Shepherd of Hermas, Mandatum (Mandates)* 11, 1, in *PG* 2:943.

41. Ignatius, *Epistle to the Magnesians* 5, in *PG* 5:648; Clement, *Second Epistle to the Corinthians* 6, in *PG* 1:336–37; Barnabas, *Catholic Epistle* 5, in *PG* 2:733; 18, in *PG* 2:776; see Kirsopp Lake's note on the *Shepherd of Hermas* in his *Apostolic Fathers*, Loeb ed. (1912), 2:21, n. 1; reprinted Classic Library Series, vols. 9, 10 in two vols. (Cambridge, Mass.: Harvard University Press, 1970).

42. Clement, *First Epistle to the Corinthians* 1, in *PG* 1:201–8; 3, in *PG* 1:213–16; 19, in *PG* 1:248; 24, in *PG* 1:260–61; Ignatius, *Epistle to the Trallians* 7, in *PG* 5:764–65; *Epistle to the Ephesians* 9, 5, in *PG* 5:713; 17, in *PG* 5:749–52; *Shepherd of Hermas, Visions* 3, 3, in *PG*

2:901; 10, in *PG* 2:907. Cf. Testament of Hezekiah 2:3B-4:18 in *OTP* 2:159-61.

43. Barnabas, *Catholic Epistle* 16, in *PG* 2:771-76; Didache 16:3; Enoch 89; 56; 66-67; Logion 14, in "Prétendues sentences de Jésus," in *PO* 4:176-77; cf. "Le Salut - les vieux sages," in *PO* 9:227-28.

44. *Shepherd of Hermas, Visions* 3, 3-7, in *PG* 2:901-6.

45. Ibid., 3, 11-13, in *PG* 2:907-10.

46. *Shepherd of Hermas, Similitudes* 3, in *PG* 2:955; 4, in *PG* 2: 955-58; 9, in *PG* 2:979-1010; Clement, *First Epistle to the Corinthians* 58, in *PG* 5:328; Eusebius, *HE* III, 31, 3, in *PG* 20:280-81; V, 24, 2, in *PG* 20:493-508.

47. A. D. Nock, "The Vocabulary of the New Testament," *Journal of Biblical Literature* 52 (1933): 135.

48. Hilary, *Liber contra Auxentium (Against Auxentius)* 4, in *PL* 10:611B.

49. K. Holl, "Urchristentum und Religionsgeschichte," *Zeitschrift für systematische Theologie* 2 (1924): 403-5; Suzanne de Dietrich, *Le Dessein de Dieu*, 2nd ed. (Neuchatel: Delachaux & Niestle, 1948), 19, finds only one case, Mark 5:19, in which Christ did not avoid publicity.

50. Origen, *Contra Celsum (Against Celsus)* 2, 76, in *PG* 11:848; 4, 28, in *PG* 11:1068; Minucius Felix, *Octavius* 7-11, in *PL* 3:262-81; Lactantius, *Divine Institutes* V, 7, in *PL* 6:991.

51. Minucius Felix, *Octavius* 9-10, in *PL* 3:270-76; Justin, *Dialogue with Trypho* 52, in *PG* 6:589-92 (the Parousia a secret); 90, 2, in *PG* 6:689-92; Tertullian, *Apologeticus adversus Gentes pro Christianis (Apology)* 7, in *PL* 1:358-62; *Clementine Recognitions* 1, 52, in *PG* 1:1236; Clement of Alexandria, *Stromata* 1, 12, in *PG* 8:753; 5, 10, in *PG* 9:93-101.

52. Matthew 13:9-17; *Clementine Recognitions* 2, 60, in *PG* 1:1264; 3, 1, in *PG* 1:1281-82; Tertullian, *De Praescriptionibus (The Prescription against Heretics)* 25-26, in *PL* 2:43-46; Origen, *Against Celsus* I, 1, 1-7, in *PG* 11:651-69; Ignatius, *Epistle to the Trallians* 5, in *PG* 5:781-84.

53. Origen, *Peri Archōn (On First Things)* I, 2, in *PG* 11:130-45; I, 4, in *PG* 11:155; I, 6-8, in *PG* 11:165-83.

54. Origen, *Against Celsus* 2, 70, in *PG* 11:905-8; Albert Schweitzer, *Geschichte der Leben-Jesu-Forschung* (Tübingen: Mohr, 1951), 396. This is an edition of the earlier *Von Reimarus zu Wrede;* cf. English translation, *The Quest of the Historical Jesus* (New York: Macmillan, 1961). Herman Gunkel, *Zum religionsgeschichtlichen Verständnis des Neuen Testaments* (Göttingen: Vandenhoeck &

Ruprecht, 1903), 78–79; Kirsopp Lake, *Introduction to the New Testament* (New York: Harper, 1937), 37.

55. Irenaeus, *Contra Haereses (Against Heresies)* IV, 33, 7, in *PG* 7:1076–77; II, 27, 1–3, in *PG* 7:802, insists that nothing has been lost, cf. I, 8, 1, in *PG* 7:519, etc., yet speaks with awe of the knowledge of the apostles, I, 13, 6, in *PG* 7:588; III, 2, 2, in *PG* 7:847, which Ignatius implies far exceeds his own, *Epistle to the Ephesians* 3, in *PG* 5:645; *Epistle to the Magnesians* 5, in *PG* 5:648; *Epistola ad Romanos (Epistle to the Romans)* 4, in *PG* 5:689. Later fathers were intrigued by the great unwritten knowledge of the apostles, Gottfried Thomasius, *Die christliche Dogmengeschichte als Entwicklungsgeschichte des kirchlichen Lehrbegriffs*, 2nd ed. (Erlangen: Deichert, 1886–89), vol. 1, *Dogmengeschichte der alten Kirche* (Erlangen: Deichert, 1886), 209, 297–98.

56. Joachim Jeremias, *Jesu Verheissung für die Völker* (Stuttgart: Kohlhammer, 1956), 15–16, 61–62 = *Jesus' Promise to the Nations*, tr. S. H. Hooke (London: SCM Press, 1958).

57. Albert Dufourcq, *Epoque syncrétiste. Histoire de la fondation de l'église, la révolution religieuse* (Paris: Blond, 1909), 220; Jeremias, *Jesu Verheissung für die Völker*, 17, 21, 60–61. Note 38 above.

58. Didache 10:5; Ignatius, *Epistle to the Romans* 7, in *PG* 5:693: "deuro pros ton patera"—literally.

59. Discussed by Olof Linton, *Das Problem der Urkirche in der neueren Forschung* (Uppsala: Almquist & Wiksell, 1932), 198–200.

60. Robert Eisler, *Iesous Basileus ou Basileusas*, 2 vols. (Heidelberg: Winter, 1930), 2:237.

61. Brandon, *The Fall of Jerusalem and the Christian Church*, 7–11.

62. *Homiliae Clementinae* XI, 16, 21, in *PG* 2:384A; Hippolytus, *De Consummatione Mundi* (spuria) *(On the Consummation of the World)* 10–11, in *PG* 10:913A–C; Athanasius, *Vita Antonii (Life of Antony)* 82, in *PG* 26:957.

63. *Acta Pilati* 15, in *PO* 9:108–9; James Rendell Harris, *Gospel of the Twelve Apostles*, 28, 33, 35, 38; A. W. Wallis Budge, *Contendings of the Apostles* 2 vols. (London: Oxford University Press, 1899–1901) 2:62, 53–55, 59.

64. Lake, *Introduction to the New Testament*, 62.

65. Robert M. Grant, *Second Century Christianity* (London: Society for Promoting Christian Knowledge, 1946), 9.

66. Eusebius, *HE* III, 32, 7–8, in *PG* 20:281–84.

67. Robert L. P. Milburn, *Early Christian Interpretations of History* (London: Black, 1954), 25–26.

200 MORMONISM AND EARLY CHRISTIANITY

68. Gustave Bardy, in *Revue des Sciences Religieuses* 12 (1932): 1, quoting Tertullian, *Apology* 18, 4, in *PL* 1:362-65.

69. Eugéne de Faye, *Étude sur les origines des églises de l'age apostolique* (Paris: Leroux, 1909), 111.

70. E.g., *Shepherd of Hermas*, Visions 1, 3, in *PG* 2:891-93; 2, 2, in *PG* 2:895-97; 3, 9, in *PG* 2:897; *Similitudes* 9, 19, in *PG* 2:997; *Mandates* 11-12, in *PG* 2:943; Clement, *First Epistle to the Corinthians* 21, in *PG* 1:256. Cf. Eusebius, *HE* V, 28, in *PG* 20:512; *Clementine Recognitions* 1, 1-5, in *PG* 1:1207-9.

71. See Marlé, "Le Christ de la Foi et le Jésus de l'Histoire," 67-76.

72. Origen, *Against Celsus* 8, 72 and 74, in *PG* 11:1624-29; Tertullian, *Apology* 38, in *PL* 1:526-31; *Apostolic Constitutions* 7, 39, in *PG* 1:1037-40; Barnabas, *Catholic Epistle* 2, in *PG* 2:729; 4, in *PG* 2:731; 1 Corinthians 7:29-32.

73. Origen, *Against Celsus* 8, 17-20, in *PG* 11:1540-49; Zeno, *Liber (Commentary)* 1, *Tractatus (Tractate)* 14, in *PL* 11:354B-358A; Minucius Felix, *Octavius* 10, in *PL* 3:274; Jerome, *Epistolae (Letters)* 130, 15, in *PL* 22:1119A; Arnobius, *Against the Heathen* 6, 1, in *PL* 5:1162B.

74. *Shepherd of Hermas*, *Similitudes* 1, 1, in *PG* 2:951; Clement, *Second Epistle to the Corinthians* 5, in *PG* 1:336; Cyprian, *Liber de Mortalitate (Treatise on Mortality)* 25, in *PL* 4:623B.

75. Hans Lietzmann, *Geschichte der alten Kirche* (Berlin: de Gruyter, 1932-34) 2:41-42 = *A History of the Early Church*, vol. 2, *The Founding of the Church Universal*, tr. Bertram Woolf (London: Nicholson & Watson, 1950); Ernst Käsemann, *Das wandernde Gottesvolk* (Göttingen: Vandenhoeck & Ruprecht, 1939), 51-52.

76. Tertullian, *The Prescription against Heretics* 27-29, in *PL* 2:46-48; Polycarp, *Epistle to the Philippians* 9, in *PG* 5:1012-13.

77. Acts 17:6; 2 Timothy 4:6-8. Conversion not the object, 1 Corinthians 1:17.

78. Oscar Cullman, in Davies & Daube, *Background of the New Testament and Its Eschatology*, 415.

79. 1 Corinthians 9:16; John 15:22; Matthew 23:34-35; 27:25; Luke 11:49-51; Acts 5:28; 18:6; *Clementine Recognitions* I, 8, in *PG* 1:1211, "tacere non possumus."

80. Oscar Cullman, *Urchristentum und Gottesdienst* (Zürich: Zwingli, 1950), 39-56.

81. Ignatius, *Epistle to the Romans* 6-8, in *PG* 5:691-94; *Epistle to the Ephesians* 11, 1, in *PG* 5:654; *Passio s. Perpetuae* 6; 18; 21. Quote from *Apostolic Constitutions* V, 5, in *PG* 1:833.

82. Eusebius, *HE* VI, 45, in *PG* 20:633.

83. Tertullian, *Apology* 1, in *PL* 1:305–8; Cyprian, *Treatise on Mortality* 12, in *PL* 4:611–12.

84. Eduard Norden, *Die antike Kunstprosa* (Leipzig: Teubner, 1898) 2:418–19, contrasts the early and later Christian concepts of martyrdom. The transition is clear in Cyprian, who must warn, "non martyres Evangelium faciant," *Letters* 24 (22), in *PL* 4:293A.

85. Cyprian, *Letters* 8, in *PL* 4:255A; *De Duplici Martyrio (On the Twofold Martyrdom)* 35, in *PL* 4:982A; Clement of Alexandria, *Stromata* IV, 7, in *PG* 8:1268–80; Leo, *Sermo* 47, 1, in *PL* 54:295B-C.

86. So Asterius Urbanus, *Fragmenta contra Montanistas (Against the Montanists)*, frg. 3; 6; 8, in *PG* 10:149B, 153A-B.

87. So Optatus, *De Schismate Donatistarum (On the Donatist Schism)* 17; 24–26, in *PL* 11:968–69, 979B-986A.

88. Cyprian, *Epistola ad Fortunatum (Letter to Fortunatus)*, Praefatio, in *PL* 4:678–82.

89. Clarence T. Craig, *The Beginnings of Christianity* (New York: Abingdon-Cokesbury, 1943), 328.

90. Pieter A. van Stempvoort, "Het onstaan van het Kerkbegrip en de oudste Kerkorganisatie," in J. H. Waszink et al., eds., *Het Oudste Christendom en de antieke Cultuur*, 2 vols. (Haarlem: Tjeenk Willink, 1951), 2:331; Brandon, *The Fall of Jerusalem and the Christian Church*, 9–11. The imagery goes back to Eusebius, *HE* I, 1, 3, in *PG* 20:48–53.

91. Brandon, *The Fall of Jerusalem and the Christian Church*, 10; Eduard Schwartz, *Kaiser Constantin und die christliche Kirche* (Leipzig: Teubner, 1913), 17–18; Hans Lietzmann, *Kleine Schriften* (Berlin: Akademie-Verlag, 1958–62) 1:97.

92. Theodore Brandt, *Die Kirche im Wandel der Zeit* (Leipzig: MBK-Verlag, 1933), 79.

93. E. C. Blackman, "The Task of Exegesis," in Davies & Daube, *Background of the New Testament and Its Eschatology*, 13.

94. Gustave Bardy, *La conversion au christianisme* (Paris: Aubier, 1949), 296.

95. Dufourcq, *Epoque syncrétiste. Histoire de la fondation de l'église*, 250; Maurice Goguel, *Les premiers temps de l'église* (Neuchatel: Delachaux et Niestlé, 1949), 139; and Maurice Goguel, "La seconde génération chrétienne," *Revue de l'Histoire des Religions* 136 (1949): 36–37.

96. Eusebius, *HE* III, 37, in *PG* 20:292–93; III, 39, in *PG* 20:292–302; Clement, *First Epistle to the Corinthians* 47, in *PG* 1:305–8; Polycarp, *Epistle to the Philippians* 3, in *PG* 5:1008; Ignatius, *Epistle to the Romans* 5, in *PG* 5:809–12; Irenaeus, *Against*

202 MORMONISM AND EARLY CHRISTIANITY

Heresies III, 3, 4, in PG 7:851; Methodius, Ex Libro de Resurrectione (From the Treatise on Resurrection) 6, in PG 18:313B.

97. Eusebius, HE III, 39, 1–4, in PG 20:297; V, 10, 4, in PG 20:453–56; XI, 3–5, in PG 20:456–57; Justin, Dialogue with Trypho 82, in PG 6:669–72; Origen, Against Celsus II, 8, in PG 11:805–8.

98. Eusebius, HE III, 32, 7–8, in PG 20:281–86; II, 1, 3, in PG 20:140–41; Irenaeus, Against Heresies I, in PG 7:437–45.

99. Polycarp, Epistle to the Philippians 3, in PG 5:1008; Barnabas, Catholic Epistle 1, 5, in PG 2:727; the case of Ignatius is discussed by Jean Réville, "Études sur les origines de le'épiscopat," Revue de l'histoire religieuse 22 (1890): 285–88.

100. D. Busy, in Recherches de science religieuse 24 (1934): 431.

101. Bardy, La conversion au christianisme, 306; Grant, Second Century Christianity, 9–18.

102. "Singuli quique coetus haereticorum se potissimum Christianos, et suam esse Catholicam Ecclesiam putant," Lactantius, Divine Institutes IV, 30, in PL 6:540–44; Eusebius, HE V, 13–18, in PG 20:460–81; Sozomen, HE V, 9, in PG 67:1237–40; V, 20, in PG 67:1277–80; VI, 26, in PG 67:1361–66; VIII, 20, in PG 67:1568–70, etc. Origen, Against Celsus III, 10–12, in PG 11:932–36.

103. Justin, Apology 8, in PG 66:338–40; Dialogue with Trypho 35, in PG 6:549–53; 42, in PG 6:565; 80, in PG 6:664–80; cf. Origen, Against Celsus VI, 11, in PG 11:1305–8.

104. Eusebius, HE V, 16, in PG 20:464–72; Justin, Quaestiones (Inquiries), nos. 100, 5, in PG 6:1344–45, 1256AB.

105. Sulpicius Severus, Historia Sacra (Sacred History) II, 46, in PL 20:155; II, 50, in PL 20:157–58. Eusebius worried too, Walther Völker, "Von welchen Tendenzen liess sich Eusebius bei Abfassung seiner 'Kirchengeschichte' leiten?" Vigiliae Christianae 4 (1950): 170–71.

106. Adolf von Harnack, Lehrbuch der Dogmengeschichte, 5th ed. 3 vols. (Tübingen: Mohr, 1931), 1:250; Eusebius, HE V, 15–16, in PG 20:172–73.

107. The Reformation itself attempted revival of "prophetic, eschatological Christianity," Heinrich Bornkamm, Grundriss zum Studium der Kirchengeschichte (Gütersloh: Bertelsmann, 1949), 63.

108. Adolf von Harnack, Das Mönchtum (Giessen: Ricken, 1895), passim. The church fathers did not encourage pilgrimages, Bernard Kötting, Peregrinatio Religiosa (Münster: Regensberg, 1950), 421.

109. Goguel, Les premiers temps de l'église, 34, 180, 192–94.

110. Bardy, *La conversion au christianisme*, 304; so Lietzmann, *Geschichte der alten Kirche* 1:226; Harnack, *Das Mönchtum*, 25.

111. Robert Frick, "Die Geschichte des Reich-Gottes-Gedankens," *ZNTW*, Beiheft 6 (1928): 154, 152–55; Goguel, *Les premiers temps de l'église*, 35; Harnack, *Das Mönchtum*, 25.

112. Bultmann, "History and Eschatology in the New Testament," 15.

113. Goguel, *Les premiers temps de l'église*, 191.

114. Milburn, *Early Christian Interpretations of History*, 26.

115. Gustave Bardy, *L'Eglise et les derniers Romains* (Paris: Laffont, 1948), 48.

116. F.-M. Braun, "Où en est l'eschatologie du Nouveau Testament," *Revue Biblique* 49 (1940): 53; Henri Leclercq, "Églises," in *DACL* 4:2281.

117. J. de Zwaan, "Some Remarks on the 'Church Idea' in the Second Century," in *Aux sources de la tradition Chrétienne, Mélanges offerts à M. Maurice Goguel à l'occasion de son soixante-dixiéme anniversaire* (Neuchatel: Delachaux & Niestlé, 1950), 278.

118. Tertullian, *De Pudicitia (On Modesty)* 21, in *PL* 2:1080B.

119. Bultmann, "History and Eschatology in the New Testament," 15.

120. Wilhelm Christ, *Geschichte der griechischen Literatur*, 6th ed. 2 vols. (Munich: Beck, 1912–20) 2:2:955.

121. "In the end therefore, it was the Christian doctrine and practice which underwent the change, and society which remained," Kirsopp Lake, "The Shepherd of Hermas and Christian Life in Rome in the Second Century," *Harvard Theological Review* 4 (1911): 25.

122. L. Duchesne, *Origenes du culte chrétien* 2nd ed. (Paris: Thorin, 1898), 52–53 (5th ed. [1920], 55).

123. Lake, *Introduction to the New Testament*, 22; Dufourcq, *Epoque syncrétiste. Histoire de la fondation de l'église*, 221.

124. Goguel, *Les premiers temps de l'église*, 209; Reinhold Seeberg, *Textbook of the History of Doctrines*, 2 vols. (Grand Rapids: Baker Book House, 1952) 1:118; Karl Adam, *Das Wesen des Katholizismus* (Düsseldorf: Schwann, 1934), 194 = *The Spirit of Catholicism*, tr. D. McCann (London: Sheed & Ward, 1929).

125. Norden, *Die antike Kunstprosa* 2:479–81.

126. Linton, *Das Problem der Urkirche in der neueren Forschung*, 160, 164–66; O. Kuss, "Zur Senfkornparabel," *Theologie und Glaube* 41 (1951): 40–46; Jeremias, *Jesu Verheissung für die Völker*, 58–59; cf. English ed., 68–69.

127. So Bardy, *La conversion au christianisme*, 6; Bornkamm, *Grundriss zum Studium der Kirchengeschichte*, 20.

128. Stanley Bonner, *Roman Declamation* (Liverpool: Liverpool University Press, 1949), 59.

129. "Animae emptae a Christo non potuerunt vendi," Optatus, *On the Donatist Schism* 3, 11, in *PL* 11:1024–25; E. Fascher, "Dynamis Theou," *Zeitschrift für Theologie und Kirche* 19 (1938): 108; Chrysostom exposes the fallacy, *In Epistolam ad Galatas Commentarius* (*Commentary on the Epistle to the Galatians*) 3, 2, in *PG* 61:649–50.

130. Bardy, *La conversion au christianisme*, ch. 8 entire. Refuted by John Chrysostom, *On the Epistle to the Hebrews* 5, Homily 8, in *PG* 63:73, and Salvianus, *De Gubernatione Dei* (*On the Government of God*) IV, 1, 61.

131. Justin, *Dialogue with Trypho* 35, in *PG* 6:549–53; Origen, *Against Celsus* III, 12, in *PG* 11:933–36.

132. Matthew 7:22; 24:5; Mark 9:39; 13:6; Luke 21:8; Acts 17:15.

133. E.g., the gloating attacks on the dead Julian, Norden, *Die antike Kunstprosa* 2:563.

134. Ibid., 2:460–62, 465, 476–77, 529–32, 680–83; Frend, "Failure of the Persecutions in the Roman Empire," 12.

135. Hippolytus, *Fragmenta in Danielem* (*Fragments on Daniel*) 5, 7, in *PG* 10:681D; *Demonstratio de Christo et Antichristo* (*On Christ and the Antichrist*) 29, 57–58, in *PG* 10:749B, 776B–777A; *On the Consummation of the World* 11, in *PG* 10:913C.

136. Hilary, *De Trinitate* (*On the Trinity*) 10, 55, in *PL* 10:387.

137. Quote is from John Chrysostom, *Commentary on Matthew* 46, 1, in *PG* 58:476.

138. Johannes Straub, "Christliche Geschichtesapologetik in der Krisis des römischen Reiches," *Historia* 1 (1950): 64.

139. Basil the Great, *Epistolae* (*Letters*) 150, 2, no. 139, in *PG* 32:584A. Tertullian, *The Prescription against Heretics* 27–28, in *PL* 2:46–47, must console himself with the argument of numbers. Even before Eusebius, *Praeparatio Evangelica* (*Preparation for the Gospel*) 1, 3, in *PG* 21:33, Hegesippus sought to reassure himself that there was an absolute continuity, according to L. Duchesne, *Le Liber Pontificalis* (Paris: Thorin, 1886–92) 1:1, who vainly seeks the same assurance, Henri Leclercq, "Historiens du Christianisme," *DACL* 6:2697.

140. Eusebius, *HE* X, 4, 12–16, in *PG* 20:857–60; VIII, 1, 8-ii, in *PG* 20:740–44; VIII, 1–3, in *PG* 20:744; cf. Sozomen, *HE* III, 17, in *PG* 67:1093–96. The church was overcome by its own sins, Cyprian,

Letters 7, in *PL* 4:246–51, cf. *Liber de Lapsis*, (*Book on the Apostates*), in *PL* 4:478–510. On the Restoration motif, see Michael S. Seidlmayer, "Rom und Romgedanke im Mittelalter," *Saeculum* 7 (1956): 405–7; John Edwin Sandys, *History of Classical Scholarship*, 3 vols. (New York: Hafner, 1958) 1:513–14.

141. Ambrose, *Hexaemeron* 4, 32, in *PL* 14:217–18; Methodius, *Convivium Decem Virginum* (*Banquet of the Ten Virgins*) 6, in *PG* 18:148B; Jerome, *Commentarius in Isaiam Prophetam* (*Commentary on Isaiah*) 18, 66, in *PL* 24:699–702; Lactantius, *Divine Institutes* V, 7, in *PL* 6:570–71.

142. Discussed by this writer, Hugh W. Nibley, "The Unsolved Loyalty Problem: Our Western Heritage," *Western Political Quarterly* 6 (1953): 641–46.

143. The surprise is expressed by John Chrysostom, *Expositio in Psalmos* (*Exposition on Psalms*) 148, 4, in *PG* 55:483–84, and *Contra Judaeos et Gentiles, quod Christus Sit Deus* (*Against the Jews and the Gentiles, that Christ is God*) 12, in *PG* 48:829–30; cf. the perplexity in Justin, *Inquiries*, 74, in *PG* 6:1316A.

144. John Chrysostom, *Sermo antequam Iret in Exsilium* (*Discourse before Going into Exile*) 1, 2, in *PG* 52:429–30; *In Illud, Vidi Dominum, Homilia* (*Homily on the Verse "I Have Seen the Lord"*) 4, 2, in *PG* 56:121.

145. Völker, "'Tendenzen in Eusebius' 'Kirchengeschichte,' " 161–80. J. Burckhardt calls Eusebius "the first thoroughly dishonest historian," cited by Moses Hadas, "The Conversion of Constantine," *Jewish Quarterly Review* 41 (1950): 423.

146. See Nibley, "The Unsolved Loyalty Problem: Our Western Heritage," 644–46.

147. Lactantius, *Divine Institutes* V, 24, in *PL* 6:630.

148. Eusebius, *Commentarius in Lucam* (*Commentary on Luke*) 27, 27, in *PG* 24:584D–585A.

149. Hilary, *Commentarius in Matthaeum* (*Commentary on Matthew*) 26, 4, in *PL* 9:1057B.

150. Eusebius, *Commentary on Luke* 13, 32, in *PG* 24:601D–604A.

151. John Chrysostom, *De Decem Millium Talentorum Debitore Homilia* (*Homily on the Man Who Owed Ten Thousand Talents*) 3, in *PG* 51:21B.

152. First suggested by Origen, *Commentary on Matthew* 39, in *PG* 13:1653D.

153. Hilary, *Commentary on Matthew* 25, 8, in *PL* 9:1055.

154. Ibid. 26, 6, in *PL* 9:1058B.

206	MORMONISM AND EARLY CHRISTIANITY

155. Eusebius, *Commentarius in Isaiam Prophetam* (*Commentary on Isaiah*) 11, 6, in *PG* 24:172C-173A.

156. Optatus, *On the Donatist Schism* 7, 2, in *PL* 11:1085B-1086A.

157. A favorite theme with Chrysostom, e.g., *Homily on the Verse "I Have Seen the Lord"* 4, 4, 2, in *PG* 56:121; *Sermo post Reditum ab Exsilio* (*Discourse Following the Return from Exile*) 2, in *PG* 52:440, 442; *Sermo Ipsius Severiani de Pace*, in *PG* 52:425; cf. Athanasius II, *Homilia de Semente* (*Homily on the Seed*) 5, in *PG* 28:149C.

158. John Chrysostom, *De Novem Diebus* (*On the Nine Days*) 6, in *PG* 56:277-78; Basil, *Homilia de Gratiarum Actione* 4, in *PG* 31:228A; Hilary, *On the Trinity* X, 39-43, in *PL* 10:374-77.

159. Chrysostom, *On the Nine Days* 6, in *PG* 56:277-78.

160. Edward Gibbon, *Decline and Fall of the Roman Empire*, 2 vols. (New York: The Modern Library, 1932), ch. 26, note 101; 1:941.

161. John Chrysostom, *De Capto Eutropio et de Divitiarum Vanitate* (*On the Capture of Eutropius and the Vanity of Wealth*) 1, 6, in *PG* 52:397-98, 402; *Cum de Expulsione Ipsius Sancti Joannes Ageretur*, in *PG* 52:433; *Exposition on the Psalms* 147, 4, in *PG* 55:483; *Homily on the Verse "I Have Seen the Lord"* 4, 2, in *PG* 56:121; *Commentary on Matthew* 54, 2, in *PG* 58:535; ibid., 77, 1, in *PG* 58:702.

162. Chrysostom, *In Epistolam I ad Corinthios Homilia* (*Homily on the First Epistle to the Corinthians*) 32, 1, in *PG* 61:265; 6, 3-4, in *PG* 61:51-53.

163. Chrysostom, *De Sancta Pentecoste Homilia* (*Homily on the Holy Pentecost*) 1, 4, in *PG* 50:459, 453; *De Laudibus Sancti Pauli Apostoli Homilia* (*Homilies on the Praise of St. Paul the Apostle*) 4, in *PG* 50:488; *In Inscriptionem Actorum* (*Inscription on the Acts*) 2, 3, in *PG* 51:81-82; cf. 85; *Homily on the First Epistle to the Corinthians* 32, 2, in *PG* 61:265; *In Colossenses Homilia* (*Homily on Colossians*) 3, 8, in *PG* 62:358-59, etc.

164. Chrysostom, *Exposition on Psalms* 110, 4, in *PG* 55:285; Jerome, *Commentary on Isaiah* 54, 1, in *PL* 24:516B; 13, in *PL* 24:627B-629A; Origen, *Against Celsus* IV, 80, in *PG* 11:1152-53; *De Principiis* II, 4, 3, in *PG* 11:201-3.

165. Athanasius, *Oratio de Incarnatione Verbi Dei* (*Oration on the Incarnation of the Word*) 53, in *PG* 25:189; Jerome, *Letters* 66, 4, in *PL* 22:641; *Commentary on Isaiah* 60, 1, in *PL* 24:588D-589A.

166. Jerome, *Contra Joannem Hierosolymitanum* (*Against John the Jerusalemite*) 11-12, in *PL* 23:380C-381C.

167. K. Stendahl, "Implications of Form-Criticism and Tradition-Criticism for Biblical Interpretation," *Journal of Biblical Literature* 77 (1958): 34.

168. A. C. Cotter, "The Eschatological Discourse," *Catholic Biblical Quarterly* 1 (1939): 205.

169. N. A. Dahl, "Christ, Creation, and the Church," in Davies & Daube, *The Background of the New Testament and Its Eschatology*, 422.

170. Schweitzer, *Geschichte der Leben-Jesu-Forschung*, 375.

171. Robert M. Grant, " 'Development' in Early Christian Doctrine," *Journal of Religion* 39 (1959): 121.

172. Jeremias, *Jesu Verheissung für die Völker*, 47.

173. So Johannes Weiss, "Das Problem der Entestehung des Christentums," *Archiv für Religionswissenschaft* 16 (1913): 435.

174. Alfred Fawkes, "The Development of Christian Institutions and Beliefs," *Harvard Theological Review* 10 (1917): 115-16.

175. Linton, *Das Problem der Urkirche*, 121, 159.

176. A. Feuillet, "La Synthése Eschatologique de Saint Matthieu," *Revue Biblique* 57 (1950): 180-211; Millar Burrows, *An Outline of Biblical Theology* (Philadelphia: Westminster Press, 1946), 199-201.

177. Van Stempvoort, "Het ontstaan van het Kerkbegrip en de oudste Kerkorganisatie," 250; T. F. Glasson, "The Kerygma: Is Our Version Correct," in *Hibbert Journal* 51 (1953): 129, 131-32; Frederick A. M. Spencer, "The Second Advent According to the Gospels," *Church Quarterly Review* 126 (1938): 6.

178. Goguel, "La seconde génération chrétienne," 190; G. Bornkamm, *In Memoriam Ernst Lohmeyer* (Stuttgart: Evangelisches Verlagswerk, 1951), 116, 118, 121; E. Stauffer, "Agnostos Christos," in Davies & Daube, *The Background of the New Testament and Its Eschatology*, 281-82.

179. Eisler, *Iesous Basileus* 1:26; cf. S. Franck, "Le Royaume de Dieu et Le Monde," *Dieu Vivant* 7 (1951): 17-34.

180. Clement, *First Epistle to the Corinthians* 23, in *PG* 1:236; Clement, *Second Epistle to the Corinthians* 11-12, in *PG* 2:344-48; Barnabas, *Catholic Epistle* 4, 16, in *PG* 2:731-33; cf. Luke 18:7.

181. R. C. Petry, "Medieval Eschatology and St. Francis of Assisi," *Church History* 9 (1940): 55; F. Bäthgen, *Der Engelpapst* (Halle: Nieymeyer, 1933), 76.

182. The old dispensation theory: Origen, *Against Celsus* IV, 11-12; in *PG* 11:1039-41; Milburn, *Early Christian Interpretations of History*, 29-31. The Jews had lost and regained the temple more than once.

208 MORMONISM AND EARLY CHRISTIANITY

183. Epiphanius, *Adversus Haereses (Against Heresies)* III, 2, 6, in *PG* 42:784; Lactantius, *Divine Institutes* IV, 1, in *PL* 6:447-51.

184. H. Clavier, "Problème du Rite et du Mythe dans le quatrième Evangile," *Revue d'Histoire et Philosophie Religeuses* 31 (1951): 292; Linton, *Das Problem der Urkirchen in der neueren Forschung*, 132-33; Dahl, "Christ, Creation and the Church," 422-43.

185. Ambrose, *Expositio in Lucam (Commentary on Luke)* 2, 88, in *PL* 15:1667-68; John Chrysostom, *Homilia in Apostolicum Dictum: Hoc Scitote, Quod in Novissimis Diebus Erunt Tempora Gravia (Homily on the Apostolic Saying: "This Know Also, that in the Last Days Perilous Times Shall Come" [2 Timothy 3:1])* 5, in *PG* 56:276.

186. Origen, *Commentary on Matthew* 56, in *PG* 13:1688D, attacks this view, held by M. Brunec, in *Verbum Domini* (1952), 265, 269, 277, 323-24.

187. Hippolytus, *On the Consummation of the World* 24-25, in *PG* 10:937B-C.

188. F. F. Bruce, "Eschatology," *London Quarterly and Holborn Review* 183 (1958): 99, with a survey of the literature, 101-3.

189. G. Florovsky, "Eschatology in the Patristic Age," *Studia Patristica* 2, in *Texte und Untersuchungen* 64 (1957): 235-38.

190. Oscar Cullman, "Rudolf Bultmann's Concept of Myth and the New Testament," *Concordia Theological Monthly* 27 (1956): 24; M. Burrows, "Thy Kingdom Come," *Journal of Biblical Literature* 74 (1955): 2, 1-18.

191. H. J. Schoep, "Die ebionitische Wahrheit des Christentums," in Davies & Daube, *Background of the New Testament and Its Eschatology*, 123.

6

The Way of the Church

The Question

Granted that Jesus founded a church, was that church expected by its founder and members to remain upon the earth for a limited time only, to be removed and restored at a later date, or was the "apostolic church" the ultimate and final foundation of God on earth, destined "to remain firm and steadfast until the end of the world"? That is one of the most important questions that confront students of church history today.

Every day it becomes more apparent that on its solution depends the whole nature and history of the Christian church. The solution is not far to seek: By the simple, almost mechanical, process of extracting from the literature of the ancient church those passages dealing specifically with the church's future, or what the saints thought would be its future, placing these passages in chronological order, and reading them over, anyone who has the requisite time and patience may discover the answer. That is what the present study intends to do.

It has not been done heretofore because when churchmen have found themselves confronted by the above question, with its alarming implication that all the churches of

"The Way of the Church," originally appeared as a series in the Improvement Era, 58 (Jan.-Dec. 1955): 20–22, 44–45, 86–87, 104, 106–7, 152–54, 166, 168, 230–32, 258, 260–61, 306–8, 364–66, 384–86, 455–56, 502–04, 538, 570–71, 599–600, 602–6, 650–53, 708–10, 817, 835–38, 840–41, 902–3, 968.

Christendom might conceivably be astray, they have dismissed the awful thought with a shudder. What! cries Tertullian, can all those martyrs have shed their blood for nothing?[1]—carefully evading the declaration of the martyrs
themselves, that the only reward they ever think of is a crown
in heaven, where they have been repaid a thousandfold for
their brief sufferings here below. Conventional church history is resolved never to raise the question of whether the
church of Christ actually survived as the best way to avoid a
disastrous answer. Thus at the present time leading church
historians would forestall any embarrassing questions touching the main issue by devising ingenious titles for their studies: "The Infant Church,"[2] "A World Being Born,"[3] *The
Unquenchable Light,*[4] etc., titles as "loaded" as Neander's
Planting and Training of the Christian Church.[5]

They are "loaded" because they suggest and permit
research only along one carefully channeled course. The mere
title "Infant Church" as used by these authors fixes unalter-
ably the whole course of church history in advance: If the
early church was by very definition an infant church or a
world being born, we can tell no other story than one of
growth and advancement regardless of what happened—calam-
itous failures are merely setbacks; success in any direction is
growth; the story can have only one outcome; within a the-
matic framework we can ask all the questions we want to,
but the main question of whether the church really *was* an
infant church and not something totally different, must never
be raised. And what other tale can one tell of an "Unquenchable Light," again an expression of those authors, save that it
never goes out?[6] That wonderul title has forestalled any embarrassing questions as to whether the light was to overcome the
darkness or the other way around—for merely to ask such a
question is to remind oneself of John's terribly emphatic
answer, that the "Unquenchable Light" was by no means to
remain among men.

"The task of church history," writes the author of the latest large church history to appear, "is to give a clear, comprehensive, scientifically established over-all picture of the evolution of the visible institution of salvation founded by Christ."[7]

This is very much as if he were to say, "Our business is to describe the triumph of the church," as if that triumph were inevitable. Like the classic question, "Have you stopped beating your mother-in-law?" it cleverly avoids a very important question by asking a less important one resting on the assumption that the other has been answered. The assignment of describing the evolution of the institution established by Christ assumes (1) that there was such an institution, (2) that it remained on the earth, and (3) that it underwent an observable process of evolution. All this is taken for granted, yet until very recently the bulk of scholars have regarded the first proposition as unproven, and they have only just begun to think about the second. The third point is, thanks to the systematic avoidance of the second, never questioned.

The Nature of the Evidence

The study of church history has in the past been of interest to but a few, and their interest has been a strenuously partisan one. Who writes church histories? Churchmen. Who reads them? Divinity students. It would be hard to find another branch of science or the humanities in which so few scholars ever engage in the study of the things for its own sake. Even the rare researcher of disinterested motives must end up taking sides, for the nature of the thing requires it.

"Only one who is personally convinced of the truth of the gospel," writes Heinrich Bornkamm, "can fully grasp its historical manifestations and what is lasting or changing in them. There is no such thing as pure objectivity in the history of thought, which in fact would be rendered sterile by such."[8] In 1699 Gottfried Arnold published his *Impartial*

History of the Church and Heresy, to show that the true
church through the ages has been that of the persecuted mystics and heretics—whether his theory is right or not, it cannot by any effort of the imagination be called impartial.

Recently Professor Pfeiffer has vigorously deplored any
side-taking at all in the study of religion; he thinks one can
maintain perfect scientific detachment by "keeping facts and
faith, history and revelation, historical research and theological speculation separate and distinct."[9] But is not this appeal
for a double bookkeeping that shall "distinguish sharply
between true facts and true doctrines"[10] simply a device for
placing one's own particular beliefs beyond the reach of objective investigation? Is it fair of the doctors to denounce with
moral indignation those who have not yet given up those
partisan strivings in which they themselves engaged for generations, and only gave up with reluctance when years of
determined seeking led to unforeseen and embarrassing conclusions? It is altogether too convenient when one's own
methods of soapmaking have failed, to declare to the world
that soap simply cannot be made and heap contempt on
those who are still trying and abuse on those who have
succeeded.

When the professor finds that his facts do not square
with *his* doctrines, then, but not until then, he announces to
the world as a general moral principle that *no one* should
ever try to compare facts with doctrines. That lets him out.
But the escape is altogether too convenient; the cause of cool
and scientific detachment is defended with such surprising
heat and censure; and the announcement of these so liberal
and so obvious principles has come so suddenly and so late
(for until now church scholars have all admitted to a degree
of partisan interest) that one is forced to the conclusion that
all this pleading to keep religion out of religious studies is
possibly just an extreme form of partisan pleading, an attempt
to save face by the related declaration that the rules do not
hold any more—that religious and historical facts have

absolutely nothing to do with each other. Since the rules no longer favor us, we will abolish them!

The modern scientific credo is thus no exception to the rule that an ulterior motive has marked the writing of church history from the very beginning. "It is dangerous to enquire after truth among later writers," wrote the great Baronius, "who are often found to write that which false rumors, vain imaginings, private affection and sometimes Flattery suggested to their Minds, to the great prejudice of Historical Truth."[11] But what about the earlier writers? "The age was one of rhetoric," writes Harnack of the period from the fourth century on, "which did not draw back at artifice and unveracity of every kind. . . . Forgery was the order of the day. . . . Already in the fourth century a spirit of lying prevailed mightily in the official documents . . . and in the fifth and sixth centuries it ruled the Church." At that time "no one any longer put any faith in any written record or official document or report."

After giving various examples of the use of falsification by the most illustrious fathers as a partisan weapon, and describing the controversial literature as "a morass of lies and rascality," Harnack concludes that "one cannot escape the fear that present-day historians are still altogether too trusting in their attitude towards this whole literature. . . . We stand almost everywhere more or less helpless in the face of a systematically fabricated tradition."[12]

Recently Walther Völker has shown that the great church history of Eusebius was actually a "tendentious" writing designed to prove a particular point.[13] The events culminating in the riotous councils of the fourth century led thinking men of the time to doubt whether the church was still on earth or not: It was to silence his own doubts on this head that Eusebius undertook the researches that resulted in the ecclesiastical history. By the simple process of excerpting "only what agreed with his fundamental thesis," Eusebius, according to Völker, "altered the appearance of the old church history. All the tensions were removed, all the conflicts smoothed over."[14] This work, which rightfully won for its author the title of "Father of Church History," laid down the line which church historians have followed ever since, namely the implicit and unquestioning defense at all times of the basic proposition that the Christian church of today is actually the "apostolic church" of the beginning, no matter how strangely and wonderfully altered. To this proposition all conventional church history is dedicated; it is the axiom which may never be questioned and which predetermines the direction of all research, the bed of Procrustes into which all the evidence must be made to fit, cost what it may.

Before we address ourselves to our proper task, which is (1) to set forth in order the early references to the future of the church, and (2) to show what modern scholars have to say on the subject, it is necessary to get some idea of the nature of the documents with which we have to deal, and of the extent to which church historians have controlled those documents, actually inventing the past which they claim, and often sincerely, to be only discovering. The reader should be warned that the thesis of the present study runs counter to the massive consensus of church history for over a thousand years.

Long ago Socrates showed what a hollow thing consensus is. More recently, in 1932, Olaf Linton published his now famous study of what he calls "the Consensus" of church history in the nineteenth century. Therein he shows how the scholars when they think they are being most sound, most objective, and most scientific in their construction of church history, are actually doing little more than faithfully reflecting their own background and conditioning. As they are liberal, democratic, congregational, individualist, so must the "primitive church" be; if they like ritual, so did it; if they eschewed it, so did the early Christians.[15] But what the general public dreams not of, and even the experts underestimate, is that the invention of history has been a major industry for many centuries, one of the primary concerns of scholars having been in every age to *control the past*. This is a serious, but not criminal charge, for as we shall presently see, it is virtually impossible for anyone to handle ancient records without in some way having to control them; and so, as the records have been handed on from one generation to the next, there has been exercised over them a cumulative, all-pervasive, and thorough control.

Hand-Picked Evidence

To begin with, anyone who writes church history has the inescapable and dangerous obligation of deciding somehow just what evidence shall be made available to his readers and what shall not; obviously, he cannot include it all. Now anyone who takes it upon himself to withhold evidence is actually determining what the reader's idea of church history is going to be—he is controlling the past. And when the evidence held back is a thousand times more extensive than what is brought before the jury, it is plain that the historian is free to build up any kind of case he desires.

Is there no alternative to this commission of all but absolute power to a few notoriously partial authorities? There is none. The only completely fair presentation of church history would be a *full* display of *all* known evidence laid out before the public in chronological order—all the written stuff: histories, letters, sermons, tomes of philosophy, all the artifacts, ruins, and inscriptions, all the traditions, rituals, liturgies, and legends would have to be there, without any attempt on the part of the custodian to interpret or control. But such a corpus would be all but useless, an impenetrable jungle of stuff beyond the capacity of any reader. To be made available even to specialists it would have to be classified, broken up into departments that could be handled by one man and, as far as the general public is concerned, each of these would have to be further reduced by sampling or condensing. If one were to include in a source book but one-tenth of one

percent of the writings in the old *Patrologiae* alone—and
they are far from exhaustive, even in their area—the reader
would be confronted by five hundred solid pages of quotation. But how representative is a selection of one page in a
thousand? One need only examine Kirch's *Enchiridion* for
the answer.[16] Aside from all policy and prejudice, sheer necessity has brought it about that what has been handed on from
generation to generation as standard church history is a
growing accumulation of carefully hand-picked evidence.

But the business of control does not end with the selecting of evidence. Once our texts have been chosen for presentation, we discover that they are all without exception in an
imperfect and fragmentary state, marred by scribal slips,
emendations, interpolations, and deletions. Generations of
careless, or (what is far more dangerous) careful and deliberate scribes have been busy day and night at the game of
controlling the past by altering the texts they were supposed to be copying, and as often as not the alterations have
been intentional. And what is the cure for this? More correction! The conscientious, modern editor proceeds to control
his text by *reconstructing* it to say what he believes the original should have said. Such reconstructions are not always
infallible. In fact, in the opinion of most scholars, the
reconstructions perpetrated by most other scholars are pretty
bad.

Once the church historian has picked out the most highly
favored passages to call to the witness stand and, as a textual
critic, carefully tidied them up and brushed their hair to
make a favorable impression for his client (the client being
the church of his choice—for most church historians are professional churchmen) a most effective control still remains;
for before the evidence can be heard by the general public, it
must be *translated*. Translation is a far more effective and
aggressive way of controlling the past than most people
suppose.

The business of selecting, restoring, and translating pertinent texts is one that calls for the constant exercise of judgment and the constant making of choices. To enable the scholar to choose between two or more equally authentic but conflicting passages, between equally plausible but conflicting readings of the passage chosen, and between equally grammatical but conflicting translations of the text thus selected and restored, he invariably adopts some rule or policy in the light of which one interpretation will always enjoy a clear priority, thus obviating the necessity of giving serious consideration to the others. Let us consider the well-established principles upon which the experts operate.

All for the Party

In George Orwell's much cited and disturbing novel *Nineteen Eighty-Four*, the tyrannical super-state of the future is operated by its masters on the proposition that "who controls the past controls the present, and who controls the present controls the future." That is the secret of power: If you can control people's ideas of the past, you control their ideas of the present and hence the future. The unhappy hero of the story works in a public relations office where the past is controlled. His task is to check all back newspapers kept in the official files of the state for any piece of news, no matter how old, that might embarrass the government if brought to light—old promises and prophecies that have failed, glorious deeds of men now out of favor with the rulers, friendly alliances with governments now odious to the state, and so forth.

When he comes upon such an item, our hero immediately cuts it out and burns it, substituting in its place a revamped version of the same story of exactly the same length but so rewritten as to make it seem that the present government has always been right, infallibly vindicated in the unfolding of events. It is a careful, deliberate controlling of the past, a rewriting of history in retrospect to suit the present interests

and support the present policies of the Party, whose authority is thus confirmed by the verdict of history.

All this seems to us very cynical and sordid, and yet,
appalling as it seems, Mr. Orwell has given a very fair description of what has been going on for thousands of years in the
learned world! Except in its cold-blooded mechanics, wherein
does the operation described differ from that of the learned
Hebrew *Meturgeman*? In his business of rendering ancient
Hebrew into contemporary Aramaic, "the most difficult passages were simplified, or explained, the incidents of the past
conformed to the ideas of the present . . . and, finally, the
laws expanded in accordance with the practice and teaching
of later times . . . the Meturgeman did not scruple to transform the text before him in the boldest fashion."[17]

His motive in this, we are told, was "to gloss over or
to modify everything which seemed inconsistent with the
accepted view of the history of the nation, to magnify and
expound everything which redounded to the credit of the
heroes of the past . . . to explain away the unworthy and to
emphasize the pious motive which guided their conduct."[18]
These learned men felt it their duty in presenting the message
of an ancient prophet to the unlearned, to restate it in such a
way as "to draw out its implicit teaching; to harmonize the
teaching of the prophet with the current interpretation of the
Jewish schools; to modify the language of the prophet where
it seemed inconsistent with the traditional view of the nation's
history and even, in certain cases, to reverse the plain meaning
of the text."[19]

Whether or not all this busy revamping of the record is
to be deplored as dishonest and unscientific does not concern
us at the moment. What does concern us is the fact that the
records have been manipulated in a deliberate attempt to
control the past. For many years scholars were convinced
that Ramses II was just about the greatest builder and war-
rior king that ever lived. Ramses planned it that way. While
his stonecutters conscientiously effaced from buildings and

monuments the names of their real builder (that is, where other enterprising monarchs had not already beaten him to it) and substituted in their place the name of the ruling Ramses, his historians were busy writing up the accounts of battles that had turned out badly for the king in such a way as to transform them into glorious victories. That was controlling the past in the grand manner, a practice as old as Egypt itself. The Fifth Dynasty, for example, based its authority on an historical account of three brothers, which is a most palpable forgery.

By now some American college professors know that conventional Roman history is largely a pious party fiction, made-to-order history that bucks the evidence at every turn. Likewise the whole body of Greek literature that has come down to us has had to pass the scrutiny of generations of narrow and opinionated men: it is not the literature of the Greeks that we have inherited but a purée made from that fraction of their writings which the doctors have felt proper to place in the hands of students after much abridgment and revisal. In compiling their college omnibuses of "standard" plays, orations, and poems, and in preparing their College Outline Series of humanities and science, the professors of Alexandria effectively consigned to oblivion any writings not on the approved list: the Greek schoolmen destroyed the Greek heritage.[20]

Wherever we look in the ancient world the past has been controlled, but nowhere more rigorously than in the history of the Christian church. The methods of control, wherever we find them, fall under three general heads, which might be described as (a) the invention, (b) the destruction, and (c) the alteration of documents. They deserve some attention.

a. *Fabrication*: Tertullian tells of a scholar in Asia Minor who "out of love for the Apostle" composed a fantastic miracle and adventure tale called "The Acts of Paul," which did great damage to the church.[21] He meant well. "We have

written these things," the Apostles are represented as protesting in the Apostolic Constitutions, "that you might get things
straight, and not receive books which are falsely circulated
in our name. . . . Simon and Cleobus have published poi-
sonous books in the name of Christ and the Apostles, [and
there are all sorts of forgeries circulating in the names of the
prophets and patriarchs]."[22] But the practice continued and
grew: "Forgery was viewed by wide circles of the ancient
Church not merely as an excusable fraud, but a thoroughly
legitimate *oeconomia* [operation, administrative measure] in
the war against the enemies of the faith." Origen, Clement of
Alexandria, Hilary, and John Chrysostom all recommend
and use the *kale apate* ("fair deception"), and justify it by
Jeremiah 4:10,[23] "—Ah, Lord God! surely thou hast greatly
deceived this people."

Just as physicians must sometimes tell fibs to patients to
help them along, and as those tending small children or the
feeble-minded can handle them and help them more effectively by making up stories as they go, so the Christian
priest was to cultivate a useful deception as an essential tool
in dealing with the laity, according to John Chrysostom.[24]
"When Jacob deceived his father," he explains, "that was not
deception but *oeconomia*."[25]

Jerome admits to employing "a sometimes useful
deception," and admires others for the same practice: "how
cunning, how shrewd, what a dissimulator!"[26] And he cites
Origen as teaching that "lying is improper and unnecessary
for God, but is to be esteemed sometimes useful for men,
provided it is intended that some good should come of it."[27]
But whoever lied with any other intent? In support of his
contention, Origen appeals to Plato's doctrine of deception
in the *Republic*—a thing which had shocked even the
pagans.[28]

It was common practice for Christian scholars in the
Middle Ages both "without scruple [to] put forward older
texts, with slight alteration, as their own compositions,"[29]

and to put forth their own compositions without scruple as ancient texts. For centuries the medieval church rested its claims to temporal power on the false Isidorian Decretals, though recognized from the first as a forgery, and its doctrinal and ritual structure on the Pseudo-Dionysius Areopagiticus, a most obvious fake.

"Whoever knows and understands the men of the Middle Ages," Böhmer writes, "how many of them, though excellent bishops, abbots, clerics, and monks by the standards of the time, practised falsification of documents, [here follows a list of important names] . . . will answer with an unqualified affirmative" the question, "could Lanfranc have been a common forger?"[30] The common purpose of such forgeries was to control the past, specifically to make it appear that certain episcopal sees, especially that of Rome, had from the earliest times enjoyed great powers and prerogatives for which in fact no real evidence existed.[31]

The zealous Thomas Comber finds that in the official editions of the Councils as in Baronius "there is such adding and expunging, such altering and disguising things in the Body of the Councils, and such excusing, falsifying, and shuffling in the Notes, that a Judicious Reader will soon perceive these Venerable Records . . . do not favor them. But these Corruptions are carried on with such Confidence and Cunning, that an unexperienced and unwary Student, may be imposed on by this specious show of Venerable Antiquity."[32]

Now in such matters the general public shows no inclination to be either experienced or wary; even so, any faint stirrings of a critical spirit have been anticipated and forestalled by ample professional restrictions and taboos. On the whole the controlling of the past with the most reliable of all human traits, mental inertia, as its chief ally has been a strangely easy business. There is, as we have pointed out elsewhere, no such thing as a clever forgery—and there does not need to be, for while no forgery can succeed without public approval, no forgery (as the clumsy Piltdown hoax has proved) can fail if it has that approval. And public approval is as sure a thing as the mass ignorance and laziness that guarantee it.

A famous letter written by Innocent I of Rome to the Bishop of Gubbio in 416 provides a commentary on this theme, which is all the more enlightening for being unintentional. The pope is deploring the fact that the church of Gubbio (actually within the metropolitan authority of Rome) observes different rites for the mass from those found at Rome: "Where everyone feels free to observe not what comes by tradition, but whatever seems good to him," writes the Bishop of Rome, "we see established observances and ways of celebrating of diverse nature, depending on the location of the churches. The result is a scandal for the people who, *not knowing that the traditions have been altered by human presumption*, think either that the Churches are not in agreement with each other, or that the Apostles established contradictory things."[33]

Whatever usage they find, the people naturally attribute to the Apostles. Why not?—are they not instructed to do so? How can they be expected to know "that the ancient traditions have been altered by human presumption"? On the ignorance and complacency of the general public the religious innovator can always rely. Sometimes, however, the public itself forces the scholars to go farther than they want to. This is especially so in the case of church history, where the demand for immediate and definite answers is constant and pressing. What is the poor researcher to do? "The sources were very scarce and fragmentary," writes Linton of the great days of "scientific" scholarship in the field; "in order to derive any definite information at all from them, it was necessary to interpret these sources and to fill them out. . . . . From the very nature of the thing the passages were read with modern eyes."[34] The public could only be satisfied at the price of controlling the past.

b. *Censorship:* But forgery is a risky business. Much
more safe and dignified, and equally effective, is the office of
the censor. When the Septuagint was accepted by the Jews as
the official text of the Old Testament it was declared to have
been revealed from heaven, and all competing texts were
officially destroyed. But later when the Hebrew text was
fixed again from "old manuscripts saved from the temple of
Jerusalem," the Septuagint was found to disagree with this
miraculous discovery and accordingly "was declared to be
the work of Satan." So carefully was the order for its destruction carried out that with the exception of two little bits of
papyrus with "fragments of a few verses of Deuteronomy,"
to this day "not a single line, neither of the 'Septuagint' nor
of any other part of the Greek Bible, written by a Jew, is so
far known to be preserved."[35] But with the passing of time
grave differences arose regarding the correct readings of this
Hebrew Bible as those readings underwent constant change
at the hands of copyists and emendators, and so it became
necessary to restore the text to its ancient purity. This was
the work of Masoretes, and since they "had no model of
classical Hebrew to which they could adapt the pronunciation of Hebrew . . . they tried to create an ideal pronunciation" which *they* believed to be correct.[36] To establish this
new, text all other—and older—Bibles were ordered destroyed,
and before many years the fact that the Masorete text stood
unchallenged was taken as clear proof that it must be the
true and original version of the Bible, for people naturally
forgot that the reason why it stood alone through the centuries was that its competitors had all been deliberately and
systematically extirpated. Kahle compares this to the claims
of the Roman church to pristine purity of doctrine in the
Middle Ages: it was, or appeared to be, the oldest surviving
doctrine only because the others had been suppressed or
destroyed.[37]

Censorship

When Joseph Smith announced that the very first words
of the Bible had been edited and their meaning changed by
"an old Jew without any authority," he knew whereof he
spoke.[38] Not that the manipulation of that particular passage has been definitely proven—there is not yet enough evidence, one way or the other—but that the common practice
of such manipulation has of recent years become an established fact, thanks to the labors of Kahle and others. The
work of the Masoretes, far from being, as it was meant to
be, the final and definitive fixing of the sacred text for all
time, simply laid the groundwork for new and daring
"reconstructions."

For the Masoretic text in its turn suffered the usual process of deterioration until, in the sixteenth century, Jacob
ben Chaiyim set himself to the task of rescuing it from the
state of corruption into which it had fallen: "He was convinced that there was only one correct Masora—the Masora
compiled by himself—and that the text arranged by him
according to this Masora was the very text which had been
established by the great Masoretic authorities of Tiberias."[39]
And so scholars accepted Jacob ben Chaiyim's text as the
authoritative one; and when through the ensuing four centuries, older and better texts turned up and showed wherein
ben Chaiyim had been wrong, what did the scholars do—
correct him? Far from it: they corrected the ancient manuscripts to agree with ben Chaiyim! His hasty, superficial,
and hopelessly out-of-date text "has been regarded as the
only authoritative text up to the present day."[40] In the nineteenth century Baer made the most notable effort to restore
the pure Old Testament. His method was simple and effective: from all the material before him he "selected . . . what
he regarded as 'correct' and what differed he declared to be
'corrupt,' 'incomplete,' or 'in confusion.' " But Baer not only

selected what he regarded as the 'correct' text from the material at his disposal, he also freely *altered* readings of his manuscripts when they did not give what he regarded as "correct."[41] So when confronted by valuable old manuscripts or even by texts corrected by the great ben Asher himself, Baer's disciples firmly rejected them, since they differed from Baer's hypothetical reconstruction of them.[42] It is not, as one might suppose, the discovery of new and revealing manuscripts that controls and guides the thinking of the scholars; it is their thinking that controls the discoveries. "They approach the texts," wrote Father Deimel, the Sumerian expert, "with a preestablished and ready-made system, and then force them to conform to this bed of Procrustes."[43] Even when the scholars have "gnashed their teeth and accepted" new discoveries, according to Housman, they have been prompt to make it appear that such findings were no surprise to them, "and the history of scholarship is mutilated to save the face of those who have impeded progress."[44]

Anyone who thinks Kahle may have exaggerated should consult Goldschmidt's introduction to his standard edition of the Babylonian Talmud. Over 400 years ago Daniel Bomberg brought out the first complete printed text of the Talmud. It was widely circulated and became the "standard text." But in the ensuing centuries, as might be expected, vast numbers of ancient Talmud manuscripts have been discovered, texts entirely unknown to Bomberg and differing very widely from his text as well as among themselves. Even without these discoveries it is apparent that the Bomberg text "swarms with mistakes" obvious even to the casual reader. In the face of this, one would expect all kinds of new and improved editions of the Talmud, since Bomberg claimed no more divine inspiration than any other editor. But not a bit of it! His text had been accepted by the doctors and that settled the matter forever. "All subsequent editions have been virtually stereotype copies of the first," Goldschmidt tells us,

and so is his! He brushes aside all the great manuscript discoveries—out of respect for the received text he will not even
consider them.[45] If even the most obvious blunder in the
Bomberg edition can possibly be justified by any argument,
Goldschmidt retains it without comment; if it cannot be justified he still lets it stand but makes a modest suggestion in a
footnote. "The present edition," he announces with pride
rather than shame, "is thus an exact reproduction of the first
Bomberg edition; all other readings, even those which are
obviously more correct, are put in footnotes as variant readings, the text itself remaining untouched." The official stamp
of approval has so sanctified a text which the doctors themselves describe as extremely inaccurate and poorly substanti-
ated that "no Talmud authority would accept as reliable any
text 'improved' from the manuscripts or by scholarly judgment, or even recognize such as a Talmud text at all."[46]
Though it is hard for the layman to believe that such things
can be, they are the rule rather than the exception.

The rigorous and arbitrary censorship of ancient texts
belongs to the common heritage of all the "people of the
book," being an established routine in every age. Antiochus
ordered all copies of the Jewish scriptures burned, and pronounced the death penalty on anyone guilty of possessing a
copy.[47] Diocletian passed a like law against all Christian
writings, and Constantine followed his example by condemning to death anyone guilty of possessing writings by the heretics Porphyr or Arius.[48] In 449 Theodosius and Valentinian
passed a law that "all that . . . any person may have written
against the pious religion of the Christians be committed to
the flames wherever found."[49] Accordingly Bishop Theodoret
of Cyprus can boast of having collected and destroyed in his
diocese more than two hundred copies of the diatessaron
New Testament.[50] When it was officially decided (for party
reasons) that Ephraim should be "regarded as the classical
Syrian poet, all older forms of Syrian poetry were regarded
as imperfect and were destroyed."[51] The Arabs, raised up in

the same tradition, upon fixing the final text of the Koran, so carefully destroyed all other texts that for 1200 years it was possible to maintain that the accepted text was the very one dictated by the Prophet, though today we know that it was nothing of the sort.[52] In this wholesale destruction of texts to control the past, it is precisely the religious who are least troubled by qualms of conscience, "for how" asks Eusebius, "*could* a man who writes against the Christians do anything but lie?"[53]

But usually the violent economy of wholesale book burning is not necessary to control the past. Skilful officials avoid it as the brutal and straightforward technique of soldiers and governors, and a risky business in the bargain—for there is no telling what slippery or forgotten pages might escape the flames, and the subsequent discovery of such has sometimes proved very embarrassing. The shrewd administrator can exercise an equally crippling censorship simply by condemning certain items wherever they appear, as when Theodosius ordered all his subjects to consider "any laws or rescripts . . . alleged" in the favor of heretics as either "fraud or forgery."[54]

To prove that an order is *fraudulent* one needs no further evidence than that the party doesn't like it: it is not distasteful to the party because it is a forgery, but is automatically declared a forgery because it is distasteful. Acting on this principle, modern scholars tried to decide whether the account of the Council of Sinuessa was spurious or not solely on the grounds of whether its acceptance would do the Church more harm than good.

One school accepted it as genuine *because* it said something they thought highly favorable to the Roman Church; the other school condemned it *because* it said something else which they thought very damaging. The whole problem was whether the story was more favorable to the Church than otherwise—in which case it would be automatically accepted as true. Hefele finds the damage greater than the benefit, and so declares it false.[55] With such principles to guide him, the clever scholar in his office of *editor* can make the past out to be pretty much what he wants it to be.

The voluminous writings of Ambrose are, according to Leander, full of things "that differ from the catholic sense," being "by no means in agreement with sound doctrine." Accordingly, every such statement was to be regarded automatically as apocryphal and removed from the text by a special committee appointed by the Pope in 1580.[56] Does that sound naive? No less a sophisticated intellectual than Gilson begins his philosophical investigation of God with the announcement, "If we believe by faith that God has spoken, since what God says is true, all that contradicts the word of God can, and must, be at once excluded as false."[57] Is it at all surprising then that M. Gilson ends up by proving his faith, since all his arguments *must* conform? He is in the position of a man who declares as an article of faith that any coin when tossed will always come down heads. This being the true faith, anything that contradicts it, such as those times when a coin comes down tails, "can and must be excluded as false." The religious censor is thus not troubled by conscience, and, once he is thoroughly conversant with the party line, has a very easy time of it.

A subtle and very effective form of censorship is the *silent treatment.* "It is permitted," writes St. Augustine, "for the purpose of building up religion in things pertaining to piety, when necessary, to conceal whatever appears to need concealing; but it is not permitted to lie, of course, and so one may not conceal by way of lying."[58] The distinction is too fine, for silence can be very mendacious. The celebrated Duchesne, according to his biographer, M. Leclercq, was honest, open, and impartial in all the questions of church history *that he treated,* "but he would not handle all the questions: for example, he built a wall around the life of Jesus and the founding of the church, and he would not allow anyone to approach it. . . . He would not tolerate any discussion or any hesitation on that subject." Yet the whole labor of his life was "to prove the validity of the Church's historic claims,"—and the whole burden of the proof rests in the life of Jesus and the foundation of the Church, the two subjects of which he would tolerate no examination, even by himself![59] Recently (1952) the *Knights of Columbus Foundation for the Preservation of Historical Documents in the Vatican Library* sent out a brochure announcing its admirable project of microfilming the entire contents of the Vatican Library and housing the films in a special building in St. Louis. Only not quite all of the mighty collection was to be thus preserved: "The documents which the Church has been collecting for nearly 20 centuries," reads the announcement, "include, of course, the ecclesiastical records from the earliest Christian era. These are housed separately in the Vatican Archives and are not to be microfilmed." Why not? one asks with surprise; and the answer is a shocker: "as they are not of general interest to scholars."

Now anyone who consults the card index of any of our big libraries can quickly discover that precisely "the earliest Christian era" has been the subject of more books and studies than all the other centuries combined. If "the ecclesiastical records from the earliest Christian era" cast anything like a favorable light on the case of the Roman Church, we could long since have expected to see them splashed on the covers of some national magazines, not "housed separately" and withheld from circulation. "Not of general interest to scholars," indeed! The editors of the *Patrologia* are more ingenuous when they explain their failure to include certain important texts in what purports to be a complete collection of sources: "The editors have not published these three letters because of certain calumnies against the pope."[60]

The silent treatment is recommended, however, only in dealing with powerfully uncooperative documents. It is usually possible to control a text simply by weeding out the objectionable matter here and there instead of condemning whole books. Why destroy all the letters of Cyprian because some of them refute Roman claims? You only need declare the unfavorable ones forgeries, as Archbishop Tizzani did, and accept all the others. When Rufinus of Aquileia, translating early Christian texts at the end of the fourth century, comes upon passages presenting the peculiar and unacceptable doctrines of the early Christians, especially concerning God, he simply leaves those passages out, as he explains with disarming frankness.[61] When he is translating Origen and finds his text saying something with which he does not agree, he just naturally assumes, he tells us, that Origen never wrote any such thing and either rewrites the offending passage or strikes it out altogether![62] When Eusebius finds anything in the records of Constantine's life which might not make edifying reading (and there is plenty!), he deliberately omits such improper stuff, he explains, lest it detract from the glory of his subject.[63] In the same way, the biographers of Mohammed boast that they have eliminated all offensive passages and accepted into their histories only such material as will cast luster upon the name and reputation of the Prophet.[64]

Sometimes, however, one can preserve an entire text almost intact simply by inserting a single syllable into it—the little word "not." Though a powerful censor, this tiny word comes so near to being nothing in itself, that editors apparently think little harm can be done by introducing it here and there where careless scribes seem to have a habit of leaving it out. Thus in the 127 Canons of the Apostles we read that the church has lost the power once enjoyed by the saints to drive out devils, raise the dead, and speak in tongues, though those powers were meant to be "signs to those who believe." This agrees perfectly with Mark 16:17, "these signs shall follow them that believe," etc. but not with the conventional Christian thesis, that the loss of the signs was not serious, since they were meant to impress only unbelievers.

And so our editor helpfully inserts the little word which the original writers somehow overlooked: "that they should be a sign to those who do *not* believe!"[65] In the same spirit of helpfulness, when Justin Martyr propounds the doctrine (to which he refers a number of times) that "God created the world out of unorganized matter," Lange, quoted in a note in the *Patrologia*, is good enough to oblige with a useful insertion: "God created the world *not* out of unorganized matter," to which by way of clarification he adds a further interpolation, "but out of nothing."[66] Why bother to condemn Justin as a heretic when his words can be so easily controlled?

c. *Emendation—the Rewrite Job*: The excision of annoying passages and the insertion of useful ones is, after all, a surgery of last resort. Most scholars prefer to display their skill and ingenuity in the more cultivated art of *emendation*, the correction of purely scribal errors. The object of the game is to make the greatest possible change in the reading of a text by the least possible alteration of the written word; the smaller the alteration and the more striking the change of reading it effects, the more "brilliant" the emendation is considered. This, however, is a three-dimensional chess game reserved for the elite: the art of rewriting texts is practiced with little enough subtlety by most churchmen, whose prime concern has ever been to do a pious rather than a convincing rewrite job. At a very early period, "when anyone, Catholic or heretic, found a statement in the New Testament which appeared to be wrong," according to Kirsopp Lake, "it would seem to him a moral duty to correct an obvious scribal error into a true statement. But who can say what are the limits of 'scribal errors'?"[67] Those limits are set by any pious reader whose duty it is to alter the text whenever he feels the scribe is off the track. This is an unlimited license to control the past.

In one of the very earliest post-apostolic writings, Ignatius reprimands those Christians who won't believe anything that can't be proved from the archives, telling the Philadelphians, "My archives are Jesus Christ, *and they can't be tampered with.*"[68] Which shows not only how soon the church took to resting its case on documents, but also how soon those documents began to be controlled.

The original version of Josephus' *Jewish War*[69] contained a very unflattering reference to Christ. For this reason the book was condemned. Yet the writings of Josephus had been raised to almost canonical rank by the Christians—how could this treasure be saved? In the oldest surviving manuscripts, the famous passage about Christ has been savagely inked out, rubbed out, or cut out, as if in hasty attempts to clear the owners of any charge of possessing illicit writings. In later manuscripts, however, this passage reemerges, but this time wonderfully altered: by the changing of a few words and a little deft insertion and deletion the insulting paragraph has now become a glowing character reference for Jesus from the mouth of an infidel![70]

Coming down to our own time, we find the emendator still at work in the same old shop. When Père Batiffol reads in the Odes of Solomon, "thou hast introduced thy person into the world," he asks, "How could God introduce his person into the world which belongs to him? Let us rather say that God introduces his 'countenance' instead: . . . not *prosopon* (person), but *morphe* (face, form)."[71] Let us say, indeed! And what has the author to say about it? This passage, Batiffol obligingly explains, "calls for a rather energetic correction in order to have sense."[72] Sense for whom? The second-year Greek student is constantly running into passages that make no sense to him, and which he feels strongly urged to "correct." But when a text fails to make sense to a reader, or makes undesirable sense to his church, the last thing he may do is to alter it to some form that he and his party can accept. And that is notoriously the first thing that religious scholars do—just look through the footnotes of almost any early volume of the *Patrologiae.*

In all his extensive writings, it is axiomatic with M. Batiffol
that anything not satisfactory to his church can only be nonsense. Armed with this supremely practical and convenient
rule of thumb, he has no difficulty or hesitation in perpetrat-
ing his "energetic corrections" whenever an ancient writing
refuses to cooperate with him or his party. The Odes of
Solomon, for example, repeatedly speaks of "the worlds" in
the plural. In one place it declares of Christ, "In Him the
worlds speak one to another," making him the common Lord
of many worlds. Such was early Christian doctrine; but not
modern: "One is surprised," writes Batiffol, "to see 'the worlds'
speaking to one another; one would expect rather that it
would be *men*. . . . I would understand verse 8a to read
'men,' not 'worlds.' "[73] To what purpose then, does an ancient
author *say* "worlds" if an editor many centuries later can
substitute any word that suits him in its place? Is a poet writing some eighteen-hundred years ago under any obligation
to put down what "one would expect" him to write today?
Apparently he is.

By What Authority?

Those who hold ancient writers to modern standards,
find their work immeasurably simplified by the use of certain favorite yardsticks. With the textual critics this yardstick is "the best manuscript." Among a dozen or more ancient
manuscripts of a text, one is certain to have fewer mistakes
in it, that is, to be nearer the original form, than any of the
others. Having located this one, a critic will turn to it and it
alone in every case of doubt, oblivious of the fact that the
best authority may at times be hopelessly wrong, just as the
worst authority may be surprisingly right.

That is another way of saying that there *are no authorities*. But the scholars insist on acting as if there were because
if they had such to appeal to, their problem of constantly
having to make decisions would be solved. And so they
solve it by creating the authorities to which they then appeal!

This procedure drives Mr. Housman to wrathful sermons: "By this time," he writes, "it has become apparent what the modern conservative critic really is: a creature moving about in worlds not realized. His trade is one which requires, that it may be practised in perfection, two qualifications only: ignorance of language and abstinence from thought. The tenacity with which he adheres to the testimony of scribes has no relation to the trustworthiness of that testimony, but is dictated wholly by his inability to stand alone." These gentlemen, he says, "use manuscripts as drunkards use lampposts—not to light them on their way, but to dissimulate their instability."[74]

But relatively few men work with original manuscripts. Far more common are those other yardsticks, the pet hypothesis and the official party line. Mr. Toynbee uses pet hypotheses just as textual critics use pet manuscripts: "Toynbee's images," writes M. Frankfort, "betray an evolutionistic as well as a moral bias which interferes with the historian's supreme duty," since he "merely projects postulates which fulfill an emotional need in the West [i.e., his own cultural standards] into human groups whose values lie elsewhere."[75] Taking his own culture as a yardstick, Toynbee has no difficulty at all in telling at a glance just how advanced or retarded everybody else has been.

This is one of the oldest and easiest games in the world, though it was not until the nineteenth century that its devotees had the effrontery to call it a science. The "evolutionistic bias" of modern scholarship has played havoc with ancient history, not only predetermining every reaction of the historian to his text, but also in most cases freeing him from any obligation toward the text at all. Many large college textbooks are brought forth by men who, it is painfully apparent, have never bothered to read through the documents on which their work is supposed to be based. Their confidence in a moth-eaten rule-of-thumb is simply sublime—why should one waste precious eyesight examining moldy evidence when everybody knows already what the answer is going to be? "Naturally," writes one of the better authorities of our time, speaking of the ancient world in general, "the earlier kingdoms were neither large nor firmly established."

What economy is here! Who would beat a weary trail to the stacks in search of early kingdoms when he can reconstruct them at will by the application of a simple and universal rule? If one knows from biological analogy that early states were *naturally* small and weak, why spoil the game by toying with evidence which might prove that *historically* they were nothing of the sort?[76]

But more damaging to the past even than the wilful and mechanical application of lazy hand-me-down "science" to its reconstruction is the *rule of vanity*. In the end, as Housman demonstrates at length, a scholar's right to reconstruct history or restore a battered text rests on the possession of personal gifts which escape analysis. Here is high art indeed! The expert feels in his bones that what he says is what is right, unaware that his bones have been undergoing constant conditioning since the day of his birth. He is trained and intelligent; he means to be perfectly scientific and detached; he is constitutionally incapable of wanton error; how then can he be wrong?

Answer: simply by being human! Purity of motive is no guarantee of infallibility; the greatest of errors are by no means intentional, and are often made by the ablest of scholars. Yet because Dr. Faugh *means* to write an honest, impartial, and objective history we are expected by his publishers to have the decency, or at least the courtesy, to believe that his history *is* honest, impartial, and objective. No scholar alive possesses enough knowledge to speak the final word on anything, and as to integrity, let us rather call it vanity.

After surveying the whole field of Ezekiel scholarship for the period 1933–43, W. A. Irwin came out with the flat announcement that "not a single scholar has succeeded in convincing his colleagues of the finality of his analysis of so

much as one passage." Why not? Because "they have given
only opinions, when the situation cries aloud for . . . evidence. . . . There is no clearly emerging recognition of a
sound method by which to assault this prime problem. Every
scholar goes his own way, and according to his private predilection chooses what is genuine and what is secondary in
the book; and the figure and work of Ezekiel still dwell in
thick darkness."[77] No common yardstick having been agreed
on, every expert is his own yardstick, to which Ezekiel must
conform. This we call the rule of vanity, when the scholar
simply sets himself up as the final court of appeal.

There are, it is true, worse things than vanity, which is
common to all men, and it often happens that the very pom-
posity of a scholar clears him of any suspicion of cynicism
or intent to deceive. As Scaliger teaches us in his table talk,
the principal weakness of the learned lies not in their slyness
or vindictiveness but in their almost childlike simplicity and
gullibility where their own gifts and talents are concerned.

Professor von Gall, for example, was perfectly sincere in
his conviction that the doctrine of the Messiah could not
possibly have been known to the Jews before the Exile; then
when he found passages in the Old Testament that made it
perfectly clear that that doctrine *was* known to them, he sol-
emnly accused such non-cooperative texts of "obscuring the
clear line of thought" which he was following; and in all
good faith he then removed those passages from the Bible:
"If we remove these," he explains, "then almost everything
falls into perfect order—unless the text is corrupt." If any
lingering traces of the Messianic teaching remain in the text
after von Gall has got through with it, he begs us to attribute
such to lurking corruptions which he has overlooked. How
disarming, and how naive![78]

Neither can we charge with malpractice those students of
history who, having become sincerely convinced that there
was no organization in the primitive church, deftly remove
as a corruption of the text anything in the New Testament

that might imply that there was such an organization.[79] Quite recently Professor Bultmann, having decided that the message of John is a purely spiritual one, is, as it were, honor bound to remove from John 3:5 those crass physical words "and of water," which for him can only be a later interpolation.[80]

These people are honest and consistent in their operations, and one need no more accuse them of bad faith than one would condemn the faithful guide in the woods because he is going north when he sincerely believes he is going east. But that simple vanity which forbids us to condemn such guides also admonishes and excuses us from following them.

"What stamps the last twenty years with their special character," wrote Housman at the beginning of this century, "is . . . the absence of great scholars. . . . They now pretend that the relapse of the last twenty years is not a reaction against the great work of their elders, but a supplement to it. To the Lachmanns and Bentleys and Scaligers they politely ascribe the quality of *Genialität:* there is a complementary virtue called *Umsicht* (circumspection, perspicacity) and this they ascribe to themselves. Why, I cannot tell."[81]

Lest the reader think such charges of vanity are exaggerated, we reproduce herewith a certificate of supreme competence, written by a famous scholar in recommendation of himself to establish beyond a doubt the authority by which he does the amazing things described in the certificate itself. In his preface to his edition of the *Divans* of the earliest Arabic poets, the celebrated Dr. Ahlwardt writes (with our italics):

> In this edition I have chiefly relied on some manuscripts of the text . . . but I have not abstained from adopting readings which appeared to me more appropriate, from other sources. *I think myself justified in claiming this privilege as a right.* As I would not hesitate, when a verse has faults in the metre or lacks its proper feet, to correct it as far as I am able to do so from the context, so likewise I

do not scruple to reject a reading that is not reconcilable with *my appreciation of the sense*, and to select another— or even to invent one.[82]

Ahlwardt claims as a right the privilege of inventing a line of his own whenever the text before him offends his "appreciation of the sense." And to what remarkable personal gifts does Professor Ahlwardt attribute his infallible judgment of Arabic poetry? Not, surprisingly enough, to any superior knowledge of Arabic language or poetic idiom, but solely to the possession of a quality of superior acumen which only those trained in a modern university possess: "I readily concede," he writes, "that the feeling of the language which the native Arabian philologians possessed is in great measure wanting in us. . . . The faculty which is especially concerned in these matters, however, is one which was wholly, or almost wholly, denied to them . . . critical acumen."[83]

This is that very *Umsicht* over which Housman makes merry. One would suppose that "the faculty which is especially concerned" with the business of reconstructing ancient verses would be that "feeling of the language" by which alone poetry can be produced or comprehended. But not so. *Umsicht* is the thing, and Ahlwardt proceeds to ascribe it to himself in lavish measure: "On this ground, as I judge, *we* have a right to reject readings even when they have been expressly sanctioned by *them*. I readily admit that we neither now nor ever can equal them in quantity of knowledge. I do not rate our *knowledge* high, but our *power*, our *method* of investigation, our critical treatment of a given subject."[84]

And why is Ahlwardt so frank and open in confessing limitations of knowledge? Because he cannot conceal them: any claim to intimate knowledge of a language may be quickly and easily put to the test, whereas in matters of "power, method, and critical acumen" every scholar is his own examiner and awards himself his own certificate: "Every scholar goes his own way, and according to his private predilection chooses what is genuine and what is secondary."

Ahlwardt claims training in a wonderful method by which the initiate can bring forth knowledge of the past; this knowledge, he says, is far inferior to that possessed by the ancients themselves but is to be preferred to theirs, since their knowledge, though superior to it, was not derived by the approved method! Incredible as it seems, this is the normal attitude of scholars to records of the past, as Paul Kahle has demonstrated at great length. In the end, the mood, the method, the ripe assurance of the individual researcher, in a word, his vanity, has priority over all evidence.

But once a text has survived the ravages of the censor and received its final, "definitive" form at the hands of editors, it still had to face new and deadly perils before being placed in the hands of the general reader. For now comes the business of interpreting, a major factor where religious documents are concerned. Without adding, removing, or altering a single letter in a document one may by simply interpreting it as it stands effectively control its message. Here is the field in which the party can bring direct influence to bear. The Council of Trent "decrees that no one, relying on his own skill, shall . . . presume to interpret the said sacred Scripture contrary to that sense which holy mother Church—whose it is to judge of the true sense and interpretation of the holy Scriptures—hath held and doth hold."[85] And there is no text on earth so clear, simple, and unequivocal but that some devout commentator cannot make it mean the very opposite to what it says. Thus Justin Martyr in the *Dialogue* (A.D. 120) can demonstrate with ease that Genesis 22:17 is really a most terrible curse against the seed of Abraham!

There is an easy way of discovering in Mansi or the *Patrologiae* those texts which run counter to the claims of the Roman church: when the text suddenly gives way to long crowded columns of commentary, it is almost a sure sign that something has been said that has to be explained away, and the more clear and unequivocal the ancient statement, the more toilsome and extensive the commentary. Seventeen pages of Mansi are devoted to getting around the simply and clearly stated thirty-seventh canon of the Council of Arles (A.D. 309) decreeing that paintings should be banned from the churches and explaining why. Schermann, in all seriousness, tells us that the remark of Aristides, that the primitive Christians rejoiced on the death of an infant "all the more, as for one that has left the earth in a sinless condition" *proves* the early Christians baptized babies![86] Now to those reared in churches that teach and practice infant baptism the passage may prove just that, but to those reared in another tradition it seems to convey the very opposite meaning, identifying sinlessness with infancy as such, since Aristides says that though there was rejoicing at the death of any faithful member, for an infant that was something special. The point here is that what looks perfectly natural and logical to Schermann is, whether right or wrong, really the reflection of his partisan training.

In a very early writing attributed to Peter, that apostle is represented as complaining to James about "the varied interpretations of my words" enjoying currency in the church: "They seem to think they can interpret my own words better than I can, pretending to report my very thoughts, when as a fact such things never entered my head. If they dare so much while I am still alive, what liberties will they not take after I am gone!"[87]

The greatest handicap an ancient writer has in trying to tell his story against intrenched opinions of the scholars is that he cannot be present to defend himself. The master himself is dead, the public in ignorance, and the field is left clear to the servants of the household to make themselves magnificent at the expense of their lord; when the master does turn up unexpectedly, as did Ben Asher, he is promptly turned out-of-doors so the masquerade can continue. Already

Tertullian complains of the technique of reading the scripture so that it says one thing and means another, as if it were all an allegory, parable, or enigma. "But this is to pervert the faith," he says, "not to believe plain evidence but to put in its place unfounded propositions—and then accept them."[88]

Thus, the plain statement in Genesis 18, that the Lord visited Abraham and ate with him, may be explained in two ways, according to writing attributed to Athanasius: (1) If it really was the Lord, then there can have been no eating, and (2) if they really ate, then it could not have been the Lord.[89] In either case the scripture is adjusted to our ideas of what the Lord should do, and under no conditions need we change our own opinions to agree with what the scripture tells us he does. Against those scriptural passages (to cite another case) which tell us that Mary had other children besides Jesus "we give this argument," writes Pope Siricus, "she *could* not have, because that would be vileness and incontinence."[90] In vain does the scripture insist—the clergy has made up its mind.

From Origen on, the fathers insist that every verse of the scripture can be read a number of different ways, an arrangement which Aquinas aptly describes as "convenient." If a passage might prove embarrassing taken as it stands, one has only to read it in some other "sense." Needless to say the sense most frequently objected to is the crass, literal, historical one—beneath the attention of minds devoted to the contemplation of higher things. In the fathers, according to Schanz, "allegorical arbitrariness and uncontrolled whimsy run riot," expressing themselves in the scholia, the homily, and the commentary.[91]

In our own day, both for Catholics and Protestants, this lavish control has boiled down to a much simpler double bookkeeping, in which, according to Professor Pfeiffer, one must "distinguish sharply between true facts and true doctrine. . . . That the points of view of science and faith should be kept distinct is admitted by a historian who is a Roman

Catholic priest, G. Ricciotti, when he recognized that *exeget-ically* 'the sun stood still and the moon stayed' at Gibeon in a literal sense, but that scientifically 'there was no real astro-nomical perturbation.' "[92] So, the sun stood still *literally* but not astronomically.

What if Constantine only saw a sundog and not a vision of the cross? This simply proves for Father Bligh "that the value of a confession is not determined by the rational suffi-ciency of the motives that produced its first steps," and "what is true for the Emperor is true for those who imitated him,"[93] which is another way of saying that though Constantine did not have a vision at all, it is just the same as if he did since in the end he became converted.

Peter the Lombard, more bound by literal mindedness, when he finds the Bible in conflict with his science, falls back on the principle propounded by Hilary: "The thing must not be subject to the word, but the word to the thing."[94] That sounds reasonable enough: but when the word is the scrip-ture and the thing is one's own limited experience, then to subject the word to the thing is to interpret any line of scrip-ture in whatever way suits one's predilections—and as such the Lombard makes full use of it. It is an unlimited license to control the past. It is the boast of the Catholic scholar Schindler that the scholastic philosophers always denounced lying.[95] Of course they did; the purpose of their art was to make it unnecessary to lie. If one can *prove* that black is white by a syllogism, why should one be guilty of blurting it out, unproven, as a lie?

The ardent Catholic apologist Arnold Lunn recently wrote: "The Church claims that her credentials can be proved from certain books in the Bible, treating them as purely human documents. The Bible consists of a series of books selected by the Catholic Church—books which the Catholic Church claims the right to interpret. It is for the church to say where the Bible records objective facts and where the Bible uses metaphor and allegory."[96] This is self-certification with a

vengeance: the church waves before us certain documents
which she claims prove her authority; these documents she
has personally selected, but even so they do not even remotely
suggest what she claims they do unless they be read and
interpreted in a *very special sense*, that sense being carefully
prescribed—by the church! Mr. Lunn is telling us in effect
that the church has a perfect right to control the past to
prove its holy calling, even though the only proof of that
calling is the doctored document itself. A reading of Denzinger
will show the surprising degree to which the reading of the
scriptures is controlled by the Roman church; in this valuable work the extreme nervousness of the clergy about letting people read the Bible for themselves or in their own
languages goes hand in hand with the frequent and frank
admission, that while the Bible seems to swarm with *anti*-
Catholic material, to make a *pro*-Catholic case out of it
requires the labor of trained specialists equipped with highly
artificial tools of interpretation.[97]

When in 1865 John Henry Newman was consulted by a
friend regarding the founding of a Catholic historical review
he replied: "Nothing would be better—but who would bear
it? *Unless one doctored all one's facts, one would be thought
a bad Catholic.*"[98] At the same time Duchesne was protesting
in vain to his fellow church historians "that it was contrary
to a sound historical method to insist on twisting the texts to
make them talk like Athanasius," that is, to control the earlier texts in support of later theology.[99] In opposing this
Duchesne was bucking the established practice of centuries.
According to De Wulf, when St. Thomas Aquinas wants to
disagree with St. Augustine, his unfailing guide and mentor,
"he does not contradict him; he does not consider him suspect . . . instead he transforms the *meaning* of his statements,
sometimes by slight corrections, sometimes by violent
interpretations which do violence to the text." Von Hertling
has listed some 250 citations from Augustine, a good portion
of them deliberately falsified.[100]

This business is easily justified among religious writers by the law of the greater good. The Mohammedan doctors established the principle that anything which Mohammed would have said could be safely attributed to him, and on this authority put in his mouth the edict, "Whatever is in agreement with this, that is from me, whether I actually said it or not."[101]

What makes this sort of highhanded control possible is the confiding of all interpretive authority in official, appointed bodies of experts, closed corporations of professional clergy that may not be challenged from outside; they are self-certified and self-perpetuating. Nowhere have the doctors enjoyed more absolute authority than among the Jews, whose awe in the presence of formal learning is just this side of idolatry; whatever a clever scholar teaches, according to Rabbi Joshua ben Levi, is to be received as if it were the word of God spoken to Moses himself on Sinai![102]

By closing ranks and presenting a proud front to the world of common men, the clergy are spared the pains of ever having to answer back to the strong arguments against their control of the past. Any who refuse to accept their verdict are by that very act disgraced and disqualified. As often as not they gain the support of princes and potentates, and then woe to the wretch who questions them!

When the immortal Pascal, one of the supremely great intellects of all time, challenged the tricky but shallow and contradictory arguments of the Jesuits, they put him in his place by accusing him of being "a brilliant farceur without 'authority,' a lay theologian, an amateur of two days' standing, 'the ladies' theologian,' " and the like, clinching their charges with the ultimate condemnation of all upstarts: "He does not even have a doctor's degree!"[103] Thus Lunn annihilates one who dared to criticize the matchless double talk of St. Liguori: "The poor man did not realize that casuistry, like other branches of law, has its technical vocabulary and, as a result, he made a very complete fool of himself." As for

Professor Haldane, though he quotes Aquinas in the clearest possible terms, he cannot for Mr. Lunn be anything but "uninstructed and amateurish."[104] This is the last and favorite resort of the clergy when they are questioned too closely: their questioners simply don't understand; they are "uninstructed and amateurish." Unless you accept our interpretation of the texts, the layman is told, you obviously do not understand them. And if you don't understand them, you have no right to question our interpretation of them!

And so the layman is put in his place. The guarded degree, the closed corporation, the technical vocabulary, these are the inner redoubt, the inviolable stronghold of usurped authority. Locked safe within the massive and forbidding walls of institution and formality lies what the Egyptians called "the King's secret," the secret of controlling the past.

"... As Far as It Is Translated Correctly."

After all has been said about the art of selecting, censoring, rewriting, and interpreting the records of the past, the fact remains that the greatest opportunity for exercising control over the documents lies not in these mechanical chores but in the business of translating the strange and unfamiliar idioms in which the texts are written. As Joseph Smith knew so well, next to revelation it is language that holds the key to the past. This key is worth a brief examination here.

The writers of fantastic fiction often overlook the very obvious. We have yet to learn of any creation of theirs that has surpassed in boldness of conception or economy of operation that astounding device by which the human race has throughout its history been able to preserve the very thoughts of men and transmit them through unlimited expanses of time and space. Writing is a thoroughly artificial thing—no more a product of evolution than feathers or water or algebra are. It is hard to believe that the first systems of writing that arose almost simultaneously in Egypt, Sumer, Elam, and India (all these cultures being at that time in contact

with each other) were each invented independently or brought
forth in response to the needs of the business world.[105] For
though writing may have been suggested by such useful mne-
monic devices as property marks and tallies,[106] busy practical people have always got along supremely well without it.
Like the calendar—long supposed to have been the invention
of farmers, who of all people are the least dependent on the
fixed and rigid setting of days[107]—writing is only useful in
everyday life because everyday uses have been found for it.
But the businessman, however capable he may be in other
things, often becomes awkward and self-conscious when he
tries to write correctly, embarrassingly aware that he is
handling a medium that is strange to his calling.

Though writing is as old as history, practical people have
never yet got used to it, but like the generality of mankind
have persisted in viewing it as a sort of magic, an affected
and artificial thing, an ornamental accomplishment designed
for ostentation rather than for use. It is inconceivable that
true writing was ever devised as a tool for these people, let
alone by them. The really marvelous things that writing does,
the astounding feats of thought-stimulation, thought-
preservation, and thought-transmission for which it has always
been valued by a small and specialized segment of society,
"the scribes," are of no interest to practical people: business
records, private letters, school exercises, and the like are
periodically consigned to the incinerator by clerks and merchants to whom eternal preservation and limitless transmission mean nothing. The contents of such documents from
the beginning show a complete unawareness, almost a visible
contempt, for the real capabilities and uses of writing. It is
another and equally ancient type of document that knows
how to prize the true merit of the written word, and it is
easy to surmise that this wonderful device came to the human
family as a gift from parties unknown whose intent was that
it should assist the race in a sort of cosmic bookkeeping. At

any rate, that actually is the principal use to which the instrument has been put since the beginning of that history which it alone has made possible.

One might as well argue that the brace and bit was invented as a crude tool for scratching leather and later discovered to be useful for boring holes in wood as to maintain that writing was conceived as a means of keeping track of heads of beef and measures of grain by people who later discovered that far more wonderful and significant things could be done with it. The great Seal of England *can* be used to crack nuts with—a simple, practical, primitive operation, suggesting a very plausible origin—but it also has other uses. The earliest uses of writing for the keeping of accounts are in temple records, sacred things; and right along with them go the ritual texts, with an equal claim to antiquity and a far greater claim to the attention of those priests who have always been the peculiar custodians of the written word. From the beginning the written words were the *divine* words, the *mdw ntr*.[108]

To state it briefly, we find writing from the first used for two kinds of bookkeeping: for terrestrial business it is not really necessary—in fact, such masters of this field as Commodore Vanderbilt found themselves better off without it; but for celestial business it is indispensable. Which, then, is the more likely to have produced it? Every indication points to the temple.

And what an instrument! By its operation we know not only what men saw and heard and did and said three and four thousand years ago, but actually what they also thought and felt. The most delicate nuances and fleeting impulses of the mind have outlasted the enormous Cyclopean foundations of world-ruling cities, and where twenty-ton blocks may have vanished without a trace, the dreams, hopes, and surmises of the fragile people who lived among them remain as fresh and clear as ever, available to the modern world in almost embarrassing abundance. Embarrassing, because this

inestimable treasure lies neglected, even by those regiments
of professional humanists who claim to be its custodians.

The cause of this neglect is to be found in the peculiar
nature of the instrument. Our thought-transmission machine
is the simple and economical apparatus it is by virtue of
being at the same time an exceedingly sensitive one. The
price of the thing is nominal in this age of great libraries and
microfilming, but its effectiveness depends entirely on the
skill and understanding with which it is operated. True writing is not picture writing; to receive its message the reader
himself must be very specially adjusted. And when such a
reader takes it upon himself to convey to others the words of
the ancients, he himself becomes a part of the transmission
machine—its most vital element, in fact. As far as the general public is concerned, the effectiveness of the miraculous
and age-old machine for thought-transmission depends entirely
on the man who is operating it.

All the documents of antiquity without exception are
written in languages that no one speaks today. What an
opportunity this offers for controlling the past! In the field
of translation the scope and ambition of operations are simply staggering. The ancient writer and the modern reader—
producer and consumer of history respectively—are alike at
the mercy of a tyrannical middleman without whose express
permission not one word can be conveyed from the past to
the present. This serious situation demands a moment's attention. Let us consider briefly the crippling disadvantages of
trying to study church history through the medium of
translations.

The Follies of Translation

Folly Number One—Destroying the Clues: Every page of
any ancient text is a densely compact, all but solid mass of
elaborately interwoven *clues*. No two people react the same
way to these clues, and no one person reacts the same way
to them twice. Yet a translation, no matter how good, is

only one man's reaction to the clues at one time of his life. The most famous and successful translation in the English language is Fitzgerald's *Rubaiyat*. Fitzgerald's, not Omar Khayyam's, for though Fitzgerald translated the whole thing again and again, producing a different Omar each time, Fitzgerald was never satisfied that any of his poems was Omar's. The translator is like an officious detective who hands us his written report of the case but refuses to let us see the evidence for ourselves. Granted that the constable is smarter than we are and more experienced at his business, still we want to see the clues for ourselves, for in them lie the charm, challenge, and instruction of the game. In the place of a teeming, living complex of hints and suggestions which is the original text the translator gives us, as he must, only a limited number of certitudes—*his* certitudes, not the author's— and whatever fails to attract *his* attention and elicit *his* response is left unrecorded. Thus the door is closed to any critical study of any text in translation, and we have the well-known dictum that the completest critical commentary on a text is a translation of it, or in other words, that a translation is not a text at all but only a commentary on it: after the translator has given us his views there is nothing more to say. He places before us his own handiwork from which all possible interpretations but his own have been removed.

Folly Number Two—Opinions for Evidence: There are two things that no translation can convey, namely *what* the author said and *how* he said it. At the beginning of his book on the translation of Greek and Latin, Wilamowitz-Moellendorf gives a well-nigh perfect definition of a translation: "A translation is a statement in the translator's own words of what he thinks the author had in mind." He cannot, of course, state what the author actually had in mind, for only the author knows that; nor can he report what the author *said* he had in mind, for the author has already done that; he can, as Wilamowitz assures us, only tell us in his own language what he thinks the author is trying to convey.

This means that any translation is at best only an
opinion—one man's opinion of what another man had in
mind. Now the importance of ancient documents as a whole
lies in their value as *evidence*, the evidence on which we
must build the whole story of the human race. But an opinion is *not* evidence. It is not admissible in the court of scholarship for the same reason that it is not admissible in a court
of law, because it always contains a conclusion of the witness. We may not ask A for B's testimony—only B can speak
for B, and when Professor Shorey pompously entitles a book
by himself *What Plato Said* he is officiously interposing his
own person between Plato and the reader, offering himself,
like an insinuating dragoman, as interpreter for one of the
most marvelously articulate men who ever lived—whether
Plato wants him or not.

Only a *perfect* translation is ever acceptable as evidence
in any situation, for if it is anything short of absolutely perfect, how can we be sure at any given moment that the translator has not slipped up? But can there be a perfect translation?
How would it deal with double meanings and puns of which
the ancients were so fond? Or how should it convey something which the original writer had no intention of telling
us? For the student of the past the great value and charm of
many a text lies in what it reveals without the author's knowledge, as when the terminology of the philosophers unconsciously reveals their social backgrounds and prejudices. The
old writings are like questionnaires which have been filled
out by the subjects with sly intent to deceive, unaware as
they are that their every word tells the skilled investigator
something about themselves which they do not wish told.
But a translation should report, according to Wilamowitz,
only what the translator thinks the author had in mind, that
is, what he *wanted* to convey. This rule is terribly confining,
but it can't be broken, for if a translator is allowed to introduce into a writing what the author neither had in mind nor
said in so many words, there is no limit to what he might

read into a text, setting forth as actual statements of the original what is to be detected only by an interpretation of clues.
The translator has no right to go beyond the writer's intent;
but the reader of an original is bound by no such obligation—there is no limit to the things that the text might legit-
imately convey to him. This is no mere rationalization: the
experience of any teacher of the classics will confirm the
observation, made with wonder and amazement by each
succeeding generation, that every reading of an ancient author
is a new experience full of the most surprising discoveries.

Folly Number Three—The Substitute Flavor: The
commonest objection to translations is that they lose much
of the "flavor" of the original. Though that is by no means
the worst charge against them, it is a serious one, for the
"flavor" is not merely weakened or denatured by translation,
it is usually destroyed altogether, and in its place is submit-
ted something far different and almost always far inferior.
That is because the commonly translated works of antiquity
are those of high literary merit, while the men who do the
translating are almost always those of low literary gifts. There
is a saying in England that translation is the lazy scholar's
refuge. The more feeble, unoriginal, and unenterprising the
mind, the more easily and naturally it falls into the vice of
simply translating the text that it has been taught to construe
since childhood. Thus most translations are made by the last
men in the world who should be allowed to make them—
academic drones who render the text in a stilted and artificial classroom jargon no matter who is speaking in it.

The verses which a translator puts down in and under
the name of a great poet can never be greater than his own
verses would be. True, he may be working under the powerful and constant stimulation of the glorious page at his elbow;
but the example and inspiration of the original, while they
may give him the uncontrollable urge to compose matchless
poetry, can, alas! never give him the ability to do so. If it

could, America would have produced as many immortal bards as it has professors of English.

But if dullness is a common defect of translators, even genius can be a danger. For if it is unfair of a translator to do a worse job than the original poet, it is both unfair and unkind of him to do a better! The only solution is for the translator to be just as great a poet—no more, no less—as the man he is translating. And what are the chances of *that* ever happening? And if it did, the result would be not two versions of the same poem, but simply two poets writing on the same theme. Homer was to the Greeks and all who followed *the* poet, the greatest master of poetic language the world has known. Yet though poets have read and translated him in every age, to this day the only readable Homer in English is not poetry at all but prose—literally Homer with Homer left out!

Folly Number Four—The Illusion of the Literal Translation: "He who translates a verse quite literally is a liar," is the rabbinical rule.[109] If two words in two different languages had exactly the same meaning in all contexts, then it would be possible to translate the one by the other in any operation. But it is almost impossible to find two words in any two languages that have this perfect one-to-one relationship! Nothing could be more obvious than that the Latin "*in*," for example, is the same as our word "in"; yet at least half the time it is impossible to translate the one "in" by the other. For a literal translation every word in one language would require a word that matched it perfectly in the other. But the meanings of words in different languages do not coincide snugly; they only overlap loosely in limited areas; for example, "to follow" may mean to accompany, to pursue, to understand another, to succeed, to come after, to chase, to obey another, etc. All these ideas overlap with the idea of following. So when a recently found ancient Christian manuscript says that miracles come after faith, and are not meant for the unbelieving, it is an easy thing for the modern translator to take the sting out of the passage by rendering "come after" (*tabat*) as "accompany," because in some cases it *can* mean that.[110] If he is taken to task for the obvious perversion of the meaning, the translator need only point with wide-eyed innocence to the dictionary, where, sure enough, "follow" does mean "accompany." Because words only overlap in meaning, the most "literal" translation can be completely misleading.

In dealing with contemporary languages something like a one-to-one relationship may be detected in limited areas, such as sports and science. Today an Arabic, Greek, Russian, English, and French newspaper will all dutifully report that a meeting is going to "take place" at such and such a time, though the expression "take place" is not native to any of those languages but one. Still they all use it, for they speak an international idiom, the sophisticated language of world civilization. This was as true two thousand years ago as it is today, and every student has wondered why Greek and Latin seem so much alike—almost like one language with two alphabets—though fundamentally they are as different from each other as they are from English. Professor Albright has commented often on the amazing uniformity of the languages of four thousand years ago—they too had their own peculiar world-idiom.[111] As Spengler observed, it is civilizations, not cultures, that keep records (*alle Geschichte ist Stadtgeschichte*); hence the language of the records is the language of civilization and at any given time reflects a fairly uniform equipment of ideas and things, which makes the translation of contemporary languages into each other comparatively mechanical and reliable.

It is when we want to translate between languages separated by a gap of thousands of years or even a few centuries that the trouble begins. So completely does any one-to-one relationship vanish between languages that reflect widely different cultures that it may be necessary to translate one line of a text by a whole page or a page by a single line![112] So much for "literal" translation. Where a synthetic language must be translated into an analytic one or vice versa, the idea of literal translation is completely annihilated, and the experts often declare any translation at all to be out of the question. A passage from Dieterici shows what we are up against:

> In sentence structure the Semites employ short, disconnected utterances, expressed only by fits or starts, which reflect the subjective concept only in the most brief and sketchy form. The Indogermanic languages on the other hand move in well-ordered, easily-unfolding periods. The Semitic sentence is but the immediate reflection of a subjective idea (*Affekt*), it is only an opinion; the Indogermanic insists on the identity of the thought conveyed with actual reality. . . . At the institution of the sacrament, Christ cannot possibly have said anything but "this: my blood, this: my flesh," and no one present could possibly have misunderstood him. . . .
>
> Such a nominal sentence (the usual thing in Semitic) is utterly untranslatable into Greek without the word "esti" (is) which of course in the original language never existed.[113]

Yet on that *esti* rests the whole doctrine of transubstantiation. At the Marburg disputation Luther, it is said, silenced the opposition by writing upon the table with a piece of chalk: *Hoc est corpus meum*, with all the emphasis on the *est*, a word which in the language of Jesus had no equivalent! Only to one writing Latin do the fine theological distinctions between *est, ens, essens, essentia, esse*, etc., have a real, if any, significance, and when M. Gilson triumphantly defines God at the end of his search as "the pure act of being," he is uttering what, to vast numbers of the human race—in whose languages "being" is not an *act* at all and often does not even exist as a verb—would be the purest nonsense. The Latin fathers often express regret that the impossibility of rendering Greek expressions into Latin makes it impossible for them to convey a clear conception of the Godhead.[114]

Folly Number Five: The Search for Shortcuts: Most of the energy and determination that should go into surmounting the language barrier between us and the past is at present being expended in ingenious efforts to circumvent it. A widespread recognition of the limitations of translation has, for example, produced a continual outpouring of bilingual editions, with the original text on one page and the English facing it on the other. Such texts are a pernicious nuisance: if one can read the original, the translation is an impertinence, if not, the original is a rebuke. But worst of all the double text is a fiendish design for crippling the mind. No one ever knows any language as well as his own, and when confronted by two texts the eye, following the law of least resistance, will infallibly gravitate to the more familiar idiom. I defy the best scholar alive to spend a week with a Loeb text without losing a good deal of his confidence and independent judgment, for the ready translation constantly anticipates and thereby conditions all one's reactions to the clues.

Then there are special handbooks and courses designed to reduce the language barrier to a minimum by confining all effort to an assault on one single book, typical offerings being *Biblical Aramaic, New Testament Greek, Homeric Greek, Legal Latin,* etc. In these special courses, special grammars and special dictionaries, we are told just what the text is going to say before we read it. If it does not say just that for us, we have learned our lesson badly. But if we know exactly what the original text is going to tell us before we open it, why bother to open it at all? We are told exactly how to react to every word, when the whole purpose of our study is to enjoy an independent reaction.

Hardly much better are standard grammars and dictionaries. They can get the student started on his way, but they accompany him only the first few steps of his journey. The excellence of the great scholars of the Renaissance and after, lay in their early discovery that there is no such thing as the correct dictionary meaning of a word. For the most part, grammars and lexicons are loaded dice: they are tip-offs on the clues, preconditioning the reader and precluding independent reaction to the text. Professor Gardiner shows us the limitation of all mechanical helps when he explains why the translation of Egyptian is so hard:

> The meaning of the large majority of the words employed is either already known, or else can be elicited through comparison with other examples; but not the precise nuances of meaning, only the kind of meaning, its general direction and its approximate emotional quality. . . . The only basis we can have for preferring one rendering to another, when once the exigencies of grammar and dictionary have been satisfied—and these leave a large margin for divergencies—is an intuitive appreciation of the trend of the ancient writer's mind. A very precarious basis, all will admit. [115]

If language followed natural laws, then the area of intuition might be reduced to nothing and a machine for perfect translation be devised. But one of the greatest charms of language is that it may be used waywardly, wantonly, whimsically, ironically, subtlely, inanely, or literally to any degree which a writer chooses—and it is the greatest masters of language that take the most liberties with it. The very purpose of literature is to annihilate boredom, and for most people the rules of grammar are a bore. The rigid rules of grammar infallibly suggest naughty tricks to the creative mind, which loves to crack the mold of usage upon which the whole regularity of language depends. And once the genius has struck off in a new direction the million promptly and gladly follow him, and in their dogmatic, unimaginative way turn the new grammatical felony into a law of grammar.[116] Thus in an endless antiphonal the spirit rebukes the letter, and the letter checks the spirit, and by the time the machine has caught up with the mind, the mind is already two jumps ahead of it.

This endless game effectively disqualifies another device by which students have hoped to circumvent the language obstacle. This is the study of linguistics. The arbitrariness of language makes all the general laws subject to change without notice. In linguistics one is everlastingly discovering and demonstrating the two principles, (1) that people are very conservative, and (2) that in spite of that, rules *do* get broken. If the human race were absolutely conservative, we could have reliable rules of language.[117] But fortunately the very men and women who take the most liberties with language are those who have the most influence upon it: The people who make the rules are the people who break them.

A belated attempt to remove the language barrier is the invention of simplified languages, such as basic English, and of new international idioms such as Esperanto, Volapuk, and Interlingua. These languages prove what we should have known long ago: that the languages men speak today are much harder than they ever need to be, that people like it that way, and that they find language devoid of challenge to be tasteless to the point of nausea. After all, language, as its name tells us, is something that is on the tongue—it must have flavor, and a body, or we spit it out. This was even truer in ancient times: "What the evidence suggests," writes Lord Raglan, "is that the originators, not of language but of all known languages, were people of acute and fertile minds who took a pride and a pleasure in working out complex grammatical systems, systems which merely as a means of communication are quite unnecessary."[118] We may find such artificiality regrettable, but let us not forget that all language is artificial—there is no rule in speech, any more than there is in music; genius must work with instruments that nature alone has created.

The language of Homer, Vergil, the Eddas, and the *Qasidas* is pure professional jargon, about as artificial as a thing can be. While the evolutionists think of language as a tool, the human race itself resents functionalism in language as it does in dress.

The value of a language is not to be measured by its efficiency: The greatest languages are the hardest. The operation of a hard grammatical apparatus requires a certain minimum of mental effort, even of those who have grown up with the language (does the fact that English is our mother tongue make the spelling of English easy for us?); it guarantees a degree of cerebration which easier languages do not. The mere statement of a thing in some languages is a mental challenge. The Romans envied the superior difficulty of Greek and did their best to make their own language like it. Their writings display a conscious mental effort which they positively enjoyed and which is the chief stimulus of Latin to this day—one never misses a sense of exercise, of stretching one's mental muscles, which is disturbingly lacking in some less vertebrate languages. Looking at a page of Latin one can readily see that almost every word has a familiar root and that the story might be very simply and easily told in Spanish or French. Yet superimposed over the whole page, like a complicated template over a map, is a grammatical pattern so laborious and arbitrary that the best scholars must spend hours trying to figure out simple sentences. And this tough and annoying apparatus is entirely unnecessary. It shows us that language does more than fill a need for elementary communication. It is mankind's other world, a dream world, the playing field, the parade ground, the shady retreat, the laboratory, the theater, the forum, the mirror of the cosmos; we must allow it infinite scope and infinite ambition. Along with that it is also a tool, a means of communication of man not only with his fellows but also with himself. This takes us:

Beyond the Gadgets

Today we have machines that do most of our calculations for us. IBM machine "702" is now ready to take over all the functions of accounting and bookkeeping in a world which lives by those disciplines. [119] At a total of only six percent of present capital outlay, it is estimated, all the big industry of the United States could be operated almost entirely by mechanical controls. Three cheers! What a machine can do, that a machine should do. But what remains for us? Science without gadgets! That we can do some things that no machine can or conceivably ever could do—therein lies our true dignity and destiny as human beings. The checking and ushering and bookkeeping, all the automatic and repetitious things that make up the day's work for most modern men, have no business being done by living people; some day they may be done as they should be, by machines, and then men can really get down to business.

Yet for most of us such a prospect is simply terrifying. The busy-work that rightfully belongs to the machine is the refuge of the timid mind, and it is to the gadgetry of scholarship—the pretentious secretarial tasks of compiling, annotating, copying, checking, abridging, and the rest—that the academic world clings today with a sort of desperation. Regiments of workers equipped with costly machinery are busy searching out, digging up, acquisitioning, classifying, cataloging, preserving, reproducing, disseminating, explaining, displaying, and even selling the documents of the past—doing every conceivable thing with the documents but reading them! They are waiting for the reading machine that will never come. Three hundred and fifty years ago Joseph Scaliger could read more ancient texts and comprehend what he read more clearly than any scholar in the world today. Scientists can stand on the shoulders of those who have gone before, but not humanists. The latest text in astronomy supersedes and supplants whole shelves of earlier textbooks, but the humanist must start with his ABCs and read on, page by page, through the very same literature that Casaubon and Lipsius had to wade through centuries ago. Summaries, condensations, and translation will help him not at all, for they are only opinions and bound to be out of date. A rapid skimming of the stuff is out of the question. What a joyful thing to contemplate—the one boundless task left to man in the universe![120]

During the past century repeated attempts have been made to handle the vast and ever-growing bulk of stuff bequeathed us by the ancients by certain ingenious experiments in *repackaging*. Against a roar of protest Lord Acton introduced the study of history at Cambridge, but this did not reduce but only added to the amount of materials to be handled by the conscientious student. Today ambitious men would grasp the whole message of the human record by repackaging it in this or that social science: the packages are impressively tied and labeled—but there is very little in them, and nothing of the original source material that makes up the vast preponderance of the field notes and lab notes of the human race. A new school of archaeology is trying to grasp the same prize, claiming that they can discover the past simply by looking at pictures—which is much easier than reading texts. Leading archaeologists are loudly deploring this tendency, which is bound to become as popular as it is futile. While any text may be meaningful without pictures (though illustrations are always welcome), no picture can convey its real meaning without reference to some text: to abolish the text is to abolish archaeology, and to abolish the original language is to abolish the text. The glamorous package, a great aid to salesmanship, has no place in scholarship: it will do nothing either to surmount or circumvent the language barrier.

But you can't expect people to learn scores of languages to be able to survey the past! They don't need to. It is one of the delightful compensations to the student willing to go the hard way that Providence, as if taking pity on his plight and concerned lest the staggering accumulations of the past go neglected in an inextricable maze of hundreds of forgotten languages, had removed the difficulty by a most marvelous device: the world language.

One wishing to study twentieth century world civilization could do so knowing one language alone—English—and he would pretty well have to know that. But English still has serious competitors as a world language, and it has only been on top for forty years. Imagine, then, how important our language would be if it had been the *only* world language, without competitors, *for a thousand years!* What if for ten centuries everything of any importance that was thought or said in the western world had to be said and written down in English. Well, for a thousand years Latin actually was the one language of the West, while at the same time Arabic ruled the East. And before that for another thousand years—the most creative period of all—Greek was the common world language of East *and* West. And before that for yet another thousand years, a common Semitic idiom was the learned and diplomatic language of the world. The greatest and most significant works of the human mind, as well as the smallest and most insignificant efforts of the schoolmen, are almost all recorded in a few languages, and the records of the past run not into innumerable linguistic puddles to be searched out and correlated but are conveniently channeled into a few vast, all-inclusive reservoirs. This should make it clear why a knowledge of certain languages is absolutely indispensable to any serious study of the past, and why their neglect has led to a serious crippling of all our efforts to get a convincing picture of what men have really been doing and thinking through the ages. The gadgets will never answer that question for us.

But if scholarship is not a slide-rule science, it has certain controls which any science might envy. Antiquity is a romantic study; it has an irresistible appeal to the glamor hunter and the poseur; everybody wants to get into the act. The result is a chaos of clashing ambitions and waspish tempers, with amateurs and "professionals" everlastingly accusing each other of stupidity and humbug. Without a governor the humanities get completely and quickly out of hand. But in language we have perfect control: The man who can read off the ancient text you place before him is not likely to be an irresponsible crackpot. The rigid check on the scholar does not lie in the judgment of his fellows—scholars band easily together into groups and schools and conform their thinking to that of prevailing movements with notorious servility— the perfect teacher of virtue is the text itself. The scholar with an ancient text before him may do with it as he chooses: He may insert any vowels he pleases if it is in a Semitic language; he may divide up consonants into whatever groups catch his fancy; he may punctuate to taste; he may give any word, allegorically, any meaning he wants to; in short, he can cheat to his heart's content. But how far will it get him? Every wrong and wilful reading must be supported by another one: If one word is arbitrarily treated, the next must be beaten into conformity with it, and the resulting sentence, all wrong, must match the next sentence, and so on. With every wrong reading the student gets himself deeper into the mud; the farther he carries the game the more humiliating it becomes; with every new syllable his position becomes more intolerable and the future more threatening. In the end he gives up and starts all over again—the text, unaided and alone, has won the day.

The more one considers the power of the written word, the more miraculous it appears. The determined and desperate efforts to control it which we have been describing are a remarkable tribute to its uncanny capacity to convey the truth regardless of designing men. Within the last decade a few simple scrolls have successfully overcome the solid and determined opposition of scholarly consensus and shattered all the fondest beliefs and firmest preconceptions of church historians. Church history must now be written all over again and it is to the most vital questions of that fascinating subject that we must now turn our attention.

In times of world crisis and widespread calamity, those churchmen who normally exhibit a bland and easy confidence in the assured and inevitable triumph of Christianity through the ages find themselves pressed by the force of events to ask questions and indulge in reflections which in better times are left strictly alone. We have suggested already that the key to conventional church history is its fair-weather determination not to face up to certain unpleasant, nay, alarming possibilities, in particular the proposition that the church of Christ did not survive in the world long after the Apostles.

But today, as at other moments of great upheaval, such authorities, Catholic and Protestant, as D. Busy, Bardy, A. G. Herbert, and F. A. M. Spencer are moved to remind us that, after all, Christianity has never come anywhere near either converting or saving the world. Instead of the moral reform which the fourth-century fathers promised with such confidence, if the empire would only turn officially Christian, came a disastrous deterioration of morals; instead of world peace (also promised), world war; instead of prosperity, economic collapse; instead of the promised intellectual certainty, violent controversy; instead of faith, speculation and doubt; instead of tolerance and love, ceaseless polemic and persecution; instead of trust in God, cynicism and power politics. The world once Christianized not only remained barbarian, but became also more and more barbaric as it passed from one century of Christian tutelage to the next. Contemporary scholars freely admit, since they can't deny it, that something went very wrong. A. G. Herbert, a Catholic writer, now even goes so far as to declare that defeat,

264 MORMONISM AND EARLY CHRISTIANITY

not victory, is "the hall-mark of authenticity" for the church of Christ on earth.

So much being conceded, the only question is not whether God would allow his church to suffer—he *has* allowed it—but how far he would allow things to go? Some Christians when pressed will allow that the rule of evil reached the point of *almost* complete extermination for the church on earth; this is the Baptist "trail of blood" theory—that the church has been reduced from time to time to an almost imperceptible trickle but never allowed to go out entirely. The last inch, of course, they cannot concede, for that would be fatal to all their claims. To save at least the tattered remnants of the true church, modern claimants fall back on three main arguments. The first is the perfectly irrelevant "gates of hell" passage (Matthew 16:18), which we shall discuss later. The second is what they like to call "the simple fact" that the church has, for all its setbacks and troubles, persisted in the world unintermittently for nigh onto two thousand years. This is worth a moment's thought.

Actually that statement of survival merely assumes what it claims to prove, namely that whatever has come through so many centuries must be the *true* church. But the fact that churches (*never* just one, and usually many) calling themselves Christ's have been found on the earth in every century since the apostles is no proof in itself that all or any of those churches really were Christ's. After all, did not the Lord himself predict a time when there would be many groups bearing his name and saying, "Lo, here is Christ, or there!" and did not he warn that at such a time *none* of those professing Christians would be authorized? (Matthew 24:23.) As the so-called Apostolic Fathers and the early apologists never tire of repeating, the *name* of Christian does *not* guarantee the Lord's approval of recognition of the individual or society bearing it, nor does its presence in the earth prove at any time that Christ's church has survived. So though we find in

every age churches claiming to be the true heirs of the apostles, and though we are under obligation to investigate them
all, we are by no means bound to accept any one of them
simply because it is big or old—least of all, simply because it
exists. Athanasius says the argument of bigness is preposter-
ous; Justin Martyr says the argument of antiquity is vicious.
The argument of mere existence is the weakest of all, when
at no time since Christ have there failed to be numbers of
Christian churches all damning each other as impostors.

The third argument, usually delivered in shocked and
outraged tones, is that God simply would not allow a complete dissolution of his church. "Can God fail?" cried an
angry priest to the writer, with a great show of indignation.
Well, God has "failed" to give the earth two moons or equip
the human race with gold teeth—but is that *failure*? One can
speak only of failure where an intended aim is not achieved;
where desirable things are dispensed with, that is not failure
but policy. "How often" would God have done things for the
people—"and ye would not!" (Matthew 23:37.) To learn what
God's intention and policy are in the matter, we must consult not our own common sense or emotions but the statements of his prophets: "My ways are not your ways!" The
ancient pagans loved to charge the Christians with believing
in a God who was either immoral because he knowingly
allowed the existence of evil or weak because he could not
prevent it. Their logical minds could not conceive how anything could happen in a universe ruled by an omnipotent
God which was not the immediate and consummate expression of that God's desire and intention. Those Christians are
guilty of the same vanity and impetuosity who insist that
because they just can't see the point in taking the church
from the earth, God would be foolish and unjust—a failure—if he permitted it. The solution of the problem lies not
in men's feelings on a subject on which they are necessarily
very ill-informed, but in God's expressed intention in the

matter. Fortunately the New Testament contains full and explicit information.

The Three Acts of the Drama:—First of all, Christ knew and explained to others the nature and outcome of his own mission: what his purpose was in coming to earth, how he would be received here, and what would happen after he left. These points are all touched upon in a single parable—the only parable in the Bible to which the Lord himself has left us a full explanation. The parable might be called a drama in three acts. Act One is the Lord's earthly mission, in which he likens himself "unto a man which sowed good in his field" (Matthew 13:24, 37), the field being the world, (Matthew 13:38). In Act Two the villain enters: "But while men slept, his enemy came and sowed tares among the wheat" (Matthew 13:25), and as a result the crop was spoiled: "when the blade was sprung up, and brought forth fruit, then appeared the tares also" (Matthew 13:26). This sorry state of things, with wheat and tares indistinguishably mixed together, does not represent the state of the church, for we are explicitly told that the ruined field is the *world*, in which the good seed ("the children of the kingdom") have not yet been brought together (Matthew 13:27–30). This time of confusion is a long one, lasting "until the harvest," which is Act Three, entitled "the end of the world" (Matthew 13:39). Here everything is set to rights again, and the wheat is finally gathered together out of the world and "into my barn" (Matthew 13:30). "A gathering out" happens to be the very meaning of the world *ekklesia*—"church." In the settling of accounts in the last act the tares are bound in bundles for the burning, and "*then* shall the righteous shine forth as the sun in the kingdom of their Father" (Matthew 13:43; italics added), "so shall it be at the end of this world" (Matthew 13:40). It is a happy ending, indeed, but a delayed one: first the Lord, then the adversary, who is the devil (Matthew 13:39), and finally the Lord again.

The parable of the vineyard tells the same story. In Act One we learn that the master of the vineyard, having been detained in a far country, has in the past sent many servants—the prophets—to receive the fruit at the hand of those he had left in charge; but his messengers have all been roughly treated and thrown out. Now he has decided to send his Beloved Son, saying, "it may be they will reverence him" (Luke 20:13; Matthew 21:37). But in the Second Act we see the Son treated even worse than the others, cast out of the vineyard and slain by villainous men who say, "Let us kill him, and let us seize on his inheritance . . ."; "let us kill him, that the inheritance may be *ours*" (Matthew 21:38; Luke 20:14). So they claim the vineyard for their own and remain in possession until Act Three, when the lord of the vineyard comes to destroy the impostors and turns the vineyard over to authorized workers (Luke 20:16). It is the same three-act theme as the other parable: first the Lord's work, then the triumph of the impostor, finally the return and triumph of the Lord.

The first two of these acts are the legitimate subject of church history, since the third either has not happened yet or opens with the restoration of the gospel, which conventional church history does not recognize. Let us consider the major steps of the drama as far as the New Testament is concerned. First of all, the Lord came into the world knowing full well that he and his message would be rejected: even as Elias had come "and they knew him not, but have done unto him whatsoever they listed. Likewise shall also the Son of man suffer of them" (Matthew 17:12); "for from the days of John the Baptist [Elias] . . . the kingdom of heaven suffereth violence, and the violent take it by force" (Matthew 11:12). At the outset of his mission he was met by "two possessed with devils," who recognized him for what he was and hailed him as the Son of God, with the request that he leave them alone and not torment them "before the time" (Matthew 8:28-29). Immediately thereafter a whole city of mortal men followed

the lead of those evil spirits "and besought him that he would
depart out of *their* coasts" (Matthew 8:34). Neither devils
nor men would accept his preaching nor did he expect them
to:

> Why do ye not understand my speech? even because
> ye cannot hear my word.
> Ye are of your father the devil, and the lusts of your
> father ye will do. . . .
> And because I tell you the truth, ye believe me not.
> Which of you convinceth me of sin? And, if I say the
> truth, why do ye not believe me?
> . . . because ye are not of God (John 8:43–47).

He expected only hatred from a world who came to testify of it "that the works thereof are evil" (John 7:7.) "I know
you," he said to his hearers, "that ye have not the love of
God in you" (John 5:42), for truly "he knew all men." He
made no effort to wheedle, persuade, or meet the world half-
way. Said his enemies:

> Master, we know that thou art true, and teachest the
> way of God in truth, neither carest thou for any man: for
> thou regardest not the person of men (Matthew 22:16;
> Mark 12:14; Luke 20:21).

If Jerusalem refused to be gathered to him, no matter
how often he would have gathered them, he would not force
them (Matthew 23:37). If his hometown people put no faith
in him, he could do no mighty works for them (Mark 6:5;
Matthew 14:2). If they wanted to go so far as to "kill the
Prince of Life" (Acts 3:15), even then he would not resist
them (James 5:6).

Either we have here a very weak character or else he has
definite reasons for his behavior. The reason and purpose of
his preaching he makes very clear; like the other prophets,
he has been sent as a *witness* by the Father: "We speak what
we do know, and testify that we have seen; and ye receive

not our witness" (John 3:11). "And what he hath seen and heard, that he testifieth; and no man receiveth his testimony" (John 3:32). As in the days of Noah, the witness was given and rejected:

> The world was made by him, and the world knew him not. He came unto his own, and his own received him not (John 1:10–11).

Even as their ancestors did not believe in Moses, "ye also have seen me, and believe not" (John 6:36); "for neither did his brethren believe in him" (John 7:5). "The world cannot receive the spirit of truth" (see John 14:17). Why then bother to preach it? The answer is clear: "For judgment I am come into this world" (John 9:39)—that judgment to take place at a later date; "the Father . . . hath committed all judgment unto the Son" (John 5:22), but during his earlier mission he did not judge. Men are free to accept or reject him as they will: "And if any man hear my words, and believe not, I judge him not: for I came not to judge the world, but to save the world.

"He that rejecteth me . . . hath one that judgeth him [lit. "one to judge him"]: the word I have spoken, the same shall judge him in the last day" (John 12:47–48). No judgment now, but "in the last day." "Therefore judge nothing before the time, until the Lord come," writes Paul (1 Corinthians 4:5), "who both will bring to light the hidden things of darkness, and will make manifest the counsels of the hearts: and *then* shall every man have praise of God" (italics added). The time of Christ and the apostles was not to be the time of judgment, but of testing; without the opportunity of freely accepting or rejecting, there could be no judgment: "If I had not done among them the works which none other man did, they had not had sin: but *now* they have both seen and hated both me and my Father" (John 15:24; italics added). That was the purpose of his preaching to them—to give them the

chance, not to convert them no matter what—"That the saying of Esaias the prophet might be fulfilled, which he spake,
Lord, who hath believed our report? . . .

"Therefore they could not believe" (John 12:38–41); "their
ears are dull of hearing, and their eyes they have closed; lest
at any time they should see with their eyes, and hear with
their ears, and should understand with their heart, and should
be converted" (Matthew 13:15). The world is not going to be
converted, but it *is* going to be judged. The first act of the
drama is all a preparation, not for the second act, but for the
last one—the second coming and the judgment; on that time
and event all the apostles fix their gaze as the reward and
vindication of all they are doing. In between lies the dark
and dismal interlude of the second act about which the Lord
and the apostles have a great deal to say.

Having been as completely as possible rejected by the
world—cast out of the vineyard and slain—the Lord was to
depart thence and leave the stage clear to the adversary for
the gloomy second act. This is a long period in which people
go about seeking the Lord in vain and falsely but loudly proclaiming themselves to be the true heirs of the vineyard.
First, the departure of the Lord, in no happy mood: "O
faithless and perverse generation, how long shall I be with
you, and suffer you?" (Luke 9:41). He is going to rise up and
"shut the door" (see Luke 13:25). "The days will come, when
the bridegroom shall be taken from them, and then shall
they fast" (Matthew 9:15). "Hereafter I will not talk much
with you: for the prince of this world cometh, and hath
nothing in me" (John 14:30).

Then, surprisingly enough, once he is gone, everyone,
the wicked as well as the righteous, will desire Christ and
seek after him—but in vain. Just as the wicked world venerated the prophets and painted their tombs after they had
been safely put to death (Matthew 23:29–33), so they would
worship Christ—at a safe distance.

Yet a little while am I with you, and then I go unto
him that sent me.

Ye shall *seek* me, and shall *not* find me: and where I
am, thither ye cannot come (John 7:33-34).

I go my way, and ye shall *seek* me, and shall die in
your sins: whither I go, ye cannot come (John 8:21).

Little children, yet a little while I am with you. Ye
shall *seek* me: and as I said unto the Jews, *Whither* I go, ye
cannot come; so now I say unto you" (John 13:33).

The days will come, when ye shall *desire* to see one of
the days of the Son of man, and ye shall not see it.

And they shall say to you, See here; or, see there: go
not after them, nor follow them (Luke 17:22-23; italics
added).

In these speeches the Lord is addressing not the wicked
but his followers; even for them the quest will be vain; plainly
there are conditions and time limits attached to the promise
"Seek and ye shall find," and "Lo, I am with you alway,
even unto the end of the world" (Matthew 28:20). In their
search they are warned not to follow after *any* of the groups
claiming to be the church—to have found Jesus. Those who
are looking admit they have not found him—they are not the
church; and all the rest are impostors! Once he has risen up
and has shut the door, then all will call upon his name and
clamor to be numbered among his followers—but then it will
be too late: he will refuse to recognize them (see Luke
13:25-27). "In vain do they worship me" (Matthew 15:9) is
not a denunciation of idolatry, but of those marching under
the banner of Christ. There is a point of no return after
which even repentance comes too late, as Esau learned to his
sorrow: "For ye know how that afterward, when he would
have inherited the blessing, he was rejected: for he found no
chance to repent [*metanoias topon*, 'place of repentance'],
though he sought it carefully with tears" (Hebrews 12:17).
He wants to repent sincerely and makes every effort to be
reinstated in his inheritance, but it is too late; he is "rejected"

even as those will be rejected who cry "Lord! Lord!" and try to get into the kingdom of Christ (Matthew 7:21). The time is coming when vast numbers shall claim Christ for their own, and when that time comes, "if *any* man shall say unto you, Lo, here is Christ, or there; believe it not" (Matthew 24:23; italics added). And that time is not far off: "the time draweth near [when many shall come *in my name*]; . . . go ye not therefore after them" (Luke 21:8). It is true, the real church is going to be there for a time, but the story is one of constantly deepening gloom until, to use Polycarp's famous phrase, after the apostles "the light went out."

The beautiful and much-quoted words "I am the light of the world" are rarely given in full, since their purpose is to make clear that the light is *not* going to remain in the world:

I must work the works of him that sent me, while it is day: the night cometh, when no man can work.
As long as I am in the world, I am the light of the world (John 9:4–5).

It is not the night of death referred to here (the scripture knows no such expression), but a night that keeps *men* from doing a particular kind of work—"the works of him that sent me," the Father's work, the work of the church. What follows the Lord's mission is not victory but darkness: "The light shineth in the darkness; and the darkness comprehendeth it not" (John 1:5).

Yet a little while is the light with you. Walk while ye have the light, lest darkness come upon you:
. . . While ye have light, believe in the light (John 12:35–36).

"And this is the condemnation [literally, 'the process of judgment'], that light is come into the world, and men loved darkness rather than light, because their deeds were evil" (John 3:19).

The Role of the Apostles: But aren't we forgetting about Christ's "successors"? A "successor" is one who comes after and takes the place of another. To be a successor it is not enough merely to outlive another or come after him, one must hold his identical office and function. Even a regent is not successor to a king—only a king can be that; when a vice president takes over on the death of a president, he does not become his successor until he, too, is president. The scriptures never call the apostles Christ's successors; there is only one successor to the Lord mentioned in the Bible, and that is the Holy Ghost, "whom the Father will send in my name, he shall teach you all things, and bring all things to your remembrance, whatsoever I have said unto you" (John 14:26). Here is a true successor, coming expressly to take the Lord's place: "if I go not away, the Comforter will not come unto you; but if I depart, I will send him unto you" (John 16:7). Sent by the same authority, he will do the very same work, speak the identical words, be a witness for the judgment, and guide the apostles in all things exactly as the Lord had done (John 16:8–15).

As for the disciples, the famous passage in Mark (13:34–37) describes them as servants left behind with authorization to do special jobs: the Lord "left his house, and gave to his servants the authority, to each one his task, and commanded the porter to watch." There is no mention of supreme authority being given to anyone, but to each the authority for his particular work. The fact that every soldier in the army acts with the authority of the commander-in-chief does not give any one of them the fulness of authority that he possesses. But what about the servants? Were they expected to carry on the work and prosper where the master was rejected?

By no means! "The servant is not greater than his lord. If they have persecuted me, they will also persecute you" (John 15:20). "If they have called the master of the house Beelzebub, how much more shall they call them of his household" (Matthew 10:25)? "If the world hate you, ye know that it

hated me before it hated you" (John 15:18). The mission of
the apostles does not bring about a new and happy turn of
events in the drama; where the master has "failed," we are
told not to look for success for the servants: "Behold, I send
you forth as lambs among wolves" (Luke 10:3; Matthew
10:16). He had gone as a lamb to the slaughter; their fate
was to be no different. They are repeatedly told that they are
to occupy a rear guard position in which they can expect no
relief in this world: "I think," says Paul "that God hath set
forth us the apostles *last*, as it were appointed to death" (1
Corinthians 4:9); and he describes the brethren as "the filth
of the world, and . . . are the offscouring of all things unto
this day" (1 Corinthians 4:13). Are the apostles rejected like
the master? They are cast off! Their orders were to endure to
the end, and, as Tertullian reminds us,[121] there was absolutely no doubt in the mind of any early Christian as to
what that meant: to endure to the end meant just one thing,
"to suffer the end," to suffer death. "And ye shall be hated *of
all men*" (Luke 21:17). "Then shall they deliver you up to be
afflicted, and shall *kill* you. But he that endures to the *end*
shall be *saved* (see Matthew 24:9, 13; italics added).

In that last sentence we are given both the expected
outcome and the reward of the apostolic preaching. As he
went to his death, Christ said to his apostles, "In the world
ye shall have tribulation: but be of good cheer; I have overcome the world" (John 16:33). His victory was in the resurrection, and in that alone the apostles put all their hope of
victory and expectation of reward.

> Knowing that he which raised up the Lord Jesus shall
> raise up us also by Jesus, . . .
> For *which* cause we faint not (2 Corinthians 4:14, 16).

"Ye shall be betrayed . . . and some of you . . . be put
to death. . . .

"But there shall not an hair of your head perish" (Luke 21:16, 18). Paul is more than willing to suffer "the loss of all things, and do count them but dung. . . .

"If by any means I might attain unto the resurrection of the dead. . . .

"I press toward the mark for the prize" (Philippians 3:8, 11, 14), the prize being "to know him and the power of his resurrection" (Philippians 3:10). So, at the conclusion of his missionary labors, Paul can claim for his work an unqualified success, and that immediately after noting that things are going to be much worse in the church after his departure (Acts 20:29), that "all they which are in Asia [the bulk of his converts] be turned away from me" (2 Timothy 1:15), and that in a recent controversy "no man stood with me, but all men forsook me" (2 Timothy 4:16). In what then does the victory and success consist? "Henceforth there is laid up for me a crown . . . which the Lord, the righteous judge, shall give me at that day" (2 Timothy 4:8). It never occurs to him or any other apostle that his success is to be measured by the converts he makes. Even spiritual power on this earth was not their objective: "Rejoice not, that the spirits are subject to you; but rather rejoice, because your names are written in heaven" (Luke 10:20). That great institution toward which the apostles are striving in no way resembles any later churches: "I appoint unto you a kingdom . . . that he may eat and drink at my table in my kingdom, and sit on thrones, judging the twelve tribes of Israel" (Matthew 19:28). "For our conversation is in heaven; from whence also we look for the Savior, . . . who shall change our vile body, that it may be fashioned like unto his glorious body" (Philippians 3:20-21).

The heavenly kingdom, the second coming, the judgment, the resurrection—it is clear what these men were working for. Never once in the days of the early church does anyone so much as hint at great expectations for the church on this earth, never is its future success and glory suggested as a

motive for their works or a comfort for their afflictions; even
in the midst of the fiercest persecutions when the saints need
"strong comfort" no one ever suggests the thought that relief
is on the way, that the church will win out in the end, that it
is their duty to stick it out so that generations yet unborn
may call them blessed (a theme familiar to all of them from
the example of *pius Aeneas*, but never used by the Christians), that they are building up the church which is to fill
the earth and save mankind, etc. These are the noisy
trumpetings of the fourth century which only make more
significant the thundering silence of the earlier period on the
future of the church. Either the apostles were remarkably
mean and self-centered men, exclusively concerned with their
individual salvation and a distant judgment, or else the victory for the church which they steadfastly refuse to promise
or even mention and for which they express no yearnings
and to which they dedicate no strivings was simply not in
the program. When Tertullian[122] in a later age, sorely perplexed by the spiritual poverty of the church, tried to comfort himself and quiet his misgivings with the thought that
the church *could* not have been taken from the earth because
in that case the martyrs would all have shed their blood in
vain, he was forgetting two all-important things: first, that
the virtues and sufferings of one man or generation do not
accrue automatically to the advantage of another—it is quite
possible, as Paul reminds the Galatians, for the church to
suffer in vain; and second, that the martyrs have received
the only reward they ever thought to get—if one wins eternal
life and glory one can hardly be said to have "run in vain"!

The program of the apostles' mission was the same as
that of the Lord's. Before they ever began to work, they were
told that they would be "hated of all men" (Mark 13:13),
betrayed and put to death as he was (John 16:2), allowed to
preach for a while, but then be thrust out of the synagogues
and put to death by pious souls who "think that they are
doing God a favor," even as the "devout and honourable

women, and the chief men of the city, . . . expelled them out of their coasts" (Acts 13:50). "Go unto this people, and say, Hearing ye shall hear, and shall not understand; and seeing ye shall see, and not perceive" (Acts 28:26). "Behold, ye despisers, and wonder, and perish: for I work a work in your days, a work which ye shall in no wise believe, though a man declare it unto you" (Acts 13:41). "We are troubled on every side, yet not distressed; we are perplexed, but not in despair; persecuted, but not forsaken; cast down, but not destroyed" (2 Corinthians 4:8–9).

Whence this indomitable optimism—in the belief that the work is going forward and the church growing? Not a word of that: "Knowing that he which raised up the Lord Jesus, shall raise up us also. . . .

"For which cause we faint not. . . . For our light affliction, which is but for a moment, worketh for us . . . eternal weight of glory;

"While we look not at things which are seen, but at the things which are not seen: . . . which are . . . eternal" (2 Corinthians 4:14, 16–18).

And what point was there in preaching to a world that would not listen to them? It is the same as with Christ and the prophets: "as it was in the days of Noah," the gospel of the kingdom was to be "preached in all the world *for a witness* unto all nations; and then shall the *end* come" (Matthew 24:14, italics added). First the witness, then the end. "But ye denied the Holy One and the Just, . . . and killed the Prince of life, whom God hath raised from the dead; whereof we are *witnesses*" (Acts 3:14–15, italics added). Paul tells us why he bothered to preach to the Jews, who he knew would not hear him, when "he shook his raiment, and said unto them, Your blood be upon your own heads; I am clean: from henceforth I will go unto the Gentiles" (Acts 18:6). To the Gentiles he preached with the same expectations and for the same reason. Though these converts later fell victims to the wolves, turned against him en masse (2 Timothy 1:15), and became his enemies because he told them the truth (Galatians 4:16), he can leave them with the same assurance of "mission accomplished" that he left the Jews: "I know that ye all . . . shall see my face no more. "Wherefore I take you to record this day, that I am pure from the blood of all men" (Acts 10:25–26). The concern of the apostles is not whether they are believed or not but only whether they bear testimony to all against the day of judgment. Those who hear and reject such a testimony are classed with Sodom and Gomorrah and reserved for "the day of judgment" (Luke 10:12). The apostles are not to judge until they sit on thrones in the kingdom: "Judge nothing before the time until the Lord cometh" (1 Corinthians 4:5) is their instruction.

The apostles were not to spend time overcoming opposition and winning people by long-term programs, as a project of conversion demands; they were rather to bear their testimonies and be on their way in all possible haste. "And whosoever shall not receive you, nor hear you, when ye depart thence, shake off the dust under your feet for a *testimony against them*" (Mark 6:11, italics added). The program outlined in Matthew 10 and Luke 9 is not that of founding solid institutions, but of last-minute emergency: "I send you forth as lambs among wolves. . . . Salute no man by the way" (Luke 10:3–4). What is wrong with a purse and scrip, and extra cloak, or overnight visits? Nothing at all, save that there is no time left for the ordinary business and amenities of life, as Paul tells the Corinthians: marriage, mourning, celebrating, business, careers—all that must be forgotten now, for "the time [literally, 'opportunity'] is short" (1 Corinthians 7:29), "for the fashion [*schema*: 'the system'] of this world passeth away" (1 Corinthians 7:31). Only for food and lodging were the missionaries to go to individual houses; otherwise, "Go not from house to house" (Luke 10:7), but "in that city that does not receive you, go your ways out into the streets of the same and say: Even the very dust . . . we do wipe off *against you*: notwithstanding be ye sure of this, that the kingdom of God is come nigh unto you" (Luke 10:10-11). After they have had their chance, the apostles' business with them is over: "Ye shall be brought before rulers and kings for my sake, *for a testimony against them* . . . and ye shall be hated of all men for my name's sake" (Mark 13:9-13). "Ye are *witnesses* for me . . . unto the uttermost part of the earth" (Acts 1:8), for "repentance and remission of sins should be preached in his name among all nations, beginning at Jerusalem. And ye are *witnesses* of these things" (Luke 24:47-48, italics added).

The Passing of the Church: But even if the apostles were to suffer the same rejection and death as the master, is not the gloom of the "second act" relieved by the survival of the church? What of the "little children" whom they taught? Alas! they are given the same promise of extinction; they, too, are required to "endure to the end" and are given the same comfort and promise—eternal life. "If *any* man will come after me," he must lose his life (Matthew 16:24-25; Mark 8:34-35; Luke 9:23-24). The whole church—not just the apostles—are to be partakers in Christ's sufferings in a physical sense, and receive the incorruptible inheritance "reserved in heaven for you . . . [and] receive the end [reward] of your faith, even the salvation of your souls" (see 1 Peter 1:4, 9). "Forasmuch then as Christ hath suffered for us in the flesh, arm yourselves likewise with the same mind" (1 Peter 4:1). What the saints can look forward to here is necessities, distresses, stripes, imprisonments, tumults, and fastings (2 Corinthians 6:4-5). The exhortation to the saints is all for a last-ditch stand; they are to "take . . . the prophets . . . for an example of suffering affliction, and of patience," with the only hope of relief in the coming of the Lord (see James 5:10). They must work in the limited time they have here, "while it is called Today; . . . For we are made partakers of Christ, *if* we hold . . . unto the end" (Hebrews 3:13-14); "whose house are we, *if* we hold fast . . . firm unto the end" (Hebrews 3:6, italics added). When the saints need a "strong consolation" what they get is the assurance that God will reward them if they "hope unto the end" (Hebrews 6:11, 18), not a promise of relief or success or ultimate triumph for the cause.

The saints were not to put up a fight: "My kingdom is not of this world: if [it] were . . . then would my servants fight" (John 18:36). They are to assemble themselves together not for "action" but to await the end—"so much the more, as ye see the day approaching" (Hebrews 10:25). When the leaders went around "confirming the souls of the disciples, and exhorting them to continue in the faith," their specific instructions were "that we must through much tribulation enter into the kingdom of God" (Acts 14:22). These people were already members of the church; it was another kingdom for which they strove. Why is it that none of the apostles wants to make the noble sacrifice and *live* for the church? Why (later churchmen ask with wonder) did they never bother to write out full instructions for the guidance of the church to come? The "foundation" which Paul lays he emphatically declares to have nothing to do with this world (1 Corinthians 3:10–21). It is all too easy to say with the pagan philosophers and fourth-century theologians that to "leave the world" means only to lay aside the lusts of the flesh. It was Christ who served as the great example in this to the early Christians; all true believers knew that they must "suffer with him [Christ], that we may be also glorified together" (Romans 8:17)—but what can this have to do with turning from lust to philosophy? The Lord never indulged in either.

We learn from the Bible that the end of the church was to come in *two* ways. The first was the extermination of those who stood fast; that is, as we have seen, the very condition of proving oneself a true saint and winning eternal life, for one had to endure to the end to be saved. For centuries the belief persisted in the church that anyone not put to death for his testimony (*martyr* means "witness") had failed to achieve the fullest glory, so emphatic and deep-rooted were the teachings of the early church on the subject. Church members were expected in all confidence to be in the most literal sense "partakers in Christ's sufferings."

But what of the rest? What of the vast majority that did not stand fast and "suffer the end"? They continued to profess Christianity, but a Christianity perverted to their own tastes:

> But I fear, lest by any means, as the serpent beguiled Eve through his subtilty, so your minds should be *corrupted* from the simplicity that is in Christ.
> For if he that cometh preacheth *another Jesus*, whom we have not preached (2 Corinthians 11:3-4; italics added).

There is no thought in these impostors of renouncing the name and claim of Christians: "For such are false apostles, deceitful workers, transforming themselves into the apostles of Christ" (2 Corinthians 11:13).

> I marvel that ye are soon removed from him that called you into the grace of Christ unto *another gospel*:
> Which is not another; but there be some that . . . would *pervert* the gospel of Christ (Galatians 1:6-7, italics added).

What surprises the apostle in this case is not what is happening, but only that it should be happening *so soon*. The Lord himself had foretold what would happen:

> For there shall arise false Christs, and false prophets, and shall shew great signs and wonders; insomuch that, if it were possible, they shall deceive the very elect (Matthew 24:24).

Such a deception could be achieved (and the scripture says "they *shall* deceive"—using the infinitive of result—not "they would if they could") not by any pagan bluster or anti-Christian propaganda, but only by a very clever imitation of the real thing.

The danger that threatens the masses, according to the
apostles, is *not* the same danger that threatens the true disciples: the latter are to lose their lives and win their glory; but
for the rest there is another fate. They will go on as followers
of "Jesus," but it is "another Jesus" they follow. In various
ways they *"pervert"* the truth—not deny it. Some would
"depart from the faith" by "forbidding to marry" (1 Timothy
4:1-3); some would be fooled by the false Gnosis (1 Timothy
6:21); some would err from the faith out of "love of money"
(1 Timothy 6:10); some would "overthrow the faith of some,"
by denying the resurrection (2 Timothy 2:18). But such people do not return to the profession of paganism—they would
be horrified at the thought! How much simpler to do it this
way:

> For the time will come when they will not endure sound
> doctrine; but after their own lusts shall they heap to them-
> selves teachers, having itching ears;
> And they shall turn away their ears from the truth,
> and shall be turned unto fables (2 Timothy 4:3-4).

Paul is greatly alarmed at this prospect which he knows
is about to be realized: "Take heed . . . unto yourselves, and
to all the flock," he says in his farewell to Ephesus, "over the
which the Holy Ghost hath made you overseers, to feed the
church of God, which he hath purchased with his own blood"
(Acts 20:28). Here we have a test case: Could one ask for a
more perfect assurance of permanence and invulnerability to
a church than the pronouncement that it is the "church of
God," that it has been "purchased with his own blood," and
that it is led by the Holy Ghost? Yet this is a solemn writing
to take heed,

> For I know this, that *after my departing* shall grievous
> wolves enter in among you, *not sparing the flock*.
> Also of your own selves shall men arise, speaking per-
> verse things [the "perversion" motive again!], to draw away
> disciples after them.

Therefore watch, and remember that by the space of
three years I ceased not to *warn every one* night and day
with tears (Acts 29–31, italics added).

Here we are told that apostolic guidance is to be
withdrawn (cf. Galatians 4:18), that as a result the wolves
will attack, and that the attack will be successful—the flock
enjoys no immunity from such, even though "purchased with
his own blood."

Paul is warning the churches in no spirit of mild fatherly
admonition; his is not the calm assurance of later church
writers that the church of God cannot fail and all will be
well: He knows differently—the salt *can* lose its savor and be
thrown out (Luke 14:34). His alarms have gone on for years,
night and day, and with tears:

I am afraid of you, lest I have bestowed upon you
labour in vain (Galatians 4:11). . . . I stand in doubt of
you (Galatians 4:20). . . . Have ye suffered so many things
in vain? (Galatians 3:4) . . .
There are contentions among you. . . .
Is Christ divided? . . .
I thank God that I baptized none of you (2 Corinthians 1:11, 13–14).

What kind of winning talk is this? Is not the important
thing to get people to join the church in numbers so they can
be taught? Apparently Paul does not think so. Where the
strong members are concerned we hear of nothing but being
put to death, enduring to the end, partaking of Christ's
sufferings, thinking only of the resurrection and hereafter,
and counting all things but dross as far as this world is concerned. Where the weak ones are concerned, the prediction
is all of perversion, corruption, and betrayal: these are not
thrown to the lions; instead (in the words of the Didache)
these sheep turn into wolves—but still claim to be sheep. As
the Son of Man was betrayed, so would the apostles be:
Betrayal is not the work of the heathen—it is an inside job:

And ye shall be betrayed both by parents, and brethren, and kinsfolks, and friends; and some of you shall they cause to be put to death (Luke 21:16).

Others died other ways, but the great danger comes from betrayal—the pagans can neither betray nor corrupt nor pervert the gospel; only members can do that. It was the Jews who betrayed and murdered the prophets who later adorned their tombs (Acts 7:52–53).

Recently a Catholic writer has declared: "The failure of the Mormon spokesmen to explain when, where, and how the present Catholic Church was founded exposes the fatal weakness of their accusation," (i.e., that there was a Great Apostasy). The New Testament is only one of many, many sources that clearly "explain when, where, and how" the Christian church completely changed its nature and the present churches came to be what they are. To speak of a *founding* in a case like this is silly, since naturally no church claiming to have originated with Christ and the apostles (and they all claim that!) is going to go about proclaiming its foundation in this or that century *after* Christ! Even the Protestants will not admit a time and place of origin after the apostolic age; they are merely reformers of the old order—new things have been inaugurated from time to time, to be sure, and old things reformed—but it was really the same church all along. Every Christian church claims to go back to the first century: in the third century Origen admits the charge of Celsus, that already the church has long been "divided into sects, each of which claimed that it was the depository of the pure old original form of Christianity passed down from the beginning, while all the others were upstarts and innovators." Whatever groups emerge from the squabble naturally go on claiming each that it is the one church founded by Christ; but in the horrible confusion of that and the following centuries, what are such claims worth?

"Let me ask," writes Father Poetzl, "was the Catholic Church established in the 20th century? You must answer 'No.' If honest, you must say that the church of today is the continuation of the church which existed in the 19th century. Very well. Was the Church established in the 19th century? . . . The Church of the 19th century was the continuance of the Church of the 18th century. Go back farther, century by century. I defy the Mormon spokesman to name any century in which the Catholic Church was established, any other century than the first."[123] With equal propriety, and using the same words, Father Poetzl might ask: "Was the French language established in the 20th century? You must answer 'No.' If honest, you must say that the French of today is the continuation of the French which existed in the 19th century. Very well. Was French established in the 19th century? . . . The French of the 19th century was the continuance of the French of the 18th century. Go back farther, century by century. I defy Mormon spokesmen to name any century in which the French language was established other than the first." Thus it can be shown that Latin never ceased to exist as the vernacular of Gaul and that the great apostasy from the old Roman tongue which the purists so deplored never took place. It is the same with space as with time. Hugo Schuchardt showed that it is quite impossible to point to any spot, line, or area on the map at which Italian ceases and French begins. Is it Livorno? Milan? Nice? It is none of them or any other area you can name. "Very well," to follow the logic of Father Poetzl, "how can you possibly maintain that different languages prevail in Paris and Rome? The failure of Mormon spokesmen to show when, where, or how the Italian language was founded is fatal to their argument that spoken Latin disappeared." And yet it did.

The sophistry of the argument (a typical and shopworn school *demonstration*) lies in the well-known trick of confining the discussion to two alternatives only, and excluding all other possibilities: either a new church was *established* or else the old church *continued*. Only those two situations are considered—"have you stopped beating your mother-in-law"—a third possibility is not allowed. But formal establishment is *not* the only way to bring a church into being, and continuity by no means proves identity. In history actual establishments are extremely rare, and even then they are but the formal recognition of conditions that already exist, while the continuation of institutions is never without change. It is as if the white-haired Columbus were to argue that his hair was really red since he was born with red hair and no one could name the date or place at which it became white.

Since Newman forced the Catholics to admit (albeit with extreme reluctance) that they have been changing things all along, they have fallen back on the argument that once the church had received divine authority there was no limit to the changes that might be introduced without danger of corruption, since the church had the authority to make the changes. But it was precisely these self-initiated changes in the church that worried the apostles; "They went out from *us*," says John of the perverters (1 John 2:19). It is entirely possible for important churchmen of high position (a number are pointed out by name in the New Testament) to "preach another Jesus" and to "pervert the gospel of Christ" and to "corrupt the word of God" (2 Corinthians 2:17), and to "wrest . . . the . . . scriptures" (2 Peter 3:16). And it is quite possible for these to enjoy great success and become the leaders of the church after the apostles are gone (2 Timothy 4:2-5). This is the process the apostles and the Lord predicted—and it takes place without any break in historical continuity (the impostors make a great to-do about being the legitimate heirs of the vineyard) and without the *establishment* of new churches: even Tertullian, the greatest authority of his day on the early church, was fooled into believing that the Montanists were the original church of Christ.

To claim that the true Church is immune to corruption no matter how much it changes is to hold all the warnings of the Lord and the apostles in contempt. They felt no such confidence: "For if God spared not the angels," what guarantee of immunity can men expect? (2 Peter 2:4-22; Jude 5-11). "For it is impossible," writes Paul, "for those who were once enlightened, and have tasted of the heavenly gift, and were made partakers of the Holy Ghost, And have tasted the good word of God, and the powers of the world to come . . . " (Hebrews 6:4-5).

At this point let us pause and ask any Christian, or, for that matter any thinking man, to finish the sentence for us: just what *is* impossible for people so richly endowed? If the sixth chapter of Hebrews were a fragmentary text broken off at this place, any thoughtful individual could supply the conclusion: obviously Paul is reassuring the saints, telling them that it is quite impossible—unthinkable, in fact—for those who have already qualified for every earthly blessing plus the sure earnest of the world to come—it is impossible for such ever to be lost. "Reason itself" demands such a conclusion, but it is all wrong—the rest of the sentence administers a stinging rebuke to Christian complacency: It is impossible, the writer continues, for those so blessed "If they shall fall away, to renew them again unto repentance" (Hebrews 6:6). The falling away is a one-way process; it cannot be reversed. Heavenly powers and gifts once lost can only come again

> when the times of refreshing shall come from the presence
> of the Lord; . . . the times of the restitution of all things
> (Acts 3:19, 21).

The heavenly inheritance *can* be lost, even to the saints; and no matter how they may seek it "carefully and with tears," once it is gone they shall "seek and not find."

The great apostasy did not happen consciously. The mentally ill ("O foolish Galatians, who hath bewitched you"? [Galatians 3:1]) do not know what is wrong with them or when it happened. What the apostles denounce most strenuously in their letters is the complete complacency and self-satisfaction of the perverters: "Lovers of their own selves, covetous, boasters, proud. . . . Traitors, heady, highminded" (2 Timothy 3:2–4). No lack of assurance here!

Like the slinging of a noose, the end comes silently, quietly, without warning, so that the victim never suspects what is happening, being the while wholly preoccupied with the "cares of this life" (Luke 21:34). It is not a process of founding new institutions that the scriptures describe, but one of becoming: "love shall turn to hate," "evil men and seducers shall wax worse and worse" (2 Timothy 3:13), "iniquity shall increase," "the sheep of the fold shall turn into wolves" (Didache)—but go right on calling themselves sheep! The false claimants never give up, "Having a form of godliness, but denying the power thereof" (2 Timothy 3:5). The end was never formally declared (heaven forbid!); in the words of Polycarp, "the lights went out."

What, then, was "the end"? The Bible has a good deal to say on the subject, and scholars have had a great deal more. At present we are considering only the former. On the mountain of the transfiguration Peter, James, and John, having just beheld Elias in conversation with the Lord and Moses, were told that Elias would at some time come and "restore *all things*," though he had already come and been rejected (Matthew 17:11–12). It was further explained that the Son of Man would suffer the same rejection; and later on Peter declares in a sermon that Christ would come again at "the times of *restitution of all things* " (Acts 3:21; italics added). Some time after that the same Peter announces to the church that "the *end of all things* is at hand" (1 Peter 4:7; italics added). Here we have "all things" brought to earth, "all things" coming to an end, and "all things" restored again. "All *what* things?" we ask, for the world itself seems to go on. Peter gives us the answer: "*All things* which God hath spoken by the mouth of all his holy prophets since the world began" (Acts 3:21; italics added); "According as his divine power hath given unto us *all things* that pertain unto life and godliness" (2 Peter 1:3; italics added). "All things" means the fulness of the gospel. That is what passes away when "the end of all things is at hand."

The apostles speak of their own times as the end of the world, and yet they talk of more history to follow: "Now once in the end of the world hath he appeared. . . . And unto them that look for him shall he appear the second time" (Hebrews 9:26, 28). *Now* is here "the end of the world," and yet it is to be followed by a time of waiting and expectation, after which the Lord will appear again. Plainly with "the end of the world," the whole story is not told. Literally "end of the world" here means "consummation of the periods, or aeons." The word *aeon* appears over a hundred times in the New Testament, nearly always as the equivalent of the Hebrew *'olam ha-zeh*, "the age in which we live." An *aeon* is, strictly speaking, a world period, and hence was sometimes loosely employed to refer to this world of ours, our times, the wicked world, etc. But never is the sense of a limited span of time completely absent when this word is employed: one can stretch a point and translate "the completion of the *aeon*" as "the end of the world," but only if it is understood that the "world" referred to is not necessarily the physical earth or the physical universe but the present age of men.

When Christ met with the eleven by special appointment on a mountain in Galilee (Matthew 28:16), he sent them out with instructions to "teach all nations," to carry out all the instructions he had given them, and gave his messengers the promise, "Behold I am with you every day until the completion of the period" (Matthew 28:19-20). The "Great Commission" is *not* an unlimited call to everyone, but specifically and privately to the eleven; it is *not* an order for them to tell all men whatever they had heard but simply to instruct them to carry out certain specific orders (the language is technical and military); above all, it is *not* a promise that the Lord is

going to stay in the world forever and ever or, as John
Chrysostom desperately translates it, "for ages without end;"
aeon is here in the singular; a definite limit is placed on the
Savior's personal support, which is to be enjoyed until the
apostles have finished their work: "until the completion
[*syntelesis*] of the *aeon*, or period." There is going to be an
end: the Lord said he would send his apostles out to preach
to all the world for a witness, that they would carry out that
assignment, "and then shall the *end* come" (Matthew 24:14).
Their mission, like the Lord's, was indeed at the end of the
world. There is no more firmly established belief or more
ancient tradition in Christendom than the conviction that
the apostles themselves actually did carry out their mission,
the Lord, as he promised, "working with them, and confirming the word with signs following" (Mark 16:20). When every
man on Pentecost heard the gospel preached in his own tongue,
Peter announced that this was actually the fulfilment of

> that which was spoken by the prophet Joel;
> . . . in the last days, saith God, I will pour out of my
> Spirit upon all flesh (Acts 2:16–17).

These were the last days, the gospel actually had been
preached to all flesh, the prophecy was fulfilled, and the end
could come. For the prophecy was that *before* the apostles
could be put to death, "the gospel must *first* be published
among all nations" (Mark 13:9–10; italics added). The apostles themselves complete the whole work of the dispensation;
after them comes not the beginning—but the end. The clear
statement of the Lord, that "this generation shall not pass
away, till all be fulfilled" (Luke 21:32) is enough in itself to
settle the issue: either Jesus was a false prophet, or the end
did come.

Why did the early Christians express the keen and anxious
concern they did for "signs of the times?" Why did they diligently study the times and seasons and everlastingly ask the
Lord and the apostles, "When will it be?" (Cf. Acts 1:7.) It is

because they were expecting an end and had been instructed
to watch even until the end. Their attitude would have been
hard to understand if they had ever been given reason to
believe that the church had been established, once and for
all, to remain firm and steadfast until the end of the world.

It has often been noted that the ancient Christians
professed two expectations: one an expectation of bliss, the
other an expectation of woe. In their calendar the woe was
to come first. Paul explains the situation when he reminds
the Thessalonians that they must indeed look forward to
"the coming of our Lord Jesus Christ, and . . . our gathering
together unto him," but not be deceived into thinking "that
the day of Christ is at hand," since before that could come
there must come "a falling away first, and that man of sin be
revealed, the son of perdition" (2 Thessalonians 2:1-3). And
Peter reminds the church, "first, that there shall come in the
last days scoffers, walking after their own lusts," and only
later will the Lord come, being meanwhile "not slack concerning his promise," since "one day is with the Lord as a
thousand years" (2 Peter 3:3-9). The joy is coming, but first
the woe. There are ends and other ends. The "signs of the
times" are significant because things follow a pattern: "When
you see these events," says the Lord, stating a general rule in
a present general condition, "know ye that the kingdom of
God is nigh at hand" (Luke 21:31); for example, you look at
the trees, and "*when* they now shoot forth, ye see and know
of your own selves that summer is now nigh at hand" (Luke
21:29-30, italics added). It is a characteristic and repeated
event, this "end of all things" and "restitution of all things,"
which we shall discuss in the next section. Whose coming
was expected by the saints? The Lord's, according to some
accounts, the adversary's, according to others. Why should
this be a cause (as it has been) of ferocious controversy?
Plainly they expected *both*; and not at one and the same
time, but first the deceiver, and then the Lord.

After the Lord left the world, who came next? "The prince of this world cometh, and hath nothing in me" (John 14:30). Who is to follow up the work of the apostles if they are "sent last" and "the end" is to come when they have completed their work? Who indeed: "After my departing shall grievous wolves enter in among you, not sparing the flock" (Acts 20:29). Those are the only "successors" mentioned. Who is to take over the place when Peter leaves it? "The devil . . . abroad as a ravening lion," completely on the loose. When John announced, "Little children, it is the last time," is he expecting the Lord? On the contrary: "Even now there are many antichrists; *whereby* we know that it is the last time" (1 John 2:18). You know the last time is here because "the mystery of iniquity doth already work," and his work is only temporarily held up by an opponent who is presently to be "taken out of the way" (2 Thessalonians 2:7).

As modern scholars, Catholic and Protestant, are beginning to realize (we shall discuss them later), the prospects were not brilliant: "When the Son of man cometh, shall he find faith on the earth?" (Luke 18:8.) It was a dark interval that lay ahead, "the Wintertime of the Just," they called it in the ancient church. There is a real element of tragedy here; the tears of the Lord and the apostles were genuine. Paul does not warn constantly and with tears for the sake of a few inevitable crackpots and backsliders: the wicked one is coming "with all power and signs and lying wonders" (2 Thessalonians 2:9); the night is coming when no man can work, the time which the closing lines of Didache describe as the long ordeal of the human race. There is no doubt that the early Christians were convinced that the glorious final act of the drama would not be played "before the time." No city ever had a better chance of hearing the gospel than Capernaum; no city ever rejected it more completely; accordingly, "in the day of judgment" Capernaum "shall be thrust down to hell." But meantime, what is the status of the cursed city to be? Quite magnificent: "exalted to heaven" (Matthew

11:23–24; Luke 10:15). That "meanwhile" is the second act of the drama, and it lasts until the judgment.

If one is determined to believe that the primary intent and purpose of the missions of Christ and the Apostles was the setting up on the earth of a mighty institution of sure salvation for all, "to remain firm and steadfast until the end of the world" (to use the proud formula of 1870—in the absence of any appropriate scripture!), then the negative course of things so clearly indicated in the Bible was a terrible mistake. Common sense rebels against the dismal prospect of the whole earth being given into the hands of "the one who leads the world astray" (as the Didache puts it)—it is a hard thing to take. And that is exactly why all the prophets of the New Testament urge the saints continually *not* to take the common-sense point of view in the matter: "In the world ye shall have tribulation: but be of good cheer!" Is that common sense? "Now is the day of salvation," Paul cries joyfully, describing the day as one of afflictions, necessities, distresses, stripes, imprisonments, tumults, labors, watchings, fastings— "as sorrowful, yet always rejoicing" (2 Corinthians 6:10). It seems like anything but fun or good sense. As to the things that common sense values, Paul says, "I count them but dung, just so I win Christ." Worldly standards are utterly misleading. Hear what Peter, James, and John have to say:

Note the emphasis in Peter's epistles on the evil times ahead and the postponement of blessings for a definite interval: "Ye are kept . . . unto salvation ready to be revealed in the last time. Wherein ye greatly rejoice, though now for a season, if need be, ye are in heaviness . . . [expecting] praise and honour and glory at the appearing of Jesus Christ" (cf. 1 Peter 1:5–7). "Be sober, and hope to the end for the grace that is to be brought unto you at the revelation of Jesus Christ" (1 Peter 1:13). "Pass the time of your sojourning here in fear" (1 Peter 1:17). "Beloved, think it not strange concerning the fiery trial which is to try you, as though some strange thing happened unto you:

"But rejoice, inasmuch as ye are partakers of Christ's suffering; that when his glory shall be revealed, ye may be glad" (1 Peter 4:12–13). "The God of all grace . . . hath called us unto his eternal glory . . . after that ye have suffered a while" (1 Peter 5:10).

"Humble yourselves . . . that He may exalt you in due time" (1 Peter 5:6), etc. The unpleasant interval is not to be taken seriously, "For all flesh is as grass" (1 Peter 1:24); we are merely "strangers and pilgrims" here (1 Peter 2:11); it is a frightening prospect, but "if you will it shall be as nothing." Peter preaches a thoroughgoing exchange of earthly values for heavenly values.

James does not mince words: "Know ye not, that the friendship of the world is enmity with God? whosoever, therefore, will be a friend of the world is the enemy of God" (James 4:4). Nor does John: "Love not the world, neither the things that are in the world. If any man love the world, the love of the Father is not in him. For all that is in the world . . . is not of the Father, but is of the world. And the world passeth away, and the lust thereof" (1 John 2:15–17). "Marvel not, my brethren, if the world hate you. . . . "We are of God: he that knoweth God, heareth us; he that is not of God heareth not us. . . . And we know that we are of God, and the whole world lieth in wickedness" (1 John 3:13; 4:6; 5:19).

These were truly the disciples of the Lord who said, "Woe unto you, when all men shall speak well of you! for so did their fathers to the false prophets" (Luke 6:26). There is no place here for a popular program. The whole consolation of the saints is in the resurrection and glory to come, "whether we wake or sleep, . . . Wherefore comfort yourselves" (1 Thessalonians 5:10–11). There is a complete disconcern for the possible success or failure of the church on earth, and a total silence on the subject of future generations—never a thought of that "inevitable triumph" which later church historians were to insist *should have* been their chief consolation. "The foundation of God standeth sure," not in a visible institution of salvation, but "having this seal, the Lord knoweth them that are his" (2 Timothy 2:19). Every opportunity to play up the church is passed by in silence.

The values of the early Christians were *not* commonsense values. The translators of the King James Version use the word *lusts* for the Greek *epithumia*, which means "desire, interest, value," in the broadest sense, and thus make it appear that all that John is condemning is vice and depravity, whereas actually he is renouncing all earthly values good and bad. The Christian point of view was not that of another philosophy; it administered a severe shock to intelligent people— "a slap in the face," to use Karl Holl's apt expression. Thinking people were not just amused, they were "scandalized" (a favorite word) and enraged, sickened, and disgusted; Tacitus, Celsus, Caecilius, and the Jewish and pagan professors cannot think of words strong enough to express their loathing and alarm.

Here we have two systems of values totally and hopelessly opposed to each other. The things Jesus talked about were entirely outside the range of normal human thought and experience; in time their reality was to be made manifest to all, but meanwhile their rejection was to be emphatic and complete, and pagans could embarrass Christians by chanting about "Jesus the King who never ruled!" A triumphant rule and a triumphant church were not on the program, but the world would settle for nothing less, and of course the world got what it wanted—a church modeled after *its* idea of what a church should be. Such an institution was as clearly prophesied as was the passing away of the true church.

One Act or Three? Few historians at the present time will maintain that the Christian church today is the result of

a smooth and unbroken transmission of institutions and doctrines without change or shadow of change since the days of
the apostles. Since no one doubts the necessity and conve-
nience of making certain major divisions in church history,
we would strongly urge that the most meaningful and logical
division is that so clearly indicated by the New Testament
itself. To accept those clearly marked periods (1) revelation,
(2) darkness, and (3) restoration, however, is to reject the
whole conventional concept of church history as one long
unbroken irresistible victory campaign.

Yet even conventional church history is now being forced
to spoil the simplicity of the accepted plot of the growing
admission that the early church was something very special.
It would be hard to find a history of the church that does not
honor the "primitive church" with a section all of its own;
but of recent years the uniqueness and peculiarities of that
church have become objects of the most intense research,
which is showing more and more how totally different the
original church of Christ was from any of the churches claiming to be derived from it or from any of the ideas which
scholars have hitherto entertained concerning it.

The term "primitive church" is itself revealing. The early
Christians, far from thinking of themselves as primitive, tell
us often that they are living at the end of an aeon in a world
ripe for destruction. Though they lived by prophecy, no
allowances or provisions were made by them for greater refine-
ments or improvements in their own institution in the years
ahead. The church of the apostles was ready for the end,
coming as it did at "the end of the aeon," not at the beginning
of a long period of progress.

Still the designation and idea of a "primitive church" are
necessary to later generations both as a salve to conscience
(this is very clear in Chrysostom) and a sop to vanity (equally
ditto in Jerome), for if the glaring differences between the
original and the later churches could not be denied, they
would have to be explained; and the only explanation that

could save the face of Christianity—let alone make it look good—was that which decided with patronizing indulgence that the early church was just "primitive" and its disappearance a necessary and inevitable phase in the growth and progress of an institution.

The folly and vanity of a theory that looks upon the church of the apostles with patronizing superiority and glories in the irrelevant and highly suspect virtues of size and sophistication as proofs of progress, needs no comment. A basic lack of conviction in the argument may be seen in desperate attempts to dress the primitive church up to look like modern churches; serious students know better, of course, but that does not keep the producers of movies and television from assuring the general public that the church really has changed hardly at all, and showing, to prove it, ancient apostles dressed up as eighth-century bishops or mouthing the sentimental commonplaces of the schools through the whiskers and robes of traveling sophists.

But looking behind such flimsy tricks, we find that earnest investigators of church history, Catholic and Protestant alike, are discovering as it were for the first time the great gulf that lies between the ancient church and conventional Christianity, and being surprisingly frank in their comments. More and more they are forcing themselves also to face up to the dark interval of the second act, though most of them still cling desperately to the old rewrite interpretations of "Advance through Storm," "Struggle and Progress," "The Certain Victory," etc.

This interpretation so deranges the plot that the third act must either be dropped out entirely or completely rewritten: naturally we can't have a "restitution of all things" if all things have been carefully preserved and steadily improved through the centuries. And so we have the third and final act, the great culminating events of world history, studiously effaced by church historians: what we have to reckon with, we are now told, was a "spiritual" second coming which has already taken place; it was "the Easter experience," some suggest—Pentecost, according to others; it was all a mistake, a tragic miscalculation, according to another school; it is fulfilled in the Real Presence, to follow another; others have maintained that since the crucifixion was the supreme event of all time, all that followed was mere anticlimax; others have made the second coming a mystical experience. And so they go: whatever it is, that third act, as we have called it, is not the great event predicted by the scriptures. Acts two and three are out!

What, then, did happen after the apostles? Do we have reliable reports for the years following? Was it all bad? How did the Christians continue to think of the world and their position in it? Did they expect the lights to go out? Were they surprised when they did? Were they disappointed when the Lord failed to come? Did they believe that what was happening actually was the end? Such questions are the special food of church history in our day. The mere fact that they are being asked now as never before is an invitation to Latter-day Saints to enter the discussion which seems at last to be turning to their own point of view.

The history of the church is not a one-act play, a single, long protracted happy ending from start to finish, with a baffled and frustrated villain vainly trying to score a telling point against a cause that is always assured of success and never in any real danger. Yet such a fantastically wishful and unreal plot is the only alternative to the one set forth in the Bible which places the happy ending at the end—"when his glory shall be revealed and all made glad"—with a time of heaviness preceding it, during which the prince of this world holds sway and all the promised glories to come are forgotten in a tragic preoccupation with the things which please men. The story of the church is unfolded not in one act but three.

This is not the discovery of modern scholars or the private hypothesis of Latter-day Saints—through the centuries the

church fathers have been aware of it, and it has worried
them a great deal. It is very important to understand that the
fate of God's people on earth, specifically, the course of "the
church" through the ages (for the idea of "the church" is a
very ancient one) has been a subject of vital concern to
certain men in every period of history.

From the most ancient prophets to the latest monograph,
men have not ceased talking and speculating on this theme.
As the Lord was not the first prophet sent into the vineyard,
neither was his church without precedent in the world. Church
history does not begin suddenly one day in Palestine, any
more than the story of the redemption begins with certain
shepherds watching their flocks. The mighty drama goes back
to the very beginning and leaves its mark in the documents
of every age. It is a far bigger thing than the seminarists and
schoolmen realize.

In the preceding articles we first indicated the strong and
undeniable bias which has controlled the writing of conventional church history since the days of Eusebius. Next we
offered a brief preliminary sketch, based on the New Testament, of another view of church history. That view may be
thus briefly summed up: the original followers of Christ sought
their reward and placed all their hopes in the other world
and the return of the Lord in judgment, believing that as far
as this world is concerned the work of the church would not
prosper but soon come to a close, being followed by a long
time of darkness that would end only with the restoration of
all things in preparation for the coming of the Lord. Such in
barest outline is the substance of "the other view" of church
history. It will be readily admitted that it is *not* the conventional view, and it remains for us now to show from the
early sources that it most certainly was the true authentic
view of church history held by the members of the early
church in apostolic times and after. We shall also show the
present trend among students of church history toward the

recognition of glaring defects in the conventional picture and
increasing awareness of the existence and the validity of the
earlier concept.

The Eschatological Dilemma

In any bibliography of present-day studies on the Christian
religion, historical or doctrinal, the word *eschatology* looms
large. For the Christian, we are told, "any real understanding of history is only possible in connection with
eschatology."[124] And what is eschatology? According to
Gressmann, one of the fathers of modern eschatological studies, it was originally whatever had to do with the end of
things, whether of the world, the society, the age in which
we live or merely of the individual—his death and resurrection.[125] But in the 1880's the German scholars began using
the word in a special sense, applying it specifically to doctrines—Jewish, Christian, or heathen—dealing with the end
and renewal of the earth.[126] Immediately and inevitably the
discussion of such teachings became involved in the terms
and problems of Messianic, apocalyptic, mythical, mystical,
historical, and prophetic nature. Whereas formerly messianism and eschatology had had nothing to do with each other,
the new speculations brought them ever closer together, until
Mowinckel was able to announce that they were one and the
same.[127] Eschatology and apocalyptic were identified in every
conceivable degree of relationship: one of the latest studies
insists that they be sharply separated, since eschatology
"according to my terminology [Lindblom speaking] is the
prophesying of a new and totally different age to come."[128]

According to an equally recent and authoritative study,
eschatology is just the opposite of that: "Eschatological thought
I take [S. B. Frost speaking] to be a form of expectation . . .
characterized by finality. The *eschaton* is the goal of the
time-process, that after which nothing further can occur: it is
the climax of teleological history. . . . It cannot even in thought
be superseded by a subsequent event. . . . The *eschaton* is

that beyond which the faithful never peers."[129] So much for the new age—and this sort of thing has been going on for seventy-five years! While one school holds that eschatology is necessarily a late development in Jewish thought, a product of the captivity and quite unknown to the prophets (Lagrange), another maintains that prophecy itself "rests from the very beginning on a . . . fully developed eschatology."[130]

Again, while some (e.g., R. H. Charles) have held that the eschatological ideas of heathen nations were first borrowed by Jews, and hence Christians, as an anchor to faith when their own darling prophecies, especially those concerning the Messiah, failed to go into fulfilment, others regard the Jews themselves as the true originators of those ideas. Today some are claiming that apocalyptic writing is simply a combination of eschatology with myth, and Mr. Frost issues the resounding statement: "Whether apocalyptic is to be dismissed as merely myth eschatologized, or whether it is to be taken seriously as eschatology in a mythological dress, is perhaps the most urgent problem confronting the Christian Church today."[131] Personally, I am glad it does not confront my church, since Frost is saying in effect: "The most urgent problem confronting the court is whether the accused forged his name to the check or merely changed the amount on it."

Forty-five years ago Father Lagrange distinguished five different eschatologies, and, in view of the completely baffling nature of the evidence, wisely refused to attempt arranging them in any of those evolutionary or developmental patterns which the scientific scholarship of the age found so irresistible. He listed: (1) a temporal cosmic eschatology without a Messiah; (2) a transcendent cosmic eschatology without Messiah; (3) a historic Messianic eschatology; (4) a transcendent Messianic eschatology; and (5) a transcendent cosmic eschatology embracing a less transcendent but historic Messiah.[132]

In such a way the eschatological discussion from the first fused and intermingled a wealth of related and conflicting

terms, periods, and peoples, and the game of deciding just
how and to what degree, if any, each element or combination of elements was related to the others offered inexhaust-
ible opportunities for learned debate: the endless variety of
changes, the nice shades and dainty nuances of meaning, the
license of bathing forever in the tepid waters of pure terminology or spinning spider-like, from the substance of one's
own esoteric secretions, lovely fragile webs of definition without end—it was all the schoolmen asked of life, and the
eschatological discussion might have gone on like the Trinitar-
ian debate for untold generations had not a series of great
and unforeseen events given a wholly new orientation to
things within the last two decades.

But behind this great outpouring of words, and what
keeps it going, is the inescapable conviction that eschatology,
that is, what people really believed about their place in the
universe, holds the key to the genuine original Christian view
of life—that it represents the unique, the peculiar, the essentially different element that sets Christian thinking apart from
all other thinking. Those very scholars, such as Harnack and
Albert Schweitzer, who insist most emphatically on the hopeless inadequacy of the evidence, are the most reluctant to
leave eschatology alone. There is something big and portentous
hiding here if we could only grasp what it is. The vague and
twittering host of broken fragments and wraith-like traditions for all its mazy confusion is definitely trying to tell us
something, and the voices are growing louder and clearer
every day. The whole eschatological issue can best be
explained, we believe, by a brief diversion into one of those
little parables for which we have always had a weakness.

Imagine, then, a successful businessman who, responding
to some slight but persistent physical discomfort and the
urging of an importunate wife, pays a visit to a friend of
his—a doctor. Since the man has always considered himself
a fairly healthy specimen, it is with an unquiet mind that he
descends the steps of the clinic with the assurance, gained

after long hours of searching examination, that he has about three weeks to live. In the days that follow, this man's thinking undergoes a change, not a slow and subtle change— there is no time for that—but a quick and brutal reorientation. By the time he has reached home on that fateful afternoon, the first shock of the news has worn off, and he is already beginning to see things with strange eyes. As he locks the garage door, his long-held ambition to own a Cadillac suddenly seems unspeakably puerile to him, utterly unworthy of a rational, let alone an immortal being. This leads him to the shocking realization, in the hours that follow, that one can be rich and successful in this world with a perfectly barren mind. With shame and alarm he discovers that he has been making a religion of his career. In a flash of insight he recognizes that seeming and being are two wholly different things, and on his knees discovers that only his Heavenly Father knows him as he is. Abruptly he ceases to care particularly whether anybody thinks he is a good, able, smart, likable fellow or not; after all, he is not trying to sell anyone anything any more.

Things that once filled him with awe seem strangely trivial, and things which a few days before did not even exist for him now fill his consciousness. For the first time he discovers the almost celestial beauty of the world of nature, not viewed through the glass of cameras and car windows, but as the very element in which he lives; shapes and colors spring before his senses with a vividness and drama of which he never dreamed.

The perfection of children comes to him like a sudden revelation, and he is appalled by the monstrous perversion that would debauch their minds, overstimulate their appetites, and destroy their sensibilities in unscrupulous plans of sales promotion. Everywhere he looks he gets the feeling that all is passing away—not just relatively because he is saying goodbye to a world he has never seen before, but really and truly: he sees all life and stuff about him involved in a huge

ceaseless combustion, a literal and apparent process of oxi-
dation which is turning some things slowly, some rapidly,
but all things surely to ashes. He wishes he had studied more
and pays a farewell visit to some friends at the university
where he is quick to discover, with his new powers of dis-
cernment, that their professional posturing and intellectual
busy-work is no road to discovery but only an alley of escape
from responsibility and criticism.

As days pass, days during which that slight but ceaseless
physical discomfort allows our moribund hero no momen-
tary lapse into his old ways, he is visited ever more frequently by memories, memories of astonishing clarity and
vividness—mostly from his childhood, and he finds himself
at the same time slipping ever more easily into speculations,
equally vivid, on the world to come and the future of this
world. The limits of time begin to melt and fuse until everything seems present but the present. In a word, *his thinking
has become eschatological.*

"What has happened to our solid citizen?" his friends ask
perplexed. He has chosen to keep his disease a secret; it
would be even more morbid, he decides, to parade his condition. But he cannot conceal his change of heart. As far as
his old associates can see, the poor man has left the world of
reality. Parties and golf no longer amuse him; TV and movies disgust him. He takes to reading books, of all things—
even the Bible! When they engage him in conversation, he
makes very disturbing remarks, sometimes sounding quite
cynical, as if he didn't really care, for example, whether pep-
permint was selling better than wintergreen or whether the
big sales campaign went over the top by October. He even
becomes careless of his appearance, as if he didn't know that
the key to success is to make a good impression on people.
As time passes, these alarming symptoms become ever more
pronounced; his sales record drops off sharply; those who
know what is good for their future begin to avoid being seen
with him—like Lehi of old, he is hurting business, and dark

hints of subversion are not far in the offing. What is wrong with the man?

As we said, his thinking has become eschatological. He lives in a timeless, spaceless world in which Jack Benny and the World Series simply do not exist. His values are all those of eternity, looking to the "latter end" not only of his own existence but of everything and everybody around him. As he hears the news or walks the streets, he sees, in the words of Joseph Smith, "destruction writ large on everything we behold." He is no longer interested "in the things of the world." The ready-smiling, easily adjustable, anxious-to-get-ahead, eager-to-be-accepted, hard-working conformist, who for so many years was such a tangible asset to Nulb, Incorporated, has ceased to exist.

Now the question arises, has this man been jerked out of reality or into it? Has he cut himself off from the real world or has cruel necessity forced him to look in the face what he was running away from before? Is he in a dream now or has he just awakened from one? Has he become an irresponsible child or has he suddenly grown up? Is he the victim of vain imaginings or has he taken the measure of "Vanity Fair?" Some will answer one way, some another. But if you want to arouse him to wrathful sermons, just try telling the man that it makes no difference which of these worlds one lives in— that they are equally real to the people who live in them. "I have seen both," he will cry. "Don't try to tell me that the silly escapist world of busy-work, mercenary back-slaps, phoney slogans, and maniacal 'careers' has anything real about it—I know it's a fake, and so do you!"

It will be noted that this eschatological state of mind does not bear the mark of just one school of thought: once it gets in the blood, all the aspects and concepts of eschatalogical thinking enter with it. Our businessman, for example, begins to wonder about certain possibilities: What about the hereafter? Will he ever really see the face of the Lord? Is there going to be a judgment? He almost panics at the thought which has never bothered him before because he has been successful. He becomes preoccupied with history and prophecy, aware for the first time that his whole life is linked not only with D Division of Nulb, Incorporated, but, for better or for worse, with all that happens in the universe; he belongs to history and it to him—"the solemn temples, the great globe itself" are as much his concern as any man's. These ideas that come to him are all essential parts of the same picture in which one can descry inextricably joined and intermingled apocalyptic, prophecy, millennialism, messianism, history, and theology—all belong to the same eschatology.

But where is *myth*, the thing that the scholars tell us is "the very essence of eschatology"?[133] That is there, too, but you will find it only in the minds of his friends and associates: they, wide-awake and practical people, know perfectly well that the man is suffering from delusions; they know that the things which have become so real to him are all just imagination. To anyone who does not experience it, the eschatological view of things is pure myth—an invention of an overwrought mind desperately determined to support its own premises. Only what they fail to consider is that those who have had both views of the world interpret things just the other way around: it is after all eschatology that looks hard reality in the face; lazy and timid people take refuge in the busy-work of everyday; only strong and disciplined minds are willing to see things as they are, and even they must be forced to it! No wonder the scholars have agreed that whatever else eschatology is, it is not real!

To conclude our parable, what happens to our man of affairs? A second series of tests at the hospital shows that his case was not quite what they thought it was—he may live for many years. Yet he takes the news strangely, for instead of celebrating at a night club or a prize fight as any normal healthy person should, this creature will continue his difficult ways. "This," he says, "is no pardon. It is but a stay of execution. Soon enough it is going to happen. The situation is not really changed at all." So he becomes religious, a hopeless case, an eschatological zealot, a Puritan, a monk, a John Bunyan, a primitive Christian, an Essene, a Latter-day Saint. In every age such people with their annoying eschatological beliefs have disturbed the placid ("perfectly-adjusted") waters of the slough of custom and paid dearly for their folly.

And that leads us to the eschatological dilemma which confronts the Christian world today.

However deplorable the maladjusted state of mind called "eschatological" may be, there can be no denying that it was the prevailing attitude of the early Christians. Accordingly, the Christian world finds itself forced to choose between accepting the extreme view, which does violence to the common sense of respectable people, or rejecting it—and with it the right to be called Christian. In theory this hard dilemma has never ceased to disturb the peace of conventional Christianity, and in times of crisis it has a way of taking on very solid forms. It was the grim reality of World War II that forced certain German ministers—become chaplains—to ask old questions with a new frankness, and at their head Rudolf Bultmann, with inexorable logic, bids the Christian world, since it is not willing to accept the old eschatology, to throw it away entirely. Thereby he has turned a discrete compromise into a cruel dilemma for the clergy.[134]

Bultmann begins with the premise that the entire New Testament eschatology is pure mythology and nothing else. There is nothing revolutionary about that: it is what the scholars have been saying for many years, only, unlike Bultmann, they have steadfastly refused to draw the logical conclusion from that conviction or face its inevitable consequences. "The picture of the world we find in the New Testament is a mythological one," we are now told; it served well enough in its time, but it is no good any more. "When the New Testament . . . describes the saving action of God in

Jesus Christ . . . it describes this action in terms of the contemporary mythological conception of the world. . . . It was
natural for the gospel to be stated in these terms, for that was
the outlook of the age."[135] But such terms are decidedly *not*
natural for our age, Bultmann insists: "It is impossible for
the man of today to accept the mythology of the New Testament. . . . As long as this is taken at its face value as literally true, Christianity remains meaningless to modern
man."[136] It is not therefore a matter of toning down or soft-
ening or adaption of the old eschatology, but of its complete
rejection: "He contends that to ask the man of today to
accept the picture of the world that is found in the New Testament would be at once pointless and to ask the impossible. . . . It is, for instance, impossible for the man of today
to interpret a case of epilepsy or schizophrenia as demoniac
possession," or, in Bultmann's own words, "It is impossible
to make use of electric light and radio, and, in case of ill-
ness, to claim the help of modern medical and clinical methods
and at the same time believe in the New Testament's spirits
and miracles."[137] Is this a shocking statement? There is nothing the least bit new or radical about it. Over a hundred
years ago Charles Dickens denounced the Mormons as hopelessly deluded and mentally incompetent because they were
actually guilty of "seeing visions in an age of railways!"[138]
Since it is agreed that railroads and visions cannot possibly
go together, why has Bultmann so upset the clergy by saying
only what they themselves have believed all along?

It is because he will not let them keep their Christianity
and deny it at the same time. "The great difference between
Bultmann's teachings and the liberalism of the 1900's," writes
Henderson, is that "*it eliminates* the mythological, instead of
interpreting it."[139] If it is a myth, Bultmann argues, why not
treat it as such? It is his conclusion, not his premise, that
shocks. Yet with the premise all the damage is done. Over
fifty years ago a professor of Old Testament could write
without shocking a single scholar: "It is impossible from the

THE WAY OF THE CHURCH

309

modern point of view to regard Abraham and Moses as historical characters"—they are simply myths. "All the accounts from Saul to Solomon are mythological-astrological presentations . . . all details concerning the persons and their deeds have been borrowed from a mythological system."[140]

For over half a century a great band of Christian scholars have flatly denied that Jesus ever lived, but they have gone on talking and writing about him just the same.[141] Scholars became proud and boastful of their "brazen scepticism," entirely forgetting, Eisler points out, to be sceptical of their own highly subjective conclusions. Their "unhistorical Jesus" was, he says, "the stillborn creature of the age of Liberalism" . . . with a capital "L."[142] Albert Schweitzer attributed to a sound instinct for self-preservation the rejection of the historical Jesus by the Christian churches—for certainly the historical Jesus contradicts their teachings on many points.[143] In the end, the only Jesus for which Christianity had any use was an unhistorical Jesus, a "de-mythologized" Jesus, to use Bultmann's expression.

Speaking of revelation, Bultmann writes: "The existence of such a voice that speaks when God, not as the idea of God . . . but as *my* God, who here and now speaks to *me* through the mouths of men, that is the 'demythologized' sense of 'the Word became flesh,' the Church's doctrine of the incarnation."[144] It is with the history of the church as with its doctrine, according to Bultmann: you only accept of that history what you personally feel is useful to you; Christianity, he says, is the "eschatological phenomenon that brings the world to an end; it is not a historical phenomenon of the past, but is the word of that Grace which destroys and in destroying makes alive."[145] The declaration that one should take and believe from the scriptures only what one wants to has led to loud protests from the churchmen.

Yet what else have they been doing with the Bible all these years? "We are thankful," wrote Schweitzer years ago, "that we have handed down to us only gospels, not biographies, of Jesus."[146] The scholars have shown by word and deed that they do not want to know any more about Christ than they do; instead of joyfully embracing the priceless discoveries which from the Didache to the Dead Sea Scrolls have brought us step by step nearer to a knowledge of the true Church of Jesus Christ as it existed anciently, they have fought those documents at every step.[147] If the resurrected Jesus were to walk among them they would waste no time beseeching him "to depart from their coasts"—they have the only Jesus they want, and they will thank you not to complicate things by introducing new evidence. In the same spirit a great German classical scholar once expressed to the author his disapproval of studying Oriental sources. They disturb the neatness, compactness, symmetry, simplicity, and permanence of our mental picture of the Greeks, he explained.

It is accepted practice to rewrite the Gospels at will, provided one employs the proper jargon. But in frankly *admitting* that he is out to reshape Christianity to something nearer to the heart's desire, Bultmann has gone too far. "I do not want my eschatology de-eschatologized," cries the eminent scholar Millar Burrows.[148] "It is one thing," he says, "for a theologian to say that demonology is for him a mythological experience of the reality of suffering and evil in the world; it is something else for an exegete to say that Jesus himself did not believe in demons. You cannot have accurate, realistic exegesis if you are not prepared and willing to find ideas that you cannot accept."[149] You cannot de-mythologize the history in the New Testament no matter how badly you want to, Oscar Cullmann protests, because after all it never was mythology or allegory and never was meant to be—it was real history.[150] What Bultmann fondly thinks is a clear, detached, objective view of things, his vaunted *Vorverständnis* is nothing but the scientific tradition he has inherited, says von Dobschütz, a thing that conditions the thinking of every scholar whether he admits it or not. And as to

this business of picking out of the scripture as the substance
of your faith whatever suits your fancy and rejecting what
does not, what does that lead to? "Bultmann floats in Bible
and theology from one concept to another," von Dobschütz
writes, "but everything remains idea without substance. One
forgets entirely that Primitive Christianity was actually a
very concrete phenomenon."[151]

It is high time these things were being said, but without
Bultmann it is hard to imagine their ever being said by modern pastors and priests, for the charges against that alarming
man are precisely those to which they are most susceptible
themselves. For Bultmann by calling a spade a spade is smok-
ing out the temporizers and spiritualizers by forcing them to
take a stand. Many years ago Bultmann himself jarred a cornerstone of "liberal" religion with the announcement that "a
revealed religion must insist that it is the only true religion,
nothing less than *the* Truth,"[152] thereby declaring that the
true church must be a "narrow," not a "liberal" one.

We believe that Bultmann is quite wrong in choosing to
throw away the old Christian eschatology in that the ministry has no chance but to oppose him; but he is quite right in
insisting on the terrible truth that if you don't throw it away
you have to believe it! There he has the ministry checkmated, or rather they have checkmated themselves, for it is
they who for over a century and a quarter have with a single
voice hurled against the Mormons the awful charge of actually believing in visions, miracles, and the visitation of angels!
And now Bultmann tells them they must believe in those
things, too, or else forget about them.

But what now complicates the game, to the embarrassment
of both players, is the increasingly frequent and madden-
ingly unpredictable introduction of new pieces onto the board.
New discoveries of documents are "compromising" modern
Christianity more deeply all the time, making it harder and
harder for anyone who would call himself a Christian to
brush the old eschatological teachings aside. At the same

time the realities of the hydrogen bomb and the very real possibility of world destruction have occasioned a world-wide resurgence of eschatological thinking.

Forty-seven years ago Father Lagrange could dismiss the apocalyptic presentation of the old eschatology with contempt: true, he admitted, it was strictly orthodox doctrine and the early Christians were all for it, but it was a mistake just the same, "a false literary *genre*, whose overheated imaginings leave hardheaded people (*les gens de sangfroid*) unimpressed." For Lagrange it was all "a huge exertion in which a few flashes of *bon sens* illuminated a brain-sick nightmare."[153]

That is how it all looked to the safe and solid world of 1909. But what do we read today in a leading Catholic journal? "We know that thou hast been with us daily until now, and that thou shalt be with us forever," writes the editor in Church Latin, making a necessary concession to the official viewpoint, which definitely frowns upon teachings of the Second Coming.[154]

Thou dwellest among us, near us, in the land which is thine and ours. . . . But now has come a time in which thou must appear to us again, and give to this generation a sign that thou canst not put off nor deny. . . . For thou seest, Christ, our need, thou knowest how great is our necessity, our helplessness, our poverty, our desperation; thou knowest how badly we need thy coming, how necessary is thy return. Come, Christ, even as lightning, and as lightning depart; only appear to us, hear our prayer: come and go and speak but one word, one coming and one departing. . . .

Send us a sign—lightning in the sky or a light by night: let the heavens be opened, let the night be lighted: give us but an hour of thine eternity; in place of thy long silence give us but one word. . . . We do not, we do not ask for a great descent in heavenly glory, nor for the splendor of the Transfiguration. . . . Often after the resurrection didst thou

appear to the living, and to those who meant to hate
thee . . . didst thou show thy countenance. . . . Thou, who
didst so often return for but a few, why dost thou not now
return but once for all of us? If they deserved to see thee . . .
surely we in our utter desperation deserve to see thee. . . .
Never has thy word been so necessary as it is today . . .
the rule of Satan has reached its full maturity . . . the only
remaining hope is in thy return.

Return, O Christ, return! . . . We expect thee, Christ, at
this end-time; we expect thee daily, although we are unworthy and although our desire is an impossible one, still we
shall expect thee. [155]

Where now is the clerical *sang froid* and *bon sens*? When
the world is topsy-turvy and the danger is real, Christians
have a way of suddenly remembering how fundamental to
the gospel are those eschatological and Messianic concepts
of which official Christianity disapproves. The ancient faith
was no summertime religion, and its preoccupation with
eschatology—the "end of all things"—no "brain-sick
nightmare" but a hard-won decision to consider things as
they are.

NOTES

1. Tertullian, *De Praescriptionibus* (*The Prescription against Heretics*) 29, in *PL* 2:47–48.

2. Pierre Batiffol, *L'église naissante et le catholicisme*, 13th ed. (Paris: Victor Lecoffre, 1909).

3. Henri Daniel-Rops, "Un monde qui naît, un monde qui va mourir," in *L'église des apôtres et des martyrs*, vol. 1 of *Histoire de l'église du Christ*, 5 vols. (Paris: Arthème Fayard, 1948), 1:353–414.

4. Kenneth Scott Latourette, *The Unquenchable Light* (London: Religious Book Club, 1945).

5. August Neander, *History of the Planting and Training of the Christian Church by the Apostles*, trs. J.E. Ryland and E.G. Robinson (New York: Sheldon, 1869).

6. Regarding Latourette's church history, E. A. Payne writes in "The Modern Expansion of the Church: Some Reflections on Dr. Latourette's Conclusions," *Journal of Theological Studies* 47 (1946): 151: "There is always danger of a metaphor once adopted becoming master instead of servant. One cannot escape the feeling that Dr. Latourette finds his diminishing periods of recession a little too neatly and easily."

7. Karl Bihlmeyer, *Kirchengeschichte: Das christliche Altertum* (Paderborn: Schöningh, 1951), 1–2.

8. Heinrich Bornkamm, *Grundriss zum Studium der Kirchengeschichte* (Gütersloh: Bertelsmann, 1949), 14.

9. R. H. Pfeiffer, "Facts and Faith in Biblical History," *Journal of Biblical Literature* 70 (1951): 14.

10. Ibid., 3.

11. Caesar Baronius, Anno 1077, quoted in Thomas Comber, *The Church History Clear'd from the Roman Forgeries* (London: Roycroft, 1695), 189.

12. Adolf von Harnack, *Lehrbuch der Dogmengeschichte*, 5th ed., 3 vols. (Tübingen: Mohr, 1931), 2:63–64.

13. Walther Völker, "Von welchen Tendenzen liess sich Eusebius bei Abfassung seiner 'Kirchengeschichte' leiten?" *Vigiliae Christianae* 4 (1950): 157, 159–60.

14. Ibid., 180.

15. Olaf Linton, *Das Problem der Urkirche in der neueren Forschung* (Uppsala: Almquist & Wiksell, 1932), 9–10.

16. Conrad Kirch, *Enchiridion Fontium Historiae Ecclesiasticae Antiquae* (Barcelona: Herder, 1947). The six hundred pages of this famous handbook are taken up entirely with short, carefully chosen excerpts, obviously and sometimes violently forced into a prearranged

historical framework. As soon as the reader begins to get interested—
and curious—regarding a passage, the text is, as it were, snatched from
his hands by the zealous editor.

17. John Fredrick Stenning, *The Targum of Isaiah* (Oxford:
Clarendon, 1949), x.

18. Ibid., xi.

19. Ibid., xiv.

20. Wilhem Schmid, *Geschichte der griechischen Literatur*, 2 vols.
(Munich: Beck, 1929), 1.1:2–8.

21. Tertullian, *De Baptismo* (*On Baptism*) 17, in *PL* 1:1326–29.

22. Clemens Romanus, *Constitutiones Apostolicae* (*Apostolic
Constitutions*) 4, 16, in *PG* 1:949–55.

23. Robert Eisler, *Iesous Basileus ou Basileusas*, 2 vols.
(Heidelberg: Winter, 1929) 1:44–45; von Harnack, *Lehrbuch der
Dogmengeschichte* 2:63, gives other examples of approved deception.

24. John Chrysostom, *De Sacerdotio* (*On the Priesthood*) I, 5, in
PG 48:624; cf. his *Homilia* (*Homily*) 56 in *Commentarius in Acta
Apostolorum* (*Commentary on the Acts of the Apostles*), in *PG* 60.

25. Ibid.

26. Jerome, *Adversus Jovinianum* (*Against Jovinian*) 2, 73, in *PL*
23:371.

27. Jerome, *Epistolae* (*Letters*) 82, in *PL* 22:740.

28. Jerome, *Apologia adversus Libros Rufini* (*Defense against the
Book of Rufinus*), in *PL* 23:412.

29. Paul E. Kahle, *The Cairo Geniza* (London: Oxford Press,
British Academy, 1947), 221; cf. 2nd ed., enlarged (1959).

30. Heinrich Böhmer, *Die Fälschungen Erzbischofs Lanfrancs von
Canterbury* (Leipzig: Dieterich, 1902), 126. For a fuller discussion see
my article "New Approaches to Book of Mormon Study,"
Improvement Era 56 (1953): 919–1003.

31. Ibid., 830, 859–62, 919–1003.

32. Comber, *The Church History Clear'd From the Roman
Forgeries*, introduction.

33. Innocent 1, *Epistolae et Decreta* (*Letters and Decrees*), in *PL*
20:551–52.

34. Linton, *Das Problem der Urkirche*, 10 (emphasis added).

35. Kahle, *The Cairo Geniza*, 138–39.

36. Ibid., 86, 108, 118, 127.

37. Ibid., 85.

38. Joseph Smith, "King Follett Discourse," *Teachings of the
Prophet Joseph Smith*, comp. Joseph Fielding Smith (Salt Lake City:
Deseret, 1977), 348. Even the motive attributed to the scribe, that he

"thought it too bad" to leave the text as he found it, is the authentic and conventional one.

39. Kahle, *The Cairo Geniza*, 71, 77; cf. 2nd ed., 130.

40. Ibid., 71–72; cf. 2nd ed., 131.

41. Ibid., 63–66; cf. 2nd ed., 115.

42. Ibid., 66; cf. 2nd ed., 118.

43. Anton Deimel, *Sumerische Grammatik* (Rome: Pontifical Biblical Institute, 1924), 8.

44. Alfred E. Housman, *Manilius*, 5 vols. (London: Cambridge, 1927), 5:xxxiv.

45. Lazarus Goldschmidt, *Der babylonische Talmud*, 12 vols. (Haag: Nijhoff, 1933) 1:13.

46. Ibid., and 1:14.

47. 1 Maccabees 1:56–57, 63.

48. Sozomen, *HE* I, 21, in *PG* 67:861–62; Socrates, *HE* I, 9, 31, in *PG* 67:33–34. The pagan Diocletian was milder against the Christians than they were against heretics, Eusebius, *HE* VIII, 11, in *PG* 20:768–69.

49. *Corpus Juris Civilis*, vol. 2: *Codex Justinianus*, Paul Krüger, ed. (Berlin: Weidmann, 1877), 1.1:3; and *Novella* 42, i, 2; *lib.* 3, *de summa trinitate.*

50. Kahle, *The Cairo Geniza*, 211.

51. Ibid., 84.

52. Ibid., 29; cf. 192–97.

53. Eusebius, *HE* VI, 19, 9, in *PG* 20:561–72.

54. *Codex Theodosius* XVI, 1, 16 tit. v leg. 6–23, discussed in Edward Gibbon's *Decline and Fall of the Roman Empire*, 2 vols. (New York: The Modern Library, 1932), ch. 27, 2:956, 1001.

55. Karl von Hefele, *Conciliengeschichte*, 9 vols. (Freiburg: im Herder, 1856–90), 1:143–44.

56. Leander, *Praefatio* (*Preface*) 1, in *PL* 18:89.

57. E. Gilson, *God and Philosophy* (New Haven: Yale University, 1942), 11.

58. Augustine, *De Mendacio* (*On Lying*) 1, 10, in *PL* 40:500–2.

59. Henri Leclercq, "Historiens du Christiánisme," in *DACL* 6:269–98. That the motive for censorship was to cover up the adverse effect of the evidence is clear from Duchesne's revealing explanation of why he did not leave the Catholic church in view of his discoveries: he could not, he explained, offend his aged mother as the price of being "true to himself." Idem.

60. Editorial note on Tertullian, *Apologeticus adversus Gentes pro Christianis* (*Apology*), in *PL* 1:1205.

61. Rufinus, *Preface* to the *Recognitiones Clementinae* (*Clementine Recognitions*), in *PG* 1:1205–8.

62. Rufinus, *Preface* to Origen's *Peri Archon* (*On First Things*), in *PG* 11:111–14.

63. Eusebius, *De Vita Constantini* (*On the Life of Constantine*) 1, 11, in *PG* 20:924–25.

64. C. Snouck-Hurgronje, "Der Islam," in Pierre Chantepie de la Saussaye, ed., *Lehrbuch der Religionsgeschichte* (Tübingen: Mohr, 1925) 1:656.

65. Jean & Augustin Perier, *Les '127 Canons des Apôtres'* 48, in *PO* 8:623–24.

66. Justin Martyr, *Apologia pro Christianis* (*Apology*) 1, 10, in *PG* 6:340.

67. Kirsopp and Silva Lake, *An Introduction to the New Testament* (New York: Harper, 1937), 99. Cf. Kahle, *The Cairo Geniza*, 157: the "Targums had no authoritative text. Every copyist could try to improve the text he copied."

68. Or, "they haven't been tampered with." Ignatius, *Epistola ad Philadelphenses* (*Epistle to the Philadelphians*) 8, in *PG* 5:833: "hou parakousai prodēlos olethros."

69. Josephus, *Jewish War* II, 110, 172; cf. *Jewish Antiquities* XVIII, 63–64.

70. This famous Josephus passage is the subject of Eisler's whole two-volume work, *Iesous Basileus ou Basileusas*. Cf. Kahle, *The Cairo Geniza*, 150.

71. Père Batiffol, "Les Odes de Salomon," *Revue Biblique* 20 (1911): 163

72. Ibid.

73. Ibid., 189, note to Odes of Solomon 12:8.

74. Housman, *Manilius* 1:30, 40, 53.

75. Henri Frankfort, *The Birth of Civilization in the Near East* (Garden City: Doubleday, 1956), 14; cf. 20–21: Toynbee, "the confessed 'empiricist' adheres to a preconceived system and disposes of the facts" to suit himself; for his "challenge and response" system he "must in each case invent a challenge to fit a historic reality which [he] labels response."

76. Joseph W. Swain, *The Ancient World*, 2 vols. (New York: Harper, 1950), 1:65, reviewed by the present writer in *The Historian* 13 (Autumn 1950): 79–81. For a blunt statement and searching criticism of the common practice of prehistorians of giving full priority to the *concept* of evolution at the expense of the *evidence* see respectively M. Jacobs, "Further Comments on Evolutionism in

318   MORMONISM AND EARLY CHRISTIANITY

Cultural Anthropology," *American Anthropologist* 50 (1948): 565–66; and W. D. Wallis, "Presuppositions in Anthropological Interpretations," *American Anthropologist* 50 (1948): 560–64.

77. W. A. Irwin, "Ezekiel Research Since 1943," *Vetus Testamentum* 3 (1953): 61. See our discussion of this in Hugh W. Nibley, "New Approaches to Book of Mormon Study," 57 (1954):148–49, 170.

78. August von Gall, *Basileia tou Theou* (Heidelberg: Winter, 1926), 14.

79. T. Schermann, *Die allgemeine Kirchenordnung*, 3 vols. in 1 (Paderborn: Schöningh, 1914–16), 2:143.

80. Rudolf Bultmann, *Das Evangelium des Johannes* (Göttingen: Vandenhoeck and Ruprecht, 1941), 98–99; cf. tr. by G. R. Beasley-Murray, *The Gospel of John: A Commentary* (Oxford: Blackwell, 1971), 138.

81. Housman, *Manilius* 1:41–42.

82. Wilhelm Ahlwardt, *The Divans* (London: Trübner, 1870), 8.

83. Ibid., 8–9.

84. Ibid.

85. *Tridentinum*, canon 4, in Philip Schaff, *Creeds of Christendom*, 3 vols. (New York and London: Harper, 1905), 2:83.

86. Schermann, *Die allgemeine Kirchenordnung* 2:269.

87. Clement, *Epistola Petri ad Jacobum* (*Epistle of Peter to James*), in *PG* 2:28.

88. Tertullian, *Adversus Gnosticos Scorpiace* (*Scorpiace*) 11, in *PL* 2:169. "Sed haec est perversitas fidei, probata non credere, non probata praesumere."

89. Athanasius (Dubia), *Confutationes Quarumdam Propositionum* (*Refutations of Certain Arguments*) 13, in *PG* 28:1377–80.

90. Siricus, *Epistolae* (*Letters*) 9, in *PL* 13:1177.

91. Martin Schanz, *Geschichte der römischen Literatur*, 5 vols. (Munich: Beck, 1914) 4:543–44.

92. Pfeiffer, "Facts and Faith in Biblical History," 3–5.

93. J. Bligh, "The 'Edict of Milan': Curse or Blessing?" *Church Quarterly Review* 153 (1952): 310.

94. Peter Lombard, *Sententiae* (*Opinions*) I, 5, 8, in *PL* 192:537.

95. F. Schindler, "Die Lüge in der patrischen Literatur," in Albert Koeniger, ed., *Beiträge zur Geschichte des christlichen Altertums* (Amsterdam: Rodopi, 1969), 432.

96. Arnold Lunn and John B. S. Haldane, *Science and the Supernatural* (New York: Sheed & Ward, 1935), 51.

97. Heinrich Denzinger, *Enchiridion Symbolorum* (Rome: Herder, 1967), nos. 1429–32, 1530–32, 1602–8.

98. Quoted by G. C. Coulton, "Catholicism and Civilization," *Hibbert Journal* 19 (1921): 336.

99. Leclercq, "Historiens du Christianisme," 2689.

100. Maurice De Wulf, *History of Medieval Philosophy*, 2 vols., tr. E. C. Messenger (London: Longmans, Green, 1926), 2:7, note 4.

101. Ignác Goldziher, *Vorlesungen über den Islam* (Heidelberg: Winter, 1925), 43.

102. Ibid., 44.

103. Albert Bayet, *Les provenciales de Pascal* (Paris: Société française d'édit one littéra res et techniques, 1931), 90.

104. Lunn & Haldane, *Science and the Supernatural*, 94.

105. This belief is held by Vere Gordon Childe, *New Light on the Most Ancient East* (New York: Praeger, 1953), though where business economy fails to produce writing or even use it when it is known, he overlooks the anomaly. "There is no evidence that the local kings felt the need of clerks to look after their revenues," 217.

106. See our series, Hugh W. Nibley, "The Stick of Judah and the Stick of Joseph," *Improvement Era* 56 (January-May 1953).

107. The independence of ancient farmers from written calendars is well-illustrated in the Talmud where, for example, the performance of ritual acts or the length of ritual periods is determined by the time when certain leaves fall, when certain plants turn dry, when winter grapes are ripe, etc.; houses are rented "until the second rain falls," TB Shebi'ith 9. Indeed Childe admits that the first set calendar, that of the Egyptians, "was patently useless for just the purpose for which it had been devised," *New Light on the Most Ancient East*, 4—another way of saying that it must have been devised for some other purpose.

108. Alan H. Gardiner, *Egyptian Grammar*, 3rd ed. (London: Oxford University Press, 1969), 1.

109. Stenning, *The Targum of Isaiah*, 9.

110. Perier, *Les '127 Canons des Apôtres'* 48, in *PO* 8:623.

111. E.g., "Recent Progress in North Canaanite Research," *Bulletin of the American Schools of Oriental Research* 70 (1938): 21.

112. Moses Mielziner, *Introduction to the Talmud* (Cincinnati: Block Printing, 1894), 89–90.

113. Friedrich Dieterici, *Die Philosophie der Araber im X. Jahrhundert nach Christ* (Leipzig: Hinrich, 1876), 18–21.

114. Thus Anselm on the enormous difficulty of interpreting a translated passage of scripture, *Cur Deus Homo* 1, 18, in *PL* 158:388.

115. Alan H. Gardiner, "The Eloquent Peasant," *Journal of Egyptian Archaeology* 9 (1923): 6.

116. This process is illustrated by Simeon Potter, *Our Language* (London: Penguin, 1953), ch. 4, 7, and *passim*, with Shakespeare leading the parade of innovators.

117. "Now, comparative philological research has definitely proved that the laws which govern one language or group of languages do not necessarily govern another, nor do the laws which control linguistic phenomena in one period of history hold true of the same phenomena in a different age." William Foxwell Albright, "Philological Method in Identification of Anatolian Place-Names," *Journal of Egyptian Archaeology* 11 (1925): 19.

118. Lord Fitz Roy Raglan, *The Origins of Religion* (London: Watts, 1949), 43.

119. *Science News Letter* 65 (June 5, 1954): 360.

120. On the closing of the other doors, Phillippe Le Corbeiller, "Crystals and the Future of Physics," *Scientific American* 188 (January 1953), 50–56. On the new "translation machine" (IBM 701) and its limitations, see Mina Rees, "Computers: 1954," *Scientific Monthly* 79 (August 1954): 118–24. This gadget is simply an electronic dictionary that gives back the one-to-one equivalents that have been built into it. Where such one-to-one relationships do not exist between languages, it will not work.

121. Tertullian, *Adversus Gnosticos Scorpiace (Scorpiace)* 10, in *PL* 2:166.

122. Tertullian, *The Prescription against Heretics* 29, in *PL* 2:47–48.

123. Matthew Poetzl, O. F. M., "Was There a 'Great Apostasy'?" (St. Paul: Radio Replies Press, 1955).

124. Paul Althaus, "Heilsgeschichte und Eschatologie," *Zeitschrift für systematische Theologie* 2 (1924): 605.

125. Hugo Gressmann, *Der Ursprung der israelitisch-jüdischen Eschatologie* (Göttingen: Vandenhoeck and Ruprecht, 1905), 1.

126. Ibid., and R. Arconada, "La Eschatologia Mesianica en los Salmos ante dos objeciones recientes," *Biblica* 17 (1936): 204–29.

127. Arconada, "La Eschatologia Mesianica," 210–14.

128. J. Lindblom, "Gibt es eine Eschatologie bei den alttestamentlichen Propheten?" *Studia Theologica* 6 (1952): 113.

129. S. B. Frost, "Eschatology and Myth," *Vetus Testamentum* 2 (1952): 70.

130. Gressmann, *Der Ursprung der israelitisch-jüdischen Eschatologie*, 152.

131. Frost, "Eschatology and Myth," 80.

132. Marie-Joseph Lagrange, Le Messianisme chez les Juifs (Paris: Gabalda, 1909), 58–59.

133. Gressmann, Der Ursprung der israelistisch-jüdischen Eschatologie, 152, "Das Mythische . . . ist das Wesentliche an der Eschatologie [Myth is the essential feature of eschatology]."

134. For the best general treatment of Bultmann and his work, see Ian Henderson, Myth in the New Testament (London: SCM Press, 1952). We have avoided using the word existentialism in this discussion to keep from becoming too involved in definitions and distinctions.

135. Ibid., 10–11.

136. Ibid., 9.

137. Ibid., 11–12.

138. See my discussion in The World and the Prophets (Salt Lake City: Deseret, 1954; reprinted Salt Lake City: F.A.R.M.S., Deseret, 1987), 16.

139. Henderson, Myth in the New Testament, 13. Italics are Henderson's.

140. Hugo Winckler, "Geschichte und Geographie," in Eberhard Schrader, Die Keilinschriften und das Alte Testament, 3rd ed. (Berlin: Reuther and Reichard, 1903), 209, 222.

141. E.g., Bauer, Kalthoff, Hoekstra, Pierson, Naber, E. Johnson, J. M. Robertson, W. B. Smith, P. Jensen, C. P. Fuhrmann, A. Drews, A. Niemojewski, P. L. Couchard, George Brandes. The subject is discussed by Eisler, Iesous Basileus ou Basileusas 1:xiv–xvii.

142. Ibid. 1:205.

143. Albert Schweitzer, Geschichte der Leben-Jesu-Forschung (Tübingen: Mohr, 1921) 3:2.

144. R. Bultmann, "Die Frage der Entmythologisierung," Theologische Zeitschrift 10 (1954): 93: "Dass es ein solches Zusprechen gibt, indem Gott nicht als Gottesidee . . . sondern als mein Gott, der hier und jetzt zu mir spricht, u.z.w. durch den Mund von Menschen, das ist der 'entmythologisierte' Sinn des ho logos sarx egeneto, der kirchlichen Inkarnationslehre." The reader will note that the author's translation, though all but incomprehensible, still lacks something of the density of the German original. The authority of mere jargon in these discussions cannot be overestimated.

145. Ibid., 94. The remarks on the preceding note apply here.

146. Schweitzer, Geschichte der Leben-Jesu-Forschung 3:12.

147. The subject is treated at length by Eisler, Iesous Basileus ou Basileusas 1:179–95.

148. M. Burrows, "Thy Kingdom Come," *Journal of Biblical Literature* 74 (1955): 8.

149. Ibid., 3.

150. Oscar Cullmann, *Urchristentum und Gottesdienst* (Zürich: Zwingli, 1950), 57.

151. Ernst von Dobschütz, "Die Kirche im Urchristentum," *Zeitschrift für die neutestamentliche Wissenschaft* 28 (1929): 108. Henderson, *Myth in the New Testament*, 13–14, makes the same objection: Bultmann "ignores the fact that Christianity is an event."

152. Bultmann, "Untersuchungen zum Johannes Evangelium," *Zeitschrift für die neutestamentliche Wissenschaft* 27 (1928): 118–19.

153. Lagrange, *Le Messianisme chez les Juifs*, 135, 39.

154. For an official statement, see Robert Koch, "Der Gottesgeist und der Messias," *Biblica* 27 (1946): 260–68.

155. Riccardo Avallone, "Veni, Christe!" *Antiquitas* 8 (1953): 17–21. This is a translation from G. Papini, which, however, the editor considers particularly applicable to the present time, 21.

7

Jerusalem: In Early Christianity

Christian concern with Jerusalem involves the ancient concept of the city as a shrine of preeminent holiness, marking the physical and spiritual center of the cosmos, the spot at which history began and at which it shall reach its apocalyptic consummation.[1] The idea of an *umbilicus mundi*, a scale-model as it were of the universe itself,[2] at which a nation or tribe would gather periodically to renew its corporate life by the observance of the now familiar year-rites, was familiar to many ancient peoples,[3] and the nations converted to Christianity had no difficulty accepting the supreme eschatological significance of Jerusalem and its Temple.[4] The city's unique status, however, raised certain questions which have never ceased to puzzle and divide Christian theologians, namely, (1) Just how literally are Jerusalem's claims and promises to be taken? (2) How can the glory of Jerusalem be disassociated from the Jews and their persistent claims to be its legitimate heirs? (3) How can the prized continuity (back to Adam) of the city's long history be maintained if Christianity is a completely new, spiritualized beginning? (4) How can Jerusalem be the Holy City par excellence without also being the headquarters of the church? (5) How can the city's prestige be exploited in the interests of a particular church or nation?

This article first appeared under "Jerusalem: In Christianity" in the Encyclopedia Judaica, 16 vols. *(Jerusalem: Macmillan, 1972) 9:1568–75. The footnotes are published here for the first time.*

These issues have all come to the fore in each of the main periods of Christian preoccupation with Jerusalem, namely, (1) the "Golden Age" of the 2nd and 3rd centuries, (2) the Imperial Age from Constantine to Justinian, (3) the Carolingian revival, (4) the Crusades, (5) the period of intrigues and grand designs, (6) the time of patronage by the Great Powers, and (7) the rise of Israel.

The question of literalism was paramount in the second and third centuries; the early Christians had been Jews of the apocalyptic-chiliastic persuasion with lively visions of a literal New Jerusalem, while an educated and growing minority (as also among the Jews) favored a more spiritual interpretation of the biblical promises and accused the old-school Christians of superstition and "Judaizing."[5] The banning of Jews from the city by Hadrian gave an advantage to the Gentile party,[6] and the "Doctors of the Church" made the Hellenized or "spiritualized" image of Jerusalem the official one.[7] Still, the millennialist teachings survived beneath the surface, occasionally bursting out in sectarian enthusiasm or becoming general in times of crisis,[8] while the doctors themselves repeatedly succumbed to the enticements of a real and earthly Holy City.[9] Hence, the ambiguities of literalism versus allegory might have been minimized were it not that the continued presence and preachings of the Jews forced the Christians in self-defense to appeal to the doctrines of a purely spiritual Jerusalem.[10]

From Origen's time to the present, churchmen of all sects have been one in insisting that the New Jerusalem is for Christians only, since the Jewish city can never rise again.[11] In the absence of scriptural support for this claim various stock arguments are used, namely, Josephus' description of the destruction of A.D. 70, with its atmosphere of gloom and finality;[12] the argument of silence—the Bible says nothing about a restitution of the city after Vespasian;[13] the ominously lengthening period of time since the expulsion of the

Jews;[14] various tortured allegorical and numerological demonstrations;[15] the appeal to history with the ringing rhetorical challenge: "Where is your city now?"[16] A favorite argument (akin to a Jewish teaching about the Diaspora) was that Jerusalem had to be destroyed so that Jews and Christians alike might be scattered throughout the world as witnesses to the fulfillment of prophecy in the new religion.[17] Against these were arguments which never ceased to annoy: Why did the city and temple continue to flourish for forty-two years after the final pronunciation of doom, and why during that time did the Christians show every mark of reverence and respect for both?[18] Why did Jesus weep for the destruction if it was in every sense necessary and desirable?[19] Why do the doctors insist that the destruction of Jerusalem by the Romans was a great crime, and yet hail it as a blessed event, saluting its perpetrators as the builders of the New Jerusalem even though they were the chief persecutors of the Christians?[20] If expulsion from Jerusalem is proof of divine rejection of the Jews, does the principle not also hold good for their Christian successors?[21] How can the antichrist sit in the temple unless the city and temple are built again by the Jews?[22] The standard argument, that only a total and final dissolution would be fit punishment for the supreme crime of deicide,[23] was frustrated by the time schedule, which suggested to many that the city was destroyed to avenge the death not of Jesus but of James the Just.[24]

But if Jerusalem was to be permanently obliterated, how could the Christians inherit it? In a spiritual sense, of course. The church *was* the New Jerusalem in which all prophecy was fulfilled, the Millennium attained, and all things became new.[25] But this raised a serious question of continuity: Has God chosen *another* people? Can one preserve the meaning of the eschatological drama while changing all the characters?[26] Can a people (the Christians) be gathered that was never scattered?[27] And what of the Heavenly Jerusalem? The

approved school solution with its inevitable rhetorical antith-
esis was to depict the Heavenly and the Earthly Jerusalems as
opposites in all things, the one spiritual, the other carnal;[28]
yet none of the fathers is able to rid himself of "corporeal"
complications in the picture, and the two Jerusalems remain
hopelessly confused,[29] for in the end the two are actually to
meet and fuse into one.[30] Palestine was the scene of busy
theological controversy and these and related mysteries when
the "Golden Age" of Christian Jerusalem came to an end
with the persecutions of A.D. 250.[31]

   After the storm had passed, Constantine the Great at
Rome, Nicaea, Constantinople, and elsewhere celebrated his
victories over the temporal and spiritual enemies of mankind
with brilliant festivals and imposing monuments.[32] But his
greatest victory trophy was "the New Jerusalem," a sacral
complex of buildings presenting the old "hierocentric" concepts in the Imperial pagan form, with the Holy Sepulchre as
the center and chief shrine of the world.[33] Jerusalem was
treated as the legitimate spoils of Christian-Roman victory
over the Jews, whose entire heritage accordingly-including
the temple—passed intact into the hands of the Christians.[34]
Henceforth, there remained no objections to giving Jerusalem
its full meed of honor.[35] Continuity back to Adam was established with suspicious ease by the rapid and miraculous discovery of every relic and artifact mentioned in the Bible;[36]
and a flood of pilgrims came to rehearse, Bible in hand (the
earliest pilgrims, Silvia [383 A.D.] and the Bordeaux Pilgrim
[333 A.D.], are markedly partial to Old Testament remains),
the events of each holy place and undertake weary walks
and vigils in a cult strangely preoccupied with caves[37] and
rites of the dead.[38] The Patriarch Macarius, who may have
contrived the convenient discoveries of holy objects with an
eye to restoring Jerusalem to its former preeminence,[39] pro-
moted a building boom which reached a peak of great activity in the sixth and seventh centuries.[40] Financed at first by
imperial bounty, the building program was later supported

by wealthy individuals, and especially by a line of illustrious
matrons whose concern for the Holy City goes back to Queen
Helen of Adiabene,[41] and whose number includes Helen, the
mother of Constantine; his mother-in-law, Eutropia; Eudocia,
the wife of Theodosius II; Verina, the wife of Leo II; Sophia,
the mother of St. Sabas; Paula, Flavia, Domitilla, and
Melania, rich Roman ladies and friends of St. Jerome.[42] By
the end of the fourth century, Jerusalem had more than 300
religious foundations, sustained by generous infusions of outside capital, until the economic decline of the fifth century
forced the government to take the initiative, culminating in
Justinian's ambitious but fruitless building program.[43] The
period was one of specious brilliance in which, A. J. Hubert
notes, everything had to be *splendens, rutilans, nitens, micans,
radians, corsucans*—i.e., brilliantly surfaced—while the actual
remains of the buildings show slipshod and superficial
workmanship.[44]

Spared the barbarian depredations suffered by most of
the world in the fifth and sixth centuries, Jerusalem was an
island of security and easy money, where the population of
all ranks was free to indulge in those factional feuds which
were the blight of the Late Empire. Points of doctrine furnished stimulation and pretext for violent contests involving
confused and shifting combinations, ambitious churchmen
and their congregations, hordes of desert monks, government and military officials and their forces, local and national,
the ever-meddling great ladies, members of the Imperial family and their followings, and the riotous and ubiquitous factions of the games.[45] The Jews of Alexandria became
associated with one of these factions of the Emperor Phocas,
who ordered his general Bonossus to suppress the correspond-
ing faction in Jerusalem by converting all Jews by force.[46]
While pitched battles raged in the streets, a Persian army
appeared at the gates, sent by Chosroes, the pro-Christian
monarch, seeking vengeance on the treacherous Phocas for
the murder of his friend Mauritius.[47] The Jews regarded this

as a timely deliverance by a nation that had succored them
before and sided with the Persians—an act not of treachery
(as Christian writers would have it) but of war, since Phocas
had already called for their extermination as a people.[48] The
Christian world was stunned when Chosroes took the cross
from Jerusalem in A.D. 614, and elated when the victorious
Heraclius brought it back in 628. Under the vehement urging
of the monk Modestus, whom he had made patriarch and
who aspired to rebuild Jerusalem as a new Macarius,
Heraclius, against his better judgment, took savage reprisals
on the Jews.[49] But within ten years the city fell to Omar,
who allowed the pilgrimages to continue while making
Jerusalem a great Moslem shrine by the revival of the temple
complex, which the Christians also, after long and studied
neglect, now claimed as their own.[50]

   Though Christians, originally as Jews and, later, on church
business, had always made pilgrimages to Jerusalem,[51] the
great surge of popular interest beginning in the fourth century alarmed some churchmen, who denounced the pilgrimage as a waste of time and means, dangerous to life and
morals, and a disruptive influence in the church.[52] Along
with monasticism, with which it was closely associated, the
pilgrimage to Jerusalem was an attempt to get back to the
first order of the church, to retrieve the lost world of visions,
martyrs, prophets, and miracles;[53] and this implied dissatis-
faction with the present order.[54] The writings of the fathers
furnish abundant evidence for the basic motivation of the
pilgrims, which was the desire to reassure oneself of the
truth of Christianity by seeing and touching the very things
the Bible told of[55] and experiencing contact with the other
world by some overt demonstration (healing was the most
popular) of supernatural power.[56] Only at Jerusalem could
one receive this historical and miraculous reassurance in its
fullness; only there did one have a right to expect a miracle.[57]
The earliest holy place visited "was not, as might have been
supposed," the Holy Sepulchre, but the footprint of the Lord

on the Mount of Olives, the spot where he was last seen of men as he passed to heaven, and would first be seen on his return.[58] Contact was the basic idea, contact with the biblical past and contact with heaven itself, of which Jerusalem was believed to be a physical fragment.[59] Tangible pieces of the Holy City, carried to distant parts of the world, gave rise to other holy centers, which in turn sent out their tangible relics like sparks from a central fire: *Sparsa sunt ligna et accensus est mundus*, says St. Augustine.[60] The Christian world was soon covered by a net of holy shrines, built in imitation of the Church of the Holy Sepulchre or the temple, and often designated by the names of Jerusalem, the temple, or the sepulchre.[61] Each became a pilgrim center in its own right, and there was a graded system of holiness measured on a scale of distance in time from the Lord and in place from Jerusalem,[62] which remained "as far above all the other cities in the world in renown and holiness as the sun is above the stars."[63]

After being fought over for two centuries by Moslem dynasties, Jerusalem in 800 was placed under the protection of Charlemagne, who was doing Hārūn al-Rashīd the service of annoying his Umayyad enemies in Spain.[64] Though Rome had come under his protection five years earlier in the same way—by the presentation of holy keys and a banner by the bishop—it was the prestige of ruling Jerusalem that warranted the changing of Charlemagne's title from king to emperor.[65] Like Constantine, Charlemagne stimulated a revival of large-scale pilgrimages to Jerusalem,[66] and a tradition of royal generosity, endowing a church, school, monastery, and library[67]—the Jerusalem hospitals for pilgrims were a tradition going back to pre-Christian times.[68] From Darius to Augustus and the emperors of the West, great rulers had courted the favor of heaven by pious donatives to the Holy City,[69] and this tradition of royal bounty was continued through the Middle Ages, when kings imposed Jerusalem taxes on their subjects and monks from Jerusalem made regular fund-gathering trips to Europe.[70] During the years of the "quasi-Protectorate of the Western Emperors" over Jerusalem and the revived Byzantine control (made possible by Moslem disunity),[71] Northern and Slavic Europe came to bathe in the Jordan, pray at the Holy Sepulchre, and endow pious foundations.[72] Stimulated by the end-of-the-world excitement of the year 1000, this stream "multiplied tenfold" in the 11th century,[73] culminating in great mass pilgrimages of thousands led by eminent lords and churchmen.[74] When the Seljuks, having defeated the Byzantine army in 1071 and occupied Jerusalem in 1075, became oppressive in their fees and controls of the holy places, Christian leadership felt obliged to "take up again the part of Charlemagne," and the armed pilgrimage led by Robert le Frison, 1085–90, was hailed throughout Europe and viewed by the Pope and the Byzantine Emperor alike as advance reconnaissance for a crusade.[75]

The Crusades were the expression of a popular religious revival in which Jerusalem, restored to its full apocalyptic status (the Crusading literature has a strongly Old Testament flavor),[76] offered a welcome door of escape to all classes from economic and social conditions which in Europe had become intolerable.[77] The Crusades have also been described as the complete feudalization of Christianity[78] by an ancient chivalric tradition with Christ as a liege lord whose injuries must be avenged and whose stronghold must be liberated.[79] We see it in the language of the Crusading literature,[80] the significant exchange of embassies, and the close resemblance of Asiatic to European arms and accoutrements, suggesting an older common "epic milieu,"[81] and the nature of the Crusades as a *Völkerwanderung.*[82] Since the fourth century the western church had accepted, along with the Roman victory-cult,[83] the concept of world polarity, dividing the human race into the Blessed (Jerusalem, Church, *ager pacatus*) and the Damned (Babylon, Unbelievers, *ager hosticus*),[84] reflected in the *jihād* concept of the Moslem countercrusade.[85] Such a

concept assumed papal leadership of all crusades, giving rise
to baffling questions of imperial, papal, and royal prerogative. [86] These came to a head in the Latin kingdom of
Jerusalem, whose Assizes, though the most perfect expression
of a model feudal society, remained but an ideal, [87] "a lawyers'
paradise," where royalty, exploiting the city's propinquity to
heaven, dramatized its own claims to divine authority, with
pageantry of unsurpassed splendor. [88] This motif was developed by the military religious orders of the Hospitalers
(founded by the Amalfi merchants in 1048 and open only to
the nobility), and the Templars, each claiming a monopoly
of the unique traditional power and glory of Jerusalem and
the temple, and hence displaying an independence of action
which in the end was its undoing. [89]

The Crusades challenged the infidel to a formal
trial-of-arms at Jerusalem, to prove which side was chosen of
God. [90] The great scandal of the Crusades is accordingly not
the cynical self-interest, betrayal, and compromise with the
enemy that blights them from the beginning, [91] but simply
their clear-cut and humiliating failure, [92] which dealt a mortal blow to medieval ideas of feudal and ecclesiastical dominion. [93] With the loss of all the East, "Operation Jerusalem"
adopted a new strategy of indirection, approaching its goal
variously and deviously by wars against European heretics, [94] by preaching missions, through which the Franciscans
held a permanent Roman bridgehead in Jerusalem, [95] and by
local crusades against Jews and Moslems as steps in grand
designs of global strategy: the grandiose plans of Charles
VIII, Alfonso of Castile, João II, Albuquerque, and Don
Sebastian all had as their ultimate objective the liberation of
the Holy Sepulchre, [96] as indeed did all of Columbus'
projects. [97] A marked cabalistic influence has been detected
in these plans, and indeed the ever-living hopes of the Jews,
fired by new prophecies and new messiahs, were not without
effect in Catholic and Protestant circles, [98] as appears in the
career of the Humanist Guillaume Postel, who, acclaimed at

the court of France for his philological researches in Jerusalem, urged the transfer of the Papacy to that city, and finally declared himself to be the *Shekhinah.*[99]

The great reformers, while mildly condemning pilgrimages,[100] placed strong emphasis on the purely spiritual nature of the New Jerusalem and the utter impossibility of the Jews' ever returning to build an earthly city.[101] This was necessary to counteract the tendency to apocalyptic excitement and renewed deference to the Jews attendant upon the Reformation's intensive preoccupation with the Bible,[102] as various groups of enthusiasts took to building their own local New Jerusalems[103] or preparing to migrate to Palestine for the task;[104] such groups flourished down through the 19th century.[105] Protestant pilgrims to Jerusalem from the 16th to the 20th centuries have consistently condemned the "mummery" of the older pilgrimages while indulging in their own brand of ecstatic dramatizations.[106] While the Catholic practice has been to identify archaeological remains as the very objects mentioned in the Bible, the Protestants have been no less zealous in detecting proof for the scriptures in every type of object observed in the Holy Land.[107] Chateaubriand's much publicized visit to Jerusalem in 1806 combined religious, literary, and intellectual interest and established a romantic appeal of the Holy Land that lasted through the century.[108] When Jerusalem was thrown open to the West in the 1830s by Mohammed Ali, European and American missionaries hastened to the spot with ambitious projects of converting the Jews with an eye to the fulfillment of prophecy in the ultimate restoration of the Holy City.[109] Even the ill-starred Anglo-Lutheran Bishopric of 1841 had that in view,[110] and Newman's denunciation of the plan as a base concession to the Jews and Protestants[111] indicated the stand of the Roman Church, which in 1847 appointed a resident patriarch for Jerusalem.[112] In the mounting rivalry of missions and foundations that followed, France used her offices as protector of Roman Catholics and Holy Places in the East (under the Capitulations of Francis I, 1535, renewed in 1740) to advance her interests in the Orient, e.g., in the Damascus ritual-murder affair of 1840;[113] and when Louis Napoleon was obliged by his Catholic constituents to reactivate French claims to holy places which France had long neglected and the Russians long cherished, "the foolish affair of the Holy Places" (as he called it) led to the Crimean War and its portentous chain of consequences.[114]

In the second half of the nineteenth century the major powers of churches were stimulated by mutual rivalry to seek commanding positions in Jerusalem through the founding of eleemosynary institutions over which they retained control.[115] Beyond the hard facts of geography and economics, the religious significance of the city continued to exert steady pressure on the policies of all the great powers, as when the German kaiser gratified his Catholic subjects with the gift of the "Dormition,"[116] proclaimed Protestant unity by the dedication of the great Jerusalem and the patronage (thwarted by his advisers)[117] of Palestinian Zionism.[118] The taking of Jerusalem by Allenby in 1917 was hailed throughout the Christian world as the fulfillment of prophecy,[119] and deplored by the Moslems as a typical Crusade against their holy city.[120] World War II was followed by increasing interest in Jerusalem as a center of oecumenical Christianity,[121] though old religious and national rivalries, of long standing and great variety, continued to flourish.[122] The twentieth-century pilgrimages acquired a touristic air in keeping with the times, interest in Jerusalem having a more sophisticated and intellectual tone.[123] Even the old and vexing problem of the priority of Jerusalem, "mother of Churches," over other Christian bishoprics is now approached in a spirit of mutual concession and with respect for the autonomy of the various bishoprics of Jerusalem.[124] This liberal attitude may be a response to what is regarded in some Christian circles as the Jewish challenge to the basic Christian thesis that only Christians can possess a New Jerusalem.[125] While the great powers for over a century cautiously sought to exploit the energies of Zionism and its sympathizers,[126] it is now openly conceded that the Jews might indeed rebuild their city—though only as potential Christians.[127] Though some Christians are even willing to waive that proviso,[128] the fundamental thesis is so firmly rooted that the progress of Israel is commonly viewed not as a refutation of it but as a baffling and disturbing paradox.[129] The Roman position, reflecting a 2000-year battle of prestige between Rome and Jerusalem,[130] is especially resistant to change.[131]

With the Israel military victories of 1948, 1956, and 1967, the Christian world was confronted by a new image of a heroic Israel. The picture was agreeable or disturbing to Christians depending on which of two main postions one chose to take, and the years of tension following the Six-Day War of June 1967 were marked by an increasing tendency among Christians everywhere to choose sides. On the one hand, the tradition of the Church Fathers and Reformers, emphasized anew by Arnold Toynbee, looked upon a Jewish Jerusalem as a hopeless anachronism, and deplored any inclination to identify ancient with modern Israel. This attitude rested on the theory, developed by generations of theologians, that only Christians could be rightful heirs to the true Covenant and the Holy City. Roman Catholics continued to hold the position, propounded by Pope Pius X to Herzl in 1904, that the return of the Jews to Jerusalem was a demonstration of messianic expectations which that church considered discredited and outmoded. Those suspicious of the progress of Israel naturally chose to minimize the moral and world-historical significance of Jerusalem, and to treat the problems of modern Israel as purely political. On the other hand were Bible-oriented Christians of all denominations in whom the successes of the Israelis inspired to a greater or lesser extent renewed hope and interest in the literal fulfillment of biblical prophecy. To such persons in varying degrees the Jewish military achievements appeared as steps toward the fulfillment of the eschatological promise to Abraham (Genesis 15:18) As interest in Jerusalem shifted from the antiquarian appeal of the 1950s to heightened eschatological allure, something of the old Christian vision of Jerusalem seemed to stir the Christian conscience.

If Jerusalem did not exist, the Christians would have to invent it—indeed they have invented it, choking with emotion at the sight of sixteenth-century walls and tracing the Lord's footsteps through late medieval streets.[132] It has always been an indispensable authentication for their faith and an abiding reminder of prophetic promises.

NOTES

1. H. W. Hertzberg, "Der heilige Fels und das Alte Testament," *Journal of the Palestine Oriental Society* 12 (1932): 32, 39–42.

2. Sibylle Mähl, "Jerusalem in mittelalterlicher Sicht," *Welt als Geschichte* 22 (1962): 19.

3. For a recent coordination with emphasis on Hebrew rites, see Samuel H. Hooke, ed., *Myth, Ritual, and Kingship* (Oxford: Clarendon, 1958).

4. Jerusalem is to all Christians what Athens is to the Greeks and Rome to the Latins, Jerome, *Epistolae* (*Letters*) 46, in *PL* 22:489. The rites of the old shrines are now transferred to the Christian center, Theodoret, *Graecarum Affectionum Curatio* 11, in *PG* 83:1095.

5. The issue is clearly stated by Jerome, *Commentarius in Isaiam Prophetam* (*Commentary on Isaiah*) XIV, 51, 7–13, in *PL* 24:487–88; XV, 54, 1–3, in *PL* 24:516; XVIII, 65, preface, in *PL* 24:627; Jerome, *Commentarius in Jeremiam Prophetam* (*Commentary on Jeremiah*) IV, 19, in *PL* 24:802, n.b; VI, 22, in *PL* 24:886, and in the note in Origen, *Contra Celsum* (*Against Celsus*) IV, 22, in PG 11:1058, n. 74.

6. "Dissertatio de Vita Sancti Cyrilli" ("Disquisition on the Life of Saint Cyril") I, 6, 34, in *PG* 33:61.

7. It is only the ignorant rabble who "promise us a rebuilding of Jerusalem," Theodoret, *In Divini Ezechielis Prophetiam* (*On the Divine Prophecies of Ezekiel*) 1045, in *PG* 81:1248; so Origen, *Against Celsus* IV, 80, in *PG* 11:1105–8; Origen, *Peri Archon* (*On First Things*) II, 4, 3, in *PG* 11:201–3; Jerome, *Commentary on Isaiah* XV, 54, 1–3, in *PL* 24:516; XVIII, 65, preface, in *PL* 24:627–29.

8. Friedrich Baethgen, *Der Engelpapst* (Halle: Niemeyer, 1933), 76–77; Ray C. Petry, in *Church History*, 10 vols. (New Jersey: Prentice-Hall, 1962–64), 9:55.

9. Justin Martyr, *Dialogus cum Tryphone* (*Dialogue with Trypho*) 80, in *PG* 6:665; Augustine, *Enarrationes in Psalmos* (*Expositions on the Psalms*) 30, 8–10, in *PL* 36:253; Augustine, *Contra Litteras Petiliani Donatistae* (*Against the Writings of Petilianus the Donatist*) IV, 25–28, in *PL* 43:409–10; Jerome, *Letters* 46, in *PL* 22:485, 489; Cassiodorus, *Expositio in Psalterium* (*Commentary on the Psalms*) 86, 7-end, in *PL* 70:474, 621; Cyril of Alexandria, *Commentarius in Isaiam Prophetam* (*Commentary on Isaiah*) 292, in *PG* 70:468.

10. When Christians are accused of Judaizing, the specific charge is "Chiliasm," which "is found wherever the Gospel is not yet Hellenized, and must be regarded as a main element of Christian preaching," Adolf von Harnack, *History of Dogma*, 7 vols. (New York: Russell & Russell, 1958), 1:167, n. 1.

11. Arguments and references in Origen, *Against Celsus* IV, 22-23, in *PG* 11:1055–60. Protestant writers are just as emphatic, note 100 below.

12. Flavius Josephus, *Jewish War* VI, 403–22.

13. Origen, *Against Celsus* IV, 22, in *PG* 11:1057; George Cedrenus, *Historiarum Compendium* (*Compendium of History*) 1, 408-10, in *PG* 121:448–49; Theodoret, *Interpretatio in Psalmos* (*Interpretation of Psalms*) 73, 1–3, in *PG* 80:1453–56.

14. With each successive writer, this argument becomes more effective, e.g., Origen, *Against Celsus* IV, 22, in *PG* 11:1081; Hilary, *Tractatus super Psalmos* (*Treatise on the Psalms*) 58, 12, in *PL* 9:381; 124, 2–3, in *PL* 9:680; 126, 1–2, in *PL* 9:693; "Index Analyticus in Cyrillum," in *PG* 33:1711; Cosmas, *Topographia Christiana* (*Christian Topography*) 111, in *PG* 88:168; Fulbert, *Tractatus contra Judaeos* (*Treatise against the Jews*) 2, in *PL* 141:312; 3, in *PL* 141: 317–18; Andronicus Comnenus, *Dialogus contra Judaeos* (*Dialogue against the Jews*) 41, in *PG* 133:869; Ernest Wilhelm Hengstenberg, *Christology of the Old Testament*, 4 vols., tr. James Martin (Edinburgh: Clark, 1858), 3:291–92.

15. Cedrenus, *Compendium of History* 1, 285–87, 423–24, in *PG* 121:321, 461–64; Michaeus Glycas, *Annales* (*Annals*) 238, in *PG* 158:449; Sulpicius Severus, *Chronicon* (*Chronicle*) 2, 33, in *PL* 20: 147–48.

16. Using almost identical words, Ambrose, *Historiae de Excidio Hierosolymitanae Urbis* (*History of the Destruction of Jerusalem*)

19-20, in *PL* 15:2323; Augustine, *Expositions on the Psalms* 73, 1-4, in *PL* 36:929, but especially 931-32; Andronicus Comnenus, *Dialogue against the Jews* 54, in *PG* 133:893; Anonymus Saeculus, *Tractatus adversus Judaeum* (*Tract against a Jew*) 39, in *PL* 213:777; Jaroslav Pelikan and Helmut T. Lehmann, eds, *Luther's Works*, 30 vols. (Philadelphia: Concordia, 1957), 2:361; or *D. Martin Luthers Werke*, 92 vols. (Weimar: Hermann Böhlau, 1883-1941; reprinted Graz: Akademische Druck- und Verlagsanstalt, 1966-83), 42:520.

17. Irenaeus, *Contra Haereses* (*Against Heresies*) IV, 3, 1, in *PG* 7:980; Justin, *Apologia pro Christianis* (*Apology*) 49, 5, in *PL* 6: 336; Augustine, *Expositions on the Psalms* 30, 8-10, in *PL* 36:253; Cyril of Alexandria, *Commentary on Isaiah* 37, in *PG* 70:72. TB, *Pesaḥim* 87b-88a.

18. Jerome bridges the gap by transferring the angelic announcement of A.D. 70 —transeamus ex his sedibus—to the time of the crucifixion, *Epistola Paulae et Eutochii ad Marcellam* (*Letter of Paula and Eutochius to Marcella*), discussed by Robert Eisler, *Iesous Basileus ou Basileusas*, 2 vols. (Heidelberg: Winter, 1929), 1:130. Cf. Walafridus Strabus, *De Subversione Jerusalem* (*On the Destruction of Jerusalem*), in *PL* 114:967; Mähl, "Jerusalem in mittelalterlicher Sicht," 13.

19. Gregorius Magnus (Gregory the Great), *Homiliae in Evangelia* (*Homilies on the Gospel*) II, 39, in *PL* 76:1294-95; Strabus, *On the Destruction of Jerusalem*, in *PL* 114:971, 965; Origen, *Homiliae in Jeremiam* (*Homlies on Jeremiah*) 13, 1-3, in *PG* 13: 400-01; Cyril of Alexandria, *Commentary on Isaiah* 407, in *PG* 70:648.

20. Hadrian is both the benefactor of the human race *and* the Abomination of Desolation: Eusebius, *HE* IV, 5-6, in *PG* 20:308-16; cf. Domitian, cited in ibid. III, 19, in *PG* 20:252; Hadrian's Aelia *was* the New Jerusalem! Cedrenus, *Compendium of History* 1, 437-38, in *PG* 121:477. Titus' attack on Jerusalem was directed especially against the Christians, Sulpicius Severus, *Chronicon* 2, 50, in *PL* 20:157-58; Vespasian feared the Christians as he did the Jews, René Basset, ed., "Le synaxaire arabe jacobite," in *PO* 16:310.

21. The Christians find themselves in exactly the same position as the Jews and are given the identical comfort, Lactantius, *Divinae Institutiones* (*Divine Institutes*) V, 23, in *PL* 6:627-28; Origen, *In Lucam Homiliae* (*Homily on Luke*) 38, in *PG* 13:1897; Jerome, *Commentarius in Ezechielem* (*Commentary on Ezekiel*) 36, in *PL* 25: 340; Cassiodorus, *Commentary on the Psalms* 59, 7-9, in *PL* 70: 422;

Haymond of Halberstadt, *Enarratio in Malachiam Prophetam* (*Exposition on Malachi*) 14, in *PL* 117:276. The principle had been laid down that whoever holds the Holy Places is the true church, since God would *never* allow them to fall into the hands of unbelievers. Athanasius, *Quaestiones ad Antiochum Ducem* (*Questions to Duke Antiochus*) 43–45, in *PG* 28:625. Below, note 91. The fathers are *pleased* to be able to identify their people with the Jews through their parallel sufferings.

22. Irenaeus, *Against Heresies* V, 25, 1–2, in *PG* 7:1189; Hippolytus, *Exegetica* 21–22, in *PG* 10:656, 921, 928; Cyril of Jerusalem, *Catecheses* (*Catechetical Lectures*) 15, in *PG* 33:889; Clement of Alexandria, *Stromatum* I, 21, 57–62, in *PG* 8:856; Hilary, *Commentarius in Matthaeum* (*Commentary on Matthew*) 25, 1–7, in *PL* 9:1053–55; Theophylactus, *Enarratio in Evangelium Marci* (*Exposition on the Gospel of Mark*), in *PG* 123:630.

23. Origen, *Against Celsus* IV, 32, in *PG* 11:1077; Hippolytus, *Demonstratio de Christo et Antichristo* (*On Christ and the Antichrist*) 2, 7, in *PG* 10:792; Augustine, *Expositions on the Psalms* 62, 18–19, in *PL* 36:759; 64, 1–2, in *PL* 36:773; Jerome, *Letters*, in *PL* 22:485–86; Chrysostom, *Contra Judaeos et Gentiles, quod Christus Sit Deus* (*Against the Jews and the Gentiles that Christ is God*) 6, 2–3, in *PG* 48:907; Chrysostom, *Commentarius in Sanctum Matthaeum Evangelistam* (*Commentary on Matthew*) 76, in *PG* 58:695, etc.

24. Discussed by Eisler, *Iesous Basileus ou Basileusas* 1:147. Many fathers give other reasons. The time scale is the decisive factor, Christians and Jews each arranging it to suit themselves. *The Trophies of Damascus* IV, 2, 1–3 and 8, in *PO* 15:262–66.

25. The view is stated by Charles Malik: "The promises made to ancient Israel were all fulfilled in Jesus Christ," so that any subsequent development "has nothing to do either with eschatology or Christian theology. . . . Any further political expectation for the Jews would mean that there is still something which has not been already completed and finally fulfilled in Jesus Christ," cited by David Polish, *The Eternal Dissent* (The Hague: Mouton, 1960), 204. Justin, Clement of Alexandria, Cyprian, Jerome, Cyril of Jerusalem, Chrysostom, etc., all say the same.

26. "Here the Christian confronts a solemn, awful question," P. Parker, *Inherit the Promise* (Connecticut: Seabury, 1957), 62. *Renovatio* has a special meaning in this case, for God really founds *another* city entirely, Augustine, *Civitate Dei* (*The City of God*) 18, 48, in *PL* 41:574–76; Eusebius, *De Vita Constantini* (*On the Life of Constantine*) 32, 16–18, in *PG* 24:321; Anonymous, *Vita Sancti*

Pachomii (Life of Saint Pachomius) I, 30, in PL 73:250; Hilary, Treatise on the Psalms 67, 30–32, in PL 9:465; Nicolas Faber, In Fragmenta Sancti Hilarrii (On the Fragments of Saint Hilary) 30–31, in PL 10:908, etc.

27. Many fathers treat the paradox: Jerusalem is "the sterile mother," Gregory the Great, In Primum Librum Regum (Commentary on the First Book of Kings) II, 15, in PL 79:84, "black but comely," Gregory the Great, Super Cantica Canticorum Expositio (Commentary on the Song of Songs) 1, 21, in PL 79:487; 6, 3, in PL 79:526. Hippolytus, De Consummatione Mundi (On the Consummation of the World) 3, in PG 10:908; Jerome, Commentarius in Zachariam (Commentary on Zechariah) I, 1, in PL 25:1426; Prosper, Expositio Psalmorum (Commentary on the Psalms) 131, 5–10, in PL 51:379; Hilary, Treatise on the Psalms 124, 2–4, in PL 9:680–81; Justin, Dialogue with Trypho 83, 3, in PG 6:672–73; Epiphanius, Adversus Haereses (Against Heresies) I, 2, 3–4, in PG 41:392–96, etc.

28. Clement of Alexandria, Stromata IV, 26, in PG 8:1381, even compares the Christian Jerusalem with the ideal cities of mythology and philosophy.

29. Augustine, De Catechizandis Rudibus (On the Catechising of the Uninstructed) 21, 37, in PL 40:336–37; he denies the title of Christian to those who would altogether reject a physical city, Contra Donatistas (Against the Donatists) IV, 10–11, in PL 43:409–10, and Jerome reluctantly warns against separating the two cities—the earthly Jerusalem is also holy, Letters 46, 7–10, in PL 22:488–89.

30. H. Rusche, "Himmlisches Jerusalem," in Michael Buchberger, ed., Lexikon für Theologie und Kirche, 9 vols. (Freiburg: Herder, 1960), 5:367; W. Schmauch, "Jerusalem: Theologie," in Heinz Brunotte and Otto Weber, Evangelisches Kirchenlexikon, 4 vols. (Göttingen: Vandenhoeck & Ruprecht, 1958), 2:260. Wolberus, Commentaria in Canticum Canticorum (Commentary on the Song of Solomon) 208, in PL 195:1209, even suggests a third Jerusalem acting as a physical link between them.

31. Michel Join-Lambert, Jerusalem (New York: Putnam, 1958), 106. During the period the great teachers "felt that their knowledge would not be complete, nor could they achieve the highest merit [virtutem]" unless they visited Jerusalem, Jerome, Letters 46, 206, in PL 22:489.

32. Eusebius, On the Life of Constantine III, 12–15; III, 33, in PG 24:600–601; Hugh W. Nibley, "The Loyalty Problem: Our Western Heritage," Western Political Quarterly 6 (1953): 641–46.

340 MORMONISM AND EARLY CHRISTIANITY

33. W. Telfer, "Constantine's Holy Land Plan," *Texte und Untersuchungen* 63 (1957): 696–700. Eusebius, *On the Life of Constantine* III, 12–15; III, 33, in *PG* 20:600. Jerome says Palestine again became the religious capital of the world, *Letters* 46, 8–10, in *PL* 22:489; "Disquisition on the Life of Saint Cyril," I, 6, 34, in *PG* 33:61. Constantine could only express these ideas "in the pagan idiom," Andrew Alföldi, *The Conversion of Constantine and Pagan Rome*, tr. Harold Mattingly (Oxford: Clarendon, 1948), 112.

34. Eutychius, *Annales* (*Annals*) 464–68, in *PG* 111:1012, compares Constantine's conquest of the Jewish capital with Hadrian's. Cf. Georgios Harmatolos, *Chronicon* (*Chronicle*) IV, 181, in *PG* 110:612, and Augustine's victory chant, *Expositions on the Psalms* 63, in *PL* 36:759. The church stands forever on the foundation of the destroyed temple, Leo, *Sermo* (*Discourse*) 3, 1-2, in *PL* 54:145, literally occupying "non urbem sed locum," Jerome, *Commentarius in Jeremiam Prophetam* (*Commentary on Jeremiah*) IV, 29, 5–10, in *PL*24:802. "Jerusalem was converted to the Christian faith in the time of Constantine," Radulfi de Diceto, "Opera Historica," in William Stubbs, ed., *The Historical Works of Master Ralph de Diceto*, 2 vols. (London: Longman, 1876), 2:76.

35. Suddenly "Aelia remembered that it had once been at Jerusalem . . . the basilicas of Constantine and of Helena . . . were reviving and exalting its venerable traditions," Louis Duchesne, *Early History of the Christian Church*, 3 vols. (London: Murray, 1931), 2:486.

36. Jacob de Haas, *History of Palestine* (New York: Macmillan, 1934), 80–81; Georgios Hermatolos, *Chronicle* 410–11, in *PG* 110:620–21; Edward Robinson, *Biblical Researches in Palestine, Mount Sinai and Arabia Petraea*, 3 vols. (London: Murray, 1841), 2:80.

37. Silvia visited two caves of Moses and Elijah, Job's cave, the caves where Christ taught, was resurrected, born, ascended to heaven and (in spite of the scriptures) held the Last Supper, John W. Crowfoot, *Early Churches in Palestine* (London: Oxford University Press, 1941), 31. The footprint of Christ in a grotto under the Temple Rock "where the dead met to worship God," Join-Lambert, *Jerusalem*, 170, was matched by the Holy of Holies, in a cave under the same rock, C. Raymond Beazley, *The Dawn of Modern Geography*, 2 vols. (London: Murray, 1901), 2:150.

38. Constantine's prime monument, the Anastasis, was "a round building on the plan of the imperial mausoleum . . . the grotto-tomb stood in the middle," Crowfoot, *Early Churches in Palestine*, 20. There

"you cannot imagine what a wailing and howling was carried on by all the people . . . day and night," to commemorate not the death, but the resurrection of Christ! (This is the author's translation from the original text.) Compare with John H. Bernard, tr. & ed., *The Pilgrimage of S. Silvia of Aquitania to the Holy Places* (London: Palestine Pilgrims' Text Society, 1891), 68, p. 65 (cf. p. 126); 57, p. 48 (cf. p. 112). Jerome explains this with the quotation: "Where the body is, thither will the eagles be gathered together," cited in E. S. Duckett, *Wandering Saints of the Early Middle Ages* (New York: Norton, 1959), 296.

39. Join-Lambert, *Jerusalem*, 108–11.

40. Crowfoot, *Early Churches in Palestine*, 160; nine-tenths of Palestine's churches were built then.

41. For the economic history, Avi-Yonah, "The Economics of Byzantine Palestine," *Israel Exploration Journal* 8 (1958): 38–51. Queen Helen, see Josephus, *Antiquities* XX, 2, 4; Eusebius, *HE* II, 12, in *PG* 20:165, was later claimed by the Christians, Flavius Lucius Dexter, *Chronicon (Chronicle)*, in *PL* 31:201; Jacob Raisin, *Gentile Reactions to Jewish Ideals* (New York: Philosophical Library, 1953), 262.

42. Join-Lambert, *Jerusalem*, 129, 134–40; Duchesne, *Early History of the Christian Church* 3:132–34, 140–43. The Lady Silvia found distinguished dames of her acquaintance inhabiting cells in Palestine, Bernard, *The Pilgrimage of S. Silvia of Aquitania to the Holy Places* 40, p. 23–24 (cf. 90–91); 54–55, p. 42–45 (cf. 107–9).

43. Avi-Yonah, "The Economics of Byzantine Palestine," 41, 47–51. "A countless host of priests and monks" came hither, "partly because of the sanctity of the two places, partly because of the fame of Jerome, and partly to enjoy the charity of rich and noble matrons," Marius Mercatius, *Fides Rufini Aquileiensis (The Faith of Rufinus of Aquileia)* preface, in *PL* 48:239. Anonymous, *De Locis Sanctis (On the Holy Places)* 11, in *PG* 133:985, puts the number of religious establishments in Jerusalem at 365.

44. Crowfoot, *Early Churches in Palestine*, 7–8; Sozomen, *HE* II, 26, in *PG* 67:26; Avi-Yonah, "The Economics of Byzantine Palestine," 41–42, 49.

45. The grand scale rioting began at the dedication of Constantine's church, *Cambridge Medieval History*, 8 vols. (Cambridge: Cambridge University Press, 1926), 1:128, and culminated in the massacre at the Holy Sepulchre in 451 A.A. For a description, Marius Mercatius, *The Faith of Rufinus of Aquileia* 12, in *PL* 48:240; "Disquisition on the Life of Saint Cyril," I, in *PG* 33:63–64.

46. *Cambridge Medieval History* 2:285, 290; De Haas, *History of Palestine*, 116.

47. William of Tyre, *Historia Rerum in Partibus Transmarinis Gestarum* (*History of Overseas Territories*) I, 2, in *PL* 201:214-15.

48. Lawrence Edward Browne, *Eclipse of Christianity in Asia* (Cambridge: Cambridge University Press, 1933), 25; de Haas, *History of Palestine*, 117. Adrian Fortescue, "Jerusalem," in Charles G. Herberman, ed., *The Catholic Encyclopedia*, 16 vols. (New York: Appleton, 1910), 8:359-60, charges treason.

49. Georgios Harmatolos, *Chronicle* 4, 22, in *PG* 110:833, treats the breaking of this oath to the Jews as a crime, formally recognized as such by the Coptic Church. Cf. de Haas, *History of Palestine*, 120.

50. Omar, "after a lapse of six centuries," revived the essential Jewish tradition of Jerusalem, Join-Lambert, *Jerusalem*, 169. On Sophronius and the Christian claims, Charles Diehl and Georges Margais, *Le monde orientale de 395 á 1081*, in Louis Lévéque, ed., *Histoire du moyen age*, 2 vols. (Paris: Les Presses Universitaire de France, 1936), 1:154-55.

51. Jerome, *Letters* 46, 8-10, in *PL* 22:489; Eusebius, *HE* VI, 2, in *PG* 20:541-44; Sulpicius Severus, *Chronicle* 2, 31, in *PL* 20:147; Basset, "Le Synaxaire arabe jacobite," in *PO* 16:303-5.

52. F. Dölger, in *Relazioni* 3:92. Among those discouraging pilgrimages are Origen, Athanasius, Hilary, Gregory of Nyssa, Jerome, Cedrenus, Sulpicius Severus, Bede, Theodoret, William of Malmesbury, Geoffrey of Vendome, Gilles of Paris, the Russian Daniel, Rupert, and Thomas à Kempis. Note 54 below.

53. Dölger, in *Relazioni* 3:88-93. They were looking for "une sorte de paradis perdu," R. Roussel, *Les pèlerinages* (Paris: Payot, 1954), 13. Pilgrimage and monastic life "met l'homme en communication directe avec Dieu," Diehl, *Le monde orientale* 3:101. They would kiss the holy objects "like thirsty people," Jerome, *Letters* 46 and 47, in *PL* 22:484-93.

54. "In the whole of patristic literature there is not one homily or other exhortation . . . to undertake pilgrimages," B. Koetting, *Peregrinatio Religiosa* (Münster: Regensberg, 1950), 42. It was a popular vote of ʾno-confidence in the church, Adolf von Harnack, *Das Mönchtum* (Giessen: Kicker, 1895). "If you really believed, you would not have to visit these places to reassure yourselves," says Gregorius Nyssenus (Gregory of Nyssa), *Epistolae* (*Letters*) 2, in *PG* 46:1013.

55. Mähl, "Jerusalem in mittelalterlicher Sicht," 14-15; Roussel, *Les pèlerinages*, 48-50. The will to *locate and materialize* everything is paramount: "This is the tomb of Moses, in spite of the fact that the

Scriptures say that no man knows his tomb," Bernard, *The Pilgrimage of S. Silvia of Aquitania to the Holy Places*, 42, p. 27 (cf. 94). Ricoldus put a live baby into the Holy Crib so he and other pilgrims could worship it, Mähl, "Jerusalem in mittelalterlicher Sicht," 16.

56. It was believed that Jerusalem was actually a bit of heaven, Harnack, *History of Dogma* 6:8; Bernardi, *Itinerarium in Loca Sancta (Journey to the Holy Places)* 10–16, in *PL* 121:572–73; Bede, *Historia Ecclesiastica (Ecclesiastical History)* III, 16–17, in *PL* 95:258. At Jerusalem the most important "letters from heaven" descended, Mathew Paris, *Chronica Majora*, 7 vols. (London: Longman, 1872), 2:462–64; Maximilian Bittner, *Der vom Himmel gefallene Brief Christi in seinen morgenländischen Versionen und Rezensionen*, in *Denkschriften der kaiserlichen Akademie der Wissenschaften in Wien*, Philosophisch-historische Klasse, 51 (1906): 71.

57. Bernardi, *Itinerarium in Loca Sancta (Journey to the Holy Places)* 10–16, in *PL* 121:572–73; Georgios Harmatolos, *Chronicle* 139–40, in *PG* 110:664; Cassiodorus, *Commentary on the Psalms* 67, 35–38, in *PL* 70:474; Mähl, "Jerusalem in mittelalterlicher Sicht," 17.

58. Stewart Perowne, "The Site of the Holy Sepulchre," *Listener* 68 (1962): 351–53; F. M. Abel, "Jérusalem," in *DACL*, 7:2311. It was the spot of the "ultima Domini vestigia," Bede, *Ecclesiastical History* III, 16–17, in *PL* 95:257.

59. A very moving description in Bede, *Ecclesiastical History* III, 17–18, in *PL* 95:258. The great central shrine was roofless in order to maintain contact with heaven, Bernardi, *Journey to the Holy Places* 10–12, in *PL* 121:572.

60. Augustine, *Sermones (Sermons)* 117, 6–7, in *PL* 38:660. Cf. Gregory of Tours, *Miraculorum de Liber Gloria Martyrum* I, 5, in *PL* 71:709.

61. M. Daniel-Rops, *L'église de la cathedrale et de la croisade*, 542. The four columns of the Holy of Holies were claimed by Mecca, Paris, *Chronica Majora* 6:349, Venice; John Evelyn, *Diary and Correspondence of John Evelyn*, 4 vols. (Oxford: Clarendon, 1955), 2:438; and Rome, ibid., 246, where they stood on the very soil of Jerusalem, sent to Rome by St. Helen herself, ibid., 272–73, n. 1. Cf. John the Deacon, *Liber de Ecclesia Lateranensi (On the Lateran Church)* 1–4, in *PL* 194:1547–48. In the eighth century Syncellus identifies Constantinople with Jerusalem in the most literal sense, Paul Alexander, "The Strength of Empire and Capital as Seen through Byzantine Eyes," *Speculum* 37 (1962): 346–47; the chief church of Spain was called simply "Jerusalem," Petrus Braida, *Dissertatio in Sanctum Nicetam (Disquisition on Saint Nicetas)* 5, in *PL* 52:952. The

Jerusalem in Rome, William of Malmesbury, *Gesta Regum Anglorum* 1, 202; 3, 172, like the Jerusalem Chamber in Westminster, Phillip Schaff, *Creeds of Christendom*, 3 vols. (London: Harper, 1905), 1:748–49, were mystically identified with Jerusalem. The Temple in London was a reproduction of Solomon's Temple, "built round in imitation of this," Samuel Purchas, *His Pilgrimes* 8:193; Walter Besant, *Mediaeval London*, 2 vols. (London: Black, 1906), 2:276–77. The same idea was followed in London's St. Sepulchre, J. C. Dickinson, *Monastic Life in Medieval England* (New York: Barnes & Noble, 1962), 82.

62. Walsingham, "The Nazareth of England," gave the pilgrim "the same spiritual privileges as would the journey to Palestine," Roussel, *Les Pélerinages*, 94. On the rule of distance, Mähl, "Jerusalem in mittelalterlicher Sicht," 16; Titus Tobler, *Dr. Titus Toblers zwei Bücher Topographie von Jerusalem und seinen Umgebungen*, 2 vols. (Berlin: Reimer, 1853–54), 1:540.

63. Giselbert, *Historia Hierosolymitana (History of Jerusalem)* IV, 35–38, in *PL* 166:555. It is "quasi alterum coelum," Peter of Blois, *De Hierosolymitana Peregrinatione (On the Pilgrimage to Jerusalem)*, in *PL* 207:1070, "a star in some other heaven," Cassiodorus, *Commentary on the Psalms* 86-87, in *PL* 70:622, an "alter paradisus delicarum," says Urban in Robert Manachus, *Historia Hierosolymitana (History of Jerusalem)* I, 1, in *PL* 155:672.

64. On the political issues, Aziz Atiya, *Crusade, Commerce, and Culture* (Mass.: Smith, 1969), 36; Crowfoot, *Early Churches in Palestine*, 162–63.

65. Sangallensis Monachus, *De Gestis Beati Carolil Magni* II, 11, in *PL* 98:1396–98; Anonymous, *Annales Veteres Francorum*, in *PL* 98:1427–28. Paris, *Chronica Majora* 1:368; Louis Halphen, *Charlemagne and the Carolingian Empire*, tr. Giselle de Nie (New York: North-Holland, 1977), 93–94; *Cambridge Medieval History* 2:620–21, 704–5.

66. Roussel, *Les pélerinages*, 14; Join-Lambert, *Jerusalem*, 176.

67. Benedict Stolz, "The Benedictines in the Holy Land," *Christian News from Israel* 11 (1960): 12.

68. A. Philipsborn, "Les premiers hôpitaux au moyen age (orient et occident)," *Nouvelle Clio* 6 (1955): 144–46. In the history of hospitals in general "le role de Jerusalem est capital," ibid., 160.

69. Paul Heinisch, *History of the Old Testament* (Collegeville, Minn.: Liturgical Press, 1952), 418. Vespasian continued the temple tax for the pagan temple, and Theodosius diverted it into the imperial

treasury, as did the German Emperors, *Cambridge Medieval History* 7:646–47.

70. In 883 and 887 King Alfred sent the monks back to Jerusalem loaded with gifts, Simeon of Durham, *Historia Regum*, in Thomas Arnold, ed., *Symeonis Monachi Opera Omnia*, 2 vols. (London: Longman, 1882), 2:62; and in 889 following the example of Charlemagne imposed a regular Jerusalem tax, collected by the clergy, Richard of Cirencester, *Speculum Historiale de Gestis Regum Angliae* (London: Longman, Roberts & Green, 1863–69), 2:41. Circa A.D. 900 "monks used to come annually to Rouen to collect alms" for Jerusalem. Stolz, "The Benedictines in the Holy Land," 12, citing Ralph Glaber. The Jerusalem (later Saladin) tax became the foundation of Papal and national taxing policy in the Middle Ages, Ibsen's review of A. Gottlob, *Die päpstlische Kreuzzugsstreuen des 13. Jahrhunderts* (Heiligenstadt: Cordier, 1892), *Historische Zeitschrift* 72 (1894): 315. This too has an old Jewish background, Cicero, *Pro Flacco* 28 (66–69).

71. Charles Beazley, *The Dawn of Modern Geography*, 3 vols. (London: Frowde, 1905), 2:120–23; René Grousset, *Histoire des croisades et du Royaume Franc de Jerusalem*, 3 vols. (Paris: Librarie Plan, 1934), 1:lviii.

72. Beazley, *Modern Geography* 2:126, 148–49, 107; Charles Homer Haskins, *Norman Institutions* (Cambridge: Harvard University Press, 1918), 266–67; Richard of Cirencester (New York: Ungar, 1960), 2:178–79, 252, 283; Giraldus, *Chronicon* 3:397–98 (St. David of Wales); *Kristnisaga* 13:2; 17:5; Are, *Islendinga-boc* 10:14; *Orvar-Odds Saga* 33:8; 34:1.

73. Beazley, *Modern Geography* 2:155–61, 165, 167, 125, 215, 405.

74. Beazley, *Modern Geography* 2:125; Ralph Glaber, *Chronicon* 4, 6, in *PL* 142:680–82; Purchas, *His Pilgrimes* 8:18; on mass pilgrimages, Beazley, *Modern Geography* 2:129–30.

75. Quote is from Beazley, *Modern Geography* 2:127. Gregory VII and the Emperor Michael VII were already thinking of a Crusade in 1073, G. Ostrogorsky, "The Byzantine Emperor and the Hierarchical World Order," *Slavonic and East European Review* 35 (1956): 14. On Robert le Frison, L. Henri Pirenne, *Bibliographie de l'histoire de Belgique* (Bruxelles: Lamertin, 1931) 1:96–100.

76. The Crusaders are God's elect, true Israel, the Chosen People, Fulcher, *Historia Hierosolymitana* (*History of Jerusalem*) 39, 4, in *PL* 155: 891; Godfrey was the new Moses, his advent announced (literally) on Sinai, Alberic, *Historia Hierosolymitana* (*History of Jerusalem*) VI, 33–35, in *PL* 166:554; his successor is designated in his

epitaph as "Rex Baldwinus Judas alter Machabeus," Purchas, *His Pilgrimes* 8:187; the first Crusaders are "the Princes of Judah bringing comfort to Jerusalem," Guibert, *Gesta Dei per Francos* (*Acts of God through the Franks*) VIII, 4, in *PL* 156:806–8, defending her "in the midst of the Gentiles," ibid., in *PL* 156:810. "*You* are now the Children of Israel," cries Urban II, "fight better than the ancient Israelites for *Your* Jerusalem," Oswald J. Reichel, *The See of Rome in the Middle Ages* (London: Longmans, Green, 1870), 320.

77. "Through the Crusades . . . the primitive Christian institutions were restored; the sacred places . . . led it to the Christ of the Gospels," Harnack, *History of Dogma* 6:9. Rodulfus Glaber, *Historia* (*History*) 3, 4, in *PL* 142:651: "Rejecta vestustate, passim candidam ecclesiarum vestem indueret." Against the will of the leaders, the masses insisted on marching straight to Jerusalem, William of Tyre, *History of Overseas Territories* VII, 2, in *PL* 201:378–79. "Sehnsucht nach Freiheit" was the motive, Martin Grabmann, *Die Geschichte der scholastischen Methode*, 2 vols. (Graz: Akademische Druck und Verlagsanstalt, 1957), 1:258; and Urban's speech lays strong emphasis on the escape motif, Fulcher, *History of Jerusalem* 1, 2, in *PL* 155:830–32.

78. Adolf Waas, "Der heilige Krieg," *Welt als Geschichte* 19 (1959): 215–16.

79. Thus Geoffrey, though anxious to avoid bloodshed, was "bound to avenge the insult [*injuriam*] to his Lord," Godefridus Rex, *Concio ad Milites Christianos* (*Call to Christian Soldiers*), in *PL* 155: 391, and so, seeking "neither Tower, nor Gold, nor Spoile, but revenge . . . clave human bodies from the head to the raines," Purchas, *His Pilgrimes* 7:449–50. Pope and Sultan exchange formal challenges and insults in the best epic and chivalric manner, John of Whethamstede, *Registra Quorundam Abbatum Monasterius St. Albanus* (London: Longman, 1872–73) 11:270–71.

80. The Crusaders adopted the epic literary idiom, and dramatized themselves as the Knights of the Round Table, Grousset, *Histoire des croisades* 3:731. Later ages saw the Crusades in an epic setting, as Torqvato Tasso, *Gerusalemme Liberata* 1:1, 12, 21, 23; 4:7; 6, 9, etc.

81. Franz Altheim, *Gesicht vom Abend und Morgen* (Frankfurt: Fischer Bücherei, 1955), 148–50. The close ties with central Asia are significant, Éduard Perrov, *Le moyen age*, in Maurice Crouzet, ed., *Histoire genérale de civilisations*, 7 vols. (Paris: Presses Universitaires de France, 1957), 3:341; Grousset, *Histoire des croisades* 3:746.

82. "Earlier crusades were armed migrations, not military invasions," Brooks Adams, *The Law of Civilization and Decay* (New York: Macmillan, 1896, 1910), 124.

83. C. Dawson, *Dynamics of World History*, 137; T. B. L. Webster, *From Mycenae to Homer* (London: Methuen, 1958), 59–61, 106. Jerome describes the fall of Rome both in terms of Jerusalem and of Troy, Grant Showerman, *Eternal Rome* (New Haven: Yale University Press, 1925), 337–38.

84. Laetitia Boehm, " 'Gesta Dei per Francos' oder 'Gesta Francorum?' " *Saeculum* 8 (1957): 44–45; Hugh W. Nibley, "The Hierocentric State," *Western Political Quarterly* 4 (1951): 226–53, and "The Unsolved Loyalty Problem: Our Western Heritage," *Western Political Quarterly* 6 (1953): 641–46. Christianity borrowed from paganism its mystique of victory, Oswald J. Reichel, *The See of Rome in the Middle Ages* (London: Longmans, Green, 1870), 344–45.

85. Waas, "Der heilige Krieg," 212–15, demonstrates at length that the Moslems took over the idea from the Christians, and *not* the other way around. Cf. Atiya, *Crusade, Commerce, and Culture*, 130–37.

86. William of Tyre, *History of Overseas Territories* IX, 16, in *PL* 201:448; XI, 11–13, in *PL* 201:497–99; Alberic, *History of Jerusalem* VII, 63–67, in *PL* 166:602–3; W. Ohnsorge, "Byzanz und das Abendland im 9. u. 10. Jahrhundert. Eine Zusammenfassung," *Nouvelle Clio* 5 (1954): 447–49; Boehm, "Gesta Dei," 44–46; D. M. Nicol, "Byzantium and the Papacy in the Eleventh Century," *Journal of Ecclesiastical History* 13 (1962) :18; Charles Brand, "The Byzantines and Saladin, 1185–1192; Opponents of the Third Crusade," *Speculum* 37 (1962): 179. On the very day of Charlemagne's coronation the monks of St. Sabas (who had brought him the keys and banner of Jerusalem) fought a pitched battle with the Benedictines of Bethlehem whose patron was Leo III, Stolz, "The Benedictines in the Holy Land," 12–13.

87. *Cambridge Medieval History* 5:303; Steven Runciman, "The Crown of Jerusalem," *Palestine Exploration Quarterly* 92 (1960): 15; Angelo S. Rappoport, *History of Palestine* (London: Allen & Unwin, 1931), 282–85.

88. Eugéne de Roziere, ed., *Cartulaire du Saint Sépulcre* 1, in *PL* 155:1106. Most royalty in time claimed the crown of Jerusalem, Runciman, "The Crown of Jerusalem," 8–9. When the patriarch of Jerusalem, the two grand masters, the pope, and the emperor met at Verona to discuss Jerusalem, an envoy of Saladin (who "claimed Jerusalem as his by hereditary right from Sara") Ishmael was present

with a letter to "his most victorious brother," the Pope, Horace Mann, *The Lives of the Popes in the Middle Ages,* 18 vols. (London: Paul, Trench, Trübner, 1925), 10:255–56.

89. The claims of the Hospitalers, back to the Maccabees, are presented by an anonymous writer, *De Primordiis et Inventione Sacrae Religionis Ierosolymorum,* in *PL* 155:1097–1104; the claims of the Templars on Solomon's Temple are apparent from St. Bernard's *PL* 182:927–28; the rapacity and independence of the orders from John of Salisbury, *Epistolae (Letters),* 1, 140, in *PL* 199.

90. So Baldric, *Historia Hierosolymitana IV,* in *PL* 166:1152. This is brought out in the exchange of letters between the pope and the Sultan in 1457, John of Whethamstede, *Registra Quorundam Abbatum Monasterius St. Albanus* 1:270.

91. Grousset, *Histoire des croisades* 2:319, 608, 693, 745–48; 3:29, 359, 393, 650; cf. Philippe de Méziére's verdict, cited in Atiya, *Crusade, Commerce and Culture,* 110–11; D. M. Bell, *Le songe du vieil pélerin,* 2 vols. (London: Cambridge University Press, 1955), 180–90: he calls for peace with the Moslem world.

92. Waas, "Der heilige Kreig," 217–18. Defeat made the Christians vulnerable to their own stock argument against the Jews, Raisin, *Gentile Reactions,* 505; Paris, *Chronica Majora* 4:345–46, says the catastrophe of 1244 was the literal fulfillment of Mark 13:2.

93. G. Hegel, *Philosophy of History* (New York & London: Cooperative Publication Society, 1900), 393, 395; Grousset, *Histoire des croisades* 1:163–64; Boehm, "Gesta Dei," 45, 47; Waas, "Der heilige Kreig," 218, 224.

94. Paetow, *The Crusades,* 209–20; F. Mourret, *Précis d'histoire de l'église* 2:9. The crusade against the Albigensians was viewed as a mystic crusade to Jerusalem, Pierre des Vaux-de Cernay, *Histoire albigéoise* (Paris: Vrin, 1951), 42.

95. Though St. Francis is credited with the gentler new method of preaching instead of fighting, Waas, "Der heilige Krieg," 221, the legend is that he challenged Saladin's religious entourage to a formal ordeal by fire in the best feudal manner, Ernest Raymond, *In the Steps of St. Francis* (New York: Kinsey, 1939), 225–26. And certainly the Franciscans were tough and aggressive, as appears in many reports in Purchas, *His Pilgrimes* 8:181–82, 300, 302–3; 9:466, 478–80. Indeed they considered their order to be the New Jerusalem, M. R. James, *Apocalypse in Art,* 67.

96. Charles VIII, Ranke, *History of the Latin and Teutonic Nations* (London: Bell, 1909), 27, 82; Alfonso and Joan I, Elaine Sanceau, *The Perfect Prince,* 107, 243, 412; Albuquerque and

Sebastian, K. G. Jayne, *Vasco da Gama*, 101, 279. Such schemes are already apparent in the 4th crusade and the career of St. Louis, and still earlier in Nicephorus Phocas fantastic letter of 964 to the court of Baghdad. Grousset, *Histoire des croisades* 1:12.

97. Salvador de Madariaga, *Christopher Columbus* (New York: Macmillan, 1940), 18, 106, 165, 359–61, 404; Samuel Elliot Morison, *Admiral of the Ocean Sea* (Boston: Little, Brown, 1942), 5, 45–46, 97, 304, 668.

98. Purchas, *His Pilgrimes* 9:497; Albert Nathaniel Williams, *The Holy City* (New York: Deull, Slon & Pierce, 1954), 353–59; Jayne, *Vasco da Gama*, 284. The Reformation itself was hailed "as the first indication of the advent of the Messianic age," L. I. Newman, *Jewish Influence on Christian Reform Movements* (New York: Columbia University Press, 1925) 1:628, the early catharist preoccupation with Jerusalem being of Cabbalistic origin, 1:175.

99. J. Bowsma, *Concordia Mundi*, 16–17, 178. On Humanist interest in Jerusalem, Boehm, "Gesta Dei," 51–53, 59.

100. Though "d'acharnes adversaires des pélerinages," they still imitated them in their old Hebrew aspect, Roussel, *Les pélerinages*, 107. Luther can conceive of "honest" pilgrimages of the old type, *Works* 31:199; *Werke* 1:598; and is impressed by the unique holiness of Jerusalem, *Works* 2:344, 378; *Werke* 42:507, 533. Calvin objects primarily to the physical impossibility of gathering the saints at Jerusalem, John Calvin, *Commentaries on the Twelve Minor Prophets*, tr. John Owen, 5 vols. (Grand Rapids: Eerdman, 1950), 5:228.

101. Luther, *Works* 2:99–100, 342, 360–61; 3:77; 13:34–35, 269, 339; 14:20, 326–27; 21:104; 23:120–21, 369; 32:162–64; 35:291–92, 303–5, 329–30; *Werke* 42:333, 506–7, 519–20; 42:603; 8:32, 33; 41:127–28, 221–22; 5:57–58; 32:386; 33:186, 598–99; 8:60–61; John Calvin, *Commentary on the Book of Psalms*, tr. James Anderson, 5 vols. (Grand Rapids: Eerdman, 1949), 2:226.

102. As is apparent from Luther, *Works* 14:6, 9, 19; 24:169–71, 237, 262; 31:198; *Werke* 1:31, 225–26, 228–29, 238; 45:615–17, 678, 701; 1:597–98; Calvin, *Minor Prophets* 5:228.

103. Luther, *Works* 2:361–62; *Werke* 42:520; C. Henry Smith, *Smith's Story of the Mennonites* (Kansas: Mennonite Publication Office, 1950), 282; G. H. Williams, *Spiritual and Anabaptist Writers* (Philadelphia: Westminster, 1957), 23, 29, 150, 255–60.

104. John Evelyn, *Diary* 5:177–78; George Fox, *The Journal of George Fox*, ed. Norman Penney, 2 vols. (Cambridge: Cambridge University Press, 1911), 2:90, 130–32, 170–72, 338, 383, 481.

105. Such were Jung-Stilling's movement, Ernst Benz, "Ost und West in der christlicher Geschichtsanschauung," *Welt als Geschichte* 1 (1955): 503-13, and the followers of Christian Offmann and Johann Lange, the Jerusalem Friends or Templers, Smith, *Smith's Story of the Mennonites*, 282. Sir Henry Finch's book, for which James I imprisoned him, calling for the Jews to return to Jerusalem and take "complete temporal dominion over the whole world," had considerable influence for over 300 years, Christopher Sykes, *Two Studies in Virtue* (New York: Knopf, 1953), 149-50.

106. Though the Quakers insisted that "wee . . . cannot owne noe other neither outwarde Jerusalem," Fox, *The Journal of George Fox* 2:131, yet they risked life and limb to reach the physical Jerusalem, 2:338, 383, 481; W. C. Braithwaite, *The Beginnings of Quakerism* (London: Macmillan, 1912), 418-19. Purchas asserts that "to ascribe sanctitie to the place is Jewish," *His Pilgrimes* 8:19, yet he was a pilgrim; and others who poured contempt on the holy places and rites were transported by the sight of the former, 10:444, 487; Braithwaite, *The Beginnings of Quakerism*, 424. So Robinson declared it un-Christian to heed "particular times and places," Edward Robinson, *Biblical Researches in Palestine* 2:72, yet was overwhelmed by the "coincidence of time, place and number" when twelve American missionaries met in a "large upper room" in Jerusalem, 1:335; and Schaff, who abhorred the superstitious "mummery" of the pilgrimage, immersed himself ten times in the Jordan and "almost imagined I was miraculously delivered from rheumatism," David Schley Schaff, *Life of Phillip Schaff* (New York: Scribner, 1897), 311.

107. Both attitudes are seen in William Thomson, *The Land and the Book* (New York: Harper, 1882), 625-26.

108. F. Bassan, *Chateaubriand et la terre saints* (1959) 209, 247. All the French travelers to Jerusalem between 1800 and 1850 "represent un oriente de fantaise," according to Bassan, who lists 67 of them, ibid., 35.

109. Williams, *The Holy City*, 365. "In 1835 the Church Missions to the Jews" set up in Jerusalem, Ruth Rouse and Stephen Charles Neill, eds., *Histoire of the Ecumenical Movement* (Philadelphia: Westminister, 1954), 289. E. Krüger, "L'effort missionaire américain dans le proche orient," *Revue d'histoire et de philosophie religieuses* 40 (1960): 278-84. Robinson, *Palestine* 1:327-28, 332-35; Arnold Toynbee, *A Study of History* 9:101-3; K. S. Latourette, *Nineteenth Century Outside Europe*, 398.

110. This is consistently overlooked by historians, but clearly stated by Gladstone, *Correspondence of Church and Religion of*

William Edwart Gladstone, 2 vols. (New York: Macmillan, 1910), 1:243, and Bunsen.

111. John Henry Newman, *Apologia pro Vita Sua* (London: Longman, Green, 1908), 128–38, 201.

112. Fortescue, "Jerusalem," 368–70. F. Mourret, *Précis d'histoire de l'église* 3:269: these moves "counterbalance as much as possible the influence of the Russian schismatics and the German Protestants."

113. Paul Goodman, *Moses Montefiore* (Philadelphia: The Jewish Publication Society of America, 1925), 62, 64–67.

114. T. A. B. Corley, *Democratic Despot* (London: Barris & Rockliff, 1961), 148–49. G. Marchal, *Guerre de Crimée*, 2–5, showing that the war was actually fought about the Holy Places.

115. Eugénie's idealist plan for uniting the crowned heads of Europe in a common undertaking to rebuild the Holy Sepulchre found no takers, Corley, *Democratic Despot*, 267. "The French government saw in the pilgrimages a force to be utilized in the penetration of the Orient," and even the anti-clerical parties supported them accordingly, Mourret, *Précis d'histoire de l'église* 3:379. It was to meet the growing power of France and Russia (which established a Jerusalem Bishopric in 1858) that the Protestants of England and Germany were appealed to for support "in the name of national interest and prestige," De Haas, *History of Palestine*, 414, 416; cf. Schaff, *Creeds of Christendom*, 311–13.

116. Wilhelm II, *My Memoirs* (London: Cassell, 1922), 210.

117. Ibid., 208.

118. In his childhood a favorite toy was "a wooden model of Jerusalem called 'Heavenly Jerusalem,' with removable domes," Wilhelm II, *My Early Life* (New York: Doran, 1926), 40. Herzl hailed him in 1898 as "an emperor of peace . . . making a great entry into this eternal city," Theodor Herzl, *The Complete Diaries of Theodor Herzl*, ed. Raphael Patai, tr. Harry Zohn, 5 vols. (New York: Yoseloff, 1960), 2:741, a white charger and his spiritual entourage dreamed of converting the Jews, 2:759; the arrogance of his staff thwarted his Zionist intentions, Israel Cohen, *Theodor Herzl* (New York: Yoseloff, 1959), 195–96, 199, 201.

119. Rappoport, *History of Palestine*, 324–25.

120. M. Crouzet, *L'époque contemporaine*, 7 vols. (Paris: Presses Universitaires de France, 1959), 7:605; T. Canaan, "Two Documents on the Surrender of Jerusalem," *Journal of the Palestine Oriental Society* 10 (1930): 29, 31; the Turks surrendered Jerusalem "for the sole purpose of protecting the holy places."

121. Francis John McConnell, *By the Way: An Autobiography* (New York: Abingdon-Cokesbury, 1952), 193-95. The Jerusalem meeting of 1928 "recall[ed] not inaptly the period of the great Oecumenical Councils," J. Wand, in Edward Eyre, ed., *European Civilization*, 7 vols. (New York: Oxford University Press, 1934-39), 6:1561, and gave "the impetus for the creation of the international Committee on the Christian Approach to the Jews," Rouse & Neil, *Histoire of the Ecumenical Movement*, 369. Such gatherings as the YMCA International Prayer Week at Jerusalem in 1951, ibid., 633, the Grand Mufti's tea in 1955, Charles Smyth, *Cyril Forster Garbett* (London: Hodder & Stoughton, 1959), 489-90 and the World Conference of Pentecostal Organizations in 1960, *Christian News from Israel* 11 (1960):12-14, are expressive of the idea.

122. The astonishing variety, set forth by John of Wurzburg, *Descriptio Terrae Sanctae (Description of the Holy Land)* 12-13, in *PL* 155:1088, still survives, Join-Lambert, *Jerusalem*, 137. "American Jesuits from Baghdad, Presbyterian missionaries grouped around the American University of Beirut, multiplied schools and attracted students by the assurance of employment in Yankee enterprise," says a resentful French observer, Crouzet, *L'époque contemporaine* 7:619. Today the Benedictine Order "seeks recruits in all countries . . . particularly in th‹ 'Jnited States," for the work in Jerusalem, Stolz, "The Benedictines in .e Holy Land," 21.

123. In 1948 the Vatican appealed for "the growth of Jerusalem as a universal Christian religious, cultural and educational center," James McDonald, *My Mission in Israel* (New York: Simon & Schuster, 1951), 210-11. The mixture of cultural with religious interest is apparent in the pilgrimages of the Holy Year 1950, the Baptist pilgrimage of 2,500 members in 1955 and "the arrival of . . . ever increasing number[s] of interdenominational, . . . [and] study-groups," Father Jean-Roger, "Christian Travel in Israel," *Christian News from Israel* 10 (1960): 21-22. The scholarly emphasis is seen in the founding of the auxiliary residence of the Pontifical Biblical Institute at Jerusalem in 1925, and amusingly demonstrated by the impeccable good taste of Cyril Forster Garbett, Bishop of York, Smyth, *Cyril Forster Garbett*, 493-94, 497, 501. Waas, "Der heilige Krieg," 211, 224, notes that World Wars I and II both began as Crusades but quickly dropped the allusion.

124. Wilhelm de Vries, "Die Entstehung der Patriarchate des Ostens und ihr Verhältnis zur päpstlichen Vellgewalt," *Scholastik* 37 (1962): 368-69.

125. Polish, *Eternal Dissent*, 203–12. By the "dramatic entry of Israel . . . the Christian tradition in the Holy Land has been violently disrupted," says Bishop E. M. E. Blyth, who takes comfort in the thought that Israel is "fulfilling Scripture in many ways, even unconsciously," E. M. E. Blyth, "The Patriarchate of Jerusalem," *Modern Churchman*, n.s. 5 (1961–62): 231. Marcel Simon, *Versus Israel* (Paris: De Boccard, 1948), 118–20, is genuinely alarmed; Eyre, *European Civilization*, 6:854, and Williams, *The Holy City*, 348, are nonplussed.

126. In 1838 Shaftesbury got Palmerston to appoint a British vice-consul in Jerusalem charged with "protection of the Jews generally," and in 1840 they sought cooperation with Russian Decabrist, Polish Liberationists, and French statesmen as part of a widespread liberation movement, Christopher Sykes, *Two Studies in Virtue* (New York: Knopf, 1953), 151. Metternich also joined, Goodman, *Moses Montefiore*, 65. The Anglo-Lutheran Bishopric of the following year was denounced by Newman as an implicit concession to the Jews in Palestine, which it was, Newman, *Apologia pro Vita Sua*, 128, 130, 132, 135, 138, 201. When the Grand Duke Frederick of Baden, who "evinced a deep interest in Zionism," arranged for Herzl's audience with the Kaiser, Zionism became "a question with which European politics must reckon," Max Margolis and Alexander Marx, *History of the Jewish People* (Philadelphia: Jewish Publication Society, 1927), 708. Even the Russian government was sympathetic, Herzl, *Diaries* 1:373.

127. Joseph Sittler, "The Abiding Concern of the Church for the Jewish People," *Ecumenical Review* 7 (1955): 221–23; cf. Herzl, *Diaries* 4:1593–94, 1603.

128. So William F. Albright, "Israel—Prophetic Vision and Historical Fulfillment," in Moshe Davis, ed., *Israel: Its Role in Civilization* (New York: Harper, 1956), 37. Chateaubriand found the Jewish community in Jerusalem to be the one wholly admirable and miraculous phenomenon in the city, Bassan, *Chateaubriand et la terre saints*, 161; *Journal*, 177–78.

129. Polish, *Eternal Dissent*, 203–12, quoting Charles Malik, 205, and the World Council of Churches, 1948: "The continued existence of a Jewish people which does not acknowledge Christ, is a divine mystery." It is "a mystery and a wonderful phenomenon," says Berdyaev, *Meaning of History* (London: Centenary, 1936), 50, refuting "the materialistic and positivistic criterion" of history, as it does Mr. Toynbee's theory of history, to his annoyance, Poish, *Eternal Dissent*, 209. See note 125 above.

130. The rivalry is expressed in many of the fathers, and in the determined attempts of the papacy to stop the pilgrimages to Jerusalem, Mähl, "Jerusalem in mittelalterlicher Sicht," 151; James Wallace, *Fundamentals of Christian Statesmanship* (New York: Revell, 1939), 333–35; *Cambridge Medieval History* 1:174–75; Luc Compain, *Étude sur Geoffroi de Vendôme* (Paris: Bouillon, 1891), 67.

131. "I [consider] only Rome an opponent [because] . . . only Roman Catholicism is as oecumenical as Judaism," Herzl, *Diaries* 3:889, cf. 1:345, 353; 4:1603. On the Roman position, Joseph Samuel Bloch, *My Reminiscences* (Vienna: Löwit, 1923), 161–62; James G. McDonald, *My Mission in Israel: 1948–51* (New York: Simon & Schuster, 1951), 35, 205–7; Esco Foundation for Palestine, *Palestine* (New Haven: Yale University Press, 1947) 1:277. During the U.N. debate of 1949 religious considerations were foremost, *Survey of International Affairs* 5 (1939–46): 307; Williams, *The Holy City*, 403.

132. How easy it is to create holy places is seen in the designation by the Husseini family late in the 19th century of "the traditional site of Moses' tomb" in Jerusalem, "Miscellany: This Year in Jerusalem," *Palestine Review* 52 (1938): 875.

8

What Is a Temple?

Those church fathers, especially of the fourth century, who proclaim the victory of Christianity over its rivals constantly speak of the church as the competitor and supplanter of the synagogue, and modern authorities are agreed that in ritual and liturgy the Christian church grew up "in the shadow of the Synagogue."[1] This is a most significant fact. While the temple stood the Jews had both its ancient ordinances and the practices of the synagogue, but they were not the same. The temple was unique, and when it was destroyed the synagogue of the Jews did not take over its peculiarly sacred functions—they were in no wise authorized to do so.[2]

The Loss of the Temple

Is it not strange that the Christian church should take its ritual and liturgy from the synagogue rather than the temple? The ready explanation for that was that the temple had been destroyed by God, the old law abolished, and a spiritual temple—a much higher and finer thing—had taken its place.[3] But if God had abandoned the temple, he had no less

This article first appeared under the title "The Idea of the Temple in History," in Millennial Star 120 (1958): 228-37, 247-49. Nibley's article was reprinted as What is a Temple? The Idea of the Temple in History (Provo: Brigham Young University Press, 1963). A second edition appeared under the same title in 1968. A German translation, "Die Templesidae in der Geschichte," was published in Der Stern 2 (1959): 43-60. The concluding section entitled "Looking Backward" was added when this article was again reprinted in Truman G. Madsen, ed., The Temple in Antiquity (Provo: Brigham Young University Religious Studies Center, 1983), 39-51.

abandoned the synagogue—why copy *it*? If a "spiritual" temple was so much superior to the crass physical thing, why did the Christians go out of their way to borrow equally physical Jewish and Gentile rites and practices of a much lower origin? Those same churchmen who expressed a fastidious disdain for the crude and outmoded rites of the temple at the same time diligently cultivated the rites of the synagogue (at best a second-class temple) with a generous and ever-increasing intermixture of popular pagan practices.[4] Plainly the Christian world was not satisfied with the rhetorical abstractions of a purely spiritual successor to the Temple. But if the boast of the church was that it took up and continued where the old law left off, why did it not continue along the line of the Temple rather than of the synagogue?[5]

The answer is, as we shall see below, that the primitive church did just that, while the later church, by all accounts a totally different thing, tried to and failed, attempting for a time to establish its own substitutes for the temple. Jerome argues that if the Jews had the temple, the Christians have the holy sepulchre, and asks, "Doesn't the Holy Sepulchre of the Lord appear more venerable to you?"[6] This was no empty rhetoric. The Christians of the fourth century looked upon the holy sepulchre in dead earnest as the legitimate successor of the temple. The great bishops of the time protested loudly but in vain against the fixed idea that to be really saved a Christian had to visit Jerusalem and the holy sepulchre,[7] and many modern studies have shown that the appointments and rites of the holy sepulchre represent a conscious attempt to continue the ways of the temple.[8] Only later was the doctrine cultivated that any church might be considered as equivalent to the temple, and it never proved very convincing. Ambrose was the first Christian writer to call a church a temple, and the editors of the *Patrologia*, commenting on this, remind us that a church is definitely not a temple in the sense of Solomon's Temple.[9] Rome itself, after centuries of bitter rivalry, was unable to supplant Jerusalem as the supreme object of the pilgrim's desire.[10] Early Christian liturgies reveal a constant concern to reproduce physically something as near as possible to the temple rites of Jerusalem. The bulk of the liturgy is taken up with the Davidic Psalms, the old ritual texts of the temple; from the introit to the acclamation of the final psalm (Psalm 150), the imagery is that of the temple; the priests are regularly referred to as Levites, and the bishop (though his office and title derive from the synagogue and not the temple) is equated with Aaron the High Priest. Students of Christian ritual and liturgy agree today that no church possesses anything near to the original rites and ordinances of the primitive church; they point to the "gaping holes" in Christian ritual, and describe at length how through the centuries these have been filled with substitute material from Jewish, classical, and Germanic sources.[11] It was not a satisfactory arrangement: the shadow of the Temple never ceased to disquiet the churchmen, who almost panic at the suggestion that the Jews might sometime rebuild their temple.[12] For since the traditions of conventional Christianity are those of the synagogue, they could no more compete with a true temple than the synagogue itself could.

What Makes a Temple? The Cosmic Plan

Though the words synagogue, *ecclesia*, and temple are commonly employed by the doctors of the church to designate the religions of the Jews, Christians, and Pagans, respectively; still the authorities do not hesitate to apply the word temple both to the temple of the Jews and to their own churches.[13] If there are unholy temples, there are also holy ones: what makes a temple different from other buildings is not its sacredness, but its form and function.

What is that form? We can summarize a hundred studies of recent date in the formula: a temple, good or bad, is a scale-model of the universe. The first mention of the word *templum* is by Varro, for whom it designates a building

specially designed for interpreting signs in the heavens—a
sort of observatory where one gets one's bearings on the universe.[14] The root *tem-* in Greek and Latin denotes a "cutting"
or intersection of two lines at right angles, "the point where
the *cardo* and *decumanus* cross," hence where the four regions
come together,[15] every temple being carefully oriented to
express "the idea of pre-established harmony between a celestial and a terrestrial image."[16] Eusebius expressed the idea
clearly long ago when he said that the church was "a great
Temple, which the divine Word . . . had established upon
earth as the intellectual image of the celestial pattern, . . .
the earthly exemplification of celestial regions in their revolutions, the supernal Jerusalem, the celestial Mt. Zion,"
etc.[17] Varro himself says that there are three temples, one in
heaven, one on earth, and one beneath the earth.[18] In the
universal temple concept these three are identical, one being
built exactly over the other, with the earth temple in the very
middle of everything representing "the Pole of the heavens,
around which all heavenly motions revolve, the knot that
ties earth and heaven together, the seat of universal
dominion."[19] Here the four horizontal regions meet and here
the three worlds make contact. Whether in the Old World or
the New, the idea of the three levels and four directions
dominated the whole economy of the temples and of the
societies which the temples formed and guided.[20]

The temple at Jerusalem, like God's throne and the law
itself, existed before the foundations of the world, according
to the Talmud.[21] Its *middoth* or measurements were all sacred
and prescribed, with strict rules for orientation.[22] Its nature
as a cosmic center is vividly recalled in many medieval representations of the city of Jerusalem and the holy sepulchre,
which are shown as the exact center and navel of the earth.[23]
It was in conscious imitation of both Jewish and Christian
ideas that the Moslems conceived of their Kaaba as

not only the centre of the earth, it is the centre of the universe. . . . . Every heaven and every earth has its centre marked by a sanctuary as its navel. . . . At each of them the same ceremonies are carried out that are carried out at the Kaaba. So the sanctuary of Mecca is established as the religious centre of the universe and the cosmic significance of any ritual act performed there is clearly demonstrated.[24]

What is bound on earth is bound in heaven.

From the temple at Jerusalem went forth the ideas and traditions which are found all over the Jewish, Christian, and Moslem worlds. Thus the earliest Christian rites and buildings show a marked concern for orientation, commenting on which Voelkl observes:

It is usual for people to locate themselves with reference to some immovable point in the universe. . . . The dogmatic tendency of the first centuries which created the "holy line" pointing East . . . reached its final form in the mystical depths of Scholasticism.[25]

What began as tangible reality petered out in the abstractions of the schoolmen, but the source of the idea is unmistakably the temple.

The Place of Contact

As the ritual center of the universe, the temple was anciently viewed as the one point on earth at which men could establish contact with other worlds. This aspect of the temple idea has been the object of intense research in the past decade. It is now generally recognized that the earliest temples were not, as formerly supposed, dwelling places of divinity, but rather meeting places at which men at specific times attempted to make contact with the powers above. "Though in time it became the dwelling of the divinity," according to Contenau, "originally it may have had the aspect of a temple of passage, a place of arrival."[26] The temple was a building

> which the gods transversed to pass from their celestial habitation to their earthly residence. . . . The ziggurat is thus nothing but a support for the edifice on top of it, and the stairway that leads from the same between the upper and lower worlds.[27]

In this respect it resembled a mountain, for "the mountain itself was originally such a place of contact between this and the upper world."[28] A long list might be made of holy mountains on which God was believed to have talked with men in ancient times, including "the mountain of the Lord's house."[29] A great many studies have appeared in the 1950s describing the basic idea of the temple as a sort of antechamber between the worlds, and particular attention has been given to the fact that in both Egypt and Mesopotamia temples had regular wharves for the landing of celestial barks.[30]

An investigation of the oldest temples, those represented on prehistoric seals, concludes that those high structures were also "gigantic altars," built both to attract the attention of the powers above (the burnt offering being a sort of smoke signal, as it were) and to provide "the stairways which the god, in answer to these prayers, used in order to descend to the earth. . . . He comes bringing a renewal of life in all its forms."[31] From the first, it would seem, men built altars in the hopes of establishing contact with heaven, and built high towers for the same purpose (see Genesis 11:4).

As the pivot and pole of the universe, the temple is also peculiarly tied to the North Star, around which all things revolve.[32] At the same time, it is the place of meeting with the lower as well as the upper world, and the one point at which passage between the two is possible.[33] That is why in the earliest Christian records the gates and the keys are so closely connected with the Temple. Scholars have often noted that the keys of Peter (Matthew 16:19) can only be the keys of the temple with its work for the dead.[34] Many studies have demonstrated the identity of tomb, temple, and palace as the place where the powers of the other world are exercised for the benefit of the human race.[35] In the fourth century there was a massive and permanent transfer of the pilgrim's goal from temples to tombs, though the two had always been connected.[36] Invariably the rites of the Temple are those of the ancestors, and appropriately the chief character in those rites is the first ancestor and father of the race.[37]

Naturally the temple at Jerusalem has been studied along with the rest, and it has been found that its rites fit easily and naturally into the general pattern.[38] Professor Albright, while noting that Solomon's Temple was not of pagan origin, describes it as a point of contact with the other world, presenting "a rich cosmic symbolism which was largely lost in later Israelite and Jewish tradition."[39] That is, the farther back we go in time, the more uniform is the concept of the temple among the ancients as a whole, with everything pointing to a single tradition. Albright duly comments on the twelve oxen as the cosmic symbol of the circle of the year and the three stages of the great altar as representing the three worlds.[40]

The Ritual Drama

The rites of the temple are always a repetition of those that marked its founding in the beginning of the world, telling how it all came to be in the first place. The foundation of the sanctuary coincides with the foundation or creation of the earth itself: "The first fixed point in the chaotic waters . . . is the place of the sanctuary, which becomes the earthly seat of the world-order, having its palladium in throne and altar. The foundation of the sanctuary, therefore, coincides with

the creation."[41] After a lifetime of study Lord Raglan assures
us that when we study all the rituals of the world we come
up with the discovery that the pristine and original ritual of
them all, from which all others take their rise, was the dramatization of the creation of the world.[42] And Mowinckel
sums up the common cult pattern of all the earliest civilizations: "It is the creation of the World that is being
repeated."[43]

This creation drama was not a simple one for, as the
above authorities remind us, an indispensable part of the
story is the ritual death and resurrection of the King, who
represents the founder and first parent of the race, and his
ultimate triumph over death as priest and king, followed by
some form of *hieros gamos* or ritual marriage for the purpose of begetting the race.[44] All this has become stock-in-
trade of students of comparative religion today, but at the
beginning of the century nobody knew anything about it.
We find this now familiar "Year-Drama" with its familiar
episodes wherever we turn—in the Memphite Theology of
Egypt (recently held to have had great influence on the Hebrew
religion), in the well-documented Babylonian New Year's rites,
in the great secular celebration of the Romans, in the ritual
beginnings of Greek drama, in the temple-texts of Ras Shamra,
in the Celtic mythological cycles, or in the medieval mystery
plays.[45] And if we ask why this drama is performed, we
always get the same answer, according to Mowinckel:
"Because the Divinity—the First Father of the Race—did so
once in the beginning, and commanded us to do the same."[46]

The temple drama is essentially a problem-play, with a
combat as its central theme. The combat at the New Year
takes various mimetic forms throughout the world—games,
races, sham-battles, mummings, dances, plays, etc.—but the
essential part is that the hero is temporarily beaten and overcome by death: "The King . . . is even trampled upon by the

powers of chaos, but he rises again and puts the false king,
the false Messiah, to death."⁴⁷ This resurrection motif is absolutely essential to the rites, the purpose of which is ultimate
victory over death.

The Initiation

But the individual who toiled as a pilgrim in a weary
land to reach the waters of life that flowed from the temple
was no mere passive spectator. He came to share in all the
blessings of knowledge and regeneration. It was not just the
symbolic immortality of a society that was sought, but the
personal attainment of eternal life and glory by the individ-
ual.⁴⁸ This the individual attempted to achieve through a
process of initiation. "Initiation," writes Professor Rostovzeff,
"is notoriously a symbol of death, . . . the symbolic act of
death and rebirth, resurrection."⁴⁹ The essence of the great
rites that marked the New Year (in Israel as elsewhere the
one time when all were expected to come to the temple) was
"transition, *rite de passage*, succession of lives, following the
revolutions of Nature"—though it should be noted that the
revolutions of nature definitely did not furnish the original
pattern for the thing.⁵⁰ The actual initiation rites have been
studied often and in detail, and found to exhibit a very clear
and consistent pattern. We can give but one illustration here,
taken from a short but remarkable writing by Bishop Cyril
of Jerusalem, a particularly valuable witness, since he is the
last church father to be in close contact with the old Jerusalem
rites.

The general impression one gets from reading the long
discussions in the Talmud is that people in the temple at
Jerusalem spent most of their time at baptisms and ablu-
tions. Certainly baptism is one specific ordinance always
mentioned in connection with the temple. "When one is
baptised one becomes a Christian," writes Cyril, "exactly as
in Egypt by the same rite one becomes an Osiris." Not only
does Cyril recognize the undeniable resemblance between

the Christian and non-Christian rites, but he also notes that
they have the identical significance, which is initiation into
immortality.[51] The baptism in question, Cyril explains, is
rather a washing than a baptism, since it is not by immersion. It is followed by an anointing, which our guide calls
"the antitype of the anointing of Christ himself," making
every candidate as it were a Messiah.[52] Elsewhere he describes
this rite specifically as the anointing of the brow, face, ears,
nose, breast, etc., "which represents," he says, "the clothing
of the candidate in the protective panoply of the Holy Spirit,"
which however does not hinder the initiate from receiving a
real garment on the occasion.[53] Furthermore, the candidate
was reminded that the whole ordinance "is in imitation of
the sufferings of Christ," in which "we suffer without pain
by mere imitation his receiving of the nails in his hands and
feet: the antitype of Christ's sufferings."[54] Bishop Cyril further insists that Moses and Solomon had both been duly
baptized in this manner: "After being washed in water, he
[Moses] was anointed and called a Christ, because of the
anointing which was a type. When Solomon came forth to
be king, the High Priest anointed him, after a bath in Gihon.
This again was a type. But with us these things are not a
type but a reality."[55] From his last remark it is plain that the
early Christians actually performed the rites described. The
Jews once taught that when Michael and Gabriel lead all the
sinners up out of the lower world, "they will wash and anoint
them, healing them of their wounds of hell, and clothe them
with beautiful pure garments and bring them into the presence of God."[56] These things are often referred to in the *earliest* Christian writings, but were soon lost in a manner we
must now describe.

Loss and Diffusion of the Temple Ordinances

No one can consider the temples and their ancient rites (at which we have merely hinted in these pages) without asking how they came to be both so widespread and so corrupt in the world. Let us first consider the question of corruption.

1. It can be shown that both the Jews and Christians suffered greatly at the hands of their enemies because of the *secrecy* of their rites, which they steadfastly refused to discuss or divulge.[57] When the key to the ordinances was lost, this very secrecy made for a great deal of misunderstanding and above all opened the door to unbridled fraud: every Gnostic sect, for example, claimed to have the lost rites and ordinances, the keys and the teachings, as they had been given to the apostles and patriarchs of old.[58]

2. It is doubtful if a religious organization ever existed which did not have its *splits and factions*. A common cause of schism, among both Jews and Christians, was the claim of a particular group that it alone still possessed the mysteries.[59] Hence from early times many competing versions of the true rites and ordinances have been current.

3. Even in good times, the rites like the doctrines inevitably become the object of various conflicting *schools of interpretation* and become darkened and obscured as a result. Indeed, it is now generally held that mythology is simply an attempt to explain the origin and meaning of rituals that men no longer understand.[60] The clouding and corruption of ritual is apparent in the oldest texts known,[61] and painfully so in Jewish and Christian literature. The Talmud tells of a pious Jew who left Jerusalem in disgust, saying, "What answer will the Israelites give to Elijah when he comes," and asks why the scholars don't agree on the rites of the temple.[62] For in Jewish and Christian tradition alike, it is Elijah who is to come and restore the rites of the temple in their purity.

4. The early fathers had a ready explanation for any suspicious resemblances between Christian and non-Christian practices. The former, they explained, had come down from the ancient Hebrews and were thus really much older than their pagan counterparts, which had been borrowed or stolen from them. Actually there is a great deal of evidence for the widespread *usurpation* of the temple rites at a very early time. One would hardly expect people to view their own highest rites as stolen and their highest god as a usurper, yet wherever we look that is what we find. Every major mythology tells of the great usurper who rules the world and who upon examination turns out to be the father and founder of the race! [63]

Since we cannot here treat them individually, we must be content to note that the archetype of all usurpers is Nimrod, who claims kingship and priesthood by right of "the cosmic garment of Adam," which his father Ham stole from Noah. [64] When in turn Esau, that other great hunter, by a ruse got this garment from Nimrod, he sold it as a "birthright" to Jacob, and then tried to get it back again "and force his way into the temple," according to the Leptogenesis. [65] Early Jewish and Christian traditions report that Nimrod it was who built the Tower of Babel, the first pagan temple, in an attempt to contact heaven; it was he who challenged the priesthood of Abraham; it was he who built the first city, founded the first state, organized the first army, ruling the world by force; he challenged God to an archery contest and, when he thought he had won, claimed to be no less than God's successor. [66] The interesting thing is that all his activities center around the temple, whose rites and whose priesthood he boldly attempts to seize for himself.

5. The same comparative studies that discovered the common pattern in all ancient religions—a phenomenon now designated as "patternism"—have also demonstrated the processes of *diffusion* by which that pattern was spread throughout the world—and in the process torn to shreds, of which

recognizable remnants may be found in almost any land and time. It would now appear that the early fathers were not far from the mark in explaining the resemblances: the rites *do* look alike wherever we find them, however modern Christians may insist on denying the fact, for they all come from a common source.[67] The business of reconstructing the original prototype from the scattered fragments has been a long and laborious one, and it is as yet far from completed. Yet an unmistakable pattern emerges more clearly every day. This raises the question of priority: How did the Mormons get hold of the temple idea?

The Question of Priority

Let the reader study some photographs of the Salt Lake Temple, a structure whose design the Mormons believe to have been revealed to the Prophet Brigham Young. Consider how perfectly this edifice inside and out embodies the temple idea. The emphasis on the three levels is apparent at once; the orientation is basic—every pioneer community, in fact, was located and oriented with reference to the temple as the center of Zion; the crenelated walls and buttresses are familiar from the oldest monumental temples as "the pillars of heaven"; the series of stars, moon, and sunstones on the buttresses indicate the levels of celestial glory; at the lowest point in the temple is a brazen sea on the back of twelve oxen, and there are the waters through which the dead, by proxy, pass to eternal life, the gates of salvation; on the center of the west towers is the North Star and its attendant constellation, a symbol recognized throughout human history as depicting the center of time and the revolution of the universe; the battlements that impart a somewhat grim air to the building signify its isolation from a hostile world; on the main tower the inscription in gold "Holiness to the Lord" serves notice that this place is set apart from the world of mundane things, as do the gates that shut out all but a few; yet the temple itself is a reminder that none can receive the highest blessings without entering its portals—so that the whole human race shall eventually repair hither, either in the flesh or by proxy. Within the building, as many visitors have seen before its dedication, are rooms obviously appointed for rites rehearsing the creation of the world, the fall of man, and his final exaltation. [68]

But it is the actual work done within the temple that most perfectly exemplifies the temple idea. For here all time and space come together; the barriers vanish between this world and the next; between past, present, and future. What is bound here is bound beyond, and only here can the gates be opened to release the dead who are awaiting the saving ordinances. Here the whole human family meets in a common enterprise; here the records of the race are assembled as far back in time as they go, for a work performed by the present generation to assure that they and their kindred dead shall spend the eternities together in the future. All time becomes one and the worlds join hands in this work of love, which is no mere mechanical bookkeeping. The work of the temple is exciting, and through the years has been rewarded and stimulated by many marvelous blessings and manifestations. In a very real sense all humanity participates in the same work of salvation—for we cannot be saved without our fathers, nor they without us. It is a grandiose concept. Here for the first time in many centuries men may behold a genuine temple, functioning as a temple should—a temple in the fullest and purest sense of the word.

Are we to believe that this uniquely perfect institution was copied from any of the thousand-and-one battered remnants of the temple and its ordinances that have survived in the world? The fundamental nature and far-reaching implications of the temple idea are just beginning to dawn upon scholars in our own day; nothing was known about them a hundred years ago—indeed, it was not until the end of the nineteenth century that Christian churches, in competitive zeal to return to the ways of the primitive church began to orient their buildings.[69] Throughout this brief study we have indicated that surviving remnants of the temple concept and rites may be found wherever there is religion and cult in the world. It is not surprising, therefore, that merely by looking about him one may discover all sorts of parallels to Mormon—or any other!—practices. Thousands of American Indians and Pacific islanders, including many of the greatest chiefs and wise men, have become Mormons in their time and engaged in the work of the temple. They have been quick to detect the often surprising parallels between the rites of the temple and the traditions and practices of their own tribes—though those have been guarded with the greatest secrecy. Far from being disaffected by this discovery, these devoted workers have rejoiced that at last they could understand the real meaning of what they had inherited from their fathers, corroded as it was by time and overlaid with thick deposits of legend and folklore. Among the first to engage in the Latter-day temple work were many members of the Masons, a society that "is not, and does not profess to be, a religion,"[70] but whose rites present unmistakable parallels to those of the temple. Yet, like the Indians, those men experienced only an expansion of understanding.[71]

So universally is religious ritual today burdened with the defects of oddness, incongruity, quaintness, jumbled complexity, mere traditionalism, obvious faking and filling in, and contrived and artificial explanations, including myths and allegories, frankly sensual appeal, and general haziness and confusion, that those regrettable traits have come to be regarded as the very essence of ritual itself. In contrast we find the Latter-day Saint rites, though full, elaborate, and detailed, to be always perfectly lucid and meaningful, forming an organic whole that contains nothing incongruous, redundant, or mystifying, nothing purely ornamental, arbitrary, abstruse, or merely picturesque. No moral, allegorical, or

abstruse symbolism has been read into these rites; no scholars and poets have worked them over; no learned divines
have taken the liberty to interpret them; they have never
been the subject of speculation and theory; they show no
signs of invention, evolution, or elaboration. Josiah Quincy
said that the Nauvoo Temple "certainly cannot be compared
with any ecclesiastical building which may be discerned by
the natural sight,"[72] and architects have said much the same
about the Salt Lake Temple. That is high, if unconscious,
tribute, advertising the clear fact that in establishing their
temples the Mormons did not adopt traditional forms: with
them the temple and its rites are absolutely pristine. In contrast the church and temple architecture of the world is an
exotic jumble, a bewildering complex of borrowed motifs, a
persistent effort to work back through the centuries to some
golden time and place when men still had the light.

   In the fourth decade of the nineteenth century the idea of
the temple suddenly emerged full-blown in its perfection, not
as a theory alone, but as a program of intense and absorbing
activity which rewarded the faithful by showing them the
full scope and meaning of the plan of salvation.

Looking Backward

   The preceding part of this article was written twenty-five
years ago when the London Temple was dedicated. Since
then the "scientific" study of ancient temples has completed
a full circle—back to where it started some three hundred
years ago. We hasten to explain.

   In the seventeenth and eighteenth centuries it was the
habit of English country gentlemen, fired with the scientific
interests of the former century and the romantic sensibilities
of the latter, to survey, sketch, describe, and speculate about
the many and mysterious prehistoric stone circles, avenues,
passage-graves, and mounds on their estates and elsewhere.
In their papers read before local learned societies and in their

letters to antiquarian journals, they debated endlessly without reaching any consensus of agreement as to whether those often imposing monuments were the work of some mysterious unknown race or that of the ancient Britons, Druids, Romans, Saxons, or Danes. But on one thing there was almost unanimous agreement, namely, that the most impressive of the structures were *temples*. In the light of local folktales and legends, immemorial rustic seasonal festivities, and other quaint customs and observances, supported by occasional illuminating passages from classical and medieval writers as well as the Bible, they could imagine vast concourses of people gathering at these great ceremonial centers at times set by sun, moon, stars, and the growing and harvesting seasons, to celebrate a new lease on life for the individual and the society.

I have called those studies "scientific" because they were undertaken in the same spirit, employed much the same methods, and reached the same conclusions as those of the present generation of researchers, who insist that *they* are scientific. Here, for example, is a recent cover story from the (very) *Scientific American* (July 1980), in which the author expresses the same conviction as did Sir William Stukeley and John Aubrey in the mid-seventeenth century.[73] He finds "a succession of what we can only call cathedral architects" at work in the third and fourth millenniums B.C. "Most emphatically," he writes, these "megalithic rings in general [were] sacred and secular meeting places," and he sees "an impelling faith" behind the immense effort and skill that produced them— "some powerful religious belief including belief in an afterlife." He notes that though the building activity stopped by 1000 B.C., "the general population" retained folk-memories of what went on, and he finds it "more than possible that the Druidic priesthood . . . used them as temples." Finally he notes that even Christian churches in some places did not disdain to build upon their ruins.

After the eighteenth century less and less attention was paid to the megalithic complexes, upon which little remained to be said until new lines of research could be opened up. The first forward step was taken by philology, predictably enough, since the learning of the times was classical and biblical. The British presence in India set such researches in a new and fruitful direction by creating a general interest in the glamour and color of the mysterious East, and by calling the attention of scholars to strange texts in strange languages. By the middle of the nineteenth century comparative philology had become the queen of studies, thanks to the great Max Mueller, who believed that he had discovered in Sanskrit the parent and original of all the Aryan family of languages from India to Ireland, and in the Vedas "the primal form of their mythology and religion." For the ancient texts on which all such study was necessarily based were profoundly religious documents, combining myth, ritual, pious exercises, edifying doctrine, and bits of history.

Shortly before Mueller, Jacob Grimm, in gathering material for his great *Deutsche Grammatik*[74], introduced the comparative study of folktales, folk songs, myths, customs, arts, and artifacts (*Grimm's Fairy Tales* have proven to be as scientifically relevant as Grimm's Law). In the process he anticipated the conclusion of Max Mueller, that if everybody from Ireland to India spoke related languages it was because originally they were all one and the same family, living in the East. Mueller held that what survived of their religion represents a letdown and deterioration from a higher order of things, an archaic original of monotheistic persuasion, from which historic religions betray a moral and intellectual decline. This is a position being taken by some eminent scholars today. Mueller's Oxford colleagues E. Tylor and Andrew Lang felt that the master was too much under the literary influences of an earlier day (e.g., Herder), and, discounting the old romantic idea of a primal "nature mythology," gave second billing to myth, viewing it as an attempt to explain cult and custom, which really had priority. After the mid-nineteenth century, evolution of course became the answer; religion, like everything else, must necessarily have had a primitive beginning—for Lang it was in primitive magic. For Theodor Waitz it was a primitive obsession with ghosts and spirits. Herbert Spencer made it a fixed principle, universally received, that religion is superstition and superstition is primitive, and that evolution required a steady ascent from religion toward the pure light of ever more rational thinking, culminating in the modern civilized man.

At the turn of the century the watchwords were animism and totemism, which for many years explained everything for many students. The determination to reduce religion, like everything else, to scientific laws actually led to simplistic solutions, and with the desire for more thorough and methodical special studies the wide-ranging pronouncements of deep-browed armchair scientists were supplanted by a swelling outpouring of regional monographs and statistical studies aspiring to the status of exact science. The great biologist J. Arthur Thompson made sport of the excesses of the solemn "brass instrument school," laboriously compiling endless columns of figures giving the physical and mental measurements of tribes and races, which in the end could tell the student no more than a casual association with the natives in question would have provided. Given patience and a body, it was no great task for a thousand investigators to fill the books and journals with information, but beyond the most pedestrian generalities no real progress was made. As Theodor Gaster observes, "It was Frazer more than anyone else who first sought to classify and coordinate this vast body of material."[75] Today most of Frazer's main assumptions and conclusions have been discredited—for example, the "magical" origins of religion, which Gaster calls "a mere product of late nineteenth-century evolutionism"; the principle of "homeopathy," by which the magical action produced a real counterpart; the yearly celebrations of the death and rebirth of vegetation, which neglected the more immediate human experience of life and death; the obsession of an earlier time with solar religion; and above all the idea of a "primitive" level of culture which remains undefined but is the same everywhere and always, the word being worked to death by Frazer's colleagues (e.g., J. Harrison), many of whom never laid eyes on a primitive. Yet most of these discredited ideas are still accepted and taught in schools everywhere.

To explain the remarkable resemblances between the prehistoric ritual centers and their rites separated by thousands of miles and as many years, Frazer and others took for granted that at a certain stage of evolution the human mind spontaneously fell into the thought patterns that would produce identical myths and rules independently in various parts of the world. Diffusionism was rejected and still is by many. This interesting psychological explanation got some support from the famous psychologist C. G. Jung, a diligent student of ancient myth and religion. Just as in the process of evolution creatures retain vestigial organs from earlier times, so the mind, Jung insisted, being subject to evolution like everything else, retains in its unconscious what he calls "archetypes" or "primordial images." They are as natural "as the impulse of birds to build nests, and present the mind with whole mythological motifs," which lead to stories and dramatizations. Where do they come from? "They are without known origin," writes Jung, "and they reproduce themselves in any time or in any part of the world"—don't ask how. Thus "the hero figure is an archetype which has existed since time immemorial," though as to "when and where such a motif originated . . . we do not even know how to go about investigating the problem." So the cause of evolutionism is saved if we do not ask too many questions.

C. P. Thiele, a Dutch theologian, came closer than anyone else since Max Mueller to combining vast scope and detail of information with meaningful summaries, striking a balance between the old romantic school of Herder, Mueller, and

Andrew Lang, and the pedantically limited studies of single tribes, families, and problems, which became as numerous as they were trivial. Few have equaled Thiele's learning, but how to take account of all that data in a convincing summary with meaningful conclusions is a problem of more urgency now than ever. A promising new development, the TV documentary, seeks to address the public on a high and authoritative level while keeping everything simple and clear, covering an immense expanse of knowledge while giving an understandable presentation of general principles.

The present writer struggled with the problem prematurely, of course, growing up on Spencer's *First Principles*, H. G. Wells, and T. H. Buckle, and practically memorizing Spengler. The first half of the twentieth century produced pretentious works purporting to convey all knowledge, such as the University of Chicago *Synopticon*, big "Western Civilization" college texts, the Cambridge histories, various encyclopedias, the Columbia University *Chapters in Western Civilization*, and so forth. More impressive were the big corroborative works combining contributions of leading scholars in different areas. Such a one was Chantepie de la Saussaye's *Lehrbuch der Religionsgeschichte*, which the present writer acquired hot off the press and perused with dogged diligence—to no avail! The facts were there, but they added up to nothing. The compilers followed the Baconian gospel, that one has simply to collect the facts and let them speak for themselves. However one may accuse the over-eager and ill-prepared of leaping to conclusions, it is precisely that leap that the scholars have never been able or willing to make; for when they finish collecting and typing their notes, they see nowhere to go—but more notes. Will Durant was a full-time philosopher who gathered nine volumes on the history of Western civilization. And what did the philosopher learn from that? Nothing at all that we had not already heard.

A good example of this is Joseph Campbell, one of the latest and best popularizers, who assures us that he is bringing together for the first time "a single picture of the new perspectives . . . in comparative symbolism, religion, mythology, and philosophy, by the scholarship of recent years."[76] This is merely an updating of the old game, reaching exactly the same conclusions as Grimm, Max Mueller, and the rural clergymen who studied the old stones of the English countryside, that "the comparative study of the mythologies of the world compels us to view the cultural history of mankind as a unit," in which the various motifs, instead of being wildly exotic, endlessly varied, and without number, as one would expect (and as German scholars once described them), are really "only a few and always the same." The old biblical picture now emerges as the latest scientific discovery.

The boldest and clearest recent statement embracing the world landscape of culture and religion is in the works of M. Eliade, and he brings it all back to the *temple.* "The Temple, . . . preeminently the sacred place, . . . a celestial prototype" and holy mountain, typifies "the act of Creation . . . [which] brought the ordered cosmos out of chaos"; it is the scene of the sacred marriage, the ritual confrontation with evil appearing as the dragon, serpent, or other figures of death and destruction, ending in the victory of the king, whose triumphant coronation inaugurates the New Year and a new age of the world. The combat is an expression of that "ambivalence and polarity" which characterize the rites in which all things must have their opposite, and where an atoning sacrifice is necessary "to restore the primal unity" between God and man, and enable the latter to regain the divine presence. The whole, according to Eliade, is suffused with "memories of paradise," the loss of which is the result of sin, converting this world into a testing ground in which "suffering always has meaning."[77]

Thus Eliade shows us how the studies of two centuries have steadily converged on the temple. But before Eliade,

your humble informant was bringing out much of the picture in a doctoral thesis which disturbed and puzzled his
committee in the 1930's. In 1940 a section of the Pacific
Coast Meeting of the American Historical Association slept
through a discourse on the feasting of the multitudes at the
holy places, and in the following year a like gathering of the
American Archaeological Association in San Diego listened
with remarkable composure to a paper on "National Assemblies in the Bronze Age." This is to show for the record that
we were getting in on the ground floor. An article comparing
the earliest Roman rites to those all over the ancient world
was held up by World War II (which was then considered
more urgent), not appearing until 1945 (in the *Classical Journal*).[78] At that time I had been to the temple only twice, once
when I was seventeen and again when I was twenty—both
times in something of a daze. So it was not until I moved to
Utah and started going to the temple and wrote a mini-series
in the *Improvement Era* on "Baptism for the Dead in Ancient
Times" (1948)[79] that it ever occurred to me that any of what
I had been doing had anything to do with Joseph Smith.
Beginning to see the light, I started pulling out the stops in a
Pi Sigma Alpha lecture given during the centennial celebra-
tion of the University of Utah in 1950. Entitled "The
Hierocentric State," it was expanded and published the fol-
lowing year in the *Western Political Quarterly*.[80]

The dedication of the London Temple in 1958 produced,
on request, the first part of this effusion. This was followed
in 1958-60 by a study in the *Jewish Quarterly Review* on
"Christian Envy of the Temple,"[81] demonstrating that "where
there is no Temple there is no true Israel," and showing how
the Christian churches have always missed the temple while
retaining various survivals of it in their rites and liturgies. In
1966 we discussed those migratory temples, wheeled and
domed structures, that moved over the steppes of Asia, and
how they took their bearings on the universe, remaining holy

centers in spite of their mobility—like the Ark of the Covenant (*Western Political Quarterly*, 1966).[82] An article on
"Jerusalem in Christian Thought" in the first edition of the
Encyclopedia Judaica (1973)[83] dealt with the role in history
of the well-known idea of Jerusalem as the holy center of the
world, thanks to the presence of the temple, and sketched
the fierce competitive drives of Christians, Moslems, and
Jews to possess it. In the same year, in a study ambitiously
titled "The Genesis of the Written Word," we pointed out
that the oldest written documents of the race are temple
records.[84] The rich Egyptian documentation justified writing
about *The Egyptian Endowment* (1975), and comparing it in
an appendix with some of the ordinances and doctrines contained in the Manual of Disciplines (1QS) from the Dead Sea
Scrolls, the Odes of Solomon, the Pearl, the Pistis Sophia,
and Cyril of Jerusalem's Lectures on the *Ordinances* (mid-
fourth century).[85] An important performance which has very
ancient parallels throughout Asia as well as the Near East
was "The Early Christian Prayer Circle" (*BYU Studies*, 1978).[86]
A long series of articles in the *Improvement Era* (1968–70)
called attention to sacrificial aspects of the later temple ordinances as anticipated in the "arrested" sacrifice of Abraham
himself, of Sarah (in Egypt), and of Isaac.[87] Finally, the
book *Abraham in Egypt* (1981) describes ties between Egyptian and Israelite wisdom and doctrine, a subject being much
studied by scholars at the present time.[88]

To resume our story, imaginary reconstructions presented
over the past three hundred years of great gatherings of people at imposing ceremonial complexes for rites dedicated to
the renewal of life on earth are, over that long stretch of
time, surprisingly uniform. In spite of the accumulation of
evidence, there has never been a drastic reversal or revision
of the picture, which always remains the same.

First, we still have the tangible evidence, the scenery and
properties of the drama: megaliths; artifical giant mounds or
pyramids amounting to artifical mountains; stone and ditch

alignments of mathematical sophistication, correlating time and space; passage graves and great *tholoi* or domed tombs; sacred roads (often discovered from the air); remains of booths, grandstands, processional ways, and gates—these still survive in awesome combination, with all their cosmic symbolism.

In the second place is the less tangible evidence of customs, traditions, legends, folk festivals, ancient writings, and so forth, which when put together conjure up (with considerable authority, thanks to their abundance and consistency) memories of dramatic and choral celebrations of the Creation; ritual contests between life and death, good and evil, and light and darkness, followed by the triumphant coronation of the king to rule for the new age, the progenitor of the race by a sacred marriage; feasts of abundance attended by ancestors and spirits; covenants; initiations (including baptism and clothing); sacrifices and scapegoats to rid the people of a year of guilt and pollution; and various types of divination and oracular consultation for the new life cycle. And what is being emphasized today, after centuries of converging studies, is that they were *all* doing it, everywhere!

To these types of evidence must be added the most impressive—and neglected—of all, those "spin-offs" of the temple which have long attracted my interest as such. The "spin-offs" are things not essential to the temple's form and function, but the inevitable products of its existence. To begin with, there was an urgent need of accommodations for all those pilgrims from far away; hence those *booths*, memorialized in the Hebrew Festival of Booths, remains or records of which we find in many parts of the world. Our words *hotel* and *hospital* go back to those charitable organizations which took care of sick and weary pilgrims to the holy places—the Hospitalers of the Crusades offered hospitality also under the name of *Templars*, for it was travelers to the *temple* that they were aiding and protecting. Since all who came had to bring food for the festival as well as animals for offerings and sacrifice, those who lived a great distance (more than three days away in Israel; see Deuteronomy 14:22–27; 26:12–14), finding the transport of such items of great difficulty, could instead bring the *money* value of those offerings to the Temple, which thus became a place of *exchange* and *banking*—our word *money* comes from the temple of Juno Moneta, the holy center of the Roman world. Along with that, the bringing of a variety of different goods and products from widely separated places inevitably gave rise to a lively barter and exchange of goods, and everywhere a fixture of the great year rites was the yearly fair, the market-booths of the merchants added to those of the visiting pilgrims, with artisans, performers, and mountebanks also displaying their wares.

The main action at the temple was the *actio*, for which the Greek word is *drama*, with parts played by priestly temple actors and royalty. Creation was celebrated with the Creation Hymn or *poema*—the word *poem* means, in fact, Creation—sung by a *chorus* which, as the name shows, formed a circle and *danced* as they *sang*. Since nothing goes unchallenged in this world, a central theme of the temple rites was the dramatization (often *athletic*) of the combat between the powers of life and death which could take many forms—wrestling, boxing, dueling, foot or chariot races, beauty contests to choose a queen, competitions in song and dance. The temple was the original center of *learning*, beginning with the heavenly instructions received there. It was the Museon or home of the Muses, each representing a branch of study, and the scene of learned discussions among the wise men who from the earliest recorded times would travel from shrine to shrine exchanging wisdom with the wise, as Abraham did in Egypt. For the all-important setting of times and seasons, careful *astronomical* observations were taken and recorded at the place with *mathematical* precision, while the measurements of fields and buildings called for sophisticated *geometry* followed by great *architectural* and engineering skill that commands the highest respect to this day. The Garden-of-Eden or Golden-Age motif was essential to this ritual paradise, and the temple grounds contained all manner of trees and animals, often collected with great *botanical* and *zoological* zeal from distant places. Central to the temple *school* for the training of priests and nobles was the great *library* containing both the holy books revealed from on high, whether as divine revelation or as star readings (both declared the glory of God), and the records of human *history* including the "Books of Life," the names of all the living and the dead—*genealogy*. Aside from memorials kept in *writing* (the art, as we have seen, originating in the economy of the temple) were the ancestral pictures—statues, busts, and paintings giving inspiration to the *fine arts*. The purpose of the rites being to establish and acknowledge the rule of God on earth through his agent and offspring the King, who represented both the first man and everyman, the temple was the ultimate seat and sanction of *government*. Our government buildings with their massive columns, domes, marble and bronze, and so forth are copies of classic Greek and Roman temples. The meeting of the people at the holy place made the New Year the time for contracts and covenants, and all of these were recorded and stored in the temple, which was of course the seat of *law*, both for the handing down of new laws and ordinances by divine authority and for the settling of disputes between mortals. The king was a Solomon sitting as Judge on the occasion, as one who had been tested to the limit and, after calling upon God from the depths, had emerged triumphant, worthy to lead the *army* of the Lord to spread his rule over the as yet unconquered realms of darkness beyond the holy influence of the temple.

All of these matters and much, much more this writer has treated somewhere or other. The fact that the one thing they all have in common is the temple is enough in itself to indicate that the temple is the source, and not one of the derivatives, of the civilizing process. If, as noted above, "where there is no temple there is no true Israel," it is equally true that where there is no true temple, civilization itself is but an empty shell—a material structure of expediency and tradition alone, bereft of the living organism at its center that once gave it life and brought it forth.

Since the Temple is the parent and original, it is only to be expected that one should find ruins and fragments of it surviving everywhere, along with more or less ambitious attempts to recapture its lost glory and authority. And since Evil cannot create or beget but can only pervert, corrupt, wrest, and destroy what Good has accomplished, it is not surprising that the most depraved of practices take their rise in the Temple. Let us recall that the mysterious "Watchers" in Enoch's day carefully kept the ordinances that had come down from Adam, and claimed sanctity by reason of possessing a knowledge which they had completely subverted. How roundly Isaiah rebukes and denounces the ordinances of the temple—the new moons, the fasts, the prayers, the offerings, and so on, when performed by the Jews in the wrong spirit! While the temple still stood in Jerusalem, the brethren of Qumran looked forward for the coming of "a true Temple" after God's own heart. When Satan assayed to try the Lord, it was to the pinnacle of the temple that he took him; did the Evil One, then, have access to the holy place? For answer we need only recall that Jesus declared that the House of his Father had been turned into a den of thieves as he drove the money changers from its courts—a reminder that large financial institutions today, as well as government buildings, occupy structures faithfully copied from the classical fanes of ancient temples and add to the bronze and marble the sanctimonious hush of holy places. Thus the temple economy has been perverted along with the rest.

When the symbolic killing and eating of beasts were supplanted by lustful and vengeful rites of human sacrifice; when the feasts of joy and abundance became orgies, and the sacred rites of marriage were perverted to the arts of the temple hierodules; when the keepers of the records and teachers of wisdom became haughty and self-righteous scribes and Pharisees—then was demonstrated the principle that any good thing can be corrupted in this world, and as Aristotle notes, as a rule, the better the original, the more vicious the corrupted version. When "two men went up into the temple to pray" (Luke 18:10), both were ostensibly going about their devotions; yet the one was bringing hypocrisy and vanity into the holy place. So we might seriously consider the proposition that whatever we see about us in the way of the institutions of civilization, good or bad, may in the end be traced to the temple.

Did Joseph Smith reinvent the temple by putting all the fragments—Jewish, Orthodox, Masonic, Gnostic, Hindu, Egyptian, and so forth—together again? No, that is not how it is done. Very few of the fragments were available in his day, and the job of putting them together was begun, as we have seen, only in the latter half of the nineteenth century. Even when they are available, those poor fragments do not come together of themselves to make a whole; to this day the scholars who collect them do not know what to make of them. The temple is not to be derived from them, but the other way around. If the temple, as the Latter-day Saints know it, had been introduced at any date later than it was, or at some great center of learning, it could well have been suspect as a human contrivance; but that anything of such fulness, consistency, ingenuity, and perfection could have been brought forth at a single time and place—overnight, as it were—is quite adequate proof of a special dispensation.

NOTES

1. Orazio Marucchi, *Handbuch der christlichen Archäologie* (Einsiedeln: Benzinger, 1912), 25.

2. On the uniqueness of the temple, see TB Megilla 9b–10a.

3. A very common theme. Thus Eusebius says that the church is the intellectual image of the temple, Eusebius, *The Ecclesiastical*

History, 2 vols., Kirsopp Lake, trans. (London: Heinemann, 1926), X, 4, 69. Moses entering and leaving the Holy of Holies is for St. Gregory "the mind as it enters and leaves a state of contemplation"; the gold on the garment of the high priest is the gleam of intellect, etc., *Epistolae (Letters)* 25, in *PL* 77:471, 474.

4. Ambrose is a good example. See Henri Leclerq, "Gallicane (Liturgie)," in *DACL* 6:485–88.

5. An instructive parallel is furnished by Islam, where the Mosque follows the pattern of the synagogue, as Christian churches do, while the Kaaba, a wholly different institution, represents the temple; Gustav E. von Grunebaum, *Mohammadan Festivals* (New York: Schuman, 1951), 20–21; Elie Lambert, "La Synagogue de Doura-Europos et les origines de la mosquée," *Semitica* 3 (1950): 67–72.

6. Jerome, *Epistolae (Letters)* 46, in *PL* 22:486.

7. Thus Gregorius Nyssenus, *Epistolae (Letters)* 2, in *PG* 46: 1012, 1016.

8. William Simpson, "The Middle of the World in the Holy Sepulchre," *Palestine Exploration Fund Quarterly* (1888): 260–63. When St. Helen built the great church "at the very spot of the Sepulchre" to contain the wood of the cross, she actually called it "the New Jerusalem, in opposition to the old one, which had been deserted," Socrates, *HE* 1, 17, in *PG* 67:117–22.

9. Ambrose, *Epistolae (Letters)* 20, note 2, discussed in *PL* 11: 307–08.

10. H. Hubert, "Le Culte des héros et ses conditions sociales," *Revue de l'Histoire des Religions* 71 (1915): 246–47. Maximus, *Homiliae (Homilies)* 72, in *PL* 57:405–06, expresses the sense of competition.

11. The "gaping hole" (*trou beant*) is Leclerq's expression, "Gallicane (Liturgie)," 6:480. On the filling in, see Louis Duchesne, *Origines du culte chrétien* (Paris: Fontemoing, 1898), 8–10, and the English translation, *Early History of the Christian Church: From Its Foundation to the End of the Fifth Century*, Claude Jenkins, tr., 3 vols. (London: Hunt, 1950), 1:8–10; and more recently, Joseph Lechner and Ludwig Eisenhofer, *Liturgik des römischen Ritus* (Freiburg: Herder, 1953), 5–6, 191–93.

12. The ardent desire to lay down the ghost of the temple once and for all is apparent in Cyprian, *Adversus Judaeos* I, 20; II, 16–18, in *PL* 4:716–17, 739, 741; Lactantius, *De Vera Sapientia (On True Wisdom)* 4, 14, in *PL* 6:487; Athanasius, *Oratio de Incarnatione Verbi*

(On the Incarnation of the Word) 40, in *PG* 25:165; Epiphanius, *Adversus Haereses (Against Heresies)* I, 2, 24, in *PG* 41:392–93; Basil, *Commentaria in Isaiam (Commentary on Isaiah)* 2, in *PG* 24:249.

13. It is rare to call a church a temple, but it causes no offence. Zeno was opposed to building imposing churches "because such a thing is not a real temple . . . the faithful people are the real Temple of God," *Tractatus (Tractate)* I, 14, in *PL* 11:356. Athanasius says the true Holy of Holies is heaven itself, not those "temples of churches erected by men," *Quaestiones in Epistolas Pauli (On the Epistles of Paul)* 127, in *PG* 28:769. Socrates reports that a pagan temple *(naos)* was converted into a Christian church, *HE* IV, 24 in *PG* 67:521–25. But the terms are used freely and interchangeably.

14. Varro, *De Lingua Latina* VII, 6–9; discussed by S. Weinstock, "Templum," *Römische Mittheilungen* 47 (1932): 100–101. Cf. Alfred Jeramias, *Handbuch der altorientalischen Geisteskultur* (Leipzig: Hinrich, 1913), 146, 185.

15. Wilhelm Kroll's statement in "Mundus," in *RE* 16:1.563; Jeremias, *Handbuch der altorientalischen Geisteskultur*, 146, 185.

16. Alfred Jeremias, *Das alte Testament im Lichte des alten Orients* (Leipzig: Hinrich, 1916), 49–51.

17. Eusebius, *HE* X, 4 in *PG* 20:848–80.

18. Varro, *De Lingua Latina* VII, 8.

19. Alfred Jeremias, "Semitische Völker in Vorderasien," in Daniel P. Chantepie de la Saussaye, *Lehrbuch der Religionsgeschichte,* 2 vols. (Tübingen: Mohr, 1925), 1:513. The concept is fully developed by E. Burrows in his chapter, "Some Cosmological Patterns in Babylonian Religion," in Samuel H. Hooke, ed., *The Labyrinth* (London: Society for the Promotion of Christian Knowledge, 1935), 45–70.

20. It should be born in mind that ancient society was sacral in structure. One of the best discussions of the temple concept is by Zelia Nuttall, *The Fundamental Principles of Old and New World Civilizations* (Cambridge: Peabody Museum, 1901).

21. TB Pesahim 54a–b.

22. TB Erubin 56a. Anonymous, "The Herodian Temple, According to the Treatise Middoth and Flavius Josephus," *Palestine Exploration Fund Quarterly* (1886): 92–113, 224–28; (1887): 116–28.

23. Simpson, "Middle of the World," 260–63. For illustrations, see Kenneth John Conant and Glanville Downey, "The Original Buildings at the Holy Sepulchre in Jerusalem," *Speculum* 31 (1956): 1–48.

24. Von Grunebaum, *Mohammadan Festivals,* 20–21.

25. L. Voelkl, "Orientierung im Weltbild der ersten christlichen Jahrhunderte," *Rivista di Archeologia Cristiana* 25 (1949): 155.

26. George Contenau, *Le Déluge babylonien* (Paris: Payot, 1952), 246.

27. André Parrot, *Ziggurats et Tour de Babel* (Paris: Michel, 1949), 208.

28. Contenau, *Le Déluge babylonien*, 246.

29. Henri Frankfort, *Birth of Civilisation in the Near East* (Garden City: Doubleday, 1956), 56, n. 5. Pierre Amiet, "Ziggurats et 'Culte de Hauteur' des origines a l'Epoque d'Akkad," *Revue d'Assyriologie* 47 (1953): 23–33.

30. André Parrot, "La Tour de Babel et les Ziggurats," *Nouvelle Clio*, vol. 2, no. 4 (1950): 159; Herbert Ricke, *Bemerkungen zur aegyptischen Baukunst des alten Reiches* (Zurich: Borchardt-Institut für Ägyptische Bauforschung und Altertumskunde in Kairo, 1944).

31. Amiet, "Ziggurats," 30; Parrot, *Ziggurat et Tour de Babel*, 209; especially see Heinrich J. Lenzen, *Die Entwicklung der Zikurrat von ihren Anfängen bis zur Zeit der III. Dynastie von Ur* (Leipzig: Harrasowitz, 1941), for the altar idea.

32. Hermann Kees, *Aegypten* (Munich: Beck, 1933), 298; Jeremias, *Handbuch der altorientalischen Geisteskultur*, 33, 53, 125, 236, 343; for Israel, Robert Eisler, *Iesous Basileus ou Basileusas*, 2 vols. (Heidelberg: Winter, 1930), 2:670.

33. Eric Burrows, "Problems of the Abzu," *Orientalia* 1 (1932): 231–56; Burrows, "Cosmological Patterns," 49–51. The concept is very familiar to classical students, J.-A. Hild, "Mundus," in Charles Daremberg and Edmond Saglio, eds., *Dictionnaire des antiquités Classiques*, 6 vols. (Paris: Hachette, 1904), 3:2021–22; Kroll, "Mundus," 561–63.

34. The classic study is Ludwig Köhler, "Die Schlüssel des Petrus," *Archiv für Religionswissenschaft* 8 (1905): 215–17; more recently Oscar Cullmann, *Urchristentum und Gottesdienst* (Zürich: Zwingli, 1950), 274–75. August Dell, "Mt. 16, 17–19," *Zeitschrift für die neutestamentliche Wissenschaft* 15 (1914): 27–29; Hermann Gunkel, *Zum religionsgeschichtlichen Verständnis des Neuen Testaments* (Göttingen: Vandenhoeck & Ruprecht, 1910), 73, n. 7; A. Sulzbach, "Die Schlüssel des Himmelreiches," *Zeitschrift für die Neutestamentliche Wissenschaft* 4 (1903): 190–93.

35. Alexandre Moret, *Historie de l'Orient* (Paris: Presses Universitaires, 1929), 1:218–37, 365, 377. The theme is treated at length in Hooke, *The Labyrinth*.

36. This is strikingly depicted in John Chrysostom, *Sermo post Reditum ab Exsilio (Discourse following the Return from Exile)*, n. 2, in *PG* 52:440.

37. A convenient presentation of this much-treated theme is in Otto Huth, *Janus: ein Beitrag zur altrömischen Religiongeschichte* (Bonn: Rohrscheid, 1932), *passim*.

38. The chapter by Aubrey R. Johnson, "The Role of the King in the Jerusalem Cultus," in Hooke, *The Labyrinth*, 73–111, is devoted to this theme.

39. William F. Albright, *Archaeology and the Religion of Israel* (Baltimore: Johns Hopkins, 1942), 154–55, 167.

40. Albright, *Archaeology and the Religion of Israel*, 150–55.

41. Arendt J. Wensinck, "The Semitic New Year and the Origins of Eschatology," *Acta Orientalia* 1 (1922): 160.

42. Lord Fitz Roy Raglan, *The Origins of Religion* (London: Watts, 1949), 58–69.

43. Sigmund Mowinckel, *Religion und Kultus* (Göttingen: Vandenhoeck & Ruprecht, 1953), 76.

44. Johnson, "The Role of the King," 99–107; Wensinck, "Semitic New Year," 160, 183; Mowinckel, *Religion and Kultus*, 73–76.

45. Theodore Gaster, *Thespis: Ritual, Myth, and Drama in the Near East* (New York: Schuman, 1950), compares the ritual dramas of Ras Shamra, the Hittites, Egyptians, Greeks, Hebrews, English Mummer's Plays, and Christian Hymns.

46. Mowinckel, *Religion and Kultus*, 94.

47. Wensinck, "Semitic New Year," 184–85.

48. Illustrated by the Babylonian formulae, e.g., "If he go to the house (temple) of the Seven, he will attain perfection." "If he go to Babylon, trouble of a day, peace of a year," etc., given by T. G. Pinches, "Pilgrimage (Babylonian)," in James Hastings, ed., *Encyclopaedia of Religion and Ethics*, 13 vols. (New York: Scribner, 1951), 10:12.

49. Mikhail I. Rostovzeff, *Mystic Italy* (New York: Holt, 1927), 76–78. An initiation is "really a pre-enactment of death and of the rising which it is desired should follow death," Adolphus Peter Elkin, *The Australian Aborigines* (Sydney: Angus & Robertson, 1954), 159.

50. This important fact is emphasized by Cyrus H. Gordon, *Ugaritic Literature* (Rome: Pontifical Biblical Institute, 1949), 57.

51. Cyril of Jerusalem, *Catechesis XXI, Mystagogica III de Chrismate (Catechetical Lecture on the Chrism)*, in *PG* 33:1088. Julius Firmicus Maternus, *De Errore Profanarum Religionum (The Error of the Pagan Religions)* 23, in *PL* 12:1031, also comments on the perfect identity of Christian and Egyptian initiation rites, and attributes it to the plagiarism of the latter.

52. Cyril of Jerusalem, *Catechesis XX, Mystagogica II de Baptismi Caeremoniis (Catechetical Lecture on the Rites of Baptism)* in *PG* 33:1077-78.

53. Ibid., in *PG* 33:1089; on the real garment, see *PG* 33:1078. Cf. Tertullian, *De Baptismo (On Baptism)* 13, in *PL* 1:1323.

54. Cyril of Jerusalem, *Catechetical Lecture on the Rites of Baptism*, in *PG* 33:1081.

55. Ibid., *Catechetical*, in *PG* 33:1093, 1068.

56. Rabbi Akiba, cited by Samuel Aba Horodezky, "Michael und Gabriel," *Monatsschrift für Geschichte und Wissenschaft des Judentums* 72 (1928): 505.

57. Thus Marcus Minucius Felix, *Octavius*, ed. Bernhard Kytzler, (Leipzig: Teubner, 1982), ix-x.

58. Hugh W. Nibley, *The World and the Prophets* (Salt Lake City: Deseret and Foundation for Ancient Research and Mormon Studies, 1987), 65-69.

59. This fact is noted in Theodosius, *Selecta de Religione Decreta (Selected Decrees Concerning Religion)* 5-19, in *PL* 13:533-37.

60. Gaster, *Thespis*, 49, states: "The function of Myth . . . is to bring out in articulate fashion the inherent durative significance of the ritual program." Gordon, *Ugaritic Literature*, 7, says: "As a rule, when a ritual is associated with a myth or legend, the ritual is the older, for the myth or legend tends to be an explanation of the already existing ritual."

61. Even in the Pyramid Texts the "others say" formula occurs. "The two plumes on his head are Isis and Nephthys . . . but others say that the two plumes are the two very large uraei . . . and yet others say that the two plumes are his eyes," in E. A. Wallis Budge, *The Book of the Dead: Papyrus of Ani*, 3 vols. (New York: Putnam, 1913), vol. 3, pl. 7, line 32.

62. TB Pesahim 70b. In his famous letter to Gubbio in 416 A.D., Innocent I complains that "when everyone feels free to observe . . . whatever practices he likes, we see established observances and ways of celebrating of diverse nature. . . . The result is a scandal for the people who, not knowing that the ancient traditions have been altered by human presumption, think . . . that the Apostles established contradictory things;" *Epistolae et Decreta (Letters and Decrees)* 25, 1-3, in *PL* 20:551-52.

63. That is why, e.g., the Priestly Corporation of Heliopolis had to sit in judgement yearly to clear the dubious title of Pharaoh and Osiris; Rudolf Anthes, "The Original Meaning of *M3ᶜ hrw*," *Journal*

of *Near Eastern Studies* 13 (1954): 49–50, 191–92; that is why the kingly title in Mesopotamia "carried in some degree the taint of usurpation, especially in early times;" Frankfort, *Birth of Civilisation in the Near East*, 80; and why Prometheus can call Zeus himself a sham and usurper; Aeschylus, *Prometheus Bound*, lines 937–43, 953–63; and why Loki can alarm Odin and the gods by threatening to reveal their secret—that they are frauds; *Poetic Edda, Lokasenna*.

64. For a preliminary account, Hugh W. Nibley, *Lehi in the Desert and the World of the Jaredites* (Salt Lake City: Bookcraft, 1952), 160–64. "Cosmic garment" is the designation of Jeremias, *Das Alte Testament*, 159.

65. Quoted in Eisler, *Iesous Basileus ou Basileusas* 1:525; cf. Book of Jasher 27:2, 7, 10; 7:24–27.

66. Hugh W. Nibley, "The Arrow, the Hunter, and the State," *Western Political Quarterly* 2 (1949): 339–41.

67. From the first, the emergence of the pattern has alarmed Catholic divines, whose explanation of the widespread uniformities of ritual and liturgy has been that they exist only in the imaginations of scholars. Thus W. Paulus, "Marduk Urtyp Christi?" *Orientalia* 29 (1928): 63–66; J. de Fraine, "Les Implications du 'patternism,' " *Biblica* 37 (1956): 59–73. While the ancients freely admitted the parallels and explained them as borrowings by the heathen from remnants of earlier dispensations of the gospel, the modern Catholic church, denying all dispensations but one, ignore the teachings of the Fathers and leave "patternism" unexplained.

68. Doyle Green, "Los Angeles Temple Dedication," *Improvement Era* 59 (April 1956): 228–32.

69. Voelkl, "Orientierung im Weltbild," 155. How little aware even scholars are of the temple concept in our own day is apparent from Sidney B. Sperry's "Some Thoughts Concerning Ancient Temples and Their Functions," *Improvement Era* 58 (1955): 814–16. If a modern Mormon student knows so little of the ideas here discussed, what are the chances of the elders of over a hundred years ago knowing anything at all about them?

70. E. L. Hawkings, "Freemasonry," in Hastings, *Encyclopaedia of Religion and Ethics* 6:120.

71. Ibid., describes Freemasonry as "a peculiar system of morality, veiled in allegory and illustrated by symbols." Pending the exhaustive study that the subject deserves, we will only say here that an extensive reading of Masonic and Mormon teachings and history should make it clear to any reader that the former is the shadow, the latter the substance. The one is literal, the other allegorical.

390 MORMONISM AND EARLY CHRISTIANITY

72. J. Quincy, *Figures of the Past: From the Leaves of Old Journals* (Boston: Little, Brown, 1910), 389.

73. Glyn Danial, "Megalithic Monuments," *Scientific American* 243 (July 1980): 88–90.

74. Jacob Grimm, *Deutsche Grammatik*, 5 vols. (Hildesheim: Olm, 1967).

75. James G. Frazer, *The New Golden Bough*, Theodor H. Gaster ed. (New York: Phillips, 1959), xv–xx.

76. Joseph Campbell, *The Masks of God: Primitive Mythology* (New York: Viking, 1959), 4–5.

77. M. Eliade, *Cosmos and History: The Myth of the Eternal Return* (New York: Harper, 1959), 7–10.

78. "Sparsiones," *Classical Journal* 40 (1945): 515–43.

79. See above, chapter 4.

80. "The Hierocentric State," *Western Political Quarterly* 4 (1951): 226–53.

81. See below, chapter 9.

82. "Tenting, Toll, and Taxing, "*Western Political Quarterly* 29 (1966): 599–630.

83. See above, chapter 7.

84. "The Genesis of the Written Word" (Provo: Brigham Young University Press, Commissioner's Lecture, 1973); reprinted *New Era* 3 (1973): 38–50

85. *The Message of The Joseph Smith Papyri: An Egyptian Endowment* (Salt Lake City: Deseret, 1975).

86. See above, chapter 3.

87. "A New Look at the Pearl of Great Price," *Improvement Era* 71 (1968): 18–24, running serially until 73 (1970): 82–89, 91–94.

88. *Abraham in Egypt* (Salt Lake City: Deseret, 1981).

9

Christian Envy of the Temple

The Question

In his justly celebrated work on the fall of Jerusalem, S.G.F. Brandon comments on the "truly amazing" indifference of Christian writers to the importance of that event in the history of the church.[1] But if the fall of the city meant for the Christians much what it meant for the Jews, i.e., "the sudden removal of the original source of authority,"[2] the loss of the temple, which was the central episode of the catastrophe, could hardly have been of less significance; yet Brandon himself, though by comparison with other scholars a positive enthusiast for the temple, minimizes its importance for the Christians as consistently as he accuses others of playing down the importance of Jerusalem.[3]

Why is this? Long ago Adam of St. Victor observed with wonder that the Christian fathers had always gone out of their way to avoid any discussion of the tabernacle of God, in spite of its great popular interest and its importance in the divine economy.[4] The reason for this strange attitude is, as Adam and his fellow Richard explain, that the very thing which makes the temple so attractive to many Christians, i.e. the exciting possibility of a literal and tangible bond

"Christian Envy of the Temple" first appeared in the Jewish Quarterly Review 50 (1959-60): 97-123, 229-240. The article was reprinted with the same title in When the Lights Went Out (Salt Lake City: Deseret, 1970), 55-88.

between heaven and earth, is precisely the thing that most alarms and embarrasses the churchmen.[5] Again, why so? Can it be that the destruction of the temple left a gaping void in the life of the church, a vacuum that the historians and theologians have studiously ignored, exactly as they have ignored such other appalling reverses to the church as the fall of Jerusalem and the cessation of the spiritual gifts?[6] If the loss of the temple was really a crippling blow to the church, the fact can no longer be overlooked in the interpretation of church history.

But was it such a blow? The purpose of this paper is to consider three facts that strongly support an affirmative reply, namely: (1) that many Christian writers have expressed the conviction that the church possesses no adequate substitute for the temple, and have yearned for its return; (2) that determined attempts have been made from time to time to revive in the church practices peculiar to the temple; and (3) that the official Christian position, that church and temple cannot coexist and hence the latter has been abolished forever, has always been weakened by a persistent fear that the temple might be restored. These three propositions reflect in the Christian mind a sense respectively of loss, inadequacy, and misgiving. What they all share in common is envy of the temple. But before the significance of that becomes apparent, we must consider the three points in order.

Good Riddance or Tragic Loss?

Whatever the conflicting views of the earliest Christians may have been,[7] the perennial controversy regarding the temple in later times is well-illustrated by the Battle of the Books that began in the third century when Bishop Nepos attacked the "allegorists" with a book in defense of a literal and earthly millennium; in reply to this "unhealthy" teaching, Dionysius, the sophisticated Bishop of Alexandria, wrote what Jerome calls "an elegant book, deriding the old fable about the thousand years and the earthly Jerusalem with its gold and jewels, the restoration of the Temple," etc.[8] This in turn brought forth a two-volume counterblast in Jerome's day by one Apollinarius, who "not only speaks for his own following but for the greater part of the people here as well, so that I can already see," says Jerome, "what a storm of opposition is in store for me!"[9] Jerome frankly admits that the opposition represents the old Christian tradition, his own liberal "spiritualizing" interpretation running counter to the beliefs of such eminent earlier authorities as Tertullian, Victorinus, Lactantius, and Irenaeus. This puts him in a dilemma: "If we accept [the Apocalypse of John] literally we are judaizers, if spiritually, as they were written, we seem to be contradicting the opinions of many of the ancients."[10] From personal experience, furthermore, Jerome can tell us how the old-fashioned Christians in Jerusalem insist on pointing out the very plot of ground on the Mount of Olives "where they say the sanctuary of the Lord, that is, the Temple, is to be built, and where it will stand forever," that is, "when, as they say, the Lord comes with the heavenly Jerusalem at the end of the world."[11]

Professor Cadbury, in a study in which he suggests that the earliest Christians may well have believed "that this site [the Mount of Olives] is to be the site of the *parousia*," concludes that "if other Christians, ancient and modern, have found the primitive emphasis on such a literal future event embarrassing, Luke gives no real countenance to any of their ways of avoiding it,"[12] which means that Jerome's dilemma remains unresolved to this day. Through the years the doctors have continued to dismiss a literal temple as an old wives' tale only to find all their arguments against it offset by arguments at least as potent in its favor.

First and foremost was the philosophical plea against a physical temple (supported by endless repetitions of Isaiah 66:1), that God is not to be contained in any crass material structure.[13] The fact that the invisible incorporeal God needs no visible corporeal temple was grasped "by no man at any

394 MORMONISM AND EARLY CHRISTIANITY

time, either Barbarian or Greek, except by our Savior alone,"
writes Eusebius, forgetting in his tendentious zeal that this
had been a stock theme of the schools for centuries, and that
Christian Clement, speaking with the pagan voice of
Alexandria, had given it his eloquent best with supporting
quotations from Plato, Zeno, and Euripides.[14] The main objection to this view, however, was not its heathen coloring but
the idea, pointed out later by Aquinas, that the temple was
not built for God but for man, who needs a tangible image
of celestial things and "special times, tabernacles, vessels,
and ministers" to inculcate understanding and reverence.[15]
"It cannot be too often emphasized," writes Canon Phythian-
Adams, "that the belief in the Presence is not to be described
as 'unspiritual' simply because Its 'tabernacle' was material."
And the same scholar, who represents a surprising but unmistakable tendency of recent years to view the temple with a
new sympathy and understanding, rebukes the hitherto common practice in Christian theology "of confusing a belief or
doctrine with low and materialistic interpretations of it."[16]
Certainly the Jews themselves were well aware of the limitations of physical buildings, and needed no Greek schoolmen,
levied as spokesmen for a new religion, to tell them what
Solomon had said long before: "The heaven of heavens cannot contain thee, how much less this house which I have
built!"[17]

Apart from its gross and earthly substance, the temple
has always been criticized by the churchmen as symbolic of
a narrow, selfish, tribal world view, incompatible with the
grandiose concept of a universal church.[18] Again the answer
was clear: What could proclaim the oneness of God's rule
and the universality of true religion more eloquently than
the temple itself, "a house of prayer for all peoples," "the
spiritual metropolis of all lands?"[19] Some scholars protested
that the authority of the temple had been virtually abolished
by the Exile and the diaspora,[20] but others pointed out with

equal assurance that those misfortunes actually had the opposite effect: "Dispersion . . . increased the significance and
the fascination of the Temple," while the Exile "only strength-
ened the universal love for it."[21] Actually the limiting of the
great central rites and ordinances to one spot was the very
thing that recommended the temple so strongly to the Christian schoolmen, enthralled as they were by "the withering
pressure of an omnipresent and monotonous idea"—the passion for oneness.[22] Nothing on earth represented the oneness
of God, his worship, and his people more perfectly than the
temple had, and the church sorely missed just such a centralizing force.[23] Thus Peter Cantor in the twelfth century deplores
the multiplication of Christian shrines and invites the church
to "note that in all Israel there was but one Temple, one Tabernacle, one Altar," and to follow that example as "the only
remedy" for "this *morbum multiplicem.*"[24]

How was such simplification to be effected? Peter and
his fellows know nothing of the later device by which in theory there is only one central mass in the church "in which all
the Church was thought to participate."[25] Instead he suggests
a compromise that had been recommended long before: "Following the example of the *one* Temple, there should be in
every city but one church, or, if it is a very large city, but a
few, and those duly subordinated to the one principal
church."[26] The objection to this, of course, is that the few
fall as far short of the perfection of the Monad as do the
many. Christian apologists had never tired of pointing out to
the heathen the absurdity of their many gods and temples;
how, then, were they to answer heathen and Christian criticism of the endless multiplication of Christian temples of
which they first boasted[27] and which they then tried to explain
away?[28]

The standard explanation was that since the church was
mystically the temple, and, being universal, was *one*, it followed that the temple was still one.[29] Because Christians do
all things in common, it was argued, they may be considered

as one single temple.[30] But this was putting the cart before the horse, for, as Thomas Aquinas observes, the temple was introduced in the first place to achieve that unity—it is not the mystical result of it. But having praised the temple as the perfect expression of God's unity and of the *unitas et simplicitas* of the worship he requires, Thomas lamely adds: "But since the cult of the New Law with its spiritual sacrifice is acceptable to God, a multiplication of altars and temples is accordingly acceptable."[31] Here the word "spiritual" is expected to answer all questions and silence all objections, but Thomas's own insistence on the unique significance of the temple as a *locus electus*, a tangible center of worship for the benefit of mortal man, makes demands that abstract terminology cannot satisfy.[32] What is everywhere is nowhere, and for the very reason that God and his church *are* everywhere, there must be some special point of contact, Stephen VI is reported to have argued, around which the church might, like Israel, center its activities.[33]

Still, the idea of a spiritual temple was made to order for the schoolmen, who from the first took to it like ducks to water. The supplanting of a stone temple by "a spiritual edifice" is for Neander nothing less than "the mightiest achievement in the history of humanity."[34] It is a simple, eloquent formula: "The Messiah's kingdom would supplant the outworn system of the past. He would raise up a new temple of the spirit."[35] *Lugeat carnalis Judaeus, sed spiritualis gaudeat Christianus!*[36] Again the argument falls flat, for the spiritual and carnal are not neatly divided between Jews and Christians, but "were to be found in both religions, and are still to be found in them."[37] If the Christian doctors knew how to spiritualize the temple, the rabbis had done a good job of de-eschatologizing long before them, and even the old-fashioned literalists knew the danger of "putting their trust in a building rather than in the God who created them."[38] In the end it was not a question of temple *versus* no temple but, as Irenaeus pointed out, one of proper values and emphasis.[39]

An inevitable corollary of the spiritual temple was the purely intellectual temple: *Templum Dei naturaliter est anima rationalis*, the human breast wherein "the rational and intellectual and impolluted and external unutterable nature of Divinity resides," that higher, purer temple built of abstract virtues, etc. [40] But aside from the fact that such ideas bore the trademark of the schools and were far over the heads of the general public, [41] there was no reason why an "intellectual" temple should not coexist with a real one: while the Lord referred to the temple as his body, the church, Israel, and even the dry bones of Ezekiel, Origen observes, the real temple was still standing. [42] Why not? The early fathers found "nothing absurd in saying that God's dwelling is in heaven and at the same time in the earthly Zion," [43] and scholastic philosophers have no difficulty in viewing the temple under various mystic, moral, and material aspects without the least sense of contradiction. [44]

Along with their philosophical and moral condemnation of the temple, the doctors never tired of laboring the historical argument—the cold fact that the temple had actually been destroyed, that God had allowed its destruction and the prophets foretold it. [45] But that had happened before, following a well-established eschatological pattern which saw in the destruction itself an earnest of restoration; [46] and while in the divine plan the temple was to have its ups and downs (the Jews themselves anticipating the worst), [47] there was no doubt in the minds of Jewish and Christian "fundamentalists" that the story would end on a note of eternal triumph for the temple, whose glory was eternal, preexistent, and indestructible. [48] And if the Jews looked forward to a dark interim between the fall of the temple and the "Return and Restoration [which were an integral part of] the divine plan," [49] so no less did the first Christians: "For the scripture says," writes one of them, "showing how the City and the Temple and the People of Israel were to be taken away, 'It shall come to pass in the last days, that the Lord will give over the sheep of his pasture, and their sheepfold and their tower to destruction.' "[50] The fathers of the fourth century were uncomfortably aware of this tradition, and Hilary states his own conviction that because of the wickedness of the times "there has for a long time been no Mountain of the Lord's House upon the earth."[51] Later churchmen are haunted by a suspicion that the church is not really the equivalent of the temple at all, but rather of the tabernacle wandering in the wilderness, while the stable and enduring temple is still to come.[52]

A favorite symbol of the transition from crass Jewish materialism to the Christian Temple of the Spirit has always been the New Testament episode of the driving out of the money-changers.[53] Yet how much this "obvious transfer" (as St. Leo calls it)[54] left to be desired is apparent from many a bitter comment that the church itself was as much "a den of thieves" as ever the temple was, with the obvious difference, already voiced by Origen, that "today Jesus comes no more to drive out the money-changers and save the rest!"[55] Furthermore, it has often been pointed out that the purging of the temple, far from being its death sentence, was rather a demonstration by the Lord "that he would not tolerate the slightest disrespect" for his Father's House.[56]

In the same way the other classic scriptural arguments against the temple have either backfired or proven highly equivocal. The famous prophecy that not one stone should remain upon another, hailed by the churchmen as a guarantee of eternal dissolution,[57] contains nothing to confirm or deny a future restoration, and may well have been spoken "with the sorrow of a patriot rather than the wrath of an iconoclast."[58] If the rending of the veil has been treated as a symbol of irreversible eradication,[59] it has suggested with equal force a broadening and expanding of revelation.[60] Jesus' invitation to "destroy this temple" and his conditioned promise to rebuild the same are often taken—but only by a liberal revamping of the text—to mean the opposite, namely, that he will destroy the temple himself, and instead of rebuilding it bring something totally different in its place: " 'Finish then,' he might have implied, 'this work of dissolution: in three days will I . . . restore . . . not a material Temple, but a living Church.' " Dean Farrar's interpretation is typical, resting as it does not on what Jesus said but on what "he might have implied."[61]

... Tamen Usque Recurret

The temple was driven out with a fork by Jerome and his intellectual friends. On one thing all the spiritual children of Alexandria—Greek, Jewish, Christian, and Moslem—have always seen eye to eye, and that is the conviction that the old eschatology with its naive literalism and its millennial temple was unworthy of thinking men, "repugnant to every principle of faith as well as reason."[62] Of these intellectuals none have been more dedicated to the party line than the Christian schoolmen, whose opinions inevitably became the official doctrine of a church which drew its leaders almost exclusively from their ranks. Yet they were not the only force to be reckoned with, and by the time "St. Augustine's *City of God* had come to replace millenarianism as the official doctrine of the church,"[63] the more tangible and sensuous aspects of the temple, enhanced by time and legend, were exercising their powerful attraction on two highly susceptible and influential bodies—a spectacle-hungry public and a power-hungry government.

As to the first of these, it is apparent from Jerome's experience that a large part of the Christian society did not lose sight of the temple after its destruction but spoke longingly of its return. Students today are more inclined than they have been in the past to concede to the temple a high place in the estimation of Jesus,[64] of the prophets before him,[65] and of the apostles and the church after him.[66] "The ethical monotheism of the Wellhausen era," that made short work of the temple and its ritualism, now yields to recognition of the importance of the ritual drama of the temple not only

as "a basic component of Israel's religion," but of early Christianity as well.[67] For both, the way to heaven led through
the temple, and if that was but an intermediate step in the
salvation of the race, it was nonetheless an indispensable
one.[68] It was all very well for the orators of the fourth century to declaim that in the church "the goal of all old Testament hopes had now come," that "the religion of promise
and pilgrimage" had given way to "one of achievement and
fulfilment"—the simpler Christians knew better: "Christians
have not yet attained their goal; they too must run their
course (Hebrews 12:1)."[69] The Christian still needed the temple, and always remained a pilgrim to Jerusalem in a very
literal sense. Even the learned doctors of the second and
third centuries "were unable to resist the fascination of the
holy places," and came with the rest to see the spot where
the Lord had left the earth and where he would return to his
temple.[70] In vain did the great fathers of the following centuries protest against the silly custom, clearly pointing out
that it was in direct conflict with the official doctrine of the
spiritual temple: the pilgrimage went right on.[71]

The Emperor Constantine's plan "to legislate the
millennium in a generation" called for the uniting of the
human race in the bonds of a single religion, under a single
holy ruler, administered from a single holy center.[72] It was
the old "hierocentric" concept of the sacral state, represented
among others by the *Roma aeterna* of which Christian Rome
claimed to be the revival,[73] but also typified from time immemorial in the temples of the East, each a scale-model of the
cosmos, which was thought literally to revolve around it.[74]
Constantine's architectural projects proclaim his familiarity
with the idea of a *templum mundi* as a physical center of the
universe,[75] just as clearly as his panegyrists hail him in the
role of Solomon the temple-builder.[76] "It is our most peace-
ful Solomon who built this Temple," cries the orator at the
dedication of one of Constantine's vast "cosmic" rotundas,
"and the latter glory of this House is greater than the former."

Just as Christ transferred "from sordid flesh to a glorified body," so the church now has a much more glorified body than before.[77] Let no one mistake this for the incorporeal temple of the doctors, who protested briefly and ineffectively against all this materialism;[78] this really fulfils the prophecy (Haggai 2:9), no longer in words only but in deeds.[79] The same rhetorical license that had vaporized the temple of Jerusalem by its appeal to higher things was not employed to justify its very solid successors, and before a rapt audience the great Christian orator could convert a monster pile, window by window and stone by stone, "into a spiritual temple structure" by the bewitching power of allegory.[80]

Immediately after his return from the Council of Nicea, Bishop Macarius of Jerusalem, by authorization of the Emperor, demolished the temple of Jupiter that the Romans had "built on the very spot where formerly the Temple of God had stood," and in the process discovered the crypts of the Cross and the Holy Sepulchre, "and," Eusebius significantly adds, "the Holy of Holies crypt," which was identical in form with the latter.[81] Over the holy spot the emperor and/or his mother had built the wonderful structure which they called "the New Jerusalem, having erected it in the place of the ancient one that had been abandoned," the Holy Sepulchre serving as the pivot and center of the whole sacred complex.[82] The temple complex was supplanted by Christian buildings. Theodoret pointedly compares the Churches of the Crucifixion, Resurrection, and Ascension with the ruined temple, and asks how the Jews in the face of that can have the effrontery even to remain in the city: "The Babylonians never came to worship at *their* Temple," he argues, "while all the world flocks to our churches," thus proving that the true House of God that draws all nations to Jerusalem is not their temple but our church.[83] Chrysostom draws a like conclusion as he ecstatically views those vast panegyrises, those gorgeous year-assemblies at the shrine of the martyrs that represent the brilliant wedding of Christianity with the ever-popular pagan cults with their feasts and markets at holy tombs: "What does this all mean?" he asks, and the answer is clear: "It means that the Temple has been abolished."[84] We don't need to go to Jerusalem anymore, John assures his people, just as his friend Gregory of Nyssa can announce that the church can "supplant the faded antique glory of our cities by our own Christian glory."[85]

Of the many duplicates of Constantine's New Jerusalem the most ambitious was Justinian's "mighty glorious Temple, the Temple of my Lord, a heaven here below which I ween amazes even the reverencing Seraphim. If God should ever condescend to abide in a house made with hands," the panegyrist continues, "this surely is the House!"[86] As a crowning gesture, the emperor had fetched from Carthage the very vessels that the Roman soldiers had plundered from the temple of Jerusalem long before. But then in an even more significant gesture, the haughty Justinian for the only time in his life heeded the advice of the hated Jews and in superstitious dread ordered the vessels returned "in haste to Jerusalem, where he had them deposited in a church."[87] It was all very well to set up a new and holier Rome on the Bosphorus, but when it came to a showdown not even a Justinian dared to arrogate the authority of the House of God at Jerusalem.[88]

The man who dared most was Pope Leo. Behind him he had the tradition of the empire, now Christian, with Rome "holy among cities" as the center of the world.[89] But how could the church have two centers? The churchmen displayed considerable ingenuity in their arguments to show how a large number of churches could carry on the tradition of a single temple,[90] but by the time of Constantine it was recognized that if there was ever to be peace in the church what was needed was not a vague universality and equality, but a highly centralized authority.[91] Leo, who did more than any other man to transform the old universal *devotio Romana* into a new *devotio Christiana*,[92] clearly saw in the temple at

Jerusalem his most serious opponent.[93] His sermons bristle with barbed and invidious remarks that betray his touchiness on the subject. In Leo's Rome, as Seidlmayer puts it, "die christliche Kirche steht auf dem Fundament des heidnischen Tempels."[94] Leo explains this away by appealing to the well-established Roman doctrine of *renovatio* with a new twist: Rome has died pagan and been resurrected Christian.[95] The tomb of Peter now performs the function that once belonged to the *templum* of Hadrian, the great round tomb by the Tiber that was designed to draw all the world to it, while Hadrian's image now stands in the temple of Jerusalem—the roles of the two cities have been neatly reversed.[96]

Leo freely admits the debt of Christian Rome to pagan Rome,[97] and sees in the great Easter and Christmas congregations of his people both the old Roman national assembly and the gathering of Israel at the temple: "Here you see the heavenly Jerusalem, built of all nations," he cries, addressing such assemblies, "purged of all impurity on this day, it has become as the Temple of God!"[98] "Now a new and indestructible Temple has been erected," with Leo himself presiding in it, ordained in honor of Christ, the prophet "after the order of Melchizedek, . . . not after the order of Aaron whose priesthood . . . ceased with the Law of the Old Testament."[99] Rome has not abolished the rites of the temple, however, but simply taken them over, every particle of the ancient ordinances and imagery having been absorbed in the Christian sacraments: "Ours today is the circumcision, the anointing of priests, etc. . . . Ours is the honor of the Temple!"[100] Thanks to the ministrations of Peter and Paul, the people of Rome are now "a holy generation, a chosen people, a priestly and royal city." In a word, Rome was now Jerusalem.[101]

But Leo protests too much. His Easter sermons, like Hilary's Tract on the Psalms, Ambrose's *De Sacramentis*, Jerome's letters from Bethlehem, and Chrysostom's great work on the Priesthood, breathe less of pious conviction than of envy. The first of these displays a positive phobia of a literal temple, against which it wages truceless war.[102] "We admire the mysteries of the Jews, given to our fathers, first for their antiquity, and then for their sanctity," says Ambrose, reassuring his followers, "But I can promise you that the Christian sacraments are both holier and older." For the former rites go back only to Moses, while Melchizedek is the author of the latter. *Quis est Melchisedek?* Who but the Justice, Peace, and Wisdom of God—is there anything more timeless or holy than a pure abstraction?[103] Jerome, explaining to a friend that the temple was always exclusively reserved to the Christians, concedes that the Holy of Holies was a wondrous thing, and promptly adds: "But doesn't the Sepulchre of the Lord appear more worshipful to you? As often as we enter it we see the Lord lying there . . . and the Angel sitting at his feet."[104] Chrysostom, constantly approached by disillusioned Christians wanting to know what has happened to the ancient glories of Israel, is able to reply with stirring rhetoric: In ancient times only Moses could approach God, but now we all see Him face to face. Moses feared God—but no one fears Him today. Israel heard the thunder and trembled—we hear God's actual voice and are not afraid.[105] We have angels all around us in the church today—you can see them if only you will open your mental eyes.[106] The priest ministering at our altar is a more awesome object than the high priest in the temple, since "he casts aside all carnal thought and like a disembodied spirit views celestial things by pure mind alone."[107] The Jewish temple was a mere shadow, the churchmen repeat: *we* have the real thing. "They had the Tabernacle, *we* see Truth face to face!"[108] Do we? Yes, indeed, "but in a higher and hidden sense."[109]

Leo's imagery manifests an awareness that in snubbing the temple the church would be missing a good thing. Actually the fathers of the preceding generation had fumbled the ball badly when they threw out the temple. But before the church could recover, a new and formidable player, Islam, had snatched it up and run the whole length of the field.

When Omar conquered and entered Jerusalem in 638 he asked first of all to be shown "the glorious Temple that Solomon had built," only to discover that the Christians had converted the place into a garbage dump.[110] The treasure that the churchmen had so foolishly thrown away the Moslems were quick to exploit, promptly rebuilding the temple and restoring it to its prestige as a center of world pilgrimage.[111] They had already harnessed its unique powers by "transferring to Mecca cosmological ideas in vogue among Jews and Christians concerning the sanctuary of Jerusalem,"[112] and though the legends of the Kaaba, of its founding and refounding by Adam and Abraham as an earthly replica of the eternal preexistent heavenly prototype, etc., were borrowed freely from Jerusalem, there is no long history of bitter rivalry between the two.[113] For Islam, Jerusalem remained *par excellence* the City of the Holy House, and as late as the eleventh century anyone who could not make the Hajj to Mecca was instructed to go to the great feast at Jerusalem instead.[114] The Moslem intellectuals, exactly as the Jewish and Christian doctors before them, protested against the glorification of a mere building, and campaigned vigorously against the pilgrimages,[115] but the temple had a powerful advocate in Christian jealousy. Like children fighting for a toy, each faction came to prize the temple more highly when it saw how much the other wanted it.

This jealous rivalry became apparent on the very day Omar entered Jerusalem and visited the temple ruins "in all humility and simplicity." The Christians, who saw in his unassuming manner "only a Satanic hypocrisy," were piously horrified at the sight, and the Patriarch Sophronius cried out: "This, surely, is the Abomination of Desolation in the Temple, of which David [sic] prophesied."[116] For the Christians it was *their* temple now, though they had turned it into a dungheap.[117] Such horror the Jews of old had expressed at

the sight of profane feet in the temple, and presently the
Moslems took up the refrain, banishing Christians and Jews
on pain of death from the sacred precincts "where the Saracens
believe, according to their law, that their prayers are more
readily answered than anywhere else."[118] The only genuine
religious clashes between Christians and Moslems, Müller
informs us of the Crusades, were the two fights for the temple, when the Christians took it in 1099 and the Moslems got
it back in 1187—"und damit war die Geschichte des
Glaubenskrieges als solches ziemlich aus."[119] Solomon's Temple was in each case, as it had been in Jewish times, the last
redoubt; there alone neither side gave or asked for quarter; it
was the ultimate all-out objective, and each conqueror in
turn entered the holy place with songs of apocalyptic joy.[120]

Actually the possession of the temple complex was more
than a mere matter of prestige. In the endless rivalries of the
Christian sects there was just one claim to supreme authority
that could neither be duplicated nor matched: "Those who
cannot be reached by scriptural and doctrinal arguments,"
says a writing attributed to Athanasius, are bound to credit
the claims of that church which holds the holy places, including "Zion, where the salvation of the world was worked
out. . . . And if the opposition say that we hold those places
by the brute force of imperial arms, let them know that . . .
Christ has never allowed His Places to fall into the hands of
heretics." It was a strong argument until Islam took over.[121]

From the fourth century on, Christians were taught to
view the Holy Sepulchre rather than the temple as the religious center of the universe. But in supplanting the temple its
Christian counterpart could never escape the claims and traditions of its predecessors—in Jerusalem the pilgrim was never
out of the shadow of the temple, as is strikingly illustrated in
the lady Aetheria's (Silvia's) full description of the Easter celebration at Jerusalem at the end of the fourth century.

According to Aetheria, the great culmination of the pilgrimage was the *dies enceniarum* commemorating the dedication of the great Churches of the Cross and the Holy Sepulchre *and* of the Temple of Solomon. The supreme consummation and fulfilment of all the pilgrim's toil and yearning, as the lady describes it, was that moment when he was permitted to come forward and kiss the true Cross on Golgotha, *"at the same time* kissing the ring of Solomon and the horn with which the kings of Israel were anointed."[122] Again, the great annual sermon attended by all the clergy and the pilgrims, the only universal compulsory assembly, had to be delivered "always in that place . . . to which on the 40th day Joseph and Mary brought the Lord in the Temple."[123] Silvia's pilgrim is never allowed to forget that he is a pilgrim to the temple.[124] Indeed, whatever was holy about the Holy City was made such by contact with the temple, which, as Photius observes, "has the power to sanctify other things . . . a sort of divine grace to make holy."[125] Thus "the temple consecrated the city," and progressively sanctified the holy mountain, the Holy City, the Holy Land, and ultimately the whole earth;[126] "the Eternal Presence renders the new Jerusalem one vast *naos*," where John saw no temple, not because there was none, but because it was all temple.[127]

In the reports of both Eastern and Western travellers the various holy places of the temple complex are constantly confused and identified with each other.[128] Especially common is the locating of the Holy Sepulchre, the Holy of Holies, and the Cross of Golgotha (directly over the skull of Adam) at one and the same spot.[129] In old maps and drawings the temple and the Holy Sepulchre are depicted alike, as a circular structure marking the exact center of the earth, with its four shrines marking the points of the compass. The two are virtually identical.[130]

Upon taking Jerusalem in 1099 the Crusaders moved straight to the object of their desire, the Holy Sepulchre, and then proceeded directly to Solomon's Temple: *ad dominicum sepulcrum, dehinc etiam ad Templum.* [131] As they marched they sang apocalyptic hymns of joy hailing the millennial day and the New Jerusalem. [132] The Crusades are a reminder that Christianity was never able to settle for a spiritual temple or forget the old one: "It is foolish and unmeet," writes an indignant churchman, "for Fulcher to distort utterances applying to the spiritual reign and to spiritual things in such a way as to make them apply to buildings or earthly localities, which mean nothing at all to God." But Fulcher knew what he was doing: "at the time," our critic confesses, "everybody was sunk in the error of that kind of gross darkness, clergy and laity, learned and military alike." [133] To explain away the disturbing veneration of the Crusaders for the temple, scholars have argued that they were really confusing it with the Holy Sepulchre; [134] but they could hardly have confused the most sacred object on earth with anything but another very sacred object, and it is absurd to suppose that when they spoke of the Temple of Solomon they had no idea of what they were talking about. [135] Typical of modern prejudice is the naive insistence that the Knights Templars took their singular title from their street address, their headquarters being by the merest coincidence near the site of Solomon's Temple. But if the title *Pauperes commilitione Christi templique Salomoniaci* means anything, it means that these gentlemen fought for Christ *and* the Temple of Solomon, and were perfectly aware that the institution of the pilgrimage, which it was their special office to render secure, went back to the days of the temple. [136]

Though freely admitting the liturgical indebtedness of the church to the synagogue, students of ritual and liturgy have displayed singular reluctance to concede anything at all to the temple. [137] Yet if the church of the fourth and fifth centuries, while embracing popular heathen cult practices everywhere, also aped the synagogue with a zeal that was almost comical, [138] we must not forget that "the worship of the early Synagogue was based on the Temple liturgy." [139]

Nay, the fathers, early and late, derive Christian worship directly from the temple, though like Hilary they may make a hair-splitting distinction between Jewish worship *in templo* and Christian worship *ad templum*.[140] They boast that the church possesses all the physical properties of the temple— the oil, the myrrh, the altar, and incense, hymns, priestly robes, etc., everything, in fact, but the temple itself, for "in the place of the tangible Temple we behold the spiritual."[141] Strange, that the solid walls should vanish and all the rest remain! Even the unleavened bread was retained in the West as an acknowledged heritage of the temple, in spite of the much more appropriate spiritual symbolism of the leavened bread preferred by the Eastern churches, "for we do not reject all the practices of the Old Law," says Rupert in explaining this, "We still offer incense . . . daily, the holy oil of anointing is among us, we have bells in the place of ancient trumpets, and many suchlike things."[142] So we find "veils of the Temple" in Christian churches,[143] inner shrines called tabernacles, awesome Holies of Holies entered only by prince and patriarch for the Year-rite,[144] buildings and altars oriented like synagogues—which imitated the temple in that respect,[145] dedication rites faithfully reproducing those of Solomon's Temple,[146] and a body of hymns "so obviously sung in the Temple that there is no need for any words to prove this."[147] In ritual texts priests are regularly referred to as Levites, and the bishop, though his office and title derive from the synagogue and not the temple, is equated with Aaron the high priest. Rabanus Maurus leaves us in no doubt of what his people were thinking when they hailed their fine church with *templum Domini, templum Domini, templum Domini est!*[148]

The Dread and Envy of Them All

Though it did not need to be pointed out to them, the Jews were ever reminded by Christian theologians that without their temple they were helpless.[149] On the other hand,

the churchmen recognized with a shudder that if they ever
got their temple back again the same Jews would be very
dangerous indeed. *"If* the Jews had [their ancient institutions],"
Athanasius observes, "then they could deny that Christ had
come . . . ; but now all prophecy is sealed, and their gift of
prophecy, their holy city, and their Temple are taken away—
forever."[150]

That ringing "forever" is the key to the whole problem.
The joy of the clergy, some of whom take genuine pleasure
in reporting every fresh disaster and indignity to the temple,
would be cold comfort indeed were this Banquo ever to rise
and push them from their stools. The most disturbing aspect
of the temple was the apocalyptic assurance of its restoration, and every device of rhetoric and logic (in the absence of
a single verse of scripture to support the thesis and a great
many to refute it) was employed to convince the world that
the prophetic "forever" applied not to the *restoration* of the
temple, but to its *destruction*.[151] The strongest argument was
the historical one, the case stated by Hippolytus, that since
the Temple *has* never been restored it should be plain to all
"by now" that it never *will* be. The greatest comfort Origen
can muster for the future is the fact that in his day the temple
cult had been interrupted for a longer period than ever before.
True, the suspended rites have always been resumed in the
past, but in this case enough time has passed to warrant one
in being so bold as to express an opinion that they will *never*
be restored.[152] Later theologians built the feeble argument
into their chief bulwark against the temple, Chrysostom rein-
forcing it with the observation that while Josephus describes
the destruction of the temple, he has nothing to say of its
restoration, which proves "that he did not dare predict that it
would be restored again," which in turn proves that it never
can be![153] Actually "the remorseless logic of history," far
from "confuting" early Christian hopes for the temple,[154] has
seriously confuted the opposition, whose program has always
called for a complete transfer of the ancient heritage to the

new church, a transfer which "the continued existence of the Jewish nation and cult" has rendered desperately overdue.[155]

How touchy an issue the temple has always been is shown clearly enough by the extreme reluctance of the churchmen to talk about it. Anything that even reminds them of it seems to rub them on a raw place. The mere sight of its ruins, instead of providing the eyes of the monks of Palestine with a gratifying spectacle and an edifying object lesson as the pagan ruins did, drove them wild with fury—"a detestable thing that causes appallment to the worshippers of Christ."[156] The Jews had to pay a heavy tariff for the luxury of mourning at those ruins, for their mourning was not only a reminder of what the temple *had* been, but also of what it *would* be.[157] No wonder the exasperated fathers ask the Jews why they insist on hanging around Jerusalem after their temple has been destroyed, and bid them take the hint and be gone: "Everything you treasured in Jerusalem now lies in ruins, and your world-renowned temple is now the city dump of a town called Aelia."[158] On the other hand, Theophylactus reports that people even in his day tried to prove from the presence of ruins on the holy mount "that Christ was a liar."[159]

This last point, and the fundamental insecurity which underlay it, is illustrated by one of the most dramatic Christian legends, in which the mere report of the Emperor Julian's intention to assist in rebuilding the temple was magnified into the greatest crime, and its failure into the greatest miracle, of post-Apostolic history.[160] The story begins with the Jews announcing to the monarch that they are paralyzed without their temple: "We cannot worship without it."[161] The wily Emperor sees that the Christians will be equally paralyzed by its restoration, and plans in the rebuilding of the temple to deliver the *coup de grâce* to Christianity by demonstrating once for all that Jesus was a false prophet.[162] For the Christians the whole issue of the truth and survival of their religion hinges on the rebuilding of the temple. To make this clear to all, the Bishop of Jerusalem, we are told, had gone about preaching that in Daniel and the Gospels the Lord had predicted that the Jews would never, to the end of time be able to place one stone of the temple upon another.[163] Since the bishop (whose extensive writings make no mention of our story) preached no such thing,[164] since no such prophecy exists in the scriptures, and since the restoration of the temple would not confute a single recorded utterance of Jesus, it is plain that the churchmen themselves have chosen to make an issue of the temple, and thereby rendered coexistence of church and temple impossible.[165] In this case only one solution was possible: a succession of stunning and theatrical miracles in the best fourth-century tradition (but also of a type of miracle story that had been growing up around the temple for many centuries)[166] frustrated the evil project at every step. Day after day the stubborn Jews persisted, and day after day great balls of fire chased them all over the temple rock, consuming them like flies, while the earth shook and the heavens gave forth with a succession of super-spectacular displays. Among all the conflicting accounts, Adler had no difficulty finding the most probable source of the legends, which grow like a snowball;[167] yet to this day Christian scholars cite the fantastic and contradictory stories not only as actual fact, but also as positive proof that Jerusalem and the temple can never be restored.[168]

When Athanasius assures us that no crime can be more monstrous than that of converting a church into a synagogue, he makes it clear that that is not because one poor synagogue more or less makes so much difference, but because such a gesture "prepares the way" for the sitting of the antichrist in the temple.[169] The antichrist-in-the-temple prophecy has always cast a dark shadow over the pages of the fathers, and though most of them prefer an allegorical interpretation, a large and influential number of them insist on taking the thing literally, however terrible the prospect. It is *definitive templum Dei*, whether we like it or not, they assure us, and before the adversary can usurp his place in the temple, that temple must be rebuilt.[170]

Church writers have done their best to brighten the gloomy picture. They have reassured us that the only really *literal* aspect of the temple was its destruction;[171] they have told comforting stories of frustrated attempts to rebuild it;[172] they report with a great sigh of relief the collapse of the Montanist project for rebuilding the New Jerusalem;[173] and, as we have seen, they taxed the resources of exegesis to discover a ray of hope in the scriptures. Yet all this but betrays rather than allays their misgivings: towards the Jews and their temple, their words and deeds remain those of men haunted by a sense of insecurity.[174] Why otherwise would they forbid the Jews even to imitate the architecture of the temple in their synagogues?[175] The intellectuals who liquidated the temple once and for all in the economy of the church fondly supposed that their own eloquence could more than take its place: while the emperors have taken upon themselves the expense and responsibility of erecting the physical edifice, Jerome assures us, it is *eloquentia* that warrants the tabernacling of the Spirit therein.[176] If the temple of the Spirit was built without hands, human tongues worked overtime on the project, and the finished structure remains a typically unconvincing production of the Age of Rhetoric.[177]

The Reformation as a reaction against ritualism could hardly be expected to capitalize on the Christian need for the temple or its equivalent, and indeed leading Protestant scholars confess that vagueness and uncertainty in ritual matters was perhaps the most serious defect in the work of the Reformers.[178] Yet the Protestant experience seems simply to be repeating the cycle, for we have seen how the doctors of ancient times condemned the temple and its rites with over-hasty zeal, and how their successors, seeking like Esau to mend the damage and "inherit the blessing" when it was all too late, introduced into the vacuum a botched and hybrid ritual. It was the pagan element in that ritual which the

Reformers found so objectionable and exposed so skillfully.[179] Neither group has grounds for complacency, and it would be hard to determine which of the two condemns the temple with greater vigor.

By loosely and inaccurately equating the temple with the synagogue, it has been possible for Christian scholars in the past to claim victory for the church without the painful necessity of mentioning the temple too much or even at all, the assumption being that the church's triumph over the synagogue answereth all things.[180] But with the current emphasis on eschatology and ritual, the temple can no longer be kept in the background. *Eschatologie hat über uns keine Macht mehr!* has been the common creed of the clergy,[181] but eschatology now returns like an unwelcome ghost, and with it comes the temple. So while some Christian scholars still denounce the temple with surprising vehemence,[182] others are markedly hesitant,[183] and still others have reached the point of unabashedly accepting "the literalness of the future temple and its sacrificial system."[184] All three of these attitudes bespeak a sense of insecurity and inadequacy.

The moral of our tale is that the Christian world has been perennially haunted by the ghost of the temple—a ghost in which it does not believe. If the least be said for it, the temple has never lost its power to stir men's imaginations and excite their emotions, and the emotion which it has most often inspired in Christian breasts has certainly been that of envy, a passion the more dangerous for being suppressed. The temple has cast a shadow over the claims and the confidence of the Christian church from early times, a shadow which is by no means diminishing in our own day. If we seem to have labored the obvious in pointing this out, it is only because the obvious has been so long and so resolutely denied or ignored in high places.

NOTES

1. Samuel G. F. Brandon, *The Fall of Jerusalem and the Christian Church* (London: Society for the Promotion of Christian Knowledge, 1951), 10–11.

2. Ibid., 250.

3. While opposing the usual tendency to minimize the temple in the economy of the early church, e.g., ibid., 29, 39, 164–65, 263, Brandon bestows upon the city of Jerusalem the laurels that rightfully belong to the temple, e.g., 19–21.

4. "Mirum est quod quase hunc locum ita praetergressi sint," Adam Praemonstratensis (Adam of St. Victor), *De Tripartito Tabernaculo* (*On the Tripartite Tabernacle*) II, in PL 198:625. Richard of St. Victor writes on the same subject by popular demand—"rogatus ab amicis," in *De Tabernaculo* (*On the Tabernacle*) I, in *PL* 196:211–12.

5. Adam of St. Victor, *On the Tripartite Tabernacle* II, in *PL* 198:625; Richard of St. Victor, *On the Tabernacle* I, in *PL* 196:211–12, and *On the Tabernacle* II, in *PL* 196:223–42; cf. *PL* 196:306.

6. Of the latter calamity Bishop John Kaye writes: "The silence of ecclesiastical history respecting the cessation . . . is to be ascribed . . . to the combined operation of prejudice and policy—of prejudice which made them reluctant to believe, of policy which made them anxious to conceal the truth," John Kaye, *Ecclesiastical History of the Second and Third Centuries, Illustrated from the Writings of Tertullian* (London: Griffith Farran, 1894), 50.

7. Discussed by Brandon, *The Fall of Jerusalem and the Christian Church*, 39, 127, 262–64. See note 66 below.

8. Eusebius, *HE* VII, 24, 1–9, in *PG* 20:692–96, quoting Dionysius at length. Jerome, *Commentarius in Isaiam Prophetam* (*Commentary on Isaiah*) 18, in *PL* 24:627.

9. "Quem non solum suae sectae homines, sed et nostrorum in hac parte dumtaxat plurima sequitur multitudo, ut praesaga mente jam cernam quantorum in me rabies concitanda sit," Jerome, *Commentary on Isaiah* 18, in *PL* 24:627.

10. Jerome, *Commentary on Isaiah* 18, in *PL* 24:627. The case for the literalists is stated by Cyril of Jerusalem, who insists that Jesus meant the real temple when he spoke of his Father's House: *tōi Christōi peisthēsometha tōi legonti peri tou hierou* [i.e., Luke 2:49, John 2:16] . . . *di' hōn saphestata ton en Hierosolymois proteron naon oikon einai tou heautou Patros hōmologei. Catechesis VII. de Patre* (*Catechetical Lecture on the Father*) 6, in *PG* 33:612.

11. Jerome, *Commentary on Jeremiah* 31, 38, in *PL* 24:920, "Judaei videlicet et nostri Judaizantes, conantur ostendere . . . ibi dicunt sanctuarium Domini, id est templum esse condendum, mansurumque in perpetuum," etc.; cf. Jerome, *Commentarium in Isaiam Prophetam* XV, 54, in *PL* 24:516.

12. H. J. Cadbury, "Acts and Eschatology," in William D. Davies and D. Daube, eds., *The Background of the New Testament and Its Eschatology* (Cambridge: Cambridge University Press, 1956), 309, 316.

13. Therefore even Solomon's Temple was "neque legitimum neque devotum," according to Zeno, *Tractatus* (*Tractate*) I, 14, in *PL* 11:355, since God "reprobat . . . tam immensum, tam insigne, tam opulens templum," etc., ibid., in *PL* 11:356-58. The same argument is used by Hilary, *Tractatus super Psalmos* (*Treatise on the Psalms*) 126, in *PL* 9:694-99; Lactantius, *Divinae Institutiones* (*Divine Institutes*) VI, 25, in *PL* 6:728-32; Isidore, *Epistolae* (*Letters*) IV, 70, in *PG* 78:1132-33; cf. I, 20, in *PG* 78:196, and ibid., I, 196, in *PG* 78:356; Procopius, *Commentarius in Isaiam* (*Commentary on Isaiah*) 6, 5, in *PG* 87:1937.

14. Eusebius, *Praeparatio Evangelica* (*Preparation for the Gospel*) 3, 13-17, in *PG* 21:220-28; Clement of Alexandria, *Stromata* V, 11, in *PG* 9:112-16; VII, 5, in *PG* 9:436-40; Theodoret, *Graecarum Affectionum Curatio Sermo* 3, in *PG* 83:885, quotes Zeno and Plato in this connection.

15. Thomas Aquinas, *Summa Theologica*, 1a2ae, Quaestio cii, Articulus iv; Dominican ed., 29:152-77.

16. William J. Phythian-Adams, *The People and the Presence* (London/New York: Oxford University Press, 1942), 60.

17. 2 Chronicles 6:18.

18. So Irenaeus, *Contra Haereses* (*Against Heresies*) IV, 34, 4, in *PG* 7:1085-86; Hilary, *Treatise on the Psalms* 118, 4, in *PL* 9:643; Lactantius, *Divine Institutes* IV, 14, in *PL* 6:1021-22; John Chrysostom, *De Sancta Pentecoste Homilia* (*Homily on the Holy Pentecost*) 1, 1, in *PG* 50:453, etc. A favorite theme with the moderns who feel that the liquidation of the Temple was indispensable to "the absolution of God's worship from all bonds of time and nationality," Bernhard Weiss, *The Life of Christ*, tr. John W. Hope, 3 vols. (Edinburgh: Clark, 1883-84), 3:261.

19. Jacob S. Raisin, *Gentile Reactions to Jewish Ideals* (New York: Philosophical Library, 1953), 225; cf. 15-16, 34, 94.

20. So Ernest Renan, *Antichrist* (Boston: Roberts, 1897), 187-88; Arthur S. Peake, ed., *The People and the Book* (Oxford: Clarendon, 1925), 281.

21. Quotes are, respectively, from Andrew M. Fairbairn, *Philosophy of the Christian Religion* (New York: Macmillan, 1902), 487, and Albert T. Olmstead, *Jesus in the Light of History* (New York: Scribner, 1942), 69-70; cf. S. A. Cook, *The Old Testament* (New York: Macmillan, 1936), 130.

22. Quote from J. B. Bury. From early times Christians debated the cosmic significance of the oneness of the temple: Clement of Alexandria, *Stromata* V, 9, in *PG* 9:112: *Palin ho Mōusēs . . . hena d'oun neōn hidrysamenos tou Theou monogenē te kosmon . . . kai ton hena, hōs ouk eti tōi Basileidēi dokei, katēngele Theon. . . .*

23. "The purpose [ratio] of the unity of the temple or tabernacle . . . was to fix in men's minds the unity of the divine faith, God desiring that sacrifice be made to him in one place only." Aquinas, *Summa Theologica* 1a2ae, Quaestio cii, Articulus iv; Dominican ed., 29:161 On the lack of a centralizing force, Louis Duchesne, *Early History of the Christian Church*, 3 vols. (London: Murray, 1931), 2:521-26. Cf. note 2 above.

24. Peter Cantor, *Verbum Abbreviatum* (*The Abridged Word*) 29, in *PL* 205:104, 106-7. The historian Socrates, *Ecclesiastical History* (*HE*) V, 22, in *PG* 67:625-45, made the same observation in the 5th century.

25. This is the "messe publique," the oldest exemplar of which Louis M. O. Duchesne calls "un cérémonial fort postérieur à l'age antique," *Origines du culte chrétien* 2nd. ed (Paris: Thorin, 1898), 154 (=5th ed. [1920], 172).

26. Cantor, *The Abridged Word* 29, in *PL* 205:104, 106-7; so also Hilary, *Treatise on the Psalms* 14, 3, in *PL* 9:301.

27. Hilary, *Treatise on the Psalms* 14, 3, in *PL* 9:301; Eusebius, *Preparation for the Gospel* 5, 1, in *PG* 21:312; Jerome, *Commentary on Isaiah* 13, 47, in *PL* 24:471-72; Leo Magnus, *Sermo* (*Discourse*) 59, 8, in *PL* 54:341; Chrysostom, *Contra Judaeos et Gentiles, quod Christus Sit Deus* (*Against the Jews and the Gentiles, that Christ is God*) 12, in *PG* 48:829-30; cf. *De Cruce et Latrone* (*On the Cross and the Thief*) 2, 1, in *PG* 49:409; *De Capto Eutropio et de Divitiarum Vanitate* (*On the Capture of Eutropius and the Vanity of Wealth*) 15, in *PG* 52:410.

28. See the discussion by A. le Nourry in *PG* 9:900-2. A writing attributed to Athanasius admits that the multiplication of shrines presents "a strange and paradoxical problem"—*xenon kai paradoxon*

to eperōtema—to which the author gives an even stranger solution. See *Quaestiones ad Antiochum Ducem (Questions to Duke Antiochus)* 26, in *PG* 28:613.

29. The temple represents the world—*ho naos de hōs oikos Theou holon ton kosmon typoi*, and since there is but "one world, above and below . . . analogous to the order of the Church," the church itself is one temple which *ho archiereus monos syn tois hierōmenois eiserchetai*; Symeon Thessalonicensis, *De Sacro Templo (On the Holy Temple)* 131, in *PG* 155:337–40. Cf. Leo, *Discourse* 54, 8, in *PL* 54: 341; Hilary, *Treatise on the Psalms* 121, in *PL* 9:662–63; and Theodoret, *Graecarum Affectionum Curatio* 6, in *PG* 83:989.

30. Fulgentius, *Contra Fabianum (Against Fabian)* 34, in *PL* 65:811–12; Photius, *Epistolae (Letters)* I, 8, 31, in *PG* 102:665; Wolbero, *Commentaria in Canticum Canticorum (Commentary on the Song of Solomon)* III, 5, 15, in *PL* 195:1203.

31. Aquinas, *Summa Theologica*, 1a2ae Quaestio cii, Articulus iv; Dominican ed., 29:161: "Et ideo, ut firmaretur in animis hominum fides unitatis divinae, voluit Deus ut in uno loco tantum sibi sacrificium offerretur. . . . Sed cultus novae legis . . . Deo acceptus," etc.

32. Ibid., Articuli iv and v. Thomas himself at the beginning of Articulus iv refutes the common doctrine of a purely spiritual temple.

33. Anastasius Bibliothecarius, *Historia de Vitis Romanorum Pontificum (History of the Lives of the Roman Pontiffs)* 112, Stephen VI, in *PL* 128:1399.

34. August Neander, *The Life of Jesus Christ*, 4th ed. (New York: Harper, 1858), 180–81.

35. Charles M. Laymon, *Life and Teachings of Jesus* (New York: Abingdon, 1955), 280.

36. Leo, *Discourse* 3, in *PL* 54:145.

37. Frederick C. Grant, *An Introduction to New Testament Thought* (New York: Abingdon-Cokesbury, 1950), 14.

38. Barnabas, *Epistola Catholica (Catholic Epistle)* 16, in *PG* 2:771–76. cf. TB *Yebamoth* 6b: *lō' mimmĭqdōš 'atēh mĭtyayrē' 'ēlā' mimmē šĕhīzhīr 'āl hammĭqdōs* "While the Temple was still standing the principle had been established that the efficacy of every species of expiation was morally conditioned," Moore quoted in *William D. Davies, Paul and Rabbinic Judaism* (London: Society for the Promotion of Christian Knowledge, 1948), 257.

39. "Neque enim domum incusabat [Jesus] . . . sed eos, qui non bene utebantur domo," Irenaeus, *Against Heresies* IV, 2, 6, in *PG* 7:978. Even Stephen's sermon (Acts 7), usually viewed as an attack on

the Temple, is rather an appeal for a proper sense of values. See William Manson, *The Epistle to the Hebrews* (London: Hodder & Stoughton, 1951), 28, 30, 34.

40. Quotes from Origen, *Commentaria in Evangelium Secundum Matthaeum* (*Commentary on Matthew*) 14, 22–23, in *PG* 13:1452–53, and *Commentaria in Evangelium Joannis* (*Commentary on John*) 10, 16, in *PG* 14:349. The Temple is built of simplicity, intellect, *veritas, pudicitia, continentia,* etc., Zeno, *Tractate* I, 14, in *PL* 11:361–62. The theme is extremely popular with theologians.

41. Jewish and Christian doctors alike "spun out abstract doctrines far beyond the ken of the common folk, and insisted that these are the truths of religion and morality. Nor are we closing the gap today," Max Kadushin, *The Rabbinic Mind* (New York: Jewish Theological Seminary of America, 1952), 87–88. "The fathers," says Edward Gibbon, "deem themselves secure and invulnerable behind the ample veil of allegory, which they carefully spread over every tender part of the Mosaic dispensation," Edward Gibbon, *The Decline and Fall of the Roman Empire,* 3 vols. (New York: The Modern Library, 1932), ch. 15, n. 31; 1:393.

42. Origen, *Commentary on John* 10, 20, in *PG* 14:369–70. *Amphotera mentoige, to te hieron kai to sōma tou Iēsou*—it is quite possible for it to be two or more things at once.

43. Cyril of Alexandria, *Commentarius in Michaeam Prophetam* (*Commentary on Micah*) IV, 1, 2, in *PG* 71:644. Cf. Symeon, *On the Holy Temple* 128, in *PG* 155:336; Photius, *Contra Manichaeos* (*Against the Manichaeans*) 2, in *PG* 102:108.

44. Thus Rupert, *Liber Regum* (*Commentary on Kings*) 3, 6–29, in *PL* 167:1147–75; Hugh of St. Victor, *Allegoriae in Vetus Testamentum* (*Allegories on the Old Testament*) 3, 9, in *PL* 175:661–63; and *De Claustro Animae* (*On the Fortress of the Soul*) 3, 17, in *PL* 176:1118–20; Alan of Lille, *Sententiae,* no. 16, 22, in *PL* 210:236–37, 240; Garnerus, *Gregorianum,* "De Templo" (*On the Temple*) XIII, 8, in *PL* 193:398–400; Adam of St. Victor, *Sermones* (*Sermons*) 40, in *PL* 198:363–71.

45. See notes 152–57 below.

46. Hilary, *Treatise on the Psalms* 126, in *PL* 9:694–95. Cf. Olmstead, *Jesus in the Light of History,* 69.

47. "From the beginning the destruction of the Temple and the eventual cessation of the sacrifices had been anticipated," Grant, *An Introduction to New Testament Thought,* 14. As early as 587 B.C. "the old dogma that it was blasphemy even to speak of the destructibility of

the temple was shattered," Raisin, *Gentile Reactions to Jewish Ideals*, 82.

48. In the Odes of Solomon the Temple is "préexistant au monde et, de plus, il subsiste hors du monde," Pierre Batiffol, "Les odes de Salomon," *Revue Biblique* 20 n.s., 8 (1911): 40. "Est ergo altare in coelis, et templum," Irenaeus, *Against Heresies* IV, 18, in *PG* 7:1024-29. Cf. Davies, *Paul and Rabbinic Judaism*, 162, n. 2.

49. L. J. Liebereich, "Compilation of the Book of Isaiah," *Jewish Quarterly Review* 46 (1956): 272. See the Testament of Levi 14-18, the Testament of Benjamin 9, and the Testament of Naphtali 4.

50. Barnabas, *Catholic Epistle* 16, in *PG* 2:771-76. That *paradōsei* here means "remove," "take out of circulation," is clear from parallel passages in Matthew 24:9, and Didache 16:4; cf. Robert Henry Charles, *The Book of Enoch* (Oxford: Oxford University Press, 1912), 198-204.

51. Hilary, *Treatise on the Psalms* 14, in *PL* 9:301-2: "Sed mons Domini nullus in terra est: omnis enim terra jam pridem per vitia hominum maledictis obnoxia est."

52. Athanasius, *Quaestiones in Pauli Epistolas* (*Questions on the Epistles of Paul*) 127, in *PG* 28:769; Peter Damian, *Dialogus inter Judaeum et Christianum* (*Dialogue between a Jew and a Christian*) 9, in *PL* 145:59; Rupert, *Liber in Numeros* (*Commentary on Numbers*) II, 21, in *PL* 167:901; Richard of St. Victor, *On the Tabernacle 1*, in *PL* 196:212; also, *Adnotationes Mysticae in Psalmos* (*Mystic Comments on Psalms*) 28, in *PL* 196:306; *In Apocalypsin Joannis* (*Commentary on the Apocalypse of John*) VII, 2, in *PL* 196:860; Aquinas, *Summa Theologica*, 1a2ae Quaestio cii, Articulus iv, conclusion; Andrew of Caesarea, *Commentarius in Apocalypsin* (*Commentary on the Apocalypse of John*) 21, 3-4, in *PG* 106:425; Wolbero, *Commentary on the Song of Solomon* 4, in *PL* 195:1275.

53. For Tertullian the glory of the temple was extinguished by the mere declaration of the Lord that it was a den of thieves, *De Pudicitia* (*On Modesty*) 1, in *PL* 2:1033-34. It was not the money-changers as such, but really the Jews, that Christ was expelling forever, according to Cyril of Alexandria, *Commentarius in Amos Prophetam* (*Commentary on Amos*) 19, in *PG* 71:443-44; Leo, *Sermones Attributi* (*Attributed Discourses*) 14, in *PL* 54:507; Rupert, *Commentarius in Zachariam Prophetam* (*Commentary on Zechariah*) II, 5, in *PL* 168:735-36; and *Commentary on Amos* II, 3-4, in *PL* 168:301. For Ernst W. Hengstenberg, *Christology of the Old Testament*, 2nd ed., 4 vols. (Edinburgh: Clark, 1856-58), 4:248, the

"den of thieves" verdict "rendered the continuance of the former [Temple] absolutely impossible."

54. "Evidens . . . translatio" Leo, *Discourse* 68, 3, in *PL* 54:374.

55. *Nun de . . . eisi hoi pōlountes kai agorazontes en tōi hierōi . . . kai oudamou Iēsous epiphainetai hina ekbalōn sōsei tous loipous,* Origen, *Commentary on Matthew* XVI, 21, in *PG* 13:1444-45, 1417, 1448: *All' eithe eiselthōn eis to hieron tou Patros . . . kataballoi Iēsous tas . . . trapezas,* cf. *Homiliae in Jeremiam (Homilies on Jeremiah)* 9, in *PG* 13:348. Cf. Gregorius Magnus (Gregory the Great), *Epistolae (Letters)* XI, 46, in *PL* 77:1166; Theophylactus, *Enarratio in Marcum (Commentary on the Gospel of Mark)* 11, 15-18, in *PG* 123:616; Photius, *Against the Manichaeans* IV, 23, in *PG* 102:229; Alcuin, *Commentaria in Sancti Joannis Evangelium (Commentary on John)* II, 4, 14-15, in *PL* 100:773.

56. Photius, *Against the Manichaeans* IV, 23, in *PG* 102:229; so Cyril of Jerusalem, *Catechetical Lecture on the Father* 7, in *PG* 33:612.

57. Thus Hippolytus, *Demonstratio adversus Judaeos (Against the Jews)* 7, in *PG* 10:792; Juvencus, *Evangelica Historia (Gospel History)* IV, 75-80, in *PL* 19:286-87. This prophecy was "the final 'Let us depart hence' of retiring Deity," according to Frederic W. Farrar, *The Life of Christ,* 2 vols. (New York: Cassell, 1903) 2:255, who notes that 35 years *later* Deity finally departed! "Those few words completed the prophecy of Israel's desolation," Isodore O'Brien, *The Life of Christ* (Paterson, N.J.: St. Anthony Guild Press, 1937), 418 (=4th ed, 472).

58. Vincent Taylor, *Jesus and His Sacrifice* (London: Macmillan, 1937), 71.

59. So Jerome, *Commentary on Isaiah* 15, 52, in *PL* 24:513-24. Leo, *Discourse* 68, in *PL* 54:374; Theophanes, *Homilia (Homily)* 27, in *PG* 132:600. A. Feuillet, "Le sens du mot Parousie dans l'Evangile de Matthieu," in Davies & Daube, *The Background of the New Testament and Its Eschatology,* 268.

60. Cassiodorus, *Expositio in Psalterium (Commentary on the Psalms)* 21, in *PL* 70:158; Rupert, *Commentarius in Apocalypsin Joannis (Commentary on the Apocalypse of John)* IX, 15, in *PL* 169:1111; Jerome, *Commentary on Isaiah* XIV, 52, in *PL* 24:498; Aquinas, *Summa Theologica,* 1a2ae, Quaestio cii, Articulus iv; Clarence T. Craig, *The Beginning of Christianity* (New York: Abingdon-Cokesbury, 1943), 183. For a recent treatment, see Dennis Sylva, "The Temple Curtain and Jesus' Death in the Gospel of Luke," *Journal of Biblical Literature* 105 (1986): 239-50.

61. Farrar, *The Life of Christ* 1:194–95. Some scholars find the passage too hot to handle and declare it to be "not in the original utterance of Jesus," but "the travesty of the false witness," B. W. Robinson, *Jesus in Action*, 77.

62. Gibbon, *Decline and Fall*, ch. 15, n. 31, 1:393; cf. Raisin, *Gentile Reactions to Jewish Ideals*, 31.

63. Quote from Gordon Leff, "In Search of the Millenium," *Past and Present* 13 (April 1958): 92.

64. Many writers present Jesus as a would-be restorer of temple worship, with the temple as his headquarters. Thus Arthur C. Headlam, *Jesus Christ in History and Faith*, 137–39; R. Bultmann, *Theologie des Neuen Testaments*, 4th ed. (Tübingen: Mohr, 1961), 1:17; cf. English translation, *Theology of the New Testament*, tr. K. Grobel (New York: Scribner, 1951); Benjamin W. Bacon, *Studies in Matthew* (New York: Holt, 1930), 242–43.

65. "Recent research has shown that prophets had a regular part in the temple cultus," Millar Burrows, *Outline of Biblical Theology*, 255.

66. For a comprehensive statement, see James Strahan, "Temple," in James Hastings, ed., *Dictionary of the Apostolic Church* (New York: Scribner, 1916–22) 2:556–57; and Brandon, *The Fall of Jerusalem and the Christian Church*, 21, 29, 39, 127, 263, even vindicating Stephen's position, 89, 127–29, 263.

67. See N. A. Dahl, "Christ, Creation, and the Church," in Davies and Daube, *The Background of the New Testament and Its Eschatology*, 430–31, 424. Quote is from K. Stendahl, "Implications of Form Criticism and Tradition-Criticism for Biblical Interpretation," *Journal of Biblical Literature* 77 (1958): 36–37.

68. For closely paralleled Jewish, Christian, and classical concepts see B. Kötting, *Peregrinatio Religiosa* (Münster: Regensberg, 1950), 57–69, 287–88. The familiar temple imagery in Christian liturgy was disseminated directly by pilgrims coming from Jerusalem, Anton Baumstark, *Abendländische Palästinapilger* (Köln: Bachen, 1906), 31, 80–83.

69. So C. K. Barrett, "The Eschatology of the Epistle to the Hebrews," in Davies & Daube, *The Background of the New Testament and Its Eschatology*, 382.

70. F.-M. Abel, "Jérusalem," in *DACL* 7:2311; cf. Sulpicius Severus, *Historia Sacra (Sacred History)* II, 48, in *PL* 20:156–57, and note 10 above.

71. Gregorius Nyssenus, *Epistolae (Letters)* 2, 3, in *PG* 46:1012–13, 1016; Basil the Great, *Moralia*, Regula 67, in *PG* 31:808; cf. 805;

John Chrysostom, *Ad Populum Antiochenum* (*To the People of Antioch*) 17, in *PG* 49:177–80, *Homily on the Holy Pentecost* 1, in *PG* 50:453–64.

72. Quote is from C. N. Cochrane, *Christianity and Classical Culture* (Oxford: Oxford University Press, 1940), 211; for the concept, Eusebius, *De Laudibus Constantini* (*In Praise of Constantine*) 4–6, 10, in *PG* 20:1332–52, 1372–76.

73. For a recent discussion, Michael S. Seidlmayer, "Rom und Romgedanke im Mittelalter," *Saeculum* 7 (1956): 395–412.

74. See our article, Hugh W. Nibley, "The Hierocentric State," *Western Political Quarterly* 4 (1951): 226–53. Professor W. F. Albright sees in Solomon's Temple "a rich cosmic symbolism which was largely lost in later Israelite and Jewish tradition," William F. Albright, *Archaeology and the Religion of Israel* (Baltimore: Johns Hopkins Press, 1942), 154–55; cf. 88–89, 167.

75. Eusebius, *In Praise of Constantine* 4–6, 10, in *PG* 20:1332–52, 1372–76; and *De Vita Constantini* (*On the Life of Constantine*) III, 33–39, in *PG* 20:1093–1100; IV, 60, in *PG* 20:1209–12.

76. Contemporaries hail him as "the new Bezeliel or Zerubabel, who builds . . . blessed temples of . . . Christ," Antiochus Monachus, *Prologus*, in *PG* 89:1428.

77. Eusebius, *HE* X, 4, 45–46, in *PG* 20:876–77.

78. So Zeno, *Tractate* 1, 14, in *PL* 11:354–62; Jerome, *Commentary on Isaiah* 1, 2, 9, in *PL* 24:49; 17, in *PL* 24:593, and *Epistolae* (*Letters*) 52, 10, in *PL* 22:535; 130, 14, in *PL* 22:1119; 46–47, in *PL* 22:492.

79. Eusebius, *HE* X, 4, 45–46, in *PG* 20:876–77: *hōs mēketi logon, all' ergon gegonenai tēn anō lechtheisan prophēteian* [Haggai 2:9], *gegonen gar kai nun hōs alēthōs estin.*

80. See the editor's enthusiastic comment on the oratory of Paulinus, *Appendix Operum Sancti Paulini* (*Appendix to the Works of Saint Paulinus*), in *PL* 61:929.

81. Abel, "Jérusalem," 2312, for the timing. It is Zonaras, *Annales* (*Annals*) 11, 23, in *PG* 134:996, who locates the Roman temple, following Socrates, *HE* I, 17, in *PG* 67:117–21. According to Eusebius, *On the Life of Constantine* 3, 28, in *PG* 20:1088–89, as the digging proceeded, *to semnon kai panagion tēs sōtēriou anastaseōs martyrion par' elpida pasan anephaineto, kai to te hagion tōn hagiōn antron tēn homoian tes tou Sōtēros anabiōseōs apelambanen eikona.* That this is not a mere parallelism is indicated by the *kai . . . te* and *homoian.*

82. Eusebius, *On the Life of Constantine* 3, 33, in *PG* 20:1093: *kai dē tou pantos hōsper tina kephalēn, prōtōn hapantōn to hieron antron*, etc., noting that this was the very New Jerusalem that had been foretold by the prophets—an eschatological structure. Cf. Socrates, *HE* I, 17, in *PG* 67:117-21.

83. Theodoret, *Explanatio in Ezechielem* (*Explanation of Ezekiel*) 48, 35, in *PG* 81:1253.

84. John Chrysostom, *Sermo post Reditum ab Exsilio* (*Discourse Following the Return from Exile*) 2, in *PG* 52:440; "Ubi aedificabo? Absolutum est templum." He is rejoicing that the growth of the church has burst all old traditional bounds such as the limitations of the temple. Cf. Chrysostom, *Interpretatio in Isaiam Prophetam* (*On Isaiah*) 2, 3, in *PG* 56:30, 97; *Homilia in Sanctum Ignatium Martyrem* (*Homily on St. Ignatius the Martyr*) 5, in *PG* 50:595-96; Basil, *Regulae Fusius Tractatae* (*Detailed Rules*) 40, in *PG* 31:1020; Theodoret, *Epistolae* (*Letters*) 66, 67 and 68, in *PG* 83:1236-37; Zeno, *Liber* (*Commentary*) 2, *Tractate* 46, in *PL* 11:520-21. Significantly, the most brilliant of these gatherings is for the feast of the Maccabees, i.e., to commemorate the rededication of the temple, Chrysostom, *Homilia in Sanctos Maccabeos* (*Homily on the Holy Maccabees*) 1, in *PG* 50:617-24.

85. Chrysostom, *To the People of Antioch* 17, in *PG* 49:177-78; and *Against the Jews and the Gentiles that Christ is God* 9, in *PG* 48:825-26; Gregorius Nyssenus, *Letters* 17, in *PG* 46:1064.

86. Constantine Manassis, *Compendium Chronicum* 3267-83, in *PG* 127:342-43. It was a conscious imitation of Constantine's "New Jerusalem," Procopius, *Buildings* 1, discussed in the footnotes to Eusebius, *The Life of Constantine*, in *PG* 20:1098-99, n. 13-14.

87. The story is told in Raisin, *Gentile Reactions to Jewish Ideals*, 361.

88. On Constantinople as the New House of God, Andras Alföldi, *The Conversion of Constantine and Pagan Rome* (Oxford: Oxford University Press, 1948), 110.

89. Seidlmayer, "Rom und Romgedanke im Mittelalter," 400-03. cf. Pliny, *Letter to Maximus* VIII, 24, 3.

90. See notes 26-28 above. For some amusing arguments, Rupert, *De Victoria Verbi Dei* (*On the Victory of the Word of God*) 10, 10, in *PL* 169:1430; Peter Damian, *Dialogue between a Jew and a Christian* 10, in *PL* 145:60-61.

91. Eusebius, *On the Life of Constantine* 4, 24, in *PG* 20:1172; 4, 42, in *PG* 20:1189-90.

92. So Seidlmayer, "Rom und Romgedanke im Mittelalter," 402-3.

93. Thus in *Attributed Discourses* 14, 4-5, in *PL* 54:507, Leo says that the *cathedra* occupied by Moses has been torn down *mystice* and become a *pestilentiae Cathedram*, the change occurring at the moment Jesus drove the money-changers from the *temple*.

94. Seidlmayer, "Rom und Romgedanke im Mittelalter," 402.

95. Ibid., 409. See Cochrane, *Christianity and Classical Culture*, ch. 5.

96. Leo, *Attributed Discourses* 16; 17, 1-2, in *PL* 54:511-13; Jerome, *Commentary on Isaiah* I, 2, 9, in *PL* 24:49: "Ubi quondam erat templum et religio Dei, ibi Adriani statua et Jovis idolum collocatum," which many Christians regard as literal fulfillment of Mark 13:14.

97. "Partim ignorantiae vitio, partim paganitatis spiritu," Leo, *Discourse* 27, 4, in *PL* 54:218-19; cf. 89, 4, in *PL* 54:446.

98. Ibid., 40, 5, in *PL* 54:271; 48, 1, in *PL* 54:298; 49, 1, in *PL* 54:301; 60, 3, in *PL* 54:344; 21, 3 and 22, 1-2, in *PL* 54:192-95; 23, 5, in *PL* 54:203; 88, 4-5; and 89, 1-2, in *PL* 54:442-46.

99. Ibid., 3, 1-3, in *PL* 54:145-56; 5, 3, in *PL* 54:154.

100. "Nihil legalium institutionum, nihil propheticarum resedit figurarum, quod non totum in Christi sacramenta transierit. Nobiscum est signaculum circumcisionis . . . nobiscum puritas sacrificii, baptismi veritas, honor templi," ibid., 66, in *PL* 54:365-66; cf. 30, 3, in *PL* 54:229. It was all too good for the Jews.

101. Ibid., 4, 1-2, in *PL* 54:149. E. Caspar, *Geschichte des Papsttums von den Anfängen bis zur Höhe der Weltherrschaft* (Tübingen: Mohr, 1930) 1:403; Seidlmayer, "Rom und Romgedanke im Mittelalter," 403.

102. The Hauptthema of this long writing is that the House of God is "non terrena et caduca," Hilary, *Treatise on the Psalms* 121, 2, in *PL* 9:661-62; in fact, if one accepts the temple passages literally, then "inanis est psalmus, et mendax Propheta!," *Treatise on the Psalms* 124, 2, in *PL* 9:680.

103. Ambrose (dubia), *De Sacramentis* (*On the Sacraments*) 1, 4, in *PL* 16:420; 4, 3, in *PL* 16:438, cf. *PL* 16:421. Ch. 4 is intensely invidious.

104. Jerome, *Letters* 46, in *PL* 22:486.

105. Chrysostom, *In Epistolam ad Hebraeos* (*On the Epistle to the Hebrews*) 12, 32, in *PG* 63:221.

106. Chrysostom, *De Sanctis Martyribus* (*On the Holy Martyrs*) 1, in *PG* 50:645-56; cf. 582. A favorite theme with Chrysostom.

107. Chrysostom, *De Sacerdotio* (*On the Priesthood*) 3, 4, in *PG* 48:642. C. Seltmann in his edition (Münster, 1887), 83–84, raises the knotty question of just how *literal* all this is supposed to be.

108. Methodius, *Convivium Decem Virginum* (*Banquet of the Ten Virgins*) 7, in *PG* 18:109.

109. "Ibi enim stamus mentis oculos figimus . . . humana mens . . . superiora illa atque coelestia utcunque in aenigmate conspicit," Garner, *On the Temple* VIII, 8, 7, in *PL* 193:397; cf. *PL* 193:936; Zeno, *Tractate* II, 63, in *PL* 11:518–19; Eusebius, *HE* X, 4, *passim*, in *PG* 20:848–80.

110. Friedrich August Müller, *Der Islam im Morgen- und Abendland*, 2 vols. (Berlin: Grote, 1885–87), 1:285; Raisin, *Gentile Reactions to Jewish Ideals*, 370.

111. Eutychius, *Annales* (*Annals*) 287–92, in *PG* 111:1100.

112. Gustav E. von Grunebaum, *Muhammadan Festivals* (New York: Schuman, 1951), 20.

113. "If Islam substituted the Kibla of Mecca for that of Jerusalem, on the other hand it renders the greatest honor to the site of the temple . . . and pure monotheism rebuilt its fortress on Mt. Moriah," wrote Renan, quoted in Raisin, *Gentile Reactions to Jewish Ideals*, 389.

114. Adam Mez, *Renaissance des Islams* (Heidelberg: Winter, 1903), 302. Cf. English translation by S. Bukhish (London: Luzac, 1937).

115. Mez, *Renaissance des Islams*, 302–3.

116. Müller, *Der Islam im Morgen- und Abendland* 1:285.

117. Just as the Christians turned the temple site into a *sterquilinium* (note 161 below), so the Moslems just as childishly called the Holy Sepulchre church not *al-qiyāmatu*, but *al-qumāmatu*, i.e., *sterquilinium!* E. Rosenmüller, ed., *Idrīsī's Syria* (Leipzig: Sumtibus Io Ambros Barthii, 1828), 10, n. 36. Though at the end of the 10th century Christians still execrated the temple site, Eutychius, *Annals* 287–92, in *PG* 111:1100, in the 13th a friend of the sultan was rudely barred from the place, being told: "such things are not revealed to such as you. Do not insult our Law!" *mōthala hādhahu-l-'umūra la takhfaya ᶜalā 'amthālika. Lā tabṭul nāmūsanā!* etc., Qazwīnī, *Cosmography*, ed. Ferdinand Wüstenfeld, 2 vols. (Göttingen: Dieterich, 1848), 2:109.

118. Fulcher, *Historia Hierosolymitana* I, 26, 9, with editorial discussion by Heinrich Hagenmeyer in his ed. (Heidelberg: Winter, 1913), 290–91.

119. Müller, *Der Islam im Morgen- und Abendland* 2:135.

120. Guibert, *Gesta Dei per Francos* (*Acts of God through the Franks*) 7, 10, in *PL* 156:795; Fulcher, *History Hierosolymitana* I, 27, 12–13. See note 133 below. For the Moslem reaction, Müller, *Der Islam im Morgen- und Abendland* 2:157.

121. Athanasius, *Questions to Duke Antiochus* 44, in *PG* 28:625.

122. Aetheria (Silvia), *Peregrinatio ad Loca Sancta* (*Pilgrimage to Holy Places*), 4th ed. (Heidelberg: Heraeus, 1939), 48:1–2; 49:1; 37:3.

123. Ibid., 26.

124. She compares the pilgrims to those who anciently came to Jerusalem to hear the law, ibid., 27:1, 6, and notes that fasting was forbidden on the temple mount and there only, ibid., 44:1, rather than at New Testament shrines. An even earlier pilgrim, Melito of Sardis, describes a strictly Old Testament pilgrimage to the East, *Fragmentum* (*Fragment*), in *PG* 5:1216.

125. Photius, *Against the Manichaeans* 2, 11, in *PG* 102:109; cf. Raisin, *Gentile Reactions to Jewish Ideals*, 31.

126. Edwyn Hoskyn and F. Davey, *The Fourth Gospel* 1:202–3; Phythian-Adams, *The People and the Presence*, 74.

127. H. B. Swete, quoted by Barrett, "The Eschatology of the Epistle to the Hebrews," 383. Revelation 21:21–27.

128. Titus Tobler, *Dr. Titus Toblers zwei Bücher Topographie von Jerusalem*, 2 vols. (Berlin: Reimer, 1853–54), 1:540ff. Origen, *Commentary on John* 10, 22, in *PG* 14:377–78, comments on the "inconsistency and confusion" of the records. Cf. Socrates, *HE* I, 17, in *PG* 67:117–21; Sozomen, *Ecclesiastical History* (*HE*) II, 1, in *PG* 67:929–33; Eusebius, *On the Life of Constantine* III, 28, in *PG* 20:1088–89. Even the holy sites of Galilee had been transported to Jerusalem at an early time, Brandon, *The Fall of Jerusalem and the Christian Church*, 197–98.

129. "The place where the dream of Jacob occurred is the place where Adam was created, namely, the place of the future Temple and the center of the earth," A. Altmann, "The Gnostic Background of the Rabbinic Adam Legends," *Jewish Quarterly Review* 35 (1945): 390–91. But "the Midrash also teaches . . . that Adam dwelt on Mt. Moriah and there 'returned to the earth from which he was taken,' " Robert Eisler, *Iesous Basileus ou Basileusas*, 2 vols. (Heidelberg: Winter, 1930), 1:523. Yet the place where Adam sleeps is Golgotha, the foot of the cross resting on his skull, Epiphanius, *Adversus Haereses* (*Against Heresies*) II, 1, 4–5, in *PG* 41:844, and many others. Christian and Moslem traditions place the Holy of Holies on the rock on which Abraham offered Isaac, Rupert, *Liber Genesis* (*Commentary on Genesis*) 6, 28–29, in *PL* 167:427–28, making it the logical spot for the

428 MORMONISM AND EARLY CHRISTIANITY

supreme culminating sacrifice of the cross. Cf. Aquinas, *Summa Theologica*, Quaestio cii, Articulus iv. 2: "Et tunc primo aedificatum fuit templum, in loco quem designaverat Abraham . . . ad immolandum," etc. Both Fulcher and Saewulf report as eyewitnesses that the original Ark of the Covenant reposed directly in the center of the Church of the Holy Sepulchre; cited by Hagenmeyer, in Fulcher, *History Hierosolymitana*, 287-88. The Arabic writers are equally confusing: Qazwīnī, *Cosmography* 2:107-9; Ibn Ajjās, *Geography*, in F. Arnold, *Chrestomathia Arabica*, 2 vols. (Halle: Pfeffer, 1853), 1:64-66; Idrīsī, *Syria* 9-12; Ibn Batuta, *Riḥla* (Cario, 1938) 1:33-34.

130. See William Simpson, "The Middle of the World, in the Holy Sepulchre," *Palestine Exploration Fund Quarterly* (1888), 260-63; C. M. Watson, "The Traditional Sites on Sion," *Palestine Exploration Fund Quarterly.* (1910), 209; C. M. Watson, tr., "Commemoratorium de casis dei vel monasteriis," in *Palestine Exploration Fund Quarterly* (1913), pl. iii, opp. p. 28. The seal of King Baldwin of Jerusalem shows the two buildings as almost identical domes, side by side within a single walled enclosure.

131. Fulcher, *History Hierosolymitana* I, 30, 4.

132. "It was another, a new creation!" cries Raimundus de Angiles, *Historia Francorum qui ceperunt Hierusalem* (Philadelphia: American Philosophical Society, 1968), 330-31; cited by Hagenmeyer, in Fulcher, *History Hierosolymitana* I, 30, 4.

133. J. Casper Barth (1720), quoted by Hagenmeyer, in Fulcher, *History Hierosolymitana*, 287.

134. The materials are given and discussed in Hagenmeyer's edition of Fulcher, *History Hierosolymitana*, 285-87, 304-6.

135. The treaty of 1229 allowed the Christians possession of the sepulchre, while the Moslems retained the *Templum Domini*, i.e., the distinction was clearly preserved, Charles Diehl, *Le Monde oriental de 395 à 1081*, vol. 3 of *Histoire du Moyen Age* (Paris: Presses Universitaire de France 1944), 2:462.

136. See the long article in the *Enciclopedia Universal Ilustrada* (Madrid: Espasa-Calpe, 1928) 60:727-41. The rules of the order closely resemble those of some Jewish sectaries; cf. Henry Daniel-Rops, *L'eglise de la cathédrale et de la croisade* (Paris: Fayard, 1952), 145, 718, 720, 730; cf. English translation by John Warrington, *Cathedral and Crusade* (New York: Dutton, 1957). It is not surprising that the order was accused of heresy, since it "urged the emigration of converts to Palestine to help prophecy to become fulfilled," E. Kautzsch, cited by E. Kraeling, *The Old Testament Since the Reformation* (New York: Harper, 1955), 133.

137. See, for instance, Duchesne, *Origines du culte chrétien*, 45 (=5th ed., 47). Cf. John Ward, "The Fall of the Templars," *Journal of Religious History* 13 (1984): 92–113, for an overview of recent research.

138. S. Kraus, "The Jews in the Works of the Church Fathers," *Jewish Quarterly Review* 6 (1893–94): 238, who paraphrases Rufinus, *Invectio (Attack)* 1, 5 and 2, 589: "If a few Jews were to institute new rites, the Church would have to follow suit and immediately adopt them."

139. W. Oesterly and T. Robinson, *An Introduction to the Books of the Old Testament* (New York: Macmillan, 1934), 194; cf. Louis Finkelstein, "The Origin of the Synagogue," *Proceedings of the American Academy for Jewish Research* 3 (1930): 49–59.

140. Hilary, *Treatise on the Psalms* 137, in *PL* 9:787. Symeon, *Expositio de Divino Templo (Exposition on the Holy Temple)* 2, in *PG* 155:701, describes the mass in terms of the temple. Malachi 1:11, the chief scriptural support for the mass, Gustav Oehler, *Theology of the Old Testament*, 519–20, deals only with the temple. Daniel-Rops, *L'eglise de la cathédrale et de la croisade*, 542–43, points out that the round churches of Europe, revived at the time of the Crusades, were direct imitations of the temple at Jerusalem.

141. Chrysostom, *In Epistolam II ad Corinthios Homilia (Homily on the Second Epistle to the Corinthians)* 2, 2, in *PG* 61:476; Epiphanius, *Against Heresies* 61, 8, in *PG* 41:1049.

142. Rupert, "De Azymo" ("On Unleavened Bread"), in *De Divinis Officiis (On Divine Duties)* II, 22, in *PL* 170:48–51; cf. Epiphanius, *Against Heresies* 30, 16, in *PG* 41:432. Cf. Leo, *Discourse* 92, in *PL* 54:453.

143. Caspar Sagittarius, in Johannes G. Graevius, ed., *Thesaurus Antiquitatum Romanarum* (Traject. ad Rhenum: Franciscus Halman, 1697) 6:465, 492–93, noting that the Christian veils "procul dubio imitati sunt morem in templo Salomonis."

144. The place of the altar is a *terribilis locus*, Rupert, *Commentary on Genesis* 7, 23–24, in *PL* 167:468–69, "inaccessible and terrible," Symeon, *Dialogus contra Haereses (Dialogue against Heresies)* 21, in *PG* 155:108; and *Exposition on the Holy Temple* 2, in *PG* 155:701, citing the case of Ambrose in the West, who barred even the emperor "both from the naos and the altar." Cf. Gregorius Nazianzenus, *Carminum Liber I, Theologica Sectio II, Poemata Moralia (Moral Poems)* 34, 220–65, in *PG* 37:961; Pachymeros, *De Andronico Palaelogo (On Andronicus Palaelogus)* 1, 5, in *PG* 144:25. In the East only the emperor could enter the tabernacle and only at

Easter and his coronation, Codinus, *De Officiis Constantinopolitanis* (*On the Offices at Constantinople*) 17, in *PG* 157:109-10; cf. Cantacusenus, *Historia* (*History*) 1, 41, in *PG* 153:280-81; Ivo, *Sermo* (*Discourse*) 4, in *PL* 162:532-33. At Constantinople and the Vatican there was even a mark on the pavement, as there had been in the temple court of Jerusalem, to show the point beyond which the vulgar might not pass, Constantine Porphyrogenitus, *De Caeremoniis Aulae Byzantinae* (*On the Ritual of the Byzantine Court*) 1, 10, in *PG* 112:161, see especially the editor's note on this.

145. Clement of Alexandria, *Stromata* VII, 7, in *PG* 9:461, with long note by le Nourry, in *PG* 9:462-63; Hippolytus, *Fragmenta in Jeremiam* (*On Jeremiah*), in *PG* 10:632. Other and later sources given by Gronovius, in Graevius, *Thesaurus Antiquitatum Romanarum* 7:160.

146. Ivo, *Discourse* 4, in *PL* 162:527-35.

147. William K. L. Clarke, *Liturgy and Worship* (New York: Macmillan, 1932), 55-59.

148. Rabanus Maurus, *Expositio super Jeremiam* (*Exposition on Jeremiah*) 4, 7, in *PL* 111:858.

149. Origen, *Commentaria in Epistolam Pauli ad Romanos* (*Commentary on the Epistle to the Romans*) 6, 7, in *PG* 14:1073; Zeno, *Tractate* II, 66, in *PL* 11:520-21; Methodius, *Banquet of the Ten Virgins* 5, 9, 1, in *PG* 18:177; Paulinus of Nola, *Poema* (*Poem*) 34, 337-48, in *PL* 61:683. With the fall of the temple "a stupor seems to have settled upon the Jews," Brandon, *The Fall of Jerusalem and the Christian Church*, 165.

150. Athanasius, *Oratio de Incarnatione Verbi Dei* (*Oration on the Incarnation of the Word*) 40, in *PG* 25:165.

151. For Eusebius the mere statement that Jerusalem will be trodden under foot "shows that the temple shall never rise again"; he admits that the text adds "*until* the time of the Gentiles be fulfilled," but when is that? Eusebius has the answer: It means *never!* *Theophania* (*Theophany*) 8, in *PG* 24:649-50. Athanasius is even more naive: We know [he argues] that Christ was a true Prophet, because Jerusalem will never rise again. And how do we know that? Because since all has been fulfilled in the coming of the true Prophet, it *cannot* rise again! Athanasius, *Oration on the Incarnation of the Word* 39, in *PG* 25:164-65. Jerome, *Commentary on Isaiah* 1, 5, in *PL* 24:29-30, insists that the words "Non est in eo sanitas" (Isaiah 1:6) refer to the time of Titus and absolutely prove that the temple can never be restored. Even more far-fetched is Eusebius's demonstration from the

30 pieces of silver, *Demonstratio Evangelica (Proof for the Gospel)* 10, in *PG* 22:745.

152. Origen, *Contra Celsum (Against Celsus)* IV, 22, in *PG* 11:1056-57: *Tharrountes d' eroumen, hoti oud' apokatastathēsontai.* The same argument is employed by Jerome, *Commentary on Isaiah* 1, 1, in *PL* 24:20-22; and Hippolytus, *Fragmenta in Danielem (On Daniel)* 8-22, in *PG* 10:648-55.

153. Chrysostom, *Against the Jews and the Gentiles that Christ is God* 5, in *PG* 48:884, 889, 896; cf. Origen, *Against Celsus* IV, 22, in *PG* 11:1057, with a long discussion in *PG* 11:1056-60, telling how Grotius developed the argument. Hengstenberg, *Christology of the Old Testament* 3:291-92, makes this the official Protestant party line; cf. Farrar, *The Life of Christ* 2:255-56: "Neither Hadrian nor Julian, nor any other, were able to build upon its site," etc.

154. So Strahan, "Temple," 557.

155. Marcel Simon, *Verus Israel* (Paris: De Boccard, 1964), 118-20, noting, p. 120, that in spite of all efforts to explain it away the danger remains real; cf. tr. McKeating (Oxford, 1986), 91ff.

156. Raisin, *Gentile Reactions to Jewish Ideals*, 370. On the usefulness of pagan ruins as object lessons, Socrates, *HE* I, 16, in *PG* 67:116-17.

157. Kraus, "The Jews in the Works of the Church Fathers," 227.

158. Jerome, *Commentary on Isaiah* 17, 64, in *PL* 24:650, citing Josephus, *Antiquities of the Jews* VI, 12, to prove that the temple will never return. Theodoret, *Explanation of Ezekiel* 48, in *PG* 81:1252-53 and 1760; and Chrysostom, *Against the Jews and the Gentiles that Christ is God* 5, in *PG* 48:884, 889, 896, express the same impatience. See Kraus, "The Jews in the Works of the Church Fathers," 90-91, 240-45, for others.

159. Theophylactus, *Commentary on the Gospel of Mark* 13, 1-4, in *PG* 123:633: *hōste peirōntai deixai pseudē ton Christon.*

160. The story is fully treated by M. Adler, "The Emperor Julian and the Jews," *Jewish Quarterly Review*, orig. ser., 5 (1893): 615-51.

161. Rufinus, *HE* 1, 37, in *PL* 21:505; Theodoret, *HE* 3, 15, in *PG* 82:1112.

162. So Theodoret, *HE* 3, 15, in *PG* 82:1112; Philostorgius, *HE* VII, 14, in *PG* 65:552.

163. Rufinus, *HE* 1, 37, in *PL* 21:505; Socrates, *HE* III, 20, in *PG* 67:428-32.

164. Adler, "The Emperor Julian and the Jews," 649. On the temple as a test case, Chrysostom, *Against the Jews and the Gentiles that Christ is God* 5, 3, in *PG* 48:888; 6, 4, in *PG* 48:909.

165. A blunt and recent statement is that of David M. Stanley, "Kingdom to Church," *Theological Studies* 16 (1955): 26: "the definitive coming of the Church . . . terminates the existence of the Temple."

166. Johannes Hempel, *Die althebräische Literatur und ihr hellenistisch-jüdisches Nachleben* (Potsdam: Athenaion, 1930), 92. A significant point overlooked by commentators.

167. Adler, "The Emperor Julian and the Jews," 637–51.

168. Ferdinand Prat, *Jesus Christ*, 2 vols. (Milwaukee: Bruce, 1950), 2:230, hails the fire-ball story as conclusive proof that Jesus' prophecy of "not one stone upon another . . . has been fulfilled to the letter." The learned le Nourry argues that while the destruction of Jewish and pagan temples by fire, especially lightning, is a sure sign of divine wrath, a like fate suffered by Christian buildings is without significance, since Christians do not believe that God dwells in houses made with hands: Note in *PG* 9:899–901.

169. Athanasius, *Historia Arianorum ad Monachos (Arian History)* 71, in *PG* 25:777: "a persecution, a prelude and a preparation *(prooimion de kai paraskeuē)* for the Antichrist." Cf. ibid., 74, in *PG* 25:781; 79, in *PG* 25:789.

170. Quote from Irenaeus, *Against Heresies* V, 25, in *PG* 7:1189. Cyril of Jerusalem says it is a dreadful thing to think of, but cannot for that reason be denied, *Catechesis XV. de Secundo Christi Adventu (Catechetical Lectures on the Second Coming of Christ)* 15, in *PG* 33:889–92.

171. Basil, *Commentarius in Isaiam Prophetam (Commentary on Isaiah)* 3, 110, in *PG* 30:296, who for the rest is very partial to a spiritual and intellectual temple, *PG* 30:289, 233.

172. See notes 165–70 above. In one attempt the workers unearthed a stone bearing the inscription: In the beginning was the Word. "This was proof positive that it is vain ever to try to rebuild [Jerusalem]— evidence of a divine and irrevocable decree that the Temple has vanished forever!" Philostorgius, *Ecclesiastica Historia (Ecclesiastical History)* 7, 14, in *PG* 65:552–53.

173. Even Eusebius had his doubts and wondered if the Montanists might be right, W. Völker, "Von welchen Tendenzen liess sich Eusebius bei Abfassung seiner 'Kirchengeschichte' leiten?" *Vigiliae Christianae* 4 (1950): 170.

174. Well expressed in Simon, *Verus Israel*, 118–24.

175. See Helen Rosenau, "The Synagogue and the Diaspora," *Palestine Exploration Fund Quarterly* (1937), 200.

176. Jerome, *Commentary on Isaiah* 17, 40, in *PL* 24:593–94.

177. See our discussions, Hugh W. Nibley, "The Unsolved Loyalty Problem: Our Western Heritage," *Western Political Quarterly* 6 (1953): 652–55; and "Victoriosa Loquacitas," *Western Speech* 20 (1956): 68–72.

178. Heinrich Bornkamm, *Grundriss zum Studium der Kirchengeschichte* (Gütersloh: Bertelsmann, 1949), 113–14.

179. While Fernand Cabrol, *Les origines liturgiques* (Paris: Letouzey et Ané, 1906), 48–56, strenuously denies that "toute cette splendeur dont le culte fut entouré" was of any but the purest Hebraic origin, such eminent Catholic authorities as Joseph Lechner and Ludwig Eisenhofer, *Liturgik des römischen Ritus* (Freiburg: Herder, 1953), 5–6, think otherwise.

180. Thomas Livius, *St. Peter Bishop of Rome* (London: Burns & Oates, 1888), while boasting (521) that his church alone in Christendom possesses the Holy City, just like the Jews and the Moslems, never mentions the temple, but always puts the synagogue in its place, e.g., "The divinely appointed Aaronical high-priesthood . . . was in the Synagogue the fountainhead of all other priesthood" (523), "The once-favored Synagogue . . . had become a widow . . . without altar or sacrifice" (527). Only once does he let slip the ugly little word, and that in a footnote (527), but it is enough to show that he knows better and is deliberately avoiding the embarrassing word, as Christian scholars consistently do.

181. So Gustaf Wingren, "Weg, Wanderung und verwandte Begriffe," *Studia Theologica* 3 (1951): 111–12.

182. "Le Temple est mort à jamais" is the cry of M. Simon, "Retour du Christ et reconstruction du temple dans la pensée chrétienne primitive," in *Aux sources de la tradition chrétienne: Mélanges offerts à M. Maurice Goguel* (Neuchatel: Delachaux et Niestlé, 1950), 252; cf. 253, 257. An interesting development is the admission that the original Christians were devoted to the temple, coupled with a rebuke for their foolishness; so Bultmann, *Theologie des Neuen Testaments* 1:54, 57, cf. Eng. tr., 53, 57; O'Brien, *The Life of Christ*, 418. Cf. Charles Briggs, *Messianic Prophecy* (New York: Scribner, 1891), 289.

183. Charles H. Dodd, *The Interpretation of the Fourth Gospel* (Cambridge: Cambridge University Press, 1953), 300–1; Barrett, "The Eschatology of the Epistle to the Hebrews," 374–76; Burrows, *Outline of Biblical Theology*, 276. Even Farrar was very cautious in condemning the temple, *The Life of Christ* 1:192–93. W. J. Phythian-Adams's whole book, *The People and the Presence*, belongs in this hesitant and compromising group.

184. J. F. Walvoord, "The Doctrine of the Millennium," *Biblioteca Sacra* 115 (1958): 106–8. "The entire sacrificial system of the Old Testament, while perhaps incongruous with western civilization aesthetics, was nevertheless commanded by God himself. . . . If a literal view of the temple and sacrifices be allowed, it provides a more intimate view of worship in the millennium than might otherwise be afforded," ibid., 107–8.

Key to Abbreviations

1QS: The Manual of Discipline. English translations may be found in Theodor H. Gaster, *The Dead Sea Scriptures* (New York: Doublday, 1956), 39–60, and in Geze Vermes, *The Dead Sea Scrolls in English* (Harmondsworth: Penguin, 1975), 72–94

ANT: Montague R. James, *The Apocryphal New Testament* (Oxford: Clarendon, 1975)

DA: J.-P. Migne, ed., *Dictionnaire des apocryphes*, 2 vols. 23–24 of *Troisieme et dernière encyclopédie théologique* (Paris: Migne, 1856–58)

DACL: Fernand Cabrol, and Henri Leclerq ed., *Dictionnaire d'archéologie chrétienne et de liturgie* (Paris: Letouzey et Ané, 1907)

HE: Historia Ecclesiastica

NA: Edgar Henneck, *Neutestamentliche Apokryphen*, ed. Wilhelm Schneemelcher, 2 vols. (Tübingen: Mohr, 1959–64)

NHLE: James M. Robinson, ed., *The Nag Hammadi Library in English* (New York: Harper & Row, 1977)

NTA: Edgar Hennecke, *New Testament Apocrypha*, ed. Wilhelm Schneemelcher and Robert McL. Wilson, 2 vols. (Philadelphia: Westminister, 1963—65)

OTP: James H. Charlesworth, ed., *The Old Testament Pseudepigrapha*, 2 vols. (New York: Doubleday, 1983 and 1985)

PG: J.-P. Migne, ed., *Patrologiae Graecae*, 161 vols.
         (Paris: Migne, 1857–)

PL: J.-P. Migne, *Patrologiae Latinae*, 221 vols. (Paris:
         Migne, 1879–)

PO: R. Graffin and F. Nau, eds., *Patrologia Orientalis*
         (Paris: Firmin-Didot, 1907–)

RE: Pauly-Wissow, *Realencyclopädie der classischen
         Altertumswissenschaft* (Stuttgart: Metzler, 1893–)

TB: The Babylonian Talmud

TU: *Texte und Untersuchungen zur Geschichte der
         altchristlichen Literatur*

ZNTW: *Zeitschrift für die neutestamentliche Wissenschaft*

Scripture References

Genesis
11:4, p. 359
18, p. 241
22:17, pp. 151, 239
24:60, p. 151

Deuteronomy
14:22–27, p. 379
26:12–14, p. 379

Judges
5:8, p. 151

1 Kings
8:37, p. 151

2 Chronicles
6:18, p. 416

Psalms
1, p. 35
24:7, p. 75
44:21, p. 151
54:2, p. 58
55:1, p. 59
107:16, p. 151
147:13, p. 151
150, p. 356

Isaiah
45:1, p. 150
66:1, p. 392

Jeremiah
4:10, p. 220
23:24, p. 151
49:10, p. 151

Ezekiel
28:2, p. 151

Haggai
2:9, p. 400

Matthew
6:13, p. 56
7:6,8, p. 30
7:21, p. 272
7:22, p. 204
7:6–7, p. 159
8:28–29, p. 267
8:34, p. 268
9:15, pp. 194, 270
10, p. 278
10:16, p. 274
10:16–22, 28, p. 194
10:23, p. 195
10:24–25, p. 194
10:25, p. 273
11:7, p. 54
11:10, p. 54
11:12, p. 267
11:12, 14–19, p. 54
11:14–15, 25–28, p. 159
11:16, p. 55
11:16–17, pp. 54, 59
11:17, p. 88
11:23–24, p. 292
12:26–29, p. 151
13:9–17, p. 198
13:10–15, p. 152
13:11–16, p. 159
13:13–30, p. 195
13:15, p. 270
13:23, p. 152
13:24, 25–30, 37–40, 43,
    p. 266
13:24–30, 38, p. 195
13:30, 39–43, p. 195
13:34–36, p. 159
14:2, p. 268

15:9, p. 271
15:16, p. 153
16:13–17, p. 149
16:17–19, pp. 34, 149
16:18, pp. 150, 264
16:19, p. 152
16:20–21, p. 158
16:24, 25, p. 279
16:24–26, p. 195
17:1–13, p. 152
17:5–6, p. 152
17:9, p. 158
17:9–13, p. 152
17:11–12, p. 288
17:12, pp. 194, 267
19:11, p. 159
19:28, p. 275
21:37, 38, p. 267
21:37–39, p. 194
21:38, p. 195
22:16, p. 268
23:29, p. 196
23:29–33, p. 270
23:31–37, p. 194
23:34–35, p. 200
23:35–39, p. 194
23:37, pp. 265, 268
24:3, p. 159
24:5, p. 204
24:5, 6, 8, 13, p. 163
24:9, pp. 194, 420
24:9, 13, p. 274
24:14, pp. 195, 277, 290
24:23, pp. 264, 272
24:24, p. 281
25:41, p. 151
26:30, pp. 47, 63
27:25, p. 200
28:16, 19–20, p. 289

437

28:17, pp. 26, 153
28:20, pp. 195, 271

Mark
3:9, p. 194
3:23-27, p. 151
4:9-12, p. 159
4:10-13, p. 152
4:20, p. 152
6:5, p. 268
6:11, p. 278
8:27-30, p. 149
8:30-31, p. 158
8:34, 35, p. 279
9:2-13, p. 152
9:7, p. 152
9:9, p. 158
9:9-13, p. 152
9:32, p. 153
9:33-34, p. 159
9:39, p. 204
11:33, p. 159
12:6-8, p. 194
12:7, p. 195
12:9, p. 195
12:14, p. 268
13:6, p. 204
13:10, p. 195
13:13, pp. 194, 276
13:9-10, pp. 195, 290
13:9-13, p. 279
13:34-37, pp. 195, 273
14:26, pp. 47, 63
15:33, p. 58
16:8, 11-14, p. 26
16:14, p. 153
16:17, p. 230
16:19, p. 360
16:20, p. 290

Luke
2:47, p. 4
2:49, p. 415
2:52, p. 3
6:26, p. 294
8:9-10, p. 152
8:10, p. 159
8:15, p. 152
8:25, p. 153
9, p. 278
9:18-21, p. 149

9:21, p. 150
9:21-22, p. 158
9:23, 24, p. 279
9:34, p. 152
9:36, p. 152
9:36, 43-45, p. 159
9:41, pp. 194, 270
9:45, p. 153
10:7, p. 278
10:10-11, p. 279
10:12, p. 278
10:15, p. 293
10:16, p. 194
10:18, p. 151
10:20, p. 275
10:21-23, p. 159
10:3, pp. 194, 274
10:3-4, p. 278
10:36, p. 158
11:1-2, p. 55
11:4, p. 56
11:18, p. 151
11:49-51, p. 200
11:51, p. 194
11:52, p. 160
12:22-34, p. 195
12:41, p. 159
13:16, p. 151
13:25, p. 270
13:25-27, p. 194
13:25-30, p. 196
14:34, p. 283
17:20-21, p. 160
17:22, p. 194
17:22-23, p. 271
17:25, p. 194
18:7, p. 207
18:8, p. 292
18:10, p. 382
18:34, pp. 153, 159
20:13, p. 267
20:14, p. 195
20:14, 16, p. 267
20:21, p. 268
21:8, pp. 204, 272
21:16, p. 284
21:16, 18, p. 275
21:17, p. 274
21:29-31, p. 291
21:32, p. 290
21:34, p. 288

22:31, p. 151
22:67-71, p. 159
24:11, 21-35, 21-43,
    p. 26
24:16, p. 153
24:25, 27, p. 153
24:25-27, 45, p. 12
24:39, p. 23
24:47-48, p. 279
28-36, p. 152

John
1:5, p. 272
1:5, 10-11, p. 194
1:10-11, p. 269
1:11-12, p. 159
2:16, p. 414
2:22-24, p. 153
3:5, p. 237
3:11, p. 269
3:11-12, p. 159
3:11-12, 19, 32, p. 194
3:12, p. 159
3:14, p. 102
3:19, p. 272
3:32, p. 269
3:32, p. 15
5:19, p. 151
5:22, p. 269
5:38, 40-47, p. 194
5:42, p. 268
6:36, p. 269
6:36, 60-67, p. 153
6:60-66, p. 159
7:7, p. 268
7:33-34, p. 271
7:5, p. 153
7:5, p. 269
7:7, p. 194
8:19, 23-24, 37-38,
    40-47, p. 194
8:21, p. 271
8:43-44, p. 159
8:43-47, p. 268
9:4, p. 164
9:4-5, p. 272
9:39, p. 269
10:24-27, p. 159
11:13, p. 153
12:16, p. 153
12:33-36, p. 194

12:34, p. 151
12:35–36, p. 272
12:38–41, p. 270
23:47–48, p. 269
13:33, pp. 194, 271
13:7, p. 153
14:4–6, p. 151
14:17, p. 269
14:26, p. 273
14:30, pp. 151, 194, 195, 270
15:18, p. 274
15:18–21, p. 194
15:20, p. 273
15:22, p. 200
15:22–25, p. 194
15:24, p. 269
16:1, 2, 33, p. 194
16:7, p. 273
16:8–15, p. 273
16:11, p. 151
16:12–18, 25, 29–30, p. 159
16:25–33, p. 153
16:33, p. 274
17:25, p. 195
18:36, p. 280
20:9, 25–29, p. 26
12:31, p. 151
14:30, p. 292
16:2, p. 276
16:12, p. 152
17:14, p. 194
17:25, p. 195
20:9, p. 159

Acts
1:3, p. 10
1:3, pp. 24, 153
1:7, p. 290
1:8, p. 279
1:9, pp. 23, 152
2:16–17, p. 290
2:16–17, 33, p. 195
3:13–15, p. 194
3:14–15, p. 277
3:15, p. 268
3:19, 21, p. 287
3:21, pp. 152, 288, 289
5:28, p. 200
7:52–53, p. 284

10:25–26, p. 278
10:41, pp. 152, 159
13:50, p. 277
14:22, p. 280
15:28, pp. 152, 159
16:25, p. 54
17:6, p. 200
17:15, p. 204
18:6, pp. 200, 277
19:2, p. 159
20:20, p. 159
20:31, p. 163
20:28, p. 282
20:29, pp. 171, 275, 292
20:29–31, p. 160
28:26, p. 277
28:26–27, pp. 159, 194
29–31, p. 283

Romans
1:16–32, p. 195
1:21–31, p. 195
2:16, p. 151
2:17–20, p. 159
2:20, p. 160
6:19, p. 159
8, p. 194
8:17, 280
11:30–34, p. 159
11:33, p. 159

1 Corinthians
1:17, p. 200
2:14, p. 159
3:1–3, p. 159
3:2, pp. 30, 152
3:10–21, p. 280
4:5, p. 278
4:8–18, p. 194
4:9, p. 194
4:9, 13, p. 274
4:9–13, p. 29
4:9–15, p. 160
5:5, p. 151
7:25, p. 159
7:29–31, pp. 163, 278
7:29–32, p. 200
8:7, p. 159
9:16, p. 200
12:8, p. 159
13:2, 8, p. 159

13:8, 13, pp. 160, 171
14:2, 9–10, p. 159
14:6, p. 159
14:22, p. 159
15:29, p. 156
15:34, p. 159

2 Corinthians
1:11, 13–14, p. 283
1:13, p. 159
2:14, p. 159
2:17, p. 286
3:3, p. 159
4:4, p. 151
4:8–9, p. 277
4:8–16, p. 195
4:14, 16, p. 274
4:14, 16–18, p. 277
6:4–5, p. 279
6:10, p. 293
11:3–4, p. 195
11:3–4, 13, p. 281
11:6, p. 159
12:2–5, p. 159

Galatians
1:6, p. 163
1:6–7, p. 281
2:2, p. 159
3:1, p. 287
3:1–4, p. 196
3:4, p. 283
4:11, 20, p. 283
4:18, p. 283

Ephesians
3:1–5, p. 159
3:19, p. 159

Philippians
3:1–21, p. 195
3:8, p. 159
3:8, 10, 11, 14, p. 275
3:8–10, p. 195
3:20–21, p. 275

Colossians
1:26, p. 159
2:2–3, p. 159

1 Thessalonians
5:10–11, p. 294

2 Thessalonians
2:1–3, p. 291
2:1–7, p. 163
2:7, p. 292
2:7–12, p. 195
2:8, p. 195
2:9, p. 292
2:9–12, p. 195
2:11, p. 160
2:22, p. 182

1 Timothy
4:1–3, pp. 195, 282
6:10, p. 282
6:20, pp. 159, 160
6:20–21, p. 195
6:21, p. 282

2 Timothy
1:15, pp. 163, 277
2:18, p. 282
2:19, p. 295
3:2–4, p. 288
3:5, 13, p. 288
4:2–4, p. 195
4:2–5, p. 286
4:3–4, pp. 160, 195, 282
4:3–4, 7–8, p. 163
4:6–8, p. 200
4:8, 16, p. 275

Hebrews
3:6, p. 280
5:11–63, p. 34
5:12, p. 152
6:4–6, p. 287
5:12–13, p. 30
6:11, p. 195
6:11, 18, p. 280
8:5, p. 99
9:26–28, p. 289
10:25, p. 280
12:17, pp. 196, 271

James
5:6, p. 268
5:7–11, p. 152
5:10, p. 279

5:10–11, p. 195

1 Peter
1:4–6, 9, p. 195
1:4, 9, p. 279
1:5–6, 20, p. 162
1:5–7, 13, p. 293
1:6, 7, 24, p. 194
1:17, 24, p. 294
2:2, p. 159
2:11, p. 294
3:19, p. 150
4:1, p. 279
4:12–13, pp. 195, 294
4:12–14, p. 195
4:6–7, p. 162
4:7, pp. 152, 288
4:7, 12, p. 162
5:1, p. 195
5:6, 10, p. 294
5:8, p. 195

2 Peter
1:3, p. 289
2:1–22, p. 195
2:4–22, pp. 162, 287
3:3–9, p. 291
3:16, 159, 286
4:4–12, p. 162

1 John
2:13, p. 151
2:15–17, p. 294
2:18, pp. 152, 163, 292
2:19, p. 286
3:1, p. 195
3:13, p. 294
4:6, p. 294
5:19, p. 294

2 John
1:12, p. 159

Jude
1:5–19, p. 162
4–11, 16–19, p. 195
5–11, p. 287

1 Nephi
1:8, p. 53
1:8, p. 73

3 Nephi
9:22, p. 56
11:37–38, p. 56
13:9–13, p. 56

Moses
1:2, 9, p. 72
7:3, p. 72
7:41, p. 59
7:59, p. 73

Abraham
3:23, p. 70

1 Clement
p. 65

1 Enoch
1:2, p. 30
6:7, 44, p. 36
20:2, p. 151
48:2–6, p. 35
62:7, p. 35
65:2, p. 89
69:11, p. 36
89:10–27, p. 28
89:68–71, p. 28
89:69, 75–77, p. 28
89:75, p. 28

1 Jeu
pp. 56–57
10, p. 92
10–11, p. 91

1 Maccabees
1:56–57, 63, p. 316

2 Baruch
15:8, 16, p. 35
19:1, p. 35
21:13, 16, p. 35
27–30, p. 28
29:2–3, p. 37
48:32–43, p. 28
70, p. 28
70:7, p. 37
30:1, p. 149
54:15, p. 36
55:2–8, p. 28

69:2–4, 75, p. 28
85:15, p. 149

2 Enoch
18, p. 36
21–22, p. 37
22:8, p. 38
30:14–15, p. 37
31:4, p. 36
34, p. 28
56:2, p. 37
61:2, p. 34

2 Jeu
pp. 51, 63–64
54, pp. 87, 90
54–55, p. 91

3 Baruch
15:1–2, p. 37

3 Enoch
pp. 65, 68, 71
39, pp. 93, 94
56, p. 198
66–67, p. 198
89, p. 198

4 Esdras
4:35–36, p. 150
7:75–99, p. 150

4 Ezra
5:1–13, p. 28
5:28–40, p. 28
6:59, p. 28
7:46, p. 28
7:57–61, p. 37
7:72, p. 36
8:1–3, 14–15, p. 28
8:55–56, p. 36
9:1–13, p. 28
9:10–11, p. 36
9:18, p. 35
10:1–54, p. 28
14:6, p. 31
14:44–46, p. 30

4 Maccabees
8, p. 41

Acts of John
pp. 45–46, 48, 52–55
1:43, p. 90
88, p. 89

Acts of Paul
p. 40

Acts of Peter
3:1, p. 40

Acts of Philip
p. 38
20, 148, p. 40

Acts of Thomas
1, p. 26
6–7, p. 38
14, p. 39
27, p. 37
32–33, 44–45, p. 36
36, p. 31

Apocalypse of Abraham
12, p. 90
12:8–9, p. 89
12:8–10, p. 91
17:11–17, p. 89

Apocalypse of Paul
p. 34

Apocalypse of Peter
p. 25
17, p. 38

Apocalypse of Thomas
p. 25

Apocryphon of James
1:8–25, p. 30
2:19–26, p. 25
2:33–39, p. 30
4:27–5:6, p. 36
5:28–16:11, p. 28
8:1–4, p. 25
11:35–12:17, p. 25

Apocryphon of Thomas
1, p. 28

Ascension of Isaiah
3:19–4:5, p. 28
4:15–17, p. 92
4:16, p. 38
11:40, p. 38

Coptic Gnostic Writing
p. 58

Didaché
10:5, p. 197
16, p. 195
16:3, p. 198
16:3–8, p. 163
16:4, p. 420

Epistle of the Apostles
13–14, 19, p. 34
19 (30), 21 (32), 25 (36),
  p. 25
36–45, p. 28

Gospel of Bartholomew
p. 49
4–5, 66–68, p. 30

Gospel of Nicodemus
15, p. 151

Gospel of Philip
102:29–31, p. 36
105:32–106:10, p. 30
113:1–26, p. 39
124:32–36, p. 35
133:17–18, p. 34

Gospel of Thomas
80:10, p. 30
81:10–14, p. 30
81:14–17, p. 26
85:25–35, p. 39
87:10–17, p. 31
88:16–18, p. 30
90:5–7, p. 34
91:34–92:1, p. 30
94:9–13, p. 30
96:30–34, p. 30
99:7–8, p. 26

Gospel of Truth
19:4-18, p. 30
21:3-6, p. 30
21:23-24, p. 34

**Hypostasis of the
Archons**
135:23-25, p. 35
140:3, p. 91

Jubilees
3:31, p. 38
10:5-9, p. 36
11:5, p. 36

Life of Adam and Eve
12-17, p. 93
42, p. 37

Manual of Discipline
pp. 67, 69
3:2-4, 13-25, p. 35
4:1-26, p. 35
10:1-3,9, p. 92

Odes of Solomon
4:8, p. 37
5, 6, p. 92
7:11-12, p. 36
8:16, p. 37
12:8, p. 317
17:8-15, p. 152
17:12, 15-16, p. 155
22:12, p. 150
22:9-10, p. 25
23:8-12, p. 37
38:9-15, p. 28
41:5-7, p. 38
42:14, 20, p. 155
42:15-20, p. 150

42:20, p. 37

Psalm of Thomas
p. 35
1:17-37, p. 36
3:5-8, p. 36
9:7-16, p. 36

Serekh Scroll
8:12-16, p. 89

Shepherd of Hermas
p. 151

Sibylline Oracles
8:310-11, p. 154

Sirach
24:32, p. 155

Testament in Galilee
1:3-6, p. 28
1:42-43, 56, p. 28
51, 54, 56, p. 28

Testament of Benjamin
9, p. 420

Testament of Hezekiah
2:38-4:18, p. 198

Testament of Job
pp. 60-61
1:1-5, p. 90
24:6-8, p. 90
28:7, p. 90
33:1-9, p. 90
36:1-6, p. 90
38:5, p. 63
38:86, p. 90

40:1-3, p. 63
40:2, p. 90
43:1-17, 112, p. 90
43:14, p. 63
44:1, p. 90
46:1-5, 8, 9, p. 90
47:3-12, p. 90
48:1-8, p. 90
49:1-3, p. 90
50:1-3, p. 90

Testament of Levi
14-18, p. 420

Testament of Moses
5:1-6, p. 28
12:9, p. 37

Testament of Naphtali
4, p. 420

**Testement of Our Lord
Jesus Christ**
pp. 47-48
1:08, p. 37
1:13, p. 35
1:23, p. 38
2:9, p. 37
8, pp. 28, 29

**Testament of the XII
Apostles**
p. 55

The Pearl
48-49, 80-85, p. 37

Tobit
12:7, p. 47

Index

Abraham, sacrifice of, as a theme in the early Christian prayer circle, 64

Acts of John, example of the early Christian prayer circle in, 45–46, 52

Adam, sacrifice of, as a theme in the early Christian prayer circle, 60

Albertus Magnus on baptism, 124

Ambrose on baptism for the dead, 126

Anselm on the degrees of glory, 117–18

Apocrypha: stories of Jesus, 4; and the Forty-Day mission of Christ, 20–22; and the early Christian prayer circle, 45

Apostles: on salvation for the dead, 103–5; mission of, in early Christianity, 273–79

Apostolic Fathers and the fall of the Church, 172–73

Augustine: on the early Christian prayer circle, 46–47, 79; on unbaptized children, 141–42

Authority in Christian documents, 233–45

Baptism: for the dead, disappearance of doctrine of, 135–49; as a temple rite, 363–64

Barbarians in Jerusalem, 327–28

Bible and censorship, 223, 224–26

Book of Breathings and the early Christian prayer circle, 83

Bultmann, Rudolf, on eschatology, 307–11

Capra, Fritjof, on the cosmic dance, 79–82

Catholicism: and the censorship of writings, 243; and the apostasy of early Christianity, 284–85

Censorship in church history, 223–31

Charlemagne and Jerusalem, 329–30

China and the use of prayer circles, 73

Chosroes in Jerusalem, 327–28

Christian prayer circle, early, 45–99

Christianity: and its apostasy, 136–37; and historiography, 264; and temples, 355–57, 391–414

Christianity, contemporary, and the Forty-Day mission of Christ, 10–22

Christianity, early: failure and apostasy of, 168–208, 279–300; survival of, 185–86; and eschatology, 200–313; permanence of, 209–11; and Jerusalem, 323–34

Chrysostom, St. John, on temples, 402–4

Church as the New Jerusalem, 325–26

Church history: veracity of, 211–15; evidences in, 215–17; and scholarship, 263

Circles, symbolism of, in the early Christian prayer circle, 66–67

Clement of Alexandria: on salvation for the dead, 102; on the degrees of glory, 117

Clergy and the censorship of documents, 244

Clothing, use of, in the early Christian prayer circle, 61–62

Cosmology: and the early Christian prayer circle, 79–82; and temples, 357–59

Creation drama and temples, 362, 380–81

Crusades: and Jerusalem, 330–31; and the temple, 408

Cyril of Jerusalem and the early Christian prayer circle, 48

Dancing, ritual, and the early Christian prayer circle, 52–55
Death and the gates of hell, 107–8
Deception in early Christianity, 181
Degrees of glory and salvation for the dead, 112, 117
Didaché on the apostasy of Christianity, 137
Diptychs, use of, in the early Christian prayer circle, 75–76

Education in early Christianity, 177
Eliade, Mircea, on temples, 376
Emendation in the documents of Christianity, 231–33
Epiphanius on baptism for the dead, 125–26
Eschatology: according to Early Christianity, 168–69; comparison of, to history, 190; and early Christianity, 300–313; types of, 301; parable of, 302–7

Fabrication in church history, 219–22
Forgery in church history, 220–22
Forty-Day mission, symbolism of, 11–12
Four as a symbolic number in the early Christian prayer circle, 65–66
Fu Hsi and the early Christian prayer circle, 74–75

Garments, use of, in the early Christian prayer circle, 61–62
Gates of hell, definition of, 105–7
Genealogy and the early Christian prayer circle, 78
Gestures in the early Christian prayer circle, 58–59
Gnosticism: and the Forty-Day mission of Christ, 14–15, 86; and the early Christian prayer circle, 45; on Christ's post-resurrection teachings, 114; on the mysteries of the gospel, 130–33; and the apostasy of Christianity, 139, 182–84
Gospel of Bartholomew, example of the early Christian prayer circle in, 49
Great Apostasy and early Christianity, 287–88

Greek Orthodox Church and ring dancing, 53

Hero-cults and the Forty-Day mission of Christ, 18
Historiography and church history, 263–64
History: comparison of, to eschatology, 190; as a control of the past, 217–23
Holy sepulchre as replacement for temple, 356–57, 406–7

Ignatius on salvation for the dead, 103
Initiation in temples, 363–64
Irenaeus: on salvation for the dead, 103; on the degrees of glory, 112
Israel, military victories of, in the 20th century, 334

Jerome on temples, 393
Jerusalem: in early Christianity, 323–34; and the temple, 405
Jesus Christ: fables and miracle stories about childhood of, 1–7; Forty-Day mission of, 10–22; secret teachings of, unknown to Christianity, 14; mission of, to the dead, 108–9, 114–21; post-resurrection teachings of, 113–14; and eschatological prophecies, 170–72
Jewish apocrypha and the Forty-Day mission of Christ, 15–16
Judaism and the temple today, 409–10

Kasr el-Wazz fragment and the early Christian prayer circle, 51–52, 55
Kerygma and the Forty-Day mission of Christ, 17–18

Languages: and the difficulty of translation, 255–58; and scholarship, 260–62
Leo (Pope) on temples, 402–4
Linguistics and the difficulty of translation, 257

Machinery and scholarship, 259–60
Marcionites and baptism of the dead, 129–30

Martyrdom in early Christianity,
178–80
Mary and the early Christian prayer
circle, 49–50
Masoretic text and censorship, 224–26
Meturgeman and history, 218
Miracle stories about the childhood of
Jesus, 3
Missionary work in the early church,
277–78
Mount of Transfiguration theophany
and secret doctrines, 109–10
Mythology and temples, 376

Names on the altar and the early
Christian prayer circle, 79
New Jerusalem and the temple, 401–2
Nimrod and usurpation of temple rites,
366
Numbers as symbolism in the early
Christian prayer circle, 65

Odes of Solomon, emendations in,
232–33
Ordinances: and the early Christian
prayer circle, 48; temple, loss and
diffusion of, 365–67
Organization in early Christianity, 176
Orwell, George, and church history,
217–18

Paganism, influence of, on the early
church, 186
Peter on salvation for the dead, 102
Peter Cantor on temples, 395
Peter the Venerable on baptism for the
dead, 127, 128
Philosophy, influence of, on the early
church, 184
Phocas in Jerusalem, 327–28
Physical resurrection and baptism for
the dead, 124–25
Physics and the early Christian prayer
circle, 79–82
Pilgrimages to Jerusalem, 326–29
Plains Indians and the early Christian
prayer circle, 65
Prayer, language of, in the early Christian prayer circle, 56–58
Prayer rolls, use of, in the early Christian prayer circle, 76–77

Primitive church and the Great Apostasy, 296–97
Prophecy: and history, 190–91; and
early Christianity, 265
Protestant Reformation: and the
importance of Jerusalem, 332–33;
and temples, 413
Protoevangelium of Jesus, 4

Ramses II and the changing of history,
218–19
Restoration of all things, 109–13, 288
Resurrection, teachings of, 13–14
Revelation according to Rudolf
Bultmann, 309
Rhetoric, influence of, on the early
church, 189
Ritual centers and temples, 372–74
Ritual dramas and temples, 361–63
Russian Orthodox Church and ring
dancing, 53

Sacrifice as a theme in the early Christian prayer circle, 60
Salt Lake Temple as example of true
temple, 367–70
Salvation for the dead and baptism for
the dead, 100–101
Satan: involvement of, in the early
Christian prayer circle, 63–64; and
the gates of hell, 107–8
Scholarship and machinery, 259–60
Second Jeu and the early Christian
prayer circle, 51
Secret doctrines and salvation for the
dead, 109–13
Septuagint and censorship, 223
Smith, Joseph: apocryphal stories
about, compared to those about
Jesus, 7; and the origin of baptism
for the dead, 148
Spirits in prison, Christ's mission to,
114–21
Suffering as a theme in the early Christian prayer circle, 59–60
Synagogues and temples, 355, 408

Talmud and censorship, 225–26
Temples: and the early Christian
prayer circle, 68–71; purpose of,
355–83; and cosmic symbolism,

357–61; rejection of, by Christian-
ity, 391–414
Temple ordinances: and the early
    Christian prayer circle, 77–78; loss
    and diffusion of, 365–67
Tertullian on baptism for the dead, 124
Testament of our Lord Jesus Christ and
    the early Christian prayer circle,
    47–48
Textual criticism and authority, 233–45
Thomas Aquinas on temples, 396–97
Translation: as a key to church his-
    tory, 245–48; follies of, 248–59; as
    opinion, 249–50
Truth and its perversion, 282
Trypho on salvation for the dead,
    101–2

Twelve as a symbolic number in the
    early Christian prayer circle, 65–66
Two Ways, doctrine of, 16

Universal salvation also for the dead,
    100–13

Vatican archives and censorship, 229
Veils, use of, in the early Christian
    prayer circle, 71–73
Vergil, state of salvation of, 143–44

Water necessary for baptism, 122–23
Writing, as artificial, 245–46

Zionism and Jerusalem, 333–34